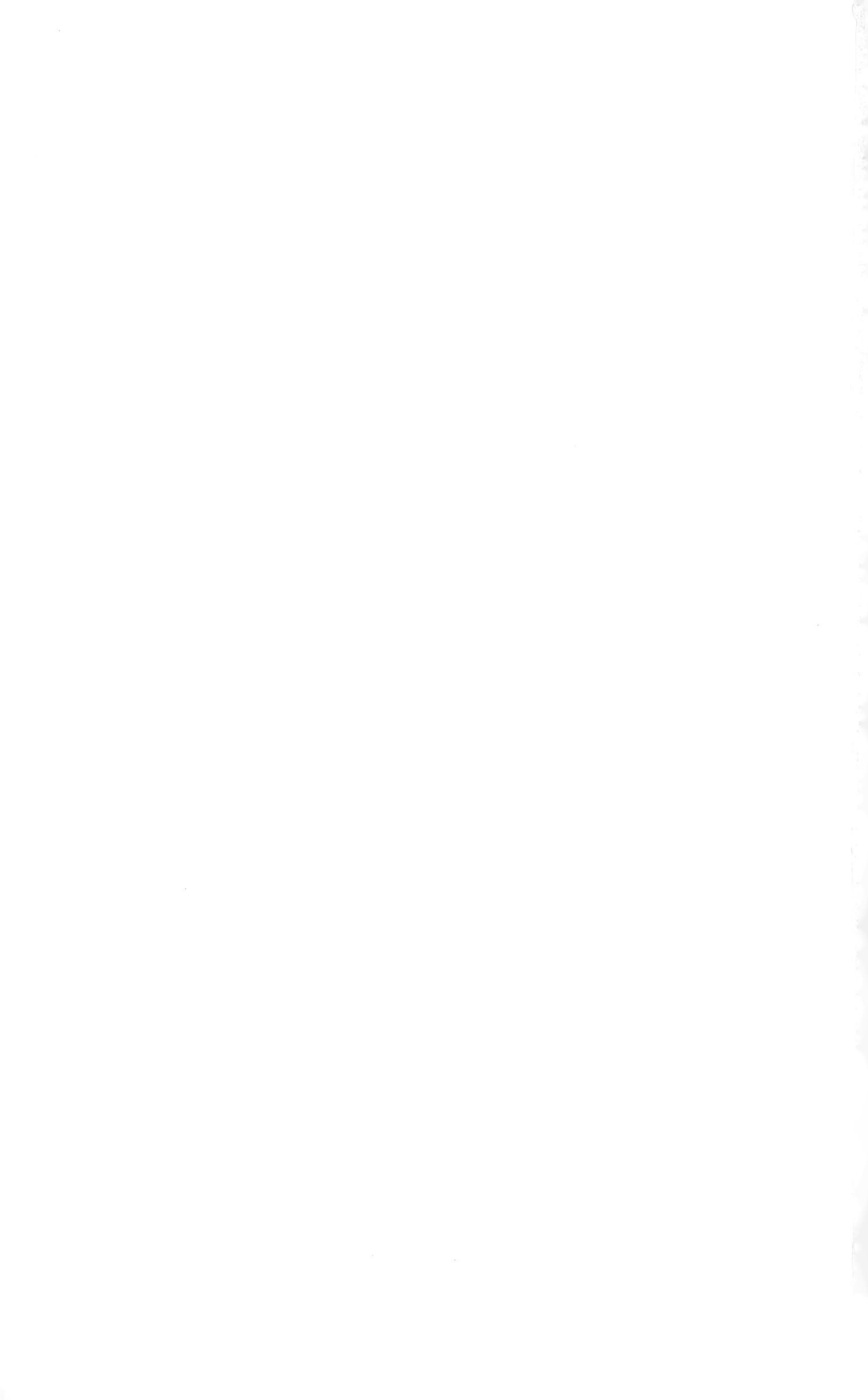

In and out of Bloomsbury

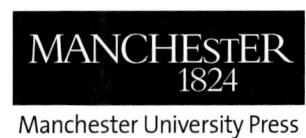

MANCHESTER
1824

Manchester University Press

In and out of Bloomsbury

Biographical essays on twentieth-century writers and artists

Martin Ferguson Smith

MANCHESTER UNIVERSITY PRESS

Published by Manchester University Press
Altrincham Street, Manchester M1 7JA

www.manchesteruniversitypress.co.uk

British Library Cataloguing-in-Publication Data
A catalogue record for this book is available from the British
Library

ISBN 978 1 5261 5744 7 hardback

First published 2021

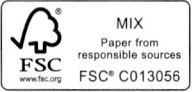

Typeset by
Servis Filmsetting Ltd, Stockport, Cheshire
Printed in Great Britain by
TJ Books Ltd, Padstow, Cornwall

Contents

List of illustrations

Preface

Note: Numbers printed in **bold** are those of the essays.

The eleven essays in this book were all written when I was in my seventies. After many years of research and writing as a classical scholar, I decided to devote some of my time and energy to a variety of more recent things that interested me. At the same time, when I ventured outside my professional field, I continued to have the same priority I had and have as a classicist, which is, so far as possible, to make known new material rather than recycle old. My main classical project, begun in 1968 and still in progress, involves the discovery and publication of pieces of the largest-known Greek inscription, in which, in the first half of the second century AD, Diogenes of Oinoanda (in modern Turkey) set out the philosophical doctrines of Epicurus for the moral benefit and salvation of the city's residents and visitors. That project has more than tripled the number of known pieces of the inscription and added several thousand words to the text of one of the most remarkable documents preserved from antiquity.

Similarly, my "modern" research has focused on extending our knowledge mainly by the presentation of previously unpublished texts, pictures, photographs, and facts, and, where the material is not new, by the independent examination of the relevant manuscripts and images.

My first such project was to edit more than a hundred previously unknown letters sent by the writer Rose Macaulay to her first cousin the poet Jean Smith.[1] The letters, described by A. N. Wilson as being "full of buried treasure", illuminate not only Rose's private life, unconventional character, and varied career, but also the literary and social scene in the years 1919–1958. Investigation of Jean's life revealed that at boarding school she had been a senior contemporary of Dorothy L. Sayers, detective novelist, religious writer, and translator of Dante, and this discovery

1 *Dearest Jean: Rose Macaulay's Letters to a Cousin.* Manchester: Manchester University Press, 2011 (paperback 2017).

naturally led on to exploration of Dorothy's teenage years (**8**, **9**). The interest in Rose Macaulay is also the origin of **7**, which presents her "new" letters to the Irish writer Katharine Tynan.

My interest in Virginia Woolf and other members of the so-called Bloomsbury Group began, naturally enough for a classicist, with the visit she made to Greece with the artist and art critic Roger Fry in 1932 (**4**), and my determination to write about it was sparked by observation of leading Woolf experts' misidentification of the Athenian temple in front of which the travellers and their companions were photographed standing. It soon became apparent that many of the photographs taken on the holiday had been wrongly or inadequately identified, and that some significant mistakes had also been made by the editors of Virginia's diary and letters.

At an early stage I was gripped by the tragic story of Roger Fry's wife, Helen Coombe, a brilliant artist who, soon after her marriage, became more and more seriously afflicted by paranoid schizophrenia. Only the outline of the story was known, and I became convinced that there was material for a book. The book is not yet finished, mainly because of demands of my classical work, but some of the material has been incorporated in three of the essays here (**1**, **5**, **6**), which give the fullest account so far of her life, personality, and artistic career.

One of those who knew Helen in London in the 1890s, when she was still single, and who gave a brief but vivid account of her in a passage of his unpublished memoir, is Richard Williams Reynolds. Curious to know more about him, I was amazed to discover where the research into this cultivated but mild and diffident Birmingham schoolteacher took me. His story is told in **10**. As for **11**, about the artist Tristram Hillier and his first visit to Portugal, my interest was aroused because I possessed a drawing he had made during it – a drawing that had belonged to Rose Macaulay.

If it is asked why this collection contains eleven pieces rather than (say) ten or twelve, the answer is that the choice seems a good compromise between extension and limit – much the same consideration as that which presumably led to the choice of eleven as the most suitable number of players on each side in several ball-games, namely cricket, association football, American football, and hockey.

MFS
Isle of Foula
Shetland
September 2020

Acknowledgements and dedication

I thank the first publishers of essays 1–8 and 10–11 for permission to reproduce them with minor revisions and alterations. Details of the original publications are given on p. 295.

I thank also the following: all who gave permission for material to be used in the original articles for authorising its reproduction in this book; the Estate of Vanessa Bell for renewing the permissions given by the previous copyright-holder, the late Henrietta Garnett; Helen Walasek for agreeing to the inclusion of essay 3, which we researched and wrote together; Odin Dekkers, Mark Hussey, and Robin Simon for their generous encouragement and assistance; my editor, Matthew Frost, for his keen interest and wise advice; and last, but certainly not least, Lucinda Ferguson Smith for making many valuable suggestions, for getting the essays into good shape for the printer, and for helping to see them through the press. To her I dedicate the book.

Introduction

Bloomsbury in this book's title denotes the so-called "Bloomsbury Group" or "Bloomsbury Set", the influential circle of innovative artists, art critics, writers, and economists, associated especially with the Bloomsbury area of London, who were active in the early decades of the twentieth century. They were linked, in varying degrees of closeness, by familial and other personal relationships and a "modern" attitude to literature, art, socio-political structures, morality, and sexual behaviour. The circle was not large, and there was and is disagreement about who belonged and who did not, about when it began, about when it ended, and even about whether it ever properly existed at all. Some of the uncertainty arises from the absence of an agreed ideology.

Essays **1–6** are chiefly about four of Bloomsbury's pivotal members – the artists Roger Fry and Vanessa Bell, the art critic Clive Bell (Vanessa's husband), and the writer Virginia Woolf (Vanessa's younger sister). They do not provide a comprehensive account of the lives and works of this quartet, but, because their focus is selective, that does not mean that it is narrow, or that the material is of marginal significance, and their impact is cumulative.

Essay **1** presents two previously unknown portraits by Roger Fry. One is a drawing of his wife, Helen, on the day of their wedding in December 1896, the other a portrait of Vanessa Bell executed during the love affair they began in the spring of 1911, at the time when his style of painting had just come under the influence of Matisse and he had introduced the British public to a new sort of art with the first of the two post-impressionist exhibitions he organised in London (November 1910, October 1912). Thus the two "new" pictures were executed at extremely important junctures of his personal life and artistic career.

The event described in **2** also belongs to the time of Roger and Vanessa's affair. A well-known manifestation of Bloomsbury's bohemianism is the readiness of its members to take off their clothes in company and be photographed in the nude. Many nude photographs of them exist, and more than a few have been published in recent years. But previously unpublished is the sequence of photographs presented and discussed in **2**. Taken out of doors by the sea at Studland in Dorset, the photographs are the record of a nude-posing session held by Vanessa and Clive Bell and Roger Fry in circumstances that were rather remarkable, in that at the time Vanessa and Roger were head over heels in love, while Clive was ignorant of their affair. These circumstances are known only because it has been possible to assign the photographs, previously dated c. 1912–1913, to early September 1911.

Despite Bloomsbury's generally liberal attitude to sexual behaviour, heterosexual and homosexual, its members were not always completely frank with one another and their families, let alone with society at large. A notorious example of this is that, when Vanessa Bell gave birth to her third child, a daughter named Angelica Vanessa Bell, on Christmas Day 1918, Clive Bell was named as her father, whereas her biological father was Duncan Grant, the Bloomsbury artist with whom Vanessa lived. Angelica was not told the truth until she turned eighteen. Another deception, certainly less serious, is that urged on Roger by Vanessa in a letter before the Studland holiday: she asks him to be careful to avoid any behaviour that might lead Clive, whom she had married in 1907, to suspect that she was in love with Roger; and this although she did not need to have too bad a conscience about the affair, given that Clive, far from being a paragon of marital fidelity, was an inveterate womaniser.

His first adulterous relationship is the subject of **3**, which, researched and written in collaboration with Helen Walasek, is the first publication and detailed discussion of the frank and entertaining account Clive gave the (Bloomsbury) Memoir Club in 1921 of his long-running affair with Annie Raven-Hill, the wife of the illustrator and *Punch* cartoonist Leonard Raven-Hill. Our publication of the paper was timed to mark the centenary of the establishment of the Memoir Club (4 March 2020), and we describe and discuss the club's history and character.

The visit Virginia Woolf and Roger Fry made to Greece in 1932 in the company of Virginia's husband, Leonard Woolf, and Roger's sister Margery Fry was much enjoyed by both of them. For Virginia it was a return, at the age of fifty, to a country she had visited in 1906, when she was in her mid-twenties. Roger, surprisingly, had not been there before. The detailed study of the visit in **4** is based on examination of the primary sources, published and unpublished. These are: Virginia's diary and letters; Roger's letters; Leonard's pocket-diary; and Virginia and Leonard's photographs. Many of the photographs are correctly identified for the first time. Moreover, examination of the manuscripts of Virginia's diary and letters enables corrections to be made of some significant errors in the published versions. The most startling and damaging of these is the misreading of an adjective she uses to describe Roger – a misreading that completely distorts her meaning, attributing to him an attitude of mind which he did not possess and she would not have admired. Seeing that she admired Roger more than almost any other friend, this is no trivial matter.

The subject of the misidentified "Greek" photographs, and especially the aforementioned one of the party standing in front of a temple in Athens, is taken up again briefly in the second part of **5**, the reason being that, after the publication of **4**, a prominent writer about Virginia Woolf, while accepting my corrections, contended that the misidentification of the temple-scene originated with Virginia herself, and argued that her alleged misidentification is psychobiographically significant. So it was necessary to show that this contention is factually incorrect.

In her essay "The Art of Scepticism" Rebecca West writes:

> Authors who write works not of the imagination, who deal with hard fact, have soon to realize that very few facts indeed are hard, and have to use the sceptical process overtime. ... There is, therefore, an inherent difficulty in the production of what is called non-fiction. ... Just how difficult it is to write a biography can be reckoned by anybody who sits down and considers just how many people know the real truth about his or her love affairs.[1]

The task of any biographer, including the psychobiographer, is challenging enough without ignoring or distorting sure facts. The policy practised throughout the present book, with its principal focus on the presentation and scrutiny of original texts, works of art, and photographs, is, wherever possible, to deal in hard facts rather than in scepticism and speculation.

The first discussion in **5** concerns Virginia Woolf's attempted suicide in September 1913 and her recuperation from the attack of mental illness that provoked it. The main focus is on the interest and advice of Roger Fry, whose wife's (Helen's) long history of mental illness invites comparison and contrast with that of Virginia: in Helen's case mental unbalance was wholly destructive, whereas in Virginia's it was by her own account a creative influence. When Virginia was convalescing, and a new nurse was required for her, Roger approached the medical superintendent of the hospital in which Helen was a patient. The letters that passed between the two are made known for the first time. The superintendent was a keen amateur artist, and the correspondence contains an interesting exchange about the effect of colour on the mind and the possibility of its therapeutic use in cases of mental illness.

Mental health issues crop up also in several other essays: in **1** and **6**, again with regard to Helen; in **7**, in relation to Pamela Hinkson's *The*

---

1 *Vogue* 120, 8, 1 November 1952, 114–115, 168, at 115.

Victors, a novel based on the depression and suicidal thoughts experienced by one of the author's soldier-brothers after the First World War; and in **11** with respect to Tristram Hillier, whose known history of depression started during the Second World War.

Essay **6**, like some of the other Bloomsbury pieces, is not entirely about Bloomsbury. Roger Fry died in 1934, Helen Fry in 1937; and after Virginia Woolf's biography of Roger was published in 1940, she received a letter from Mary Louisa Gordon strongly critical of her portrayal of Helen, and even more critical of Roger's character and conduct. Mary and Helen, neither of whom was ever a "Bloomsberry", had been friends before the latter married. In 1936 the Woolfs had published Mary's historical novel, *Chase of the Wild Goose*, about the Ladies of Llangollen. Essay **6** discusses the book, its relationship to Virginia's novel *Orlando*, and Virginia's comments on it and its author, whom she calls "the Hermaphrodite". It describes the life and remarkable career of a woman whose varied achievements have been unjustly and inexplicably neglected. A thoroughgoing feminist, Mary trained as a medical doctor at a time when the profession had only recently become open to women. She went on to combine service as the first-ever female Inspector of Prisons in England and Wales with covert moral and financial support for the suffragettes; she published a novel under a male pseudonym; and she wrote a book in which she made scathing criticisms of the prison system that are as relevant today as they were a hundred years ago. Her letter to Virginia, written just months before both writer and addressee died, was first published in 2006, but with some mistakes and no commentary. The text is now presented accurately and with explanatory notes. It is followed by an account of Helen's life, personality, and artistic talents, with discussion of Mary's assessments of her and Roger.

Essays **7–11** are less homogeneous than the Bloomsbury six, but **8** and **9** are very closely related, and there are links between the subjects of **7** and **11**. In any case, no apology is made for the varied subject-matter. Like the Bloomsbury pieces, all are based on primary source material and are, both individually and collectively, of significant biographical interest. Moreover, their variety gives a richer and more balanced picture of the cultural scene in the first half of the twentieth century.

The move out of Bloomsbury begins with Rose Macaulay (**7**), whose father, like her friend Rupert Brooke's, was a master at Rugby School. Educated first by her parents in Italy, then at Oxford High School for Girls and Somerville College, Oxford, she was from 1911 a member of a literary circle that gathered around Naomi Royde-Smith, whose work for the *Saturday Westminster Gazette* – as its literary editor from 1912 – made her an influential figure. It was a circle with which Bloomsbury had limited contact and sympathy.[2] Rose was only about six months older than Virginia Woolf, but had published seven novels before Virginia had published her first, *The Voyage Out*, in 1915.

Rose's previously unpublished letters to the Irish poet and novelist Katharine Tynan throw light on the work and lives of both writers just before, during, and after the First World War. Katharine, whose side of the correspondence does not survive, admired Rose's writing, especially her novels. Rose in turn praised Katharine's work, especially her poetry, emphasising particularly the comfort it gave her and others in wartime. She herself had lost several friends, including Rupert Brooke, and was anxious about her brother, who was serving in the army. Her eighth novel, *Non-Combatants and Others* (1916), was a book way ahead of its time, in that the main focus is on those left at home, including returned servicemen, and on the psychological damage caused by war. Katharine's two sons were in the army too. Rose took an interest in Katharine's daughter, Pamela Hinkson, who was showing early promise as a writer. In 1925 Katharine sent Rose a novel by Peter Deane. When Rose replied, she did not realise that Peter Deane was a pseudonym used by Pamela, let alone that the disturbing story was closely based on the post-war experiences of Katharine's elder son.

Dorothy L. Sayers, whose teenage years are the subject of 8 and 9, was also an alumna of Somerville College. She was twelve years younger than Rose, and it was only at the end of their lives that the two writers had much contact, when both were associated with St Thomas's Church, Regent Street, London, and its drama-loving Anglo-Catholic vicar, Patrick McLaughlin. Dorothy has received the detailed attention of several biographers, and there is a flourishing society wholly devoted to her and her work, but all overlooked her major contributions, described in 8, to a pageant in the Huntingdonshire village of Somersham in 1908, when she had only just turned fifteen.

"Pageantitis", infectious enthusiasm for historical pageants, was a widespread but largely forgotten cultural phenomenon in the late nineteenth and early twentieth centuries. The Somersham pageant, staged under professional direction, was an important local event and even attracted the attention of a national newspaper. Dorothy, as well as being one of the musical accompanists, composed the verses for at least three parts of the event, perhaps four. Her contributions, revealing a prodigious talent and singled out for special praise at the time, total a minimum of fifty-six lines.

2 See *Dearest Jean: Rose Macaulay's Letters to a Cousin*, edited by Martin Ferguson Smith. Manchester: Manchester University Press, 2011, 85, 92, 124–125.

Appropriately, given the genre of writing for which she is best known to the British public, the discovery of her prominent participation in the event involved a good deal of detective work.

A few months later, in January 1909, Dorothy entered the Godolphin School, Salisbury, as a boarder and was there for three years. Essay **9** is based on detailed research into her time at school – a time that was important for her development as a writer, thinker, and person. The main sources exploited are three: the letters, many of them unpublished, which she wrote while at the Godolphin, mainly to her parents; *The Godolphin School Magazine*; and the handwritten *School Diary*, with many items pasted in. Some use is made also of Dorothy's unfinished novel *Cat O'Mary*, which is partly autobiographical, but not always factually reliable for her.

As well as contributing much to school life, as a brilliant modern linguist and with her outstanding talents in music and drama, Dorothy benefited much from the high standard of education she received, from the civilised and stimulating atmosphere fostered by the Godolphin's able and enlightened headmistress, and from the varied contacts she had with her fellow-pupils as well as with her teachers. But she also suffered setbacks, notably when she developed pneumonia after a bout of measles and nearly died, and when she left school suddenly before the end of what was planned to be her penultimate term. The well-documented story of her Godolphin years, as well as being illuminating about her, gives a vivid picture of the activities, atmosphere, and ethos in a girls' boarding school just before the First World War.

Essay **10** is the first detailed study of the life of Richard ("Dickie") Williams Reynolds. He would no doubt have been very surprised to find himself included in a collection like this, not just because of his natural modesty, but also because his literary productions, mainly translations, were neither numerous nor distinguished. However, in the course of his life he was in close contact with several writers of importance, and he was a person, well read in several languages, who was generous with his advice to others.

The most spectacular revelation about Dickie is of his unexpectedly exotic and irregular paternity, which has not been made known before. Born in Liverpool and educated at King Edward's School (KES), Birmingham, and Balliol College, Oxford, Dickie spent the 1890s in London, where he trained to be a barrister, joined the Fabian Society, and did some high-class journalism. In 1900 he joined the staff of KES. His most famous pupil was J. R. R. Tolkien, and the two kept in touch after Tolkien left school. In 1910 he married the novelist Dorothea Deakin, a niece of Edith Nesbit, with whom he had had a long and close relationship. He and Dorothea had three daughters. In 1922 he retired from KES, and the family moved to

Capri, partly for the sake of his health, but mainly in the hope of a cure for Dorothea's tuberculosis. She soon died, leaving him to bring up their three young girls. He did that successfully, but in the mid-1930s suffered further family losses on a Greek-tragic scale, losing in quick time two of his daughters and his second wife. His youngest daughter, Pamela, a promising poet, perished in a fall down a cliff – an accident that in recent years has been misrepresented by some in Italy as suicide or even murder. On Capri the Reynolds family associated with Axel Munthe and an assortment of other resident and visiting writers and artists, their villa being known locally as the island's "little Oxford".

The collection ends (**11**), as it began, with an artist – Tristram Hillier, who, as a young man, met Roger Fry, Clive Bell, Vanessa Bell, and Duncan Grant at Cassis on the French Riviera. That was in 1928, shortly after he had left the Slade School of Fine Art at University College, London. Clive, true to form, flirted with Tristram's girlfriend, Joan Firminger, and his keen interest in her, by no means confined to flirting, continued well after her stormy relationship with Tristram ended.

Tristram made a distinctive and distinguished contribution to twentieth-century British art. In the early 1930s he was a surrealist, a member of Paul Nash's Unit One, but by the end of that decade he had moved most of the way from abstraction and surrealism to representational painting, although without ever abandoning all his surrealist inclinations.

His visit to Portugal in 1947, the first of many visits he made to that country, was of great importance. It arose out of a crisis in his private life and was from a professional point of view highly successful and productive. He had recently returned to the Roman Catholic Church, to the fury of his Irish Protestant wife, who even threatened him with divorce. It was partly to give themselves space and time to think things over that he went to Portugal for four months to draw and paint.

The essay clarifies the context, dating, and itinerary of the visit, with full use made of the Hillier files in the Tate Gallery Archive (a resource not exploited before) as well as letters in the possession of the artist's family (Hillier Archive). It focuses particular attention on the artist's portrayal of scenes in the city of Viseu, presenting and discussing his paintings of Cathedral Square and the Church of the Misericordia and the very fine drawing, made on location *en plein air*, on which the Cathedral Square painting is based. The drawing has been in private ownership since 1948 and has not been published before. It and the painting executed months later in the artist's studio make a fascinating study in comparison and contrast.

A further point of interest is that the first owner of the drawing was Rose Macaulay, who admired Tristram's work. The first of her two books about

British visitors to Portugal was published a few months before he followed in their footsteps, and in July–September 1947, during his first Portuguese travels, she spent ten weeks driving her 1934 Morris car on an adventurous journey of exploration in Spain and Portugal.[3]

Tristram Hillier died in 1983. A major retrospective exhibition of his work, recently staged in Somerset, the county in which he made his home, suggests that his reputation is on the rise.[4] What about the reputations of the others in recent decades? The "Bloomsberries" have been riding high, and Virginia Woolf especially continues to receive attention on an almost industrial scale. Dorothy L. Sayers remains best known as a detective novelist in Britain, but as a religious writer on the other side of the Pond. Dickie Reynolds has previously never received more than brief mentions in books on Edith Nesbit and Tolkien, but will henceforth be known also as the unacknowledged son of a Confederate commander in the American Civil War and as a significant but tragic participant in the social and cultural life of Capri's international community between the two World Wars. Rose Macaulay, whose writings were in vogue in her lifetime, declined in popularity in the last decades of the twentieth century. The reasons for this are not entirely clear, and in the preface to *Dearest Jean* I argued that the neglect is undeserved.[5] That was ten years ago, and since then there have been some welcome signs of a revival of interest. Tides of public taste and opinion, including in literature and art, often change. The present author will be happy if this book, as well as throwing new light on some well known figures, also increases knowledge and appreciation of some less well known ones.

---

3 Rose Macaulay wrote about her travels in *Fabled Shore: From the Pyrenees to Portugal* (London: Hamish Hamilton, 1949).

4 *Landscapes of the Mind: The Art of Tristram Hillier*. Museum of Somerset, Taunton, planned for 8 November 2019 – 18 April 2020. It closed earlier because of the Covid-19 pandemic, but a digital version is available at https://swheritage.org.uk/digitalexhibitions/landscapes-of-the-mind/.

5 *Dearest Jean*, vii–viii.

1

"New" portraits by Roger Fry of Helen Fry and Vanessa Bell

Two portraits by Roger Eliot Fry, a drawing and a painting, were recently acquired by me from separate sources in the United States. Neither has been exhibited or published before.

The earlier one (Portrait 1), drawn in pencil on paper that is now slightly foxed, is a quarter-length portrayal of a woman who looks to be in her late twenties or early thirties (Plates 1–2). The handsome face is turned slightly to the left (the viewer's right). The head is carefully drawn, as is the left hand, which is raised and turned in front of the body in such a way as to display a ring on the fourth finger, with two long, thin bands of material running over and through the fingers. The bands come loosely across the chest from a floral object, which appears incompletely at the left edge of the drawing. Although it is possible that the bands are fine chains, which were sometimes looped and pinned across the bodice, they are more plausibly interpreted as ribbons attached to the floral object, which in that case is to be identified as a bouquet rather than a floral brooch. A choker, probably a ribbon-band or possibly composed of very fine beads, with a shield-shaped front clasp or slide, is worn on the neck, and a cluster-ornament across the parting of the hair at the front. The rest of the drawing is decidedly sketchy, but it can be seen that the dress is heavily padded at the shoulders. Behind the head is the outline of what is almost certainly a cushion or pillow, and to the right of that the outline of what is probably part of a cushion or pillow or chair.

The drawing, which is unsigned, was offered for sale as *Pencil Portrait of an Unidentified Woman*. It was mounted as an oval (maximum 21 × 14 cm) inside a rectangular frame. The mount concealed a significant area of the drawing, which occupies what may be a page removed from a sketchbook. The drawing has now been remounted, no longer as an oval and with no part of it concealed. Curved lines that are just visible upper left, lower left, and on the right suggest that at some stage, perhaps when more of the drawing survived, a larger oval was planned, if not executed. Certainly these lines do not match the oval in place when the picture was

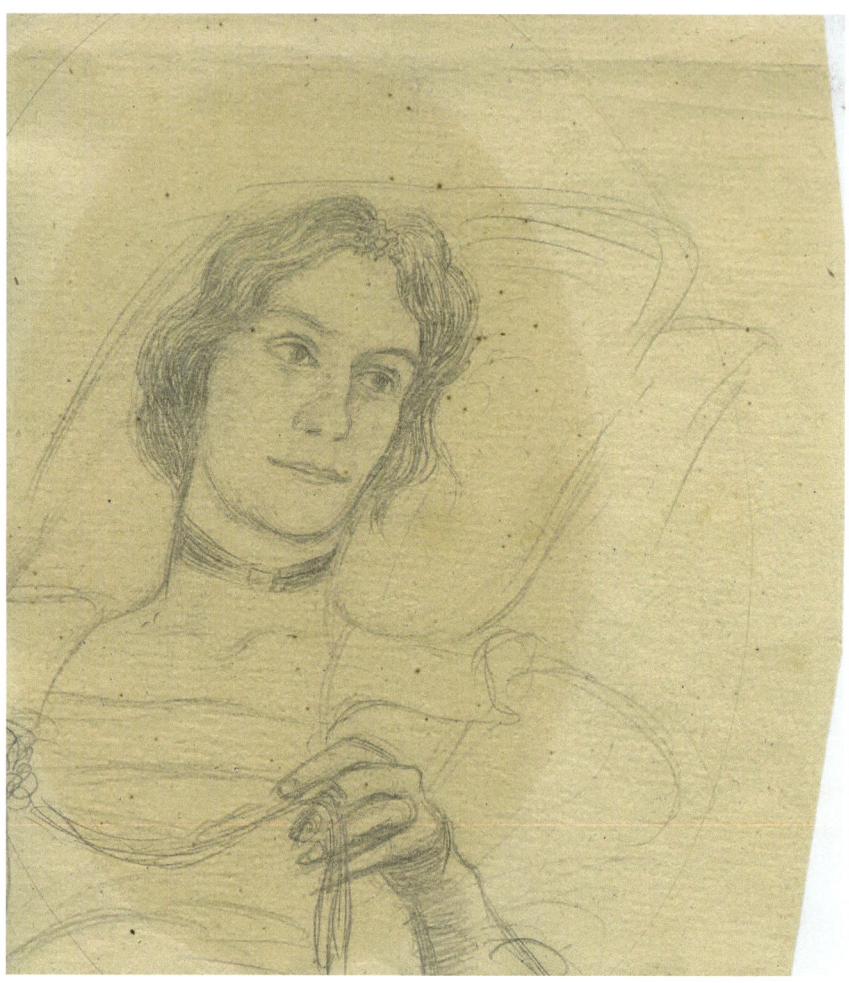

1 *Portrait of Helen Fry* by Roger Fry, 3 December 1896. Pencil on paper, 22.8 × 19.7 cm.

acquired by me. On the verso of the drawing is the start of, or a sketch for, a painted landscape with trees. On the back of the frame is the label of The Bloomsbury Workshop, 12 Galen Place, London WC1A 2JR, with the description "ROGER FRY (1866–1934) / *Head of a Woman* / Pencil / c1905". This label was attached to the frame not by The Bloomsbury Workshop, but after the drawing was acquired by the next owner, when she had it matted and framed.

The ascription of Portrait 1 to Roger Fry is correct, but the suggested date is not, and the sitter is the artist's wife, Helen Fry *née* Coombe. Being

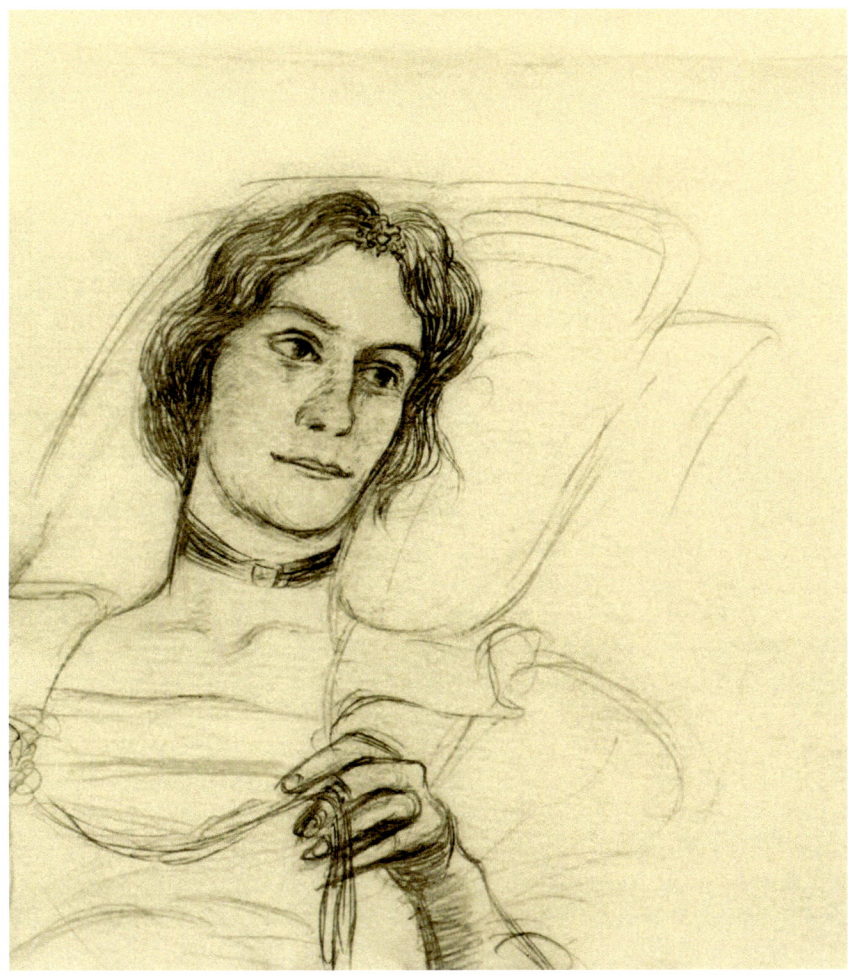

2 *Portrait of Helen Fry* by Roger Fry. The same drawing as in Plate 1, but with the image digitally restored.

familiar with drawings and photographs of her, I recognised her at once, and the identification has been endorsed by many others who have viewed the drawing alongside known images of her. But, wanting to be in the best position to combat any possible challenge, I consulted Richard Neave,[1]

1 During his forty-one-year career as Artist in Medicine and Life Sciences at the University of Manchester (1959–2000) Neave established a national and international reputation for his pioneering work in developing methods and techniques for facial reconstruction and comparison, and his expertise has been widely used

long recognised as a leading authority on facial comparison. I sent him four images: a scan of Portrait 1; two photographs of Helen with Roger[2] – one taken in autumn 1896 during their engagement (Plate 3), the other probably about a year later;[3] and a drawing of Helen by Roger in King's College Cambridge Archive Centre (REF/4/8/5). Neave devoted several hours to scientific study of the images, comparing proportions and morphology. In his detailed report of 29 January 2015 he noted numerous similarities between the "new" portrait and the other images and found no discernible dissimilarities of any significance. In making the proportional comparison, he used digital technology to produce vertically split images, combining the known portrait of Helen with each of the photographs, and carrying out a similar exercise with Portrait 1. In every case the vertical and horizontal proportions were found to be consistent. The split images that combine the head of the sitter in Portrait 1 with the head of Helen Fry in the engagement photograph are reproduced in Plates 4 and 5.

Like Roger Fry, Helen was an artist, and a very talented one. I describe and assess her life, personality, training, and career elsewhere in this book,[4] and I will be very brief here. After studying at the St John's Wood Art Schools in London, she was admitted to the Royal Academy of Arts Schools (RAS) in December 1882. On leaving the RAS at a date unknown, but not later than 1888, she turned her attention to the decorative arts. In 1896, the year of her marriage, her fine Mary-and-Martha stained-glass window, commissioned in memory of Elizabeth Martin-Leake, had been installed in the Church of the Evangelist at High Cross, Hertfordshire (16–19 March), and she had superbly decorated Arnold Dolmetsch's "Green Harpsichord" for display at the Fifth Exhibition of the Arts and Crafts Exhibition Society (7 October–5 December).

She was widely admired not only for her artistic ability, but also for her attractive personality and voice, witty conversation, deportment, and, despite bad teeth, good looks. Roger Fry had been captivated by

in both forensic and archaeological contexts. In his "retirement" he has taught in Belgium at Maastricht University and in London at The Royal College of Art and Guy's Hospital. He is a Fellow of the Medical Artists' Association, a member of the International Association for Craniological Identification, and former Chairman of the Forensic Imaging Analysis Group.

2 Tate Gallery Archive (henceforth TGA) 8010/13.

3 Both photographs were taken at Failand House, the home of Roger's parents near Bristol. The engagement photograph was taken either in late September to early October 1896 or in early November 1896, the other one probably in mid-October 1897.

4 Essay 6, Section 4. See also Essay 5, Section 1.

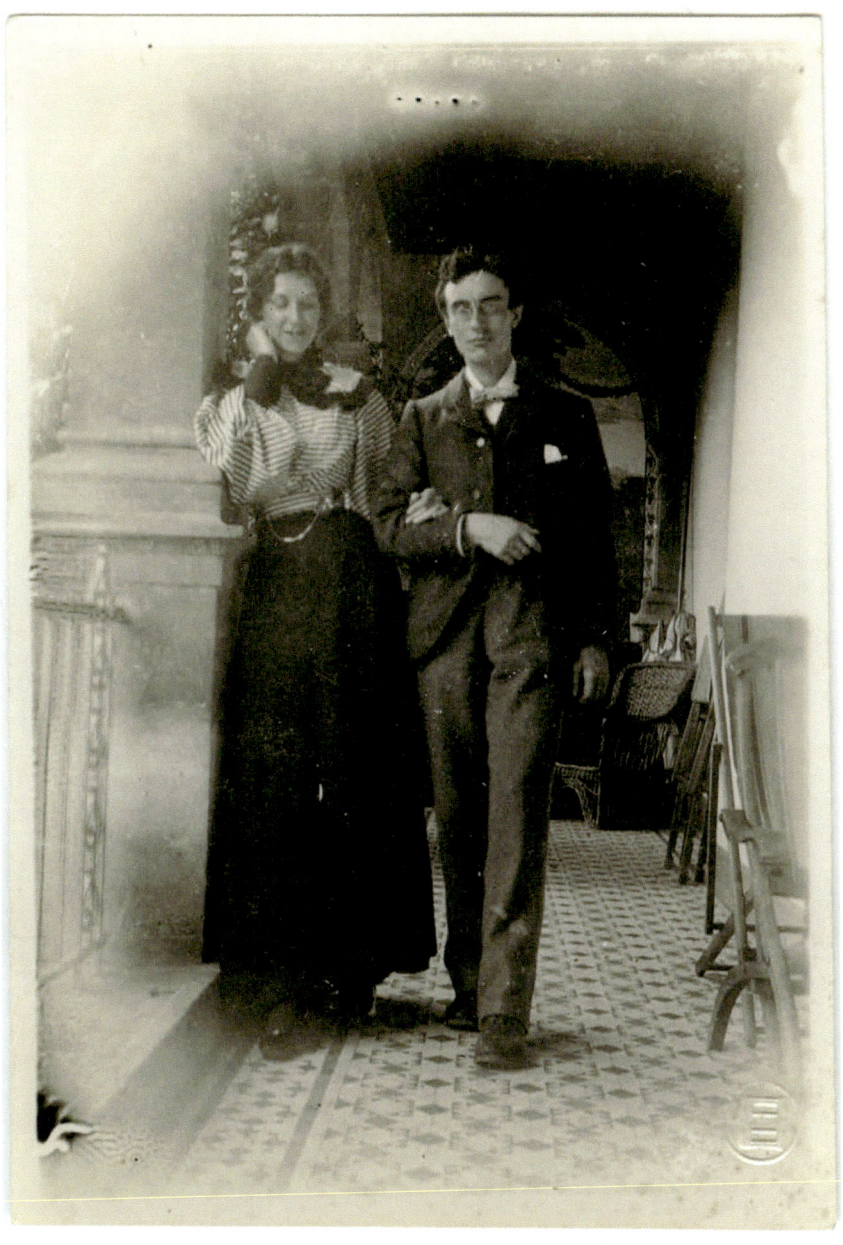

3 Helen Coombe (Fry) and Roger Fry at Failand House, Failand, near Bristol, autumn 1896. Photograph.

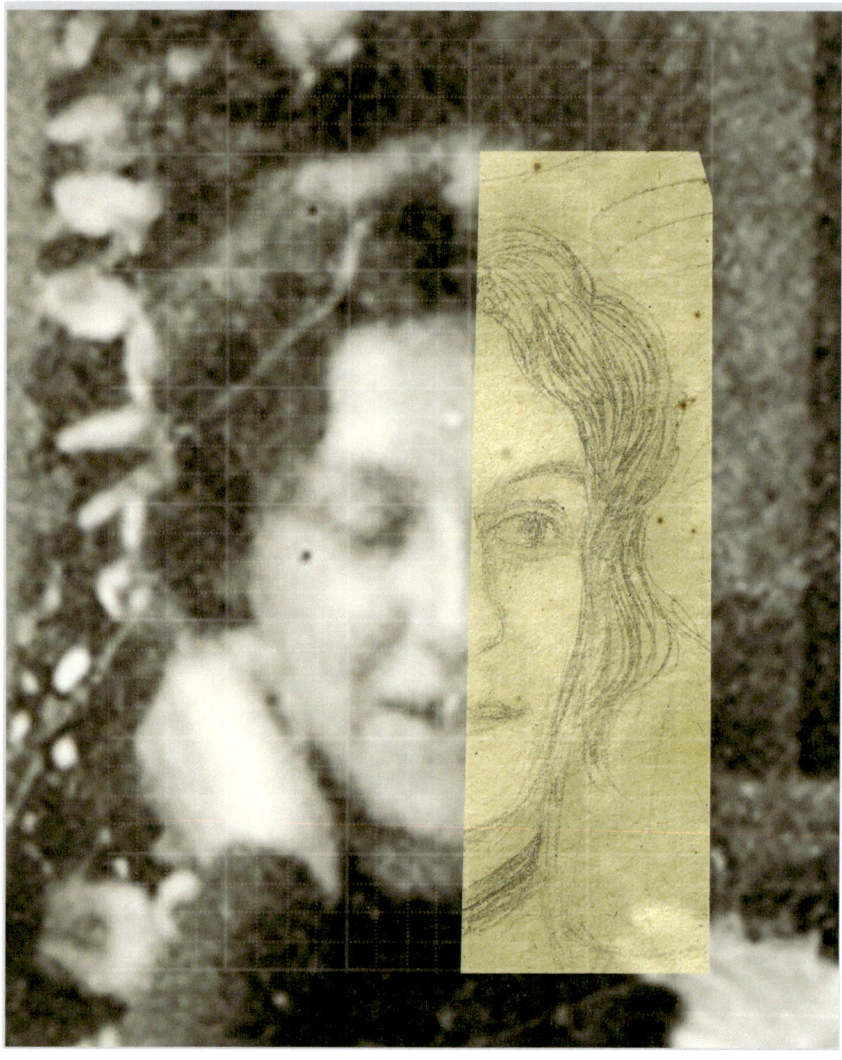

4 Vertically-split image, combining the left (viewer's right) half of the head of the sitter in Plates 1 and 2 with the right (viewer's left) half of the head of Helen Coombe (Fry) in Plate 3.

her at their first meeting, which occurred in his lodgings at 29 Beaufort Street, Chelsea, on Monday, 27 May 1895. What happened is described by the poet Robert ("Bob") Calverley Trevelyan in a letter written to Edward Marsh. Marsh, destined to become a distinguished civil servant and a notable patron of the arts, had, like Trevelyan, read Classics at Trinity College, Cambridge, and, like him and Roger Fry, was an

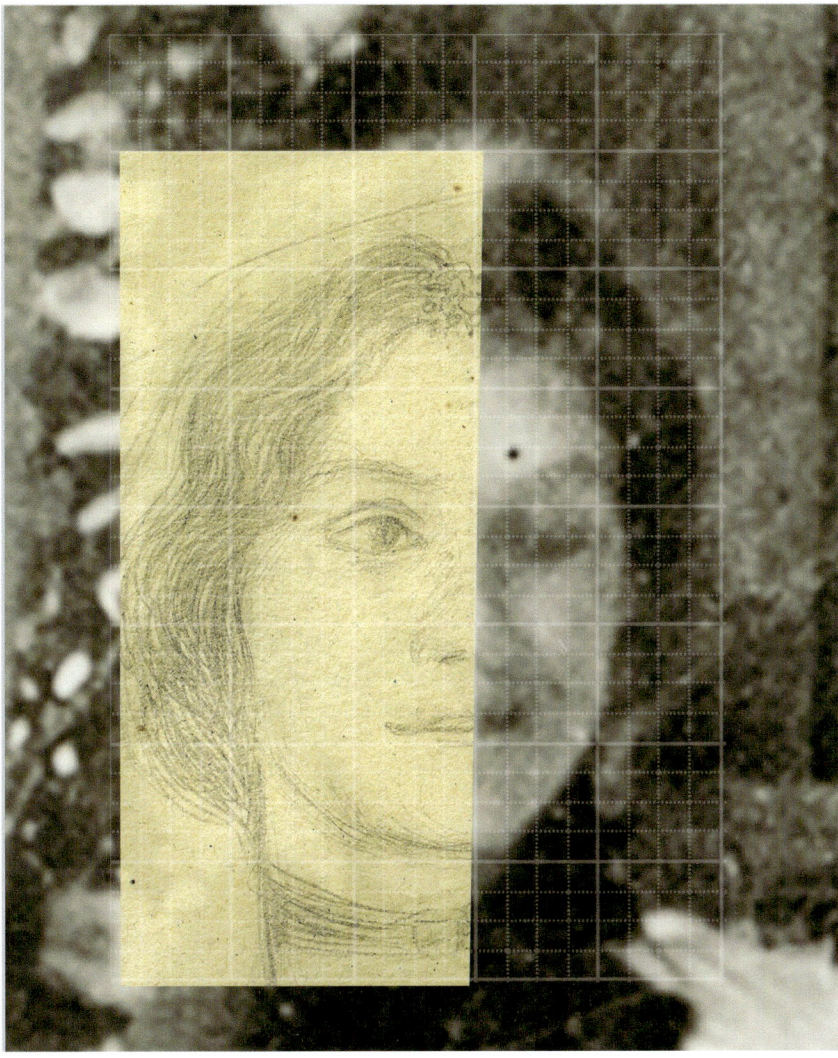

5 Vertically-split image, combining the right (viewer's left) half of the head of the sitter in Plates 1 and 2 with the left (viewer's right) half of the head of Helen Coombe (Fry) in Plate 3.

"Apostle".[5] Trevelyan had called with Helen at 30 Bruton Street, off Berkeley Square, where Marsh lived with his parents, hoping to introduce

---

5 The Apostles, properly the Cambridge Conversazione Society, a secret society founded in 1820. Originally there were twelve members – hence the name "Apostles".

her to him, but Marsh was not at home. The following day Trevelyan wrote to tell Marsh what he had missed:

> 5 Barton Str. [Westminster]
> 28 May [18]95
>
> My dear Edward,
>
> … I went round to Bruton Str yesterday morning to see if you were alive, but found that you had gone back on Sunday. You should have stayed, for I had for you a rose of Shiraz the direct descendant of the one which intoxicated Hafiz when he looked on it, and led his spirit forth like wine on the turnpikes of imagination into a land of luminous horizons. You would have had this rose, if you had been there. As it was I took it round to Fry who fell violently in love with it, and fell to painting it. Seriously it was the most perfect flower I ever set eyes on.
>
> …
>
> Yours affectionately
> R C Trevelyan[6]

Helen was much slower to fall in love with Roger, but did so in the summer of 1896, stimulated by the support and advice he gave her about the decoration of the Green Harpsichord. They were married in the Priory Church of St Bartholomew the Great in the City of London on 3 December 1896. She was aged thirty-two. He was twenty-nine, but gave his age as thirty, which he did not become until 14 December. The couple's genuine love for one another, combined with their shared interest in art, seemed to augur well for the success of their marriage, but there was soon to be much anxiety about her health – first about her physical health, then, much more alarmingly, about her mental state, as she began to display symptoms of what is now recognised to have been chronic paranoid schizophrenia. The first major episode occurred at the end of May 1898. She was in an asylum for over six months, and, although she made a recovery and had several largely trouble-free years during which she produced some more fine artistic work and two children, she had further spells in asylums in 1903 and 1907–1908, and in November 1910 was admitted to The Retreat, the Quaker asylum in York, where she was to spend the last twenty-seven years of her life.

When did Roger make the drawing under discussion? The answer is at the time of their marriage and almost certainly on the wedding day itself.

---

6 Trinity College Cambridge Library, RCT 15.276. Frances Spalding, *Roger Fry: Art and Life* (London, 1980), 57, gets the facts badly muddled. According to her, it was Marsh who tried to introduce Helen to Trevelyan, and who wrote the letter quoted above. She errs also in saying that the meeting took place "one afternoon in 1896".

There are some likely indications of this in the drawing, and they are strongly supported by a previously unpublished document.

At the time when parts of the drawing were hidden, consideration was given to the possibility that the "pillow" or "cushion" behind Helen's head is actually the thrown-back veil of her wedding-dress, and the cluster-ornament on her head an anchor for the veil. This now seems unlikely. But, whether the object partly visible below the right shoulder, at the left edge of the picture, is a bouquet with ribbons attached, or whether it is a floral cluster-brooch and the "ribbons" are fine chains looped and pinned across the bodice, they well suit a bridal context. The care that has been taken to show the wedding-ring would not of course by itself prove that Helen has just got married, but its emphasis is the more understandable if the drawing was made on her wedding-day. Given that she was not at all well off, the jewellery she is wearing suggests at the very least a special occasion, as does the dress with its padded shoulders and puffed, leg o' mutton sleeves, very much in fashion, including for wedding-dresses, in and about 1896. If the special occasion for which she was attired and ornamented was not her wedding, it is difficult to think what it could have been.

It might be questioned whether there would have been time for a sitting on the wedding-day, but Roger worked rapidly, and he was never one to waste any opportunity for a drawing or painting. As we have seen, when Helen and he met for the first time, he immediately started painting her. No wedding photographs are known to have been taken, and it is natural that he should have wanted to record how she looked on the day. The wedding service, which took place at 2 p.m., was followed by tea at Helen's mother's house in Hammersmith. Then, in the evening, the couple had dinner with four friends, including Helen's friend the artist Selwyn Image and Roger's best man, Bob Trevelyan, at Solferino's in Rupert Street near Piccadilly Circus. The establishment, known affectionately as Solfi's, was much favoured by artists and writers. It was a regular haunt of what Max Beerbohm called "the Henley Regatta" – the journalists who worked for William Henley on *The National Observer* and for *The Pall Mall Gazette*. According to William Rothenstein, the restaurant was quiet, the cooking was excellent, and "the manager was willing to give credit, though his trustfulness proved his ruin".[7]

The bill for the wedding-evening dinner, signed on the back by all six members of the party, is preserved in King's College Cambridge Archive Centre in an envelope addressed by Helen to "Roger Eliot Fry Esqre".[8] The envelope also contains a note, quoted here with key-words italicised:

---

7 *Men and Memories: Recollections of William Rothenstein 1872–1900* (London, [1931]), 285. The proprietor's name was Peter Lötzerich.
8 REF/3/58/18.

My own Sweetness –
You, Rogo are all in life to me – If you went out of it – out of life – so even should I – my lips are yours as yours are mine to all ages of ages, as all of you is mine and all of mine is yours – My Rogo I can say no more, – I want you all days and minutes given to us in all time as I understand time to be. *You are drawing me* and I am absolutely absorbed by and in you.

    Your Nell
    Your Helen
    Your Helena
    Your *Sposa*—

The note is undated, but the placing of it with the restaurant bill suggests very close synchronism between them, and "Your Sposa [Bride]" supports this. The most likely scenario is that the drawing was made between the tea and the dinner or, less probably, between dinner and bed.

Along with the engagement photograph of Helen with Roger (Plate 3), his wedding-day drawing of her shows her more relaxed, well, and happy than any other known image of her, and it is precious for this reason. To have not only the drawing, but also the movingly loving note she wrote while it was being made, is something truly special.

Provenance of Portrait 1

Roger Fry to his daughter, Pamela Diamand; from Pamela Diamand, after her death, to her younger daughter, the artist and poet Betty Taber; from Betty Taber c. 1996 to The Bloomsbury Workshop, London; from The Bloomsbury Workshop to Dr Linda Elisabeth Beattie (now LaPinta) of Louisville, Kentucky, July 1998; from Dr Beattie to William Reese Company of New Haven, Connecticut, 30 May 2013; from William Reese to me, 4 November 2013.

The other "new" picture by Roger Fry (Portrait 2), executed in pencil and gouache on paper, is of Vanessa Bell (Plate 6). Both artist and sitter are identified in notes on the verso. At the top Roger's daughter has written in pencil: "This portrait of Vanessa Bell / is by my father Roger Fry. / Pamela Diamand—" (Plate 7).[9] Lower right is a pencilled note: "V Bell by REF"

9 Pamela Diamand not infrequently wrote such statements on the backs of her father's pictures and inside his books when she sold them or gave them away. For example, his oil-on-board painting *A Woodland Path, Epping Forest*, from the collection of Philip Rieff and Alison Douglas Knox, offered for sale by Freeman's of Philadelphia on 22 June 2008, is inscribed on the verso: "This picture was painted by my father

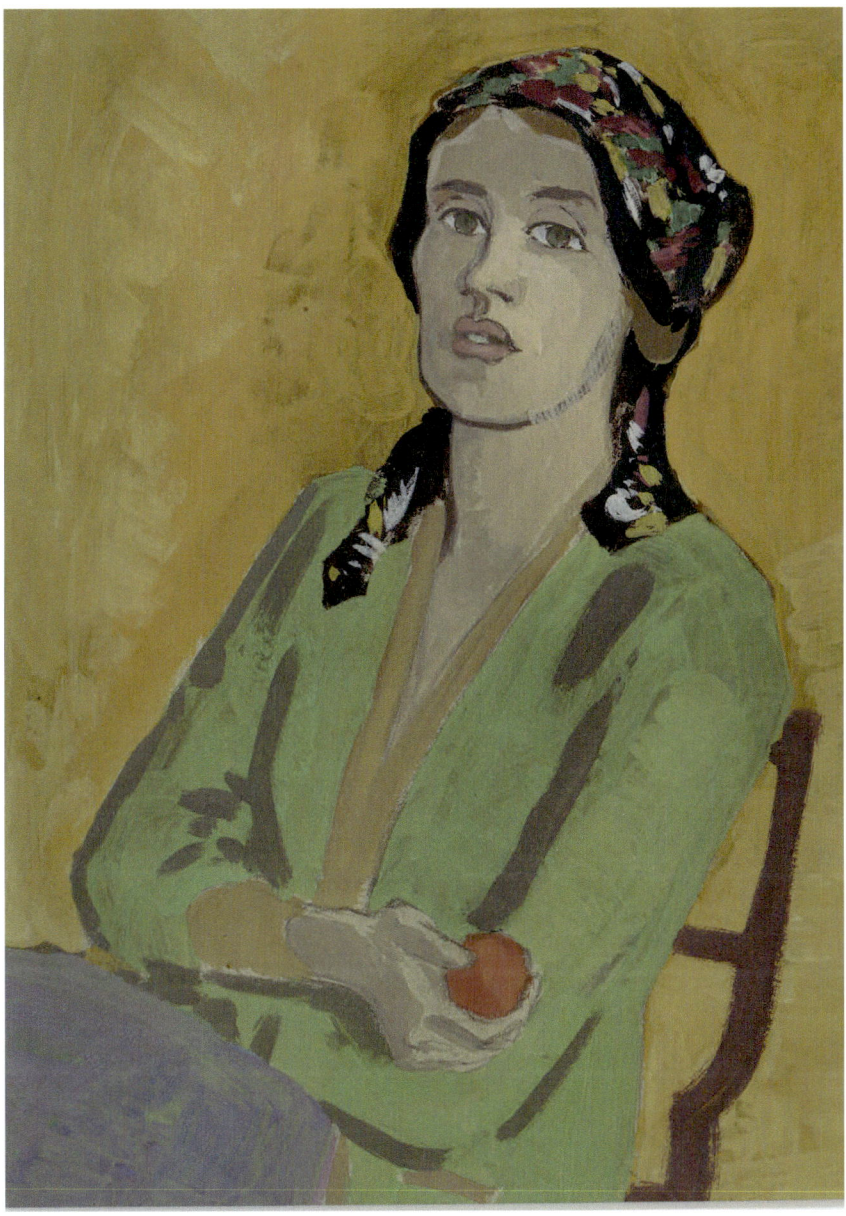

6 *Portrait of Vanessa Bell* by Roger Fry, 1911–1912. Pencil and gouache
on paper, 30.5 × 25.3 cm.

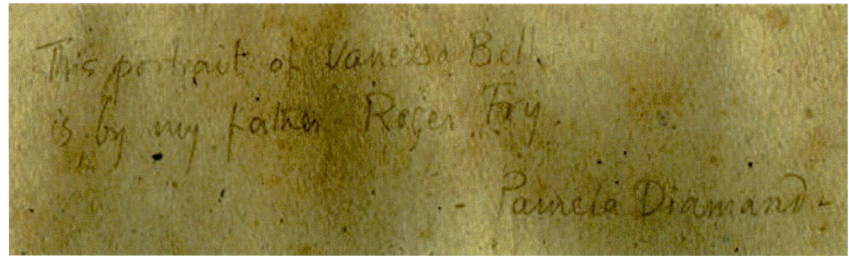

7 Autograph note by Pamela Diamand on the verso of the "new" portrait of
Vanessa Bell (Plate 6), certifying that it is the work of her father, Roger Fry.

8 Note on the verso of the "new" portrait of Vanessa Bell (Plate 6), with Roger
Fry's identification of her as the sitter.

(Plate 8). "V Bell", written in double-line letters, is in Roger's hand, as is
evident if one compares the writing with that in two letters, written by him
in 1910, in which the name "Bell" occurs – his letters to Vanessa Bell of 19
January 1910[10] and to Helen Fry of 23 January 1910.[11] The beginning of
the earlier letter, which starts "Dear Mrs. Bell", is illustrated in Plate 9, and
it can be seen that the forms of the letters and the connections and spaces
between them are identical to those in the note on the back of the portrait.
However, "by REF", which is probably preceded by a faint dash, is not
in Roger Fry's hand, but an addition made by Pamela Diamand, the "by"
being written exactly as in her note at the top.

Roger Fry – P. Diamand"; and the copy of *The Connaught Square Catechism: or,
Confessions to Mrs. Robert Witt* (London, 1915), presented to the Library of King's
College, Cambridge, on 25 September 1979, is inscribed inside: "This book belonged
to my father Roger Fry, who filled in the answers dictated by his friends as an after-
dinner entertainment. Pamela Diamand" (KCC Archive Centre, REF/7/5).

10 TGA 8010/5/590.
11 KCC Archive Centre, REF/3/58/12.

Jan. 19. 1910 .

Dear Mrs. Bell.

9 The beginning of Roger Fry's first surviving letter to Vanessa Bell.

The half-length portrait is of a pale and unsmiling Vanessa seated on, and leaning slightly back in, a wooden chair, against a yellow ochre background with visible brush-strokes. The figure is decisively outlined. The head is slightly raised and turned to the left, towards the viewer. The facial features are clearly defined. The cheekbones are pronounced, the lips full, red, and parted. The eyes are large, dark green, and somewhat asymmetrical. The expression is enigmatic, but probably to be interpreted as wistful rather than as vacant. The face and its pallor are emphasised by contrast with the gaily coloured headscarf, with its pattern of flowers and leaves and its black background and border. The colours of the pattern are red, green, white, and yellow ochre. The scarf is worn gypsy-style with two corners falling down loosely over the shoulders. It covers almost all of the medium-brown hair, which is visible only on the forehead, where it is smoothly brushed back under the scarf, and in a tuft in front of the left ear. The arms are crossed, and the sitter holds a red fruit, probably an apple, in her right hand. Her left hand is not visible. She wears a pea-green blouse or cardigan with a plunging, V-shaped neckline. The garment is trimmed with beige or fawn at the edges and cuffs, and this border gives the illusion of more exposure of flesh than there is. Whether the mauve-blue-with-some-green area lower left represents part of a skirt, as is most likely, or something else, such as a rug, it seems that the sitter's knees are raised and perhaps crossed. Her skirt, like the green of her upper garment, exhibits rapid brush-strokes. She looks similar in age to Helen Fry in Portrait 1.

Before the portrait was acquired by me, it was dated "ca. 1900–1910", but it cannot be earlier than 1910. Although Vanessa Bell met Roger Fry on two occasions before 1910, they did not become friends until that year, following a chance meeting she and her husband, Clive Bell, had with him on a platform at Cambridge railway station in mid-January.[12] By then Helen's mental health had gone from bad to worse, and before the end of the year she was permanently in an asylum in York. The Bells', and especially Vanessa's, friendship with Roger developed during the summer and autumn of that year and the winter of 1910–1911. It was based on their shared interest in art, and Roger, who had become increasingly enthusiastic about modern French art, influenced both Vanessa and Clive. He became a frequent visitor to their home at 46 Gordon Square, London, sometimes staying there when he came up to town from his home in Guildford to do editorial work on *The Burlington Magazine*, to lecture at the Slade, and to organise and curate the controversial "Manet and the Post-Impressionists" exhibition held at the Grafton Galleries from 8 November 1910 to mid-January 1911. In April 1911 Vanessa's and his relationship developed further, in a spectacular way, when she, Clive, and Roger went to Turkey with the young Vanessa-smitten Cambridge mathematician and "Apostle" Henry ("Harry") Norton. She was unwell before the trip and when they set off, and on 16 April, two days after the party had moved on from Constantinople to Bursa, she was again taken ill and suffered a miscarriage. There was no competent doctor, and the nursing care was provided in an unorthodox but effective manner by Roger, who converted Vanessa's room in the Hôtel d'Anatolie not only into a sickroom, but also into an art gallery whose exhibits were their drawings and paintings and items he bought in the bazaar. A plan to go on to Athens was abandoned and the party stayed in Turkey until early May when Vanessa had recovered sufficiently to manage the journey home, accompanied not only by Clive and Roger, but also by her sister, Virginia Stephen (later Woolf), who went out to Turkey for a week to help bring her home. By the time the party (which did not include Harry Norton, who had left it in Vienna) returned to England on 6 May, Vanessa and Roger were in love with one another.[13]

---

12 The meeting was probably on Monday morning, 17 January 1910. Vanessa Bell, *Sketches in Pen and Ink: A Bloomsbury Notebook*, ed. Lia Giachero (London, 1997), 120, is wrong in thinking that it was "early in 1908". She is also mistaken in saying that the lunch party to which Roger invited her and Clive at his home in Guildford was on a Sunday "in the early spring" (121). It was actually on 23 January 1910, as is revealed both by Roger's appointments' diary (KCC Archive Centre, REF/5/1/2) and by his letter of 23 January 1910 to Helen Fry (REF/3/58/12). The Bells did not make it to the lunch, because they could not find Roger's new house, but the engagement was rearranged, successfully, for Friday 25 February 1910.

13 Mary Ann Caws, *Women of Bloomsbury: Virginia, Vanessa, and Carrington* (New York and London, 1990), 80, would have us believe that the two fell in love before the visit to Turkey. She writes: "The relationship between them is, in the beginning, gloriously physical: February 8, 1911: 'Dear I wanted you!'." But the

After the ordeal in Turkey Vanessa remained somewhat unwell for about two years. In this situation, she found Roger's attentions a great comfort and wanted to see him as often as their family commitments and his hectic life allowed. In fact she found it frustrating that she could not see him more often. She visited him at Durbins, his home in Guildford, and later the Bells briefly rented a house in the town, Millmead Cottage (now Weir House). The affair continued strongly through 1912, but faltered in 1913, when her feelings changed in favour of Duncan Grant. Roger was very hurt, but remained a close friend.

It is highly likely that our new portrait was painted in 1911–1912. For one thing, Vanessa's youthful appearance indicates an early stage in her and Roger's friendship, when she was in her early thirties. Her face is very much as it is seen in a photograph taken of her at Durbins in 1911 (Plate 10),[14] and in five nude photographs, taken by Roger at Studland, Dorset, in September 1911. (Four of the nude photographs are reproduced as Plates 11–14). Other significant indicators of the painting having been executed while the affair was flourishing are the voluptuous red lips and the red apple. An apple is a potent symbol of love and desire, as in Dante Gabriel Rossetti's painting *Venus Verticordia*, and the red of the fruit and of the lips conveys the likely suggestion that both are ripe and ready – the apple for eating, the lips for kissing. Moreover, the showing of the tuft of hair in front of Vanessa's left ear is to be compared with a remark Roger makes in a passionate love-letter he wrote her when their affair was only weeks old.

letter from which she quotes (TGA 8010/8/97), dated just "Feb. 8" and written by Vanessa to Roger from Asheham House, Rodmell, belongs not to 1911, but to 1912. Vanessa and Virginia (Stephen) did not rent Asheham House until New Year 1912. Moreover, "Dear" is a misreading. What Vanessa actually writes, after referring to the glorious weather, is: "You will be surprised to hear I wanted you!" In the same paragraph Caws makes other mistakes. The letter (TGA 8010/8/62) in which Vanessa tells Roger "You dont [not "don't"] know how often I have wanted you since that night at [not "in"] Genoa" is to be dated 5 June [1912], not 1911. In quoting from another letter from Vanessa to Roger, dated Wednesday [6 July 1911] (TGA 8010.8.6), Caws makes her exclaim "what muse was ever as good as you", instead of "what nurse ...". She also misquotes the end of the sentence containing this remark, substituting the single word "lost" for the three words "wasted on one".

14 See also the photograph of her with Virginia Stephen and Janet Case at Firle, Sussex, almost certainly in 1911, reproduced by Maggie Humm, *Snapshots of Bloomsbury: The Private Lives of Virginia Woolf and Vanessa Bell* (London, 2006), 69. The original is in Virginia Woolf's Monk's House Photographs, circa 1867–1967 (MS Thr 564), Harvard Theatre Collection, Houghton Library, Harvard University, Series I: Loose Photographs B. (134).

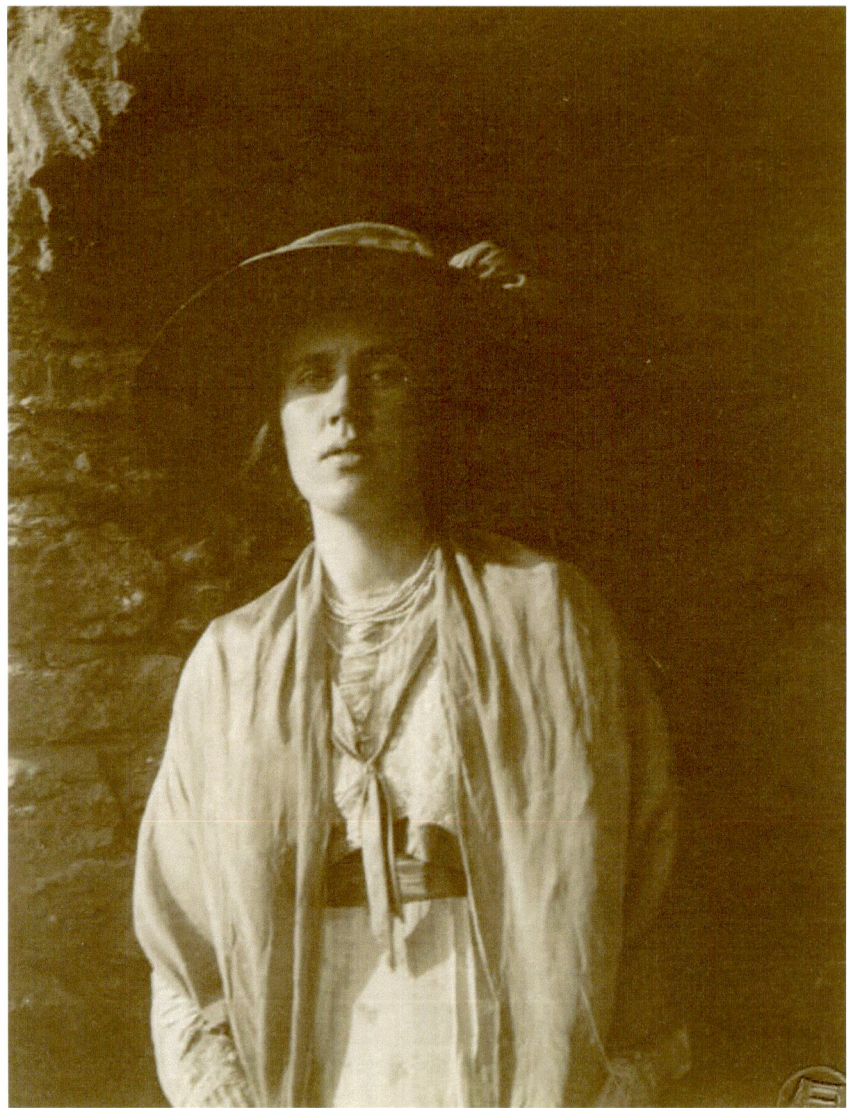

10 Vanessa Bell at Durbins (Roger Fry's house in Guildford), 1911. Photograph.

In the list of things he loves about her body he includes "the little waves of hair that ripple round your ears".[15] It may be added that her pallor well suits one who was convalescent.

15 TGA 8010/5/602 = Denys Sutton, *Letters of Roger Fry* (London, 1972), I, 349. Sutton dates the letter "[? 1911]", but one can be much more precise than that. In the

Writing to the French painter Simon Bussy, a friend of Matisse, on 23 May 1911, only just over a fortnight after returning from Turkey, Roger declares: *"maintenant je suis devenu tout à fait Matissiste."*[16] *"Tout à fait"* is an exaggeration, but the influence of Matisse is to be seen not only in his Turkish landscapes but also, to some degree, in this portrait of Vanessa. It is manifested in the way the body is depicted in decisive, simple strokes, and in the rapid brush-strokes remarked on above. It is manifested also perhaps in the colourful headscarf, which may well be one Roger bought Vanessa in Turkey and therefore another symbol of their love. Recalling the days when she was ill in Bursa, she describes how Roger cluttered her room with, among other things "every kind of object discovered and bought in the bazaars", and continues: "He found printed handkerchiefs ... of lovely colours and quality, such as no other tourist seems to have noticed then."[17] Vanessa loved colourful costumes and was to design them for Omega Workshops Ltd, the decorative-art enterprise which Roger, she, and Duncan Grant opened in July 1913. In February 1911 she and Clive, Roger, Virginia Stephen, Adrian Stephen, Duncan Grant, and James Strachey went to a fancy-dress dance at Crosby Hall, Chelsea, dressed (and undressed!) "more or less like figures from Gauguin", decked with "brilliant flowers and beads".[18] Vanessa's penchant for headscarves is confirmed by Duncan Grant in a letter he wrote to Virginia Woolf on 23 September [1912] after nearly a fortnight's stay with Vanessa at Asheham House near Lewes:

first sentence of the letter Roger refers to "my walk through Herefordshire valleys". The only visit he made to Herefordshire in 1911–1912 seems to have been on 24 May 1911, when he went to Eastnor near Ledbury and stayed the night there before proceeding to Scotland (Ardkinglas House, Argyll) on 25 May "to fix my ceiling", as he puts it in a letter to Bob Trevelyan (23 May 1911, Trinity College Cambridge Library, RCT 4.82). See his appointments' diary for April–June 1911 (KCC Archive Centre, REF/5/1/2).

16 "I have now become completely Matissist", TGA 917/9. Sutton, *Letters*, 348, misdates the letter 22 May 1911 and gives the extract he quotes from it in English, without any indication that the original is in French.

17 Bell, *Sketches*, 140.

18 Bell, *Sketches*, 133–134. She does not date the event exactly, placing it in the winter of 1910–1911, but a letter from Roger to Clive Bell dated 11 February 1911 undoubtedly refers to it. See Sutton, *Letters*, 341. Roger's letter gives the day of the ball as "Tuesday", i.e. 14 February (St Valentine's Day) 1911, but this is probably a slip for "Thursday", because in his appointments' diary he has twice written "Ball" – once in ordinary pencil, once in orange pencil – under Thursday, 16 February 1911 (KCC Archive Centre, REF/5/1/2). Bell, *Sketches*, 133–134, says that "we got stuffs I had lately found at Burnetts' made for natives in Africa with which we draped our- selves". She means B. Burnet & Co Ltd., listed in the Post Office London Directory 1911 under "Art Fabrics for Dress and Decoration" and "Theatrical Hosiers". It had

"Vanessa is in the most blooming health, like a gipsey [*sic*], and goes about with bright coloured hankerchiefs [*sic*] wound round her head."[19] Several portraits and photographs show her wearing a headscarf. The portraits include a self-portrait, dated c. 1915, in the collection of the Yale Center for British Art, Paul Mellon Fund (accession no. B.1982.16.2). The photographs include the aforementioned series of five, taken by Roger, that show her posing in the nude at Studland in September 1911.

Whatever the art-critical opinion of Roger Fry's "new" portrait of Vanessa Bell may be, it cannot be doubted that it is of considerable interest, given that both the artist and the sitter were pivotal members of the Bloomsbury Group, and that it belongs to the period when they were lovers. If, as is most likely, the portrait was painted between the summer of 1911 and the autumn of 1912, it comes between Roger's first post-impressionist exhibition of November 1910–January 1911 and his second one, also at the Grafton Galleries, of October 1912–January 1913. Both were as influential as they were controversial, and "our" portrait of Vanessa Bell, one of the British artists who wholeheartedly embraced post-impressionism and contributed work of her own to the second exhibition, was executed at a time of lively and significant change for the artist, for the sitter, and for art in the western world.

Provenance of Portrait 2

From Roger Fry to his daughter, (Agnes) Pamela Diamand, who sold it privately c. 1978–1979 to the New York art dealer Lawrence ("Larry") B. Salander of Salander–O'Reilly Galleries LLC, who gave it to his daughter, the artist Ivana Salander, in whose bedroom it hung from the day she was born; from Ivana Salander to B & B Rare Books Company of New York, June 2014; from B & B Rare Books to me, 30 October 2014. The involvement of Larry Salander in the picture's ownership is noteworthy, given that he was later to defraud customers, investors, and business-partners on a massive scale, to the tune of about $120,000,000. On 3 August 2010 he

---

premises at 22 Garrick Street in Covent Garden, at 2 Long Acre, Drury Lane, and at 198 Regent Street. The beads mentioned by Vanessa, or some of them, were probably supplied by Roger, who in the aforementioned letter to Clive writes: "I've got a splendid lot of Kaffir necklaces, etc."

19 University of Sussex Special Collections SxMs-18/1/D/62/1. Frances Spalding, *Duncan Grant: A Biography* (London, 1997), 131, mentions this passage. Her endnote on it, "Duncan Grant to Virginia Stephen, July 1911" (518, n. 10), is seriously inaccurate, not only getting the month and year wrong, but also misrepresenting Virginia, who was on her honeymoon at the time, as still unmarried.

received a prison sentence of six to eighteen years. In my possession is a very detailed and rather amusing description of the visit he made with William O'Reilly, his business partner at that time, to Pamela Diamand's home on the day he bought the picture. On 20 March 2019 the picture was sold by Sotheby's, London, in its "Made in Britain" sale L19144, lot 112.

Acknowledgements

I most gratefully acknowledge the assistance of the following: Jane Abram; Karen Arathoon; Philip Athill of Abbott & Holder Ltd, London; B & B Rare Books Ltd, New York City, and its proprietors, Josh Mann and Sunday Steinkirchner; Linda Elisabeth Beattie (now LaPinta); The Berg Collection, New York Public Library, and its former Curator, Isaac Gewirtz; Tony Bradshaw; Victoria Chance; Sally Dowding; Fran Dyson-Sutton; the late Henrietta Garnett, the copyright holder, for permission to quote from Vanessa Bell's letters and *Sketches in Pen and Ink*; Penelope Gear; Sheila Gear; Peter Grogan of Peter Grogan, Rare Books & Manuscripts, London; Terry Halladay of William Reese Company, New Haven, Connecticut; King's College Cambridge Archive Centre and its Archivist, Patricia McGuire; Jenny Lister, Curator, Department of Fashion and Textiles, Victoria and Albert Museum; Jan Marsh, National Portrait Gallery, London; Philip Mould of Philip Mould & Company, London; Richard Neave; Clare Phillips, Curator, Department of Sculpture, Metalwork, Ceramics and Glass, Victoria and Albert Museum; Jon Richardson of Jon S. Richardson Rare Books, Concord, Massachusetts; Dorota Rychlik of Vaila Fine Art, Lerwick, Shetland; Lucinda Ferguson Smith; Tate Gallery Archive; Trinity College Cambridge Library; University of Sussex Special Collections.

2

A complete strip-off:
A Bloomsbury threesome in the nude
at Studland

From 1 to 29 September 1911 Vanessa and Clive Bell and their children stayed in Studland on the coast of Dorset. They had stayed there three times before – in September 1909, March–April 1910, and September–October 1910. On all four occasions Vanessa's sister Virginia Stephen (later, Woolf) too stayed in Studland, although only on the second of them, when her mental state was shaky and the Bells took her away for a break, did she stay in the same house.

The establishment patronised by Vanessa and Clive was a lodging-house called Harbour View on Beach Road. Owned by the Payne family of Studland boatmen, who lived in the adjacent Vine Cottage, it had been run since September 1903 by tenants Jacob[1] ("Jake") William Gibbons and his wife, Lottie Jane Gibbons, *née* Puckett. Lottie was related to James Hammett, one of the Tolpuddle Martyrs. Jake, who also worked as a gardener at the Studland Bay country home of Sir Eustace Fiennes,[2] had been declared bankrupt early in 1909. The reasons he gave in court for his insolvency were "illness of self, wife, and children" and "bad letting seasons of 1906 and 1907".[3] In April 1912 he was to sign up as a second-class steward on the S.S. *Titanic*. According to his wife, he went to sea in the hope of curing the peritonitis from which he was suffering.[4] He survived the disaster, but unsurprisingly did not sign up again for such employment.[5] Harbour View, which is now a private residence called Seacombe, is conveniently situated about 300 yards from the sea, but the accommodation

---

1 Not Joseph, as stated by Frances Spalding, *Vanessa Bell* (London, 1993), 87, and Lisa Tickner, "Vanessa Bell: *Studland Beach*, Domesticity, and 'Significant Form'," *Representations* 65 (Winter 1999), 63–92, at 71.
2 Grandfather of the explorer Sir Ranulph Fiennes.
3 *Western Gazette*, 19 February 1909, 3.
4 Rodney Legg, *The Book of Studland* (Tiverton, 2002), 78.
5 He served with the Red Cross in France during the First World War, then worked for the Canadian Pacific Railway (in Canada) before returning to Harbour View.

was somewhat cramped. For a start, Jacob and Lottie had five children by the time of the 1911 visit.[6]

In Essay 1 I have described how Vanessa and Roger fell in love during a visit to Turkey with Clive Bell and Harry Norton in the spring of 1911.[7] On their return to England, Vanessa and Roger saw one another as often as they could, but not as often as they wished. She visited him at his Guildford home, Durbins, and in late July and early August she and Clive stayed nearby in Millmead Cottage, before moving on, on 14 August, with their sons, Julian and Quentin, aged three-and-a-half and one respectively,[8] to Clive's parents' home in Wiltshire, Cleeve House in the village of Seend, near Melksham. From there between 15 and 31 August Vanessa wrote to Roger (at least) fourteen times. As this epistolary bombardment, undoubtedly welcome to its target, suggests, she was missing him terribly. Her first letter makes clear that the two had made love in the morning of the fourteenth: "I seem to be hundreds of miles from you and everything exciting. Yesterday morning especially seems very remote! Oh Roger, how delicious it was though. I cant help thinking here how horrified they'd all be if they knew."[9] He missed her too. In a note that is undated but was written on 14 or 15 August he writes: "I want to know that you got safe to Seend and aren't jiggery – very much indeed. I thought I could let you go for a bit but I want you back ever so much."[10] "Jiggery" is a word the two of them use to mean something like "rocky" or "wobbly". At this time her health continued to be unsatisfactory, and, on the day of the train journey to Seend, the weather was hot (up to 30°C in southern England) and severe labour unrest was threatening transport systems; in fact, the country's first national rail strike was imminent. In response to Vanessa's declarations of love and longing and her confidences about her health problems, including

---

6 Next door to Harbour View was Full Stop, now called Sandyholme, the home of Alexander Hellier Berens, an Old Etonian who led a varied and adventurous life abroad before settling c. 1900 with his second wife in Studland, where in collaboration with Louisa Churchill, a local woman who was employed by the Berenses first as parlourmaid, then as housekeeper, he practised a wide range of arts and crafts. In 1921 the two established a business called Studland Art Industries. Berens was a versatile man (brilliant with animals for one thing) and a colourful character, and visitors to Harbour View could hardly have been unaware of the owner of the house next door. On Louisa Churchill and her family, see Joyce Meates, *Goathorn, Studland, Dorset: A Forgotten Clayworking Community* (Swanage, 2013).

7 See p. 22.

8 Julian was born on 4 February 1908, Quentin on 19 August 1910.

9 Vanessa Bell to Roger Fry, 15 August [1911] (Tate Gallery Archive [henceforth TGA] 8010/8/12).

10 TGA 8010.5.598.

daily updates on the progress of her period, Roger had to be restrained, because she was with Clive and felt obliged to read out to him at least parts of the letters she received. The main thing that kept her going at Seend was the thought that she would see Roger at Studland, and she urged him to arrange his affairs so that he could spend as much time there as possible.

In the event she did not see nearly as much of him as she had hoped. There were three reasons for this, revealed in her letters to him and in his appointments' diary.[11] First, he was often elsewhere for professional or family reasons, and it is indicative of this that between 5 and 28 September she wrote to him at least eleven times. Secondly, even when he was in Studland, with or without his family, he was not staying at Harbour View, except for the three nights of 1–3 September.[12] In fact, when his children, Julian and Pamela, aged ten and nine respectively, arrived with their Swiss governess, Madeleine Savary,[13] on 4 September, the family lodged for a week in Swanage rather than in Studland, before transferring to accommodation in Studland on 11 September. Thirdly, Vanessa was worried that Clive would smell a rat: "Next week when you come I must, however absurd it may seem, not sketch with you more than I should do naturally – for if he gets jealous now it will put an end to everything."[14] A few days earlier she had given Roger another warning – to avoid giving Virginia any excuse to "make mischief between you and him [Clive] by making him think I am in love with you".[15]

Writing soon after Roger's death twenty-three years later (1934), Vanessa recalls the time in Studland and the difficulty she had in seeing him. She remembers "painting with him once or twice", and mentions that "some snapshots exist of him and the children there".[16] What she does not mention is any photography by him or any photographs taken at Studland of him and her in the nude. But such photographs exist.

11 King's College Cambridge Archive Centre (henceforth KCC) REF/5/1/2.
12 See Vanessa's letters to Roger of Tuesday [29 August 1911] (TGA 8010/8/20), 31 August [1911] (TGA 8010/8/22), and 7 September [1911] (TGA 8010/8/23). In the possession of a descendant of the Gibbonses is the Harbour View visitors' book, but unfortunately it goes back no earlier than the 1930s.
13 Madeleine Savary had recently become a Quaker. In 1920 she organised the first regular Quaker meeting in Geneva and served as its clerk in the early years.
14 Vanessa Bell to Roger Fry, 13 September [1911] (TGA 8010/8/26).
15 Vanessa Bell to Roger Fry, 5 September [1911] (TGA 8010/8/24).
16 Vanessa Bell, *Sketches in Pen and Ink: A Bloomsbury Notebook*, ed. Lia Giachero (London, 1997), 147. For photographs of Roger and his children, Julian and Pamela, at Studland in 1911, see Maggie Humm, *Snapshots of Bloomsbury: The Private Lives of Virginia Woolf and Vanessa Bell* (London, 2006), 93–94.

The photographs are in the Henry W. and Albert A. Berg Collection of English and American Literature in The New York Public Library. They are in "An Archive of Bloomsbury Photographs and Negatives, 1908–1965 bulk (1910–1913)", acquired by the Berg from R. A. Gekoski, dealer in rare books and manuscripts, in 2005. Full details of the archive's provenance are shown at the end of this essay. The Berg's Curator, Dr Isaac Gewirtz, explains that "1908–1965 bulk (1910–1913)" means that "the entire collection spans the years 1908–1965, but the majority of the photographs in the collection date from 1910–1913".[17] The collection comprises 134 items, of which 116 are photographic negatives and prints – 36 negatives, all original, and 80 photographic prints, 53 of them "vintage", the rest "old" or "modern".[18]

Many of the portraits in the archive show their subjects nude. Those subjects include Oliver Strachey, Philippa ("Pippa") Strachey, Duncan Grant, Clive Bell, Katherine ("Ka") Cox, and Marjorie Strachey. There are five original negatives of nude photographs of Vanessa Bell, said to have been taken by Roger Fry at Studland c. 1912–1913, and five original negatives of nude photographs of Roger, said to have been taken by Vanessa at Studland c. 1912–1913.

The nude photographs of Vanessa and Roger were not taken in 1912 or 1913. Although she fancied the idea of arranging a painting party at Studland in July 1912,[19] it did not happen, and it was only in September 1911 that she and Roger are known to have coincided there. In her memoir of him she only mentions that one occasion,[20] and there is, so far as I can find, no mention of another occasion in any other source.[21]

The five portraits of Vanessa show her in different poses. The only items she is seen to be wearing in all five are a headscarf and a necklace. In Plate 11, the only photograph in which her feet appear, she is wearing a pair of court shoes (pumps).[22] In Plate 12 she is holding a dark sheet with a

17 Email to the author, 5 October 2016.

18 Thanks to the kindness of Peter Grogan, I have been able to consult, in addition to the Berg's catalogue, the detailed inventory of the archive prepared in advance of its sale by Gekoski.

19 Vanessa Bell to Roger Fry, 27 September [1911] (TGA 8010/8/32); Vanessa Bell to Duncan Grant, 27 September [1911] (TGA 20078/1/44/5).

20 Bell, *Sketches*, 117–147. She recalls the 1911 visit to Studland at 147.

21 Roger's appointments' diary for 1913 is missing, but the *argumentum ex silentio* is still very powerful. Richard Shone, *Bloomsbury Portraits* (revised and enlarged edition, London, 1993), 47, mistakenly assigns Vanessa's and Roger's portraits of Lytton Strachey at Studland to 1912. They were painted in September 1911, as stated by Elizabeth P. Richardson, *A Bloomsbury Iconography* (Winchester, 1989), 105–106. The sitting was sometime between 15 and 23 September.

22 The shoes are perhaps of patent leather.

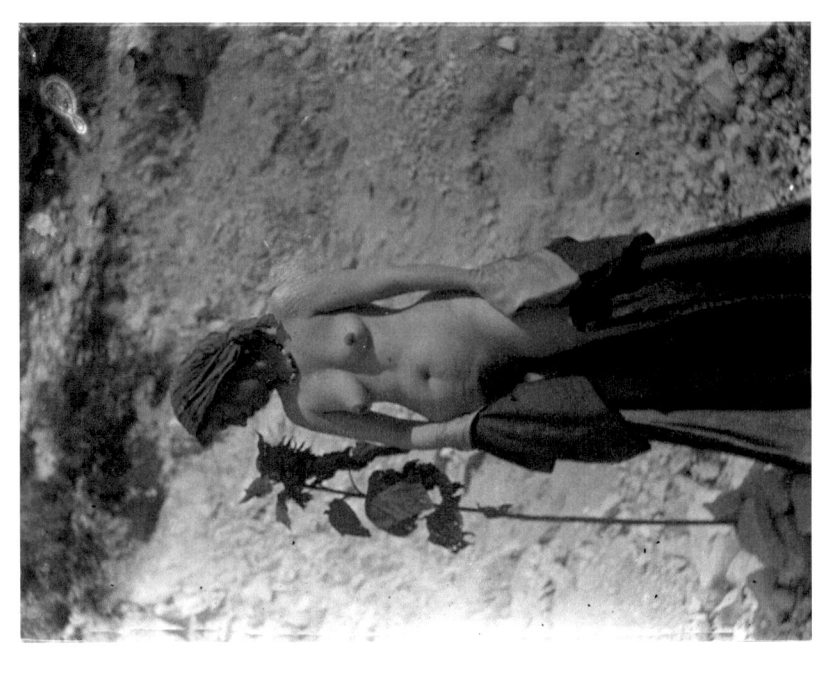

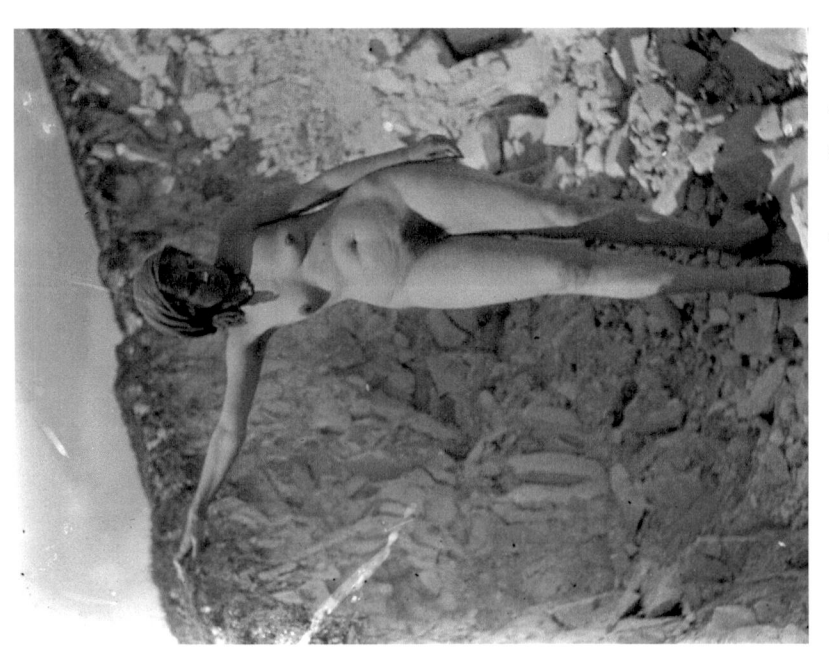

11–12 Vanessa Bell at Studland, Dorset, September 1911. Photographs by Roger Fry.

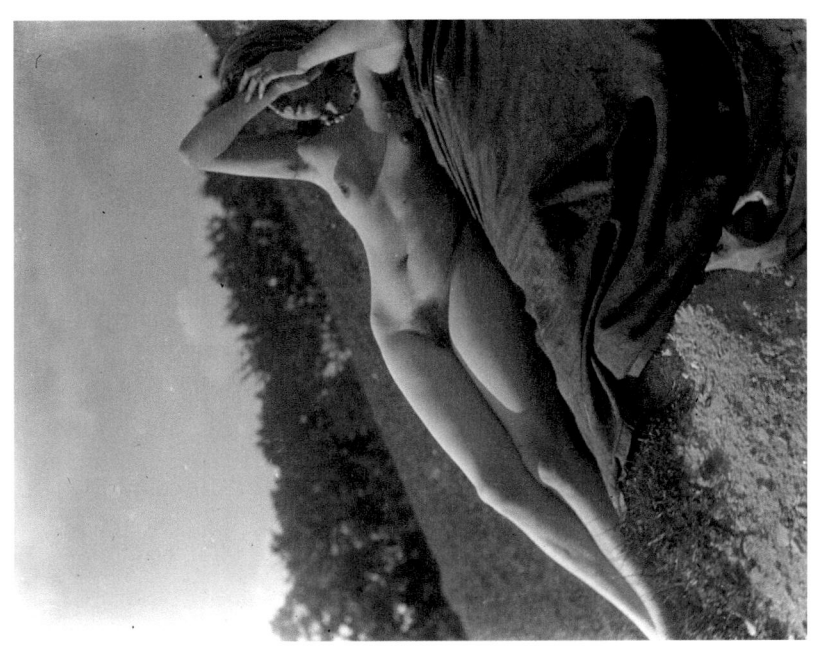

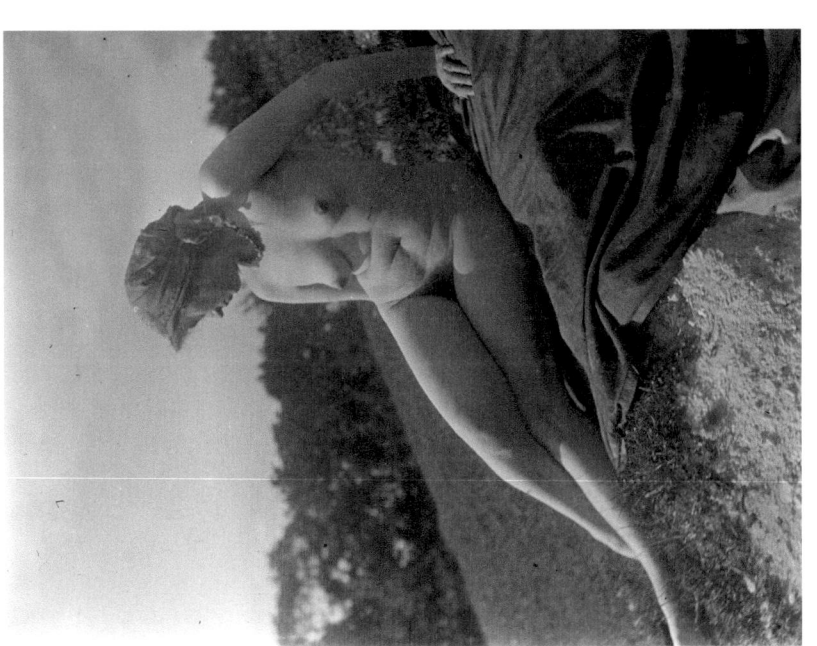

13–14 Vanessa Bell at Studland, Dorset, September 1911. Photographs by Roger Fry.

lighter-coloured lining, presumably the same sheet as the one on which she is sitting or reclining in Plates 13 and 14, draped round the lower part of her body, but in such way as to leave exposed all that is between her legs.

The headscarf is plainer than the one she is wearing in Roger's "new" gouache portrait of her,[23] but is arranged in a not dissimilar fashion, so as to reveal some tufts of hair. It is possibly the same article as the one she is wearing in a photograph of her with Virginia Stephen and Janet Case in Firle Park, Sussex.[24] The bead necklace looks similar to one seen in several other portraits of her. The earliest is an oil and pencil image executed by Duncan Grant on page 7 of the 7 August 1911 issue of *The Times*, although the sketchiness of the composition makes certainty impossible.[25] One may compare also the necklace seen in a photograph of Vanessa taken at Asheham House,[26] and in the portraits of her executed by Roger Fry and Duncan Grant at the same sitting c. 1916.[27] Their paintings suggest that the beads or nuggets are of amber and turquoise and/or lapis lazuli.

The nude photographs of Vanessa at Studland were taken in three locations, all probably in very close proximity to one another. One (Plate 11) shows her standing immediately in front of a steep and crumbly bank of chalk, two (one of them Plate 12) standing in front of what is likely to be a continuation of the same bank, and two (Plates 13 and 14) reclining on a nearby grassy slope. The sunflower (Plate 12 and another photograph), supported by an arrangement of stones, as well as facilitating different poses and expressions, has symbolic significance: since sunflowers, when young, tilt their heads to follow the sun across the sky, they connote fidelity and devotion. Moreover, they were a favourite subject of artists, including Paul Gauguin, Vincent van Gogh, and Gustav Klimt. Sunflower paintings by Gauguin and van Gogh had been among the works included in Roger Fry's "Manet and the Post-Impressionists" exhibition at the Grafton Galleries in

23 Plate 6.
24 For details of this photograph, see Essay 1, n. 14.
25 The image is reproduced by Richard Shone, *The Art of Bloomsbury: Roger Fry, Vanessa Bell and Duncan Grant* (Princeton, 1999), 248. In discussing the composition, Shone does not mention that on 7–8 August 1911 Duncan Grant was seeing Vanessa in Guildford, staying either at Durbins, Roger Fry's house, or at Millmead Cottage, the house rented by the Bells. See Vanessa's letter to Roger of 8 August [1911] (TGA 8010/8/7).
26 Reproduced in Frances Spalding, *Duncan Grant* (London, 1997), between 144 and 145, and Spalding, *Vanessa Bell*, opposite 81.
27 Duncan Grant's picture is reproduced in Shone, *Bloomsbury Portraits*, 149, Roger Fry's in Christopher Green (ed.), *Art Made Modern: Roger Fry's Vision of Art* (London, 1999), 65.

November 1910–January 1911.[28] The appearance of the sunflower in two of the photographs of Vanessa suggests that the shoot was carefully planned in advance.[29]

The photographs of Roger show him in front of a steep chalk bank, higher than the one seen behind Vanessa in Plate 11, and probably a little further to the right (north) of it. Four of them, including the three reproduced in this book (Plates 15–17) were taken at (almost) exactly the same spot. They show him in various poses, including one from the back. His hair is wet, and there is sand on parts of his body, including his feet, legs, and back. In the fifth photograph, a view from the back, he is making as if to climb the bank: he is leaning forward with his right leg advanced and his right hand on his right knee. He has lowered his head so far that it is invisible. He is wearing shoes with light-coloured uppers, whereas in the other photographs his feet are bare.

Given that Vanessa was on holiday with Clive, it would be sensationally remarkable if she and Roger had risked and got away with taking nude photographs of one another unchaperoned. Compelling evidence that this was not the case is the presence in the same Berg archive of a group of eleven vintage photographic prints of Clive in the nude. The photographs, clearly taken at Studland on the same occasion and at the same location, prove that the strip-off for the camera was a threesome. They also reveal that there was a fourth person present – a man fully dressed. The man is Gerald Frank Shove, who was educated at Uppingham and King's College, Cambridge. He took a first class in economics in 1910. The previous year he had been elected an "Apostle".[30] He was close to another King's Apostle, the economist Maynard Keynes,[31] his senior by several years. It was through Maynard and the Apostles that Gerald became associated with the Bloomsbury Group. In the photographs under discussion he is smartly (and, in the context of the event he was observing, incongruously) dressed in a dark striped suit and smoking a pipe.[32]

---

28 See Anna Gruetzner Robins, "'Manet and the Post-Impressionists': A Checklist of Exhibits", *The Burlington Magazine*, 152 (December 2010), 782–793, at 787, 790.

29 The headscarf Vanessa is seen wearing in the Firle Park photograph (see above), which may be the same as the one she wore at Studland, displays a single sunflower-head as decoration. No such decoration is visible in the Studland photographs, but may just be concealed from view. In any case, one can justifiably conclude that sunflowers were favoured by Vanessa.

30 See Essay 1, n. 5.

31 Keynes studied (and took a first in) mathematics rather than economics.

32 On Gerald Shove's high sartorial standards, see Vanessa Bell's exceptionally vulgar letter of 19 April [1914] to Maynard Keynes in Regina Marler, *Selected Letters of Vanessa Bell* (London, 1993), 163. In the summer of 1911, Duncan Grant painted Gerald's portrait in Cambridge. For a colour photograph, see Shone, *The Art of Bloomsbury*, 95.

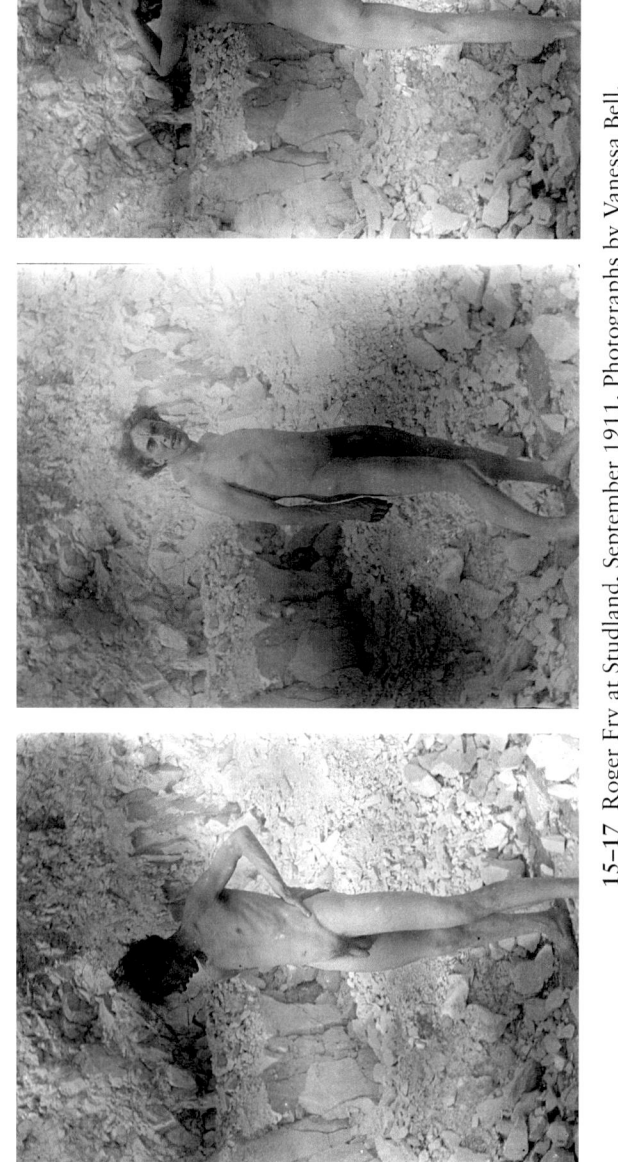

15–17 Roger Fry at Studland, September 1911. Photographs by Vanessa Bell.

Clive, like Roger, has wet hair and sand on his body. The photographs, seemingly taken at a spot very close to that where those of Vanessa were taken, show him in a variety of positions and situations, some of them so undignified that one can hardly call them "poses". In three of them he is receiving attention from Vanessa, who is wearing the headscarf and a long, long-sleeved, darkish dress (or beach-robe) with a pattern of small flowers (?) and a black belt with a large bow at the back. In one of the three she stands to the viewer's right of him, bending sideways to assist him. The picture is too blurred for one to be sure exactly what is going on, but Clive is doing a mini-squat, leaning forward towards the camera, with his head down, while Vanessa, side on to the camera, helps him either with the taking-off or putting-on of a shirt or with use of a towel. The scene is observed by an amused Gerald, pipe in mouth, right hand in pocket. In the two other photographs in which she appears, she is kneeling in front of Clive with her back to the camera, seemingly giving attention to one or both of his feet, perhaps to a shoe or a cut. In one of these, he is seen in half-profile, bending to the viewer's left, with both arms dropped, while on the extreme right Gerald, back to camera, watches, left hand on hip. In the other (Plate 18), in which Gerald does not appear, Clive, although bending slightly forward, looks at the camera. Both his arms are extended downwards, his right hand on his right thigh, his left hand on Vanessa's right shoulder for support while she attends to his left foot, which is not visible, but evidently slightly raised.

All but one of the eight photographs of Clive that remain to be described show him on his own. The exception is a waist-up portrait of him and Gerald standing together (Plate 19). Clive on the left is seen in profile, naked, head lowered, arms crossed. Gerald on the right faces the camera, fully clothed, pipe in mouth. Three photographs show Clive's rear. Of these, one is a close-up view of his sand-coated buttocks and his back; another, taken a little further away and showing him looking down, takes in his body from the back of the thighs to the back of the head; and the third, perhaps taken earlier than the other two, because there is a lot of sand not only on his buttocks, but also on his back and shoulders, shows him turned a little to the right, head slightly lowered, arms akimbo, and standing on a dark sheet (Plate 20). The sheet exhibits a lighter-coloured lining, indicating that it is either the same sheet as the one that Vanessa is holding in Plate 12 or its twin. This is useful confirmation that the photographs of her and Clive were taken on the same occasion. What is undoubtedly the same sheet, despite its lining not being visible, is seen in three other photographs of Clive. In one of these, he is bending forward, head lowered, hands on knees, legs close together and seemingly coated with sand; in another, he is seen in three-quarter rear profile, standing with his head lowered and his

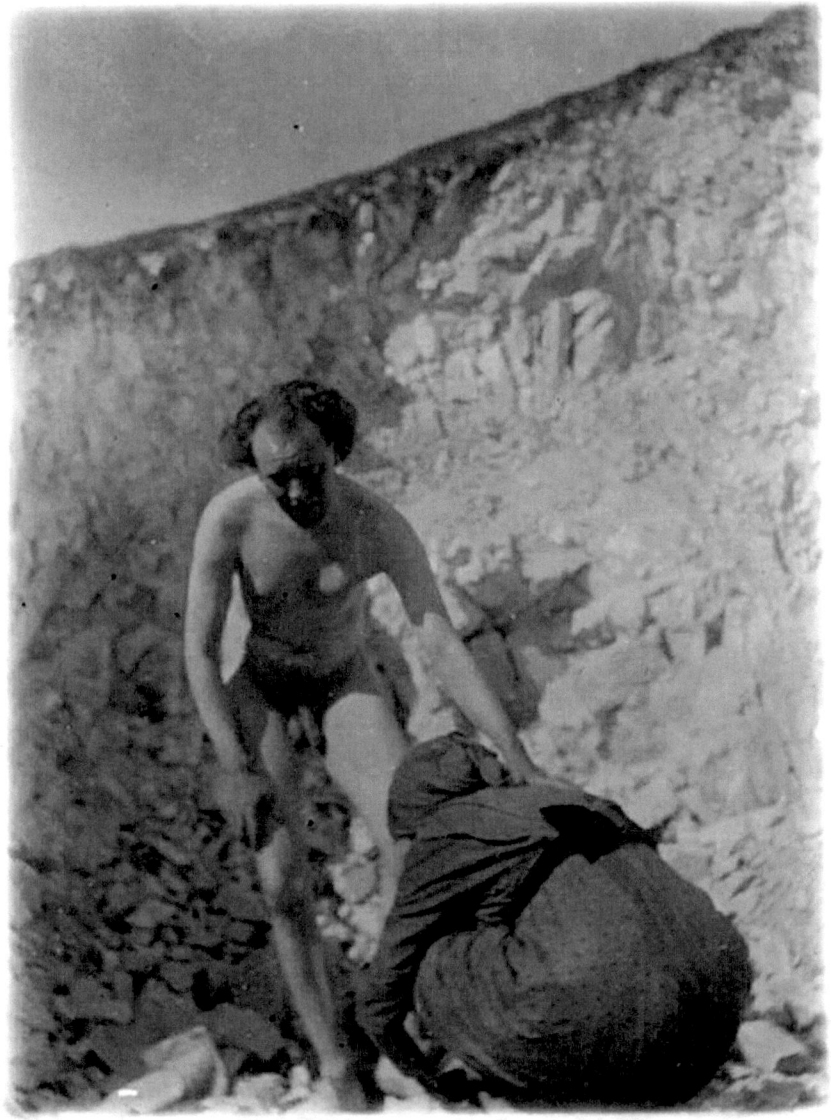

18 Clive Bell and Vanessa Bell at Studland, September 1911.
Photograph by Roger Fry.

right arm lowered in front of his body, with the hand out of sight. No doubt it was not intended so, but he looks as though he might be about to relieve himself – an unflattering pose, anyhow. It is remarkable that in the great majority of photographs he has his head down. Another such photograph,

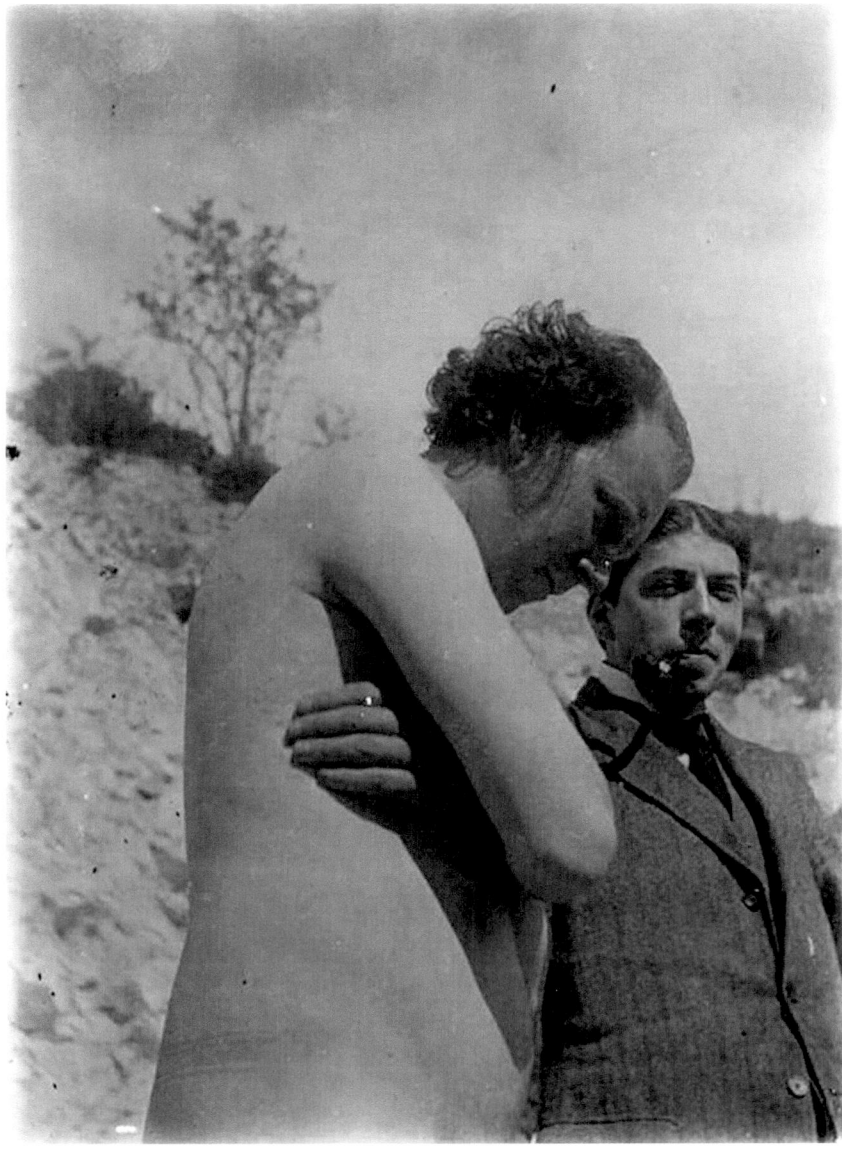

19 Clive Bell and Gerald Shove at Studland, September 1911.
Photograph by Roger Fry (or Vanessa Bell?).

not yet mentioned, shows him in three-quarters front profile, standing with his left hand on his hip. The only exception is a closer-up shot, taken at the same spot and from virtually the same angle, taking in his body from the top of his head to the top of his thighs (Plate 21). Here too he stands with

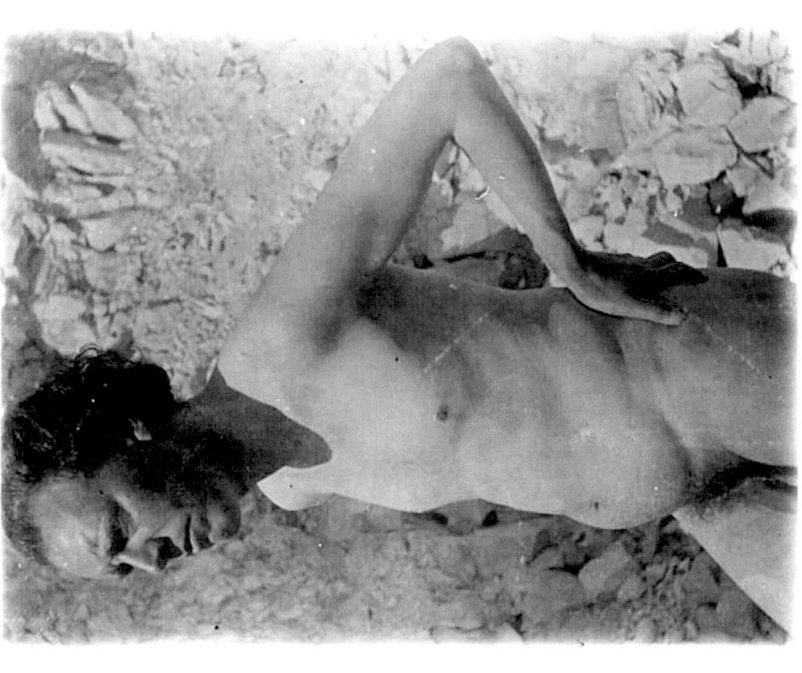

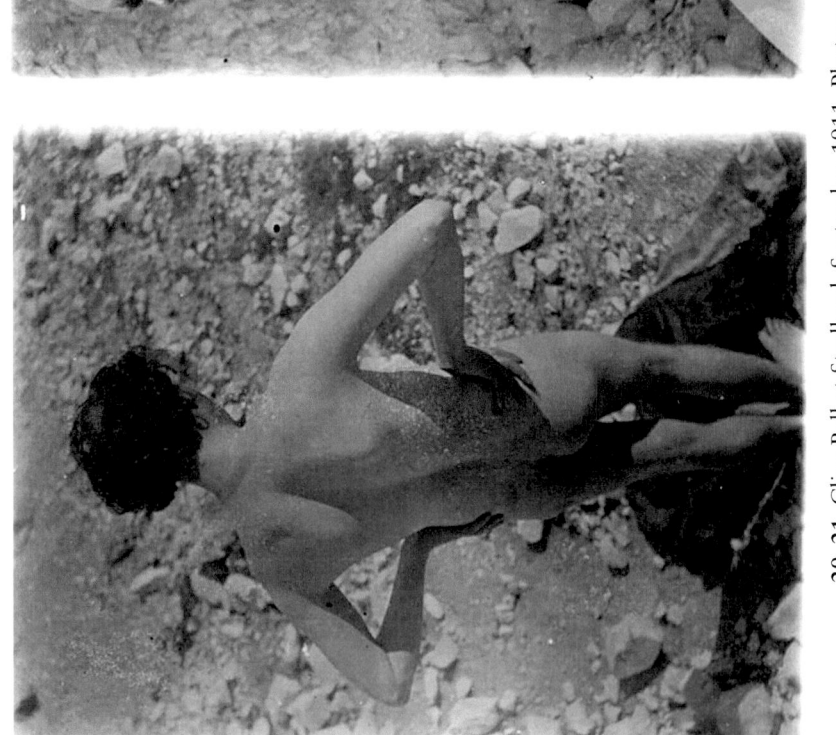

20–21 Clive Bell at Studland, September 1911. Photographs by Roger Fry (or Vanessa Bell?).

his left hand on his hip, but, instead of looking down, he is looking nearly straight ahead of him, that is to say (since the view is in three-quarters front profile), to the left of the camera.

It can be assumed that the photographs of Clive in which Vanessa also appears were taken by Roger. There is no indication that anyone else was present except Gerald, who is not known to have had any interest in photography. Vanessa was a very keen photographer, as her albums and negatives in the Tate Gallery Archive abundantly testify,[33] and, although it is perhaps most likely that Roger took all the photographs of Clive, one cannot rule out the possibility that she took some of them.

Photographs by Roger are uncommon, and these ones of Vanessa and Clive are perhaps the earliest of his that are known. When he did wield a camera, he was capable of achieving excellent results. Five years later Virginia Woolf paid this compliment to him: "The photographs certainly are masterpieces – the one of Leonard is far the best that I've ever seen of him – How does that minute camera produce such large pictures?"[34] His photographs of Vanessa in the nude at Studland may not be masterpieces, but he appears to have taken more trouble with them, or at least to have been more successful with them, than with his photographs of Clive. One almost wonders if he did not take a rather mischievous pleasure in capturing her husband in rather undignified positions.

The photographs were taken in the morning, and early. Studland faces east, and Plate 13 shows Vanessa using her right arm to shield her eyes from what is evidently a low sun.[35] Sunrise at Studland in September 1911 ranged from about 05.15 to about 05.55. The most obvious advantage of doing the deed very early would have been to avoid being seen. Before the Second World War a naturist area (unofficial at first) was established at Studland and, like the rest of the beach and the heathland behind it, was bequeathed, along with the rest of the Bankes Estate, to the National Trust in 1981,[36] but no such arrangement existed in 1911, and matters of dress and undress had recently given cause for concern. At a meeting of Studland Parish Council on 15 April 1907, chaired by the Rev. Frederick Swift Algeo, rector of the village's Church of St Nicholas:

> A resolution was passed calling the notice of the Trustees of the Bankes Estates to the unsatisfactory state of the beach as regards bathers and campers, the

33 TGA 9020.
34 Virginia Woolf to Roger Fry, [8 October 1916], *The Letters of Virginia Woolf*, edited by Nigel Nicolson, assisted by Joanne Trautmann, II (London, 1976), 121.
35 In none of the photographs is Vanessa looking at the camera, but the low sun is unlikely to be the (main) explanation for this.
36 *The Times*, 19 December 1981, 1.

Council considering it detrimental to the health of the village through the absence of any sanitary arrangements for the latter and the neglect of wearing proper costume as regards the former.[37]

It was suggested that the Trustees be asked to erect notice boards with the following rules:

(1) No person above the age of 10 years shall bathe within view from any street or public path without wearing a proper dress or regulation costume.
(2) No person shall bathe from the beach between the hours of 10. a.m. and 7. p.m. without using tent or bathing machine.
(3) The above to apply to a limit not exceeding 300[38] yds. north of Knoll Hill Road, and the Pilots path on the South.[39]

The worthies on the Parish Council would have deplored the Bells' and Roger's behaviour, if they had heard about it, but at least the visitors had the consideration to do what they did early in the morning and out of sight of the village. It has not been possible to identify the exact location of the shoot, the biggest problem being that the coastline has undergone considerable erosion during the past hundred years, and some features, including the Pilots Path, have disappeared completely, but the chalk seen in the photographs shows that it was southeast of Studland village on the way to the headland known as The Foreland or Handfast Point and Old Harry Rocks, and probably either above the south end of South (or Little) Beach or not far beyond that point. The place would have been easily reached from Harbour View.

Although the Bells were in Studland for almost the whole of September 1911 and Roger was there or nearby at various times up to and including the 25th, the event can be dated, with a high degree of confidence, to Saturday the 2nd, Sunday the 3rd, or Monday the 4th. This conclusion may seem rather bold, but is straightforwardly reached by a process of elimination, having regard to Roger's movements and numerous absences, weather conditions, and the presence of Gerald Shove. Those days, the first three after the Bells' and Roger's arrival in Studland, have two great advantages. One is that Roger was in Studland without his family and, as we have seen,

---

37 Presumably the Parish Council took the view that lack of sanitation would adversely affect the *physical* health of villagers, the absence of proper costume their *moral* health.
38 Misread as "500" by Richard Vine, *Studland: A Historical and Social Record of a Dorset Coastal Village* (Wimborne, 2003), 76.
39 *Studland Parish Council Minute Book, 1894–1927*, Dorset History Centre, Dorchester, ref. PC/STD/1/1/1, by kind permission of Sam Johnston, County Archivist.

staying with the Bells at Harbour View. The other is that the prolonged heatwave that had begun in early July was still in progress. It was to end on 12 September. On 2 September a temperature of 31°C was recorded in London and about 25°C over a wide area of southern England; 3 September brought some cloud, but was still very warm, and in Bournemouth, very close to Studland, eight hours of sunshine were recorded.[40] The weather remained warm on 4 September. That was the day Roger went to Swanage for the arrival of his family there, before departing the following day for work on *The Burlington Magazine* and at Hampton Court, but Vanessa makes clear that he was in Studland until at least the morning of 4 September.[41] He was away from Dorset 5–8 and 13–15 September and in Dorset but not in Studland on 9–10 September. On 11 September he moved his family from Swanage to Studland. And so 2–4 September were the only possible dates for him in the first half of the month.

What about Gerald Shove? Is there any mention anywhere of his having been in Studland in early September? If there is, I have not located it, but it is known that around this time he spent several days in the neighbouring county of Devon. From 1 September Lytton Strachey was also in Devon, staying at Becky (or Beckey) House, Manaton. Writing from there to Maynard Keynes on 10 September, he reports that he had a visit of "a few days" from Gerald.[42] Gerald also visited a "neo-pagan" camp organised by Justin Brooke at Clifford Bridge, Drewsteignton, about eight miles northwest of Manaton. Apparently he spent just one night there.[43] Among the campers was Rupert Brooke (unrelated to Justin). While in camp, Gerald was photographed with Rupert by Maynard Keynes,[44] who arrived on or about 26 August[45] and departed not later than 5 September.[46]

---

40 Information about temperatures and other features of the weather in September 1911 is derived from reports in *The Times*.

41 Vanessa Bell to Roger Fry, 7 September [1911] (TGA 8010/8/23). From her letter to him of 5 September [1911] (TGA 8010/8/24), it is clear that she drove with him in a cart to Swanage the previous day and drove back to Studland on her own.

42 KCC JMK/PP/45/316/4/205. Lytton here calls Gerald "His Lordship". as in his letters to Maynard of 24 August 1911 (KCC JMK/PP/45/316/4/197) and 30 August 1911 (KCC JMK/PP/45/316/4/201); Maynard does the same in his letters to Lytton of 29 August 1911 (KCC JMK/PP/45/316/4/198) and 20 September 1911 (KCC JMK/PP/45/316/4/206). See also n. 44 below.

43 Michael Holroyd, *Lytton Strachey* (London 1995), 236.

44 KCC PP/RCB/Ph/158 (sleeve no. 54). The print is inscribed on the back, by Geoffrey Keynes, "Rupert + his Lordship (Gerald Shove) taken by Maynard".

45 Letter from J. M. Keynes to Lytton Strachey, 22 August 1911 (KCC JMK/PP/45/316/4/193–4).

46 Letter from J. M. Keynes to Lytton Strachey, 29 August 1911 (KCC JMK/PP/45/316/4/198): "We shall probably be here until about Septr 5". That Maynard

In the photograph Gerald is half sitting up from a reclining position. Pipe in hand, he is wearing a trilby hat and a suit – almost certainly the one he is seen wearing at Studland. The photograph was taken sometime between 29 August and 5 September – not earlier because in a letter of 29 August Maynard told Lytton that Gerald had still not replied to invitations to visit the camp.[47]

It can be confidently assumed that Gerald visited Studland immediately before going to Manaton and Clifford Bridge. He cannot have done so on the way back, because, even if the photo-shoot in Studland took place in the early morning of 4 September, the latest possible time for Roger Fry to be present in the first half of the month, and even if Gerald's stay of "a few days" in Manaton began on 1 September, the earliest possible date, he would have had only one full day with Lytton before having to leave for Studland on 3 September, and there would have been no time for the night at Clifford Bridge.

Lytton was to transfer from Manaton to Studland on 15 September. But there is no possibility that Gerald too visited it in the second half of the month, because in the morning of 15 September he and Maynard left London for Dublin with other members of a group from the Liberal-Party-supporting Eighty Club.[48] The group made a fortnight's tour of Ireland, not returning to London until the morning of 1 October.[49] If Gerald was in Studland before his visit to Devon, he would have had to leave not later than 4 September in order to reach Clifford Bridge before Maynard departed for London.

"Bloomsberries" were not shy of being seen and photographed in the nude. But the nude-photography threesome engaged in by Vanessa, Clive, and Roger at Studland is remarkable even by Bloomsbury standards, given the relationships between the participants at the time.

Vanessa and Clive had been married for four and a half years.[50] At first they were very close, but became less so after the birth of Julian. Vanessa

meant to be in London on 5 September is shown by the sole entry in his appointments' diary for that day: "Lb. [= lift boy] of Vauxhall" (KCC JMK/PP/41), in reference to a homosexual encounter.

47 KCC JMK/PP/45/316/4/198.
48 Letters from J. M. Keynes to Lytton Strachey, 8 and 20 September 1911 (KCC JMK/PP/45/3/316/4/202–3, 206). For the diary entries made during the visit by Cecil Harmsworth, see Andrew Thorpe and Richard Toye (eds), *Parliament and Politics in the Age of Asquith and Lloyd George: The Diaries of Cecil Harmsworth, MP, 1909–1922* (Cambridge, 2016), 96–101.
49 The National Library of Ireland has a copy of the programme in its Ephemera Collection at EPH B441.
50 They were married on 7 February 1907.

was wholly absorbed in the baby, and Clive, who had no inclination to be a hands-on father, felt excluded. In the spring of 1908 he and Virginia, who also felt excluded by her sister's preoccupation with the baby, flirted with one another during a holiday in Cornwall. That did not involve any love-making, but was still hurtful to Vanessa, and not many more months had passed before Clive found solace in the welcoming arms of Annie Raven-Hill, who had been his first lover. His affair with her began in August 1899, when she was thirty-five and he was not quite eighteen and about to go up to Trinity College, Cambridge. A stylish and attractive married woman with a strong libido, she had taken the lead with him and initiated him in the *ars amatoria*. The affair stopped when Clive fell in love with Vanessa, and, after its resumption, ran on until 1914. Frank details of it are contained in a paper he read to the (Bloomsbury Group) Memoir Club on 2 February 1921. The paper is presented and fully discussed in Essay 3.

In view of Clive's infidelities, he was in no position to complain if Vanessa looked elsewhere for love and sexual satisfaction. But, although the two were no longer in love, they were still good and affectionate friends; she knew that he was not in love with Annie, and, as we have seen, she did not want him to know just how close she and Roger were.[51]

It is most probable that the nude-posing expedition was Vanessa's suggestion. As Clive's spouse and, unknown to Clive, Roger's lover, she was best placed to make it, and she was the one most interested in photography. If it was her initiative, it can be reconciled with her wish, communicated to Roger in advance of the Studland holiday, to avoid making Clive jealous, because it was a threesome, with Gerald Shove observing, and could be justified on the ground that the photography was for art's sake. But it is hard to believe that it was not in fact an act of bravado on her part. However that may be, the emotional scenario for her and Roger at the time will have been a highly charged one. The two were madly in love and hungry for one another's bodies. It must have felt most peculiar to be revealing their all to one another in the presence of Clive – exciting and deliciously naughty, but also deeply frustrating, given that they knew that there was unlikely to be any opportunity during the Studland holiday for the sexual union they both craved.

---

51 Lytton Strachey noticed, during his stay at Studland, that Roger was in love with Vanessa, but not that she was in love with him. Letter to James Strachey, 24 September 1911. See Paul Levy (ed.), *The Letters of Lytton Strachey* (London, 2005), 203.

Provenance of the Bloomsbury archive of photographs and negatives in the Berg Collection

From Duncan James Corrowr Grant to his friend the art historian Simon Watney; from Watney to R. A. Gekoski, dealer in rare books and manuscripts, October 2004; from Gekoski to the Berg Collection, New York Public Library, April 2005.[52]

Acknowledgements

I gratefully acknowledge the assistance of the following: the late Henrietta Garnett, copyright holder, for permission to receive copies of photographs taken by Vanessa Bell and for permission to publish them and make quotations from letters written by her; The Berg Collection, New York Public Library, its former Curator, Isaac Gewirtz, Librarian Joshua McKeon, and Andrea Felder of its Permissions and Reproduction Services, for supplying prints made from the negatives of photographs of Vanessa Bell and Roger Fry taken by Roger Fry and Vanessa Bell respectively, and copies of photographic prints of Clive Bell; Jane Abram; Karen Arathoon; Tony Bradshaw; Victoria Chance; Dorset History Centre, Dorchester, and the Dorset County Archivist, Sam Johnston; Sally Dowding; Peter Grogan of Peter Grogan, Rare Books & Manuscripts, London; King's College Cambridge Archive Centre and its Archivist, Patricia McGuire, for much information and generous assistance; Joyce Meates for giving me the benefit of her detailed knowledge of Studland; Jon Richardson of Jon S. Richardson Rare Books, Concord, Massachusetts; Lucinda Ferguson Smith; Susan Stares of Swanage; Tate Gallery Archive; Trinity College Library, Cambridge.

52 The Berg catalog(ue) incorrectly names Colin Mills as a "former owner". He was in fact the photographer who produced some of the modern prints in the collection. I owe this information to Peter Grogan (email of 20 October 2016).

3

Clive Bell's memoir of Annie Raven-Hill

Co-written with Helen Walasek

I. Introduction

1. *The Memoir Club*

The first meeting of the Bloomsbury Memoir Club was held on 4 March 1920. The Club was established by Mary ("Molly") MacCarthy as a successor to the short-lived Novel Club, which she had founded in March 1913. One of her intentions, and perhaps the main one, was to encourage her literary-journalist husband, Desmond MacCarthy, to produce a substantial piece of work. From this point of view, her initiative was a failure. Membership of the Memoir Club was small and mainly consisted of leading members of the Bloomsbury Group, in total only about thirteen.

The pattern was to meet in the evening in a member's (or members') house, have dinner, and afterwards hear and discuss candid autobiographical memoirs, which, it was hoped, would be the bases of chapters of books. The inaugural meeting was held in the MacCarthys' house, which was actually located not in Bloomsbury, but in Chelsea, at 25 Wellington Square.[1] The memoirs must have been short at this first meeting, for there were seven. We are told this by Virginia Woolf,[2] who names six of the contributors – Clive Bell, Vanessa Bell, Roger Fry, Duncan Grant, Molly MacCarthy, and Sydney Waterlow. It is not known who the seventh was. It is not known, either, what Clive's contribution was about. The only comment we have on it is a two-word one of Virginia Woolf, and it is not complimentary: she calls it "purely objective".[3]

---

1 Leonard Woolf, 114, manages to get both the date and the venue wrong.
2 Virginia Woolf 2, 23.
3 Virginia Woolf 2, 23. That her comment implies disappointment is clear from her verdict, in the same place, on Roger Fry's memoir: "Roger well composed; story of a coachman who stole geraniums and went to prison. Good: but too objective."

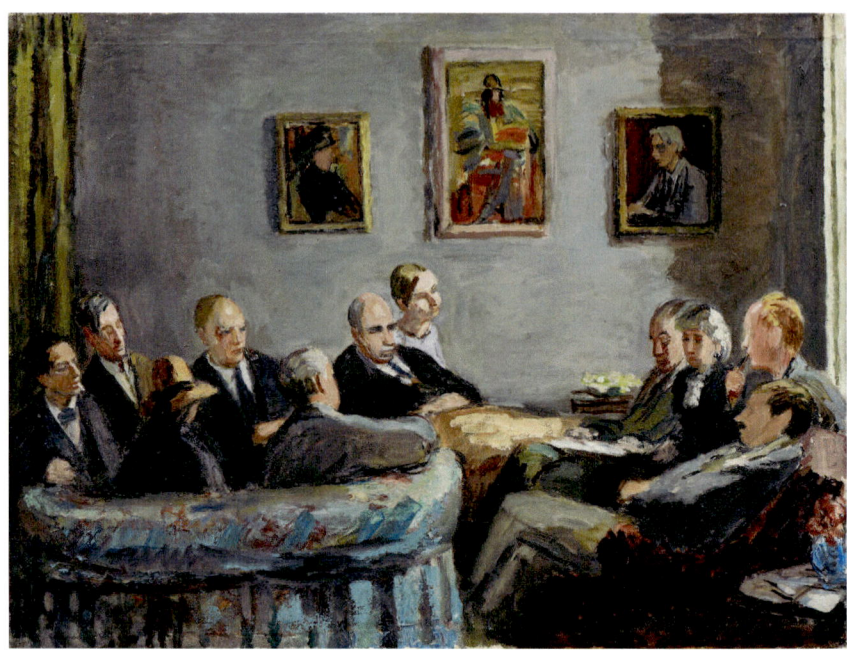

22 *The Memoir Club*, by Vanessa Bell, c. 1943. Oil on canvas, 60.8 × 81.6 cm.

The original intention was to hold monthly meetings, but this turned out to be too ambitious. Although the second meeting was held on 15 March 1920, less than a fortnight after the first, when memoirs were read by E. M. Forster, Leonard Woolf, and Virginia Woolf, the next recorded meeting was on 7 July 1920, when the contributors were Clive Bell, Duncan Grant, Maynard Keynes, and Molly MacCarthy.[4] Then there seems to have been another four-month gap until meetings on 17 November and 8 December 1920.

Meetings continued to take place at irregular intervals, and after a meeting on 19 June 1922 there was probably a six-year gap, which ended on 4 July 1928, when Virginia Woolf contributed a memoir of "Old Bloomsbury".[5] The Club continued to meet on and off until Clive Bell's death in 1964. Naturally new members were recruited as old ones died. In a painting executed c. 1943, Vanessa Bell portrayed an imaginary meeting of the Club (Plate 22), and cleverly managed to include three deceased members – Lytton Strachey, Roger Fry, and Virginia Woolf[6] – by painting pictures of them

4 Molly's memoir was read, in her absence, by her husband, Desmond.
5 The memoir has often been dated about six years earlier, but see Rosenbaum, 151.
6 Strachey died in 1932, Fry in 1934, Woolf in 1941.

on the wall. She also included herself among the participants. In December 1917, over two years before the Memoir Club was founded, Roger Fry had mentioned to Vanessa an idea just put to him by Clive:

> He suggested a great historical portrait group of Bloomsbury. I think I shall have a shot at it – It would be rather fun. Lytton, Maynard, Clive, Duncan, me, you, Virginia, Mary [Hutchinson], Molly, Desmond. Is there anyone else that ought to be in? P'raps Walter Sickert coming in at the door and looking at us all with a kind of benevolent cynicism.
>
> But p'raps its [*sic*] too hideously difficult and p'raps you ought to do it, as being so brilliant at likeness, though I seem to be getting rather better.[7]

So it seems that Clive and Roger together helped to inspire the picture Vanessa painted a quarter of a century later.

2. The presentation and reception of Clive Bell's memoir of Annie Raven-Hill

Although Clive Bell's memoir of Annie Raven-Hill[8] has not been previously published, it is not unknown, but most mentions of it are brief,[9] as are the few quotations made from it. The author's typescript copy of the untitled memoir is preserved among his papers in the Library of Trinity College, Cambridge. It occupies fifteen pages. There are a few manuscript alterations, each of which we note *ad locum* in our commentary. A pencilled note, in Clive's hand, after the end of the typescript, states: "Written in January 1921". But it is unlikely that this note was added in January 1921. It was almost certainly written in 1930, at the same time as a note added immediately below and dated to that year, mentioning that Annie Raven-Hill had been dead for some years. The two notes look as though they were written with the same pencil.

Clive's memoir of Annie was the second instalment of an account of his early life and experiences. The first instalment was read at the meeting of

---

7 Letter from Roger Fry to Vanessa Bell, 12 December 1917, in Fry, *Letters* 2, 423.

8 Clive Bell does not hyphenate "Raven Hill". Annie's husband Leonard Raven-Hill's surname at birth was Hill, his given names Leonard Raven. But as there were already several Hills "in the profession", as Leonard wrote to his father in a letter reproduced in his memoir, he began to adopt "Raven Hill" as a surname early in his career. Although he is shown on his marriage certificate and for some time after without a hyphen, he gradually adopted one, but not all official listings followed suit – he is sometimes listed in directories under "Hill". In the *Punch* magazine index (which named contributors from 1902) he is always "Raven-Hill". For consistency we use this spelling throughout, except when quoting Clive and any others who omit the hyphen.

9 An exception is Rosenbaum, 80–83.

the Memoir Club on 7 July 1920. Desmond MacCarthy, who, in Molly's absence, read her paper for her, afterwards wrote her a letter in which he describes how the evening went. After telling her how well her memoir was received, he continues:

> Maynard was very interesting. Both he and Clive stopped like serial writers at the thrilling point. Maynard's fragment was an account of a journey with Foche[10] [*sic*] to meet the German delegates and next time he promises us – revelations! Clive stopped on the threshold of his first amour – the one with Mrs Raven Hill. The beginning of his fragment was a little mannered and *affektiert*,[11] but it became interesting.[12]

Clive's first instalment does not survive, but he refers to it in the opening sentence of his memoir of Annie: "I was talking about Jenny – a white pony – before I began to talk about Dorothea and the loves of my nonage." So the piece related to the period before the start of Clive's affair with Annie, shortly before his eighteenth birthday, and there was apparently a focus on the girls he knew while he was still at school – girls he could only have met in the holidays, given that the boarding school he attended (Marlborough College) then admitted only boys.

Clive and Maynard delivered the second instalments of their memoirs at the meeting of the Club hosted by Vanessa Bell at 46 Gordon Square on 2 February 1921. Clive performed first, then Maynard. Virginia Woolf's and Morgan Forster's comments on the papers survive. Virginia writes:

> We had the Memoir Club on Wednesday. Clive and Maynard read; both elaborate and polished, Clive mellow and reminiscent about Mrs Raven Hill (he had her 2 years after his marriage, and for the last time in 1914. She is now imbecile. This was a surprise to me.[13] She coincided with his attachment to me then. But she was a voluptuary. He was not 'in love'.) Maynard, of course, was the solid piece of the evening, so long indeed that we had to leave before the end.[14]

She goes on to single out Maynard's character-drawing for special praise.

Morgan Forster, like Virginia, clearly regarded Maynard as the star performer. In his diary-entry for 4 February 1921 he gives far more space to his memoir than to Clive's. After summarising the former, he writes: "A

---

10 Marshal Ferdinand Foch.
11 "Affected."
12 Desmond MacCarthy to Molly MacCarthy, July 1920, quoted by Cecil, 202.
13 Virginia, of course, means not Mrs Raven-Hill's "imbecility" (in fact, incapacity due to a stroke), but the fact of Clive's having had her two years after his marriage, a time when Virginia was engaged in a flirtation with Clive.
14 Virginia Woolf 2, 89–90.

most wonderful paper. Privilege to listen to it, and even to Clive Bell on his copulations with Mrs. Ravenhill [*sic*], wife of the Punch artist, though this was repulsion also." After mentioning that he slept the night at 46 Gordon Square, he adds: "I don't think those people are little; but they belittle all who come into their power unless the comer is strong, which I am not. Great as is my admiration of the Club, I shall resign I think."[15] Morgan's homosexuality may partly explain the "repulsion" he felt at hearing Clive's frank description of his heterosexual experiences. Whether his comment on the way Memoir Club members belittle all who come into their power had any specific reference to Clive's memoir is doubtful. If it did, his thought was probably provoked by some of the less flattering of Clive's remarks about his lover. Despite the last words of his diary-entry, he did not resign and in fact was to be one of the Club's most prolific contributors. What was the effect on others who heard Clive's second instalment? We can only guess.

They included (as well as Maynard Keynes) Vanessa Bell, Mary Hutchinson, Sydney Waterlow, Leonard Woolf, and probably Roger Fry[16] and Molly and Desmond MacCarthy. If all these were present, it is notable that all four women who heard Clive give a detailed account of his first lover and his sexual relations with her had been sexually and/or emotionally involved with him at one time – Vanessa as his wife (she and he had married on 7 February 1907); Virginia Woolf in a flirtatious episode in 1908 that had not involved any love-making, but had caused great distress to Vanessa; Molly MacCarthy in 1913 in a brief affair that nevertheless did lasting harm to her marriage; and the writer Mary Hutchinson, who became his lover after he stopped seeing Annie in October 1914 and continued to be that, on and off, until 1927. At the time of the 2 February 1921 meeting of the Memoir Club Mary and Clive's relationship had recently entered an off-phase, as Virginia Woolf makes clear:

> Mary was there; and I note that one likes her better, partly for showing fight; partly, perhaps, for not being the mistress any longer. I am in hot water for having told Sydney [Waterlow], which I did deliberately, without malice, as conversation, thinking it allowed. Oh what a goose Sydney is! What does he do but march up and congratulate Clive in front of everyone![17]

15 Our quotations of Morgan Forster's diary are based on our reading of the manuscript in King's College Cambridge Archive Centre, EMF/12/8, p. 46. Quotations we have seen in print are not completely accurate.
16 "Memoir Club" is the only entry under 2 February 1921 in Fry's engagement diary in King's College Cambridge Archive Centre, KCC/PP/REF/5.
17 Virginia Woolf 2, 90.

It is hard to believe that Mary at any rate was passionless as she listened to Clive's memoir. Molly is unlikely to have been much affected, partly because of her lesser involvement with Clive, partly because of her deafness. To Vanessa, who had known Annie and probably also quite a lot about Clive's relationship with her, little of what he said in his memoir is likely to have come as a great surprise, let alone a great shock.

Clive himself must have thought well of his paper, for he read it again to a meeting of the Memoir Club thirty years later, on 20 September 1950. This reading was not without incident: he had almost reached the climax (in more than one sense of the word) when a sudden interruption gave rise to great hilarity, as Frances Partridge describes in her diary:

> In the evening the Memoir Club, one of the nicest meetings I remember. After eating the tenderest of ducklings cooked with cherries – a great improvement on our usual fare – we repaired to Duncan's[18] rooms, and listened to two excellent Memoirs: Clive's on losing his virginity and Bunny's[19] on getting to know Indians at school. Just as in near darkness Clive was describing the crucial moment on the sofa with Mrs Raven Hill, and his anxieties and doubts whether he could properly carry out what was expected of him, a feeble knock was heard on Duncan's door, and Marjorie's[20] silver head poked in, saying in a faint, hoarse whisper: "Duncan are you in bed?" "No," replied Duncan in an equally subdued tone.
>
> "Well, is there any competent male present?" A roar of laughter greeted this; it came so aptly to Clive's reading.[21]

It turned out that Marjorie Strachey's problem was, in Quentin Bell's words, that "she was unable to twist the cock": a gasworkers' strike had much reduced the flow of gas, and, for safety's sake, Marjorie had been trying to turn it off at the main. It may be assumed that the words Quentin chose to report the problem gave rise to a second wave of laughter.

Rosenbaum, pointing to the note Clive added at the end of his typescript in 1930, suggests that he may also have read his paper about Annie to a meeting of the Memoir Club at that time.[22] This is possible, although there does not seem to be any record of his having done this. A further indication of the memoir having being in his mind in the early 1930s is a letter which the writer and literary critic Lyn Lloyd Irvine wrote to him in July 1931. Twenty years younger than Clive, she had come to know the Woolfs and

---

18 Duncan Grant.
19 "Bunny" is David Garnett.
20 Marjorie Strachey, sister of Lytton and Oliver Strachey.
21 Partridge, 125–126. Frances Partridge was later to become the last secretary of the Memoir Club.
22 Rosenbaum, 83.

other Bloomsberries in the late 1920s, and in 1932 the Woolfs' Hogarth Press was to publish her book of essays entitled *Ten Letter-Writers*. Her letter to Clive begins:

> I found your memoir very interesting. Have you written no sequels to it? It moved me to a number of comments and reflections which I should like to tell you – if I had reached the enviable age when one can be frank about one's experiences.[23]

She goes on to reflect on the difficulty of accurately recalling one's early experiences, with the exception of the embarrassing ones. Further on she writes:

> By the way, a remark made by Mrs. Raven Hill – that you were very nice about not showing how bored you were the next morning – although a hint, confirmed my suspicion that you are one of those rare but terrible people who have trained themselves to conceal boredom. I shall never be happy in your company unless I can discover, or you will tell me, some tiny signal, some infinitely small reaction to boredom which has escaped your control. Never quite happy, that's to say.

It is very unlikely that Lyn Irvine would have been invited to attend a meeting of the Memoir Club. She is writing to Clive while on holiday in Braemar, Scotland, and the natural assumption is that he has lent her the paper to read. Of course he might have done that anyhow, but he is perhaps more likely to have done it if he had recently reread it to the Memoir Club.

3. Clive Bell: A selective chronology

1881

16 September: (Arthur) Clive Heward Bell born at East Shefford House, East Shefford, Berkshire, the third of the four children (two sons and two daughters) of William Heward Bell and Hannah Taylor Cory.

1883

His father, who had derived most of his wealth from the coalmines of Merthyr Tydfil, buys Cleeve House in the Wiltshire village of Seend and largely rebuilds it, adding a huge hall crammed with hunting trophies from home and abroad.[24]

---

23 Lyn Lloyd Irvine to Clive Bell, 26 July 1931, Washington State University, Manuscripts, Archives, and Special Collections, Clive and Vanessa Bell Papers 1907–1957, Cage 5068.

24 On the house, its owners, and their family, see Quentin Bell, 22–27.

c. 1890–1894

Attends, as a boarder, Waynflete,[25] a boys' preparatory school at Durdham Down, Bristol.

1895

January: Enters Marlborough College.

1899

July: Leaves Marlborough College.

August: Has his first sexual encounter with Annie Raven-Hill.

October: Enters Trinity College, Cambridge. During his first term, founds the Midnight Society, an undergraduate reading-group, with Saxon Sydney-Turner, Leonard Woolf, Lytton Strachey, Thoby Stephen, and Ainslie John Robertson. Influenced by the philosopher George Edward Moore.

1902

Summer: Graduates with a "second" in History.

October–August 1903: Having been awarded the Earl of Derby Studentship by Trinity College, Cambridge, works in the Public Record Office, Chancery Lane, London, researching the Congress of Verona (1822). Takes rooms at 6 King's Bench Walk, Temple, and retains them until he marries in 1907.

1903

Late summer–November: Goes "most unwillingly" with his father to shoot animals in British Columbia.

1904

January: Goes to Paris, supposedly to continue his research in the Archives Nationales, but instead makes daily visits to the Louvre. Meets and learns from the artists Gerald Kelly, James Wilson Morrice, and Roderic O'Conor, friend of Gauguin.

Late April or early May: Introduces Thoby, Vanessa, and Virginia Stephen to artist-friends in Paris.

---

25 In 1897, to mark Queen Victoria's diamond jubilee, the school was renamed Queen Victoria House.

1905

Spends time living in the hamlet of St Symphorien in the Loire Valley.
August: Proposes marriage to Vanessa Stephen, but is rejected.

1906

Introduced to Maynard Keynes by Lytton Strachey.
31 July: Second proposal of marriage to Vanessa Stephen rejected.
20 November: His friend Thoby Stephen, brother of Vanessa and Virginia, dies of typhoid.
22 November: Third proposal of marriage to Vanessa Stephen accepted.

1907

7 February: Marries Vanessa Stephen at St Pancras Register Office.

1908

4 February: Vanessa's and his elder son, Julian Heward Bell, born.
Late April and early May: He and Virginia flirt on holiday in St Ives, Cornwall.

1910

Mid-January: Vanessa and he chance to meet Roger Fry at Cambridge Railway Station and soon become close friends with him.
19 August: Vanessa's and his younger son, Quentin Claudian Stephen Bell, born. November–January 1911: Assists Roger Fry with the First Post-Impressionist Exhibition at the Grafton Galleries, London.

1911

April–6 May: Vanessa and he visit Turkey (Istanbul and Bursa) with Roger Fry and Harry Norton. Vanessa is taken ill and suffers miscarriage, and she and Roger fall in love.

1912

October 1912–January 1913: Second Post-Impressionist Exhibition at the Grafton Galleries.

1913

Affair with Molly MacCarthy.

1914

February: Presents his aesthetic theory in *Art*, London: Chatto & Windus.
October: Last fling with Annie Raven-Hill. Soon afterwards, begins an affair with Mary Hutchinson.

1915

Publishes *Peace at Once* (Manchester & London: National Labour Press), advocating peace with Germany, and sees copies seized and destroyed by the authorities. Maintains pacifism in both world wars.

1918

25 December: Agrees, on the birth of Vanessa Bell's and Duncan Grant's daughter, Angelica, to present himself as her father.

1920

4 March: Contributes to the inaugural meeting of the Memoir Club.
7 July: Reads the first part of a two-part memoir to the Memoir Club.

1921

2 February: Reads to the Memoir Club the second part of the memoir begun on 7 July 1920, this part describing his affair with Annie Raven-Hill.
Poems. London: Hogarth Press.

1922

26 April: Death of Annie Raven-Hill, aged fifty-seven.
Since Cézanne. London: Chatto & Windus.

1923

On British Freedom. London: Chatto & Windus.

1927

February: Affair with Mary Hutchinson ends.
21 June: Death of William Heward Bell, aged seventy-eight.
Landmarks in Nineteenth-Century French Painting. London: Chatto & Windus.

1928

Civilization. London: Chatto & Windus.
Proust. London: Chatto & Windus

1931

An Account of French Painting. London: Chatto & Windus.

1934

9 September: Death of Roger Fry, aged sixty-seven.

Enjoying Pictures: Meditations in the National Gallery and Elsewhere. London: Chatto & Windus.

1936

Appointed Chevalier de la Légion d'Honneur.

1937

18 July: Death of Julian Heward Bell, aged twenty-nine, killed while serving as an ambulance-driver in the republican cause in the Spanish Civil War.

1941

28 March: Death (by suicide) of Virginia Woolf, aged fifty-nine.

1942

14 February: Death of Hannah Taylor Bell, aged ninety-one.

1950

20 September: Gives another reading of the memoir of Annie Raven-Hill.

1956

Old Friends: Personal Recollections. London: Chatto & Windus.

1961

7 April: Death of Vanessa Bell, aged eighty-two.

1964

17 September: Dies of cancer, the day after his eighty-third birthday, in the Fitzroy House Nursing Home, Fitzroy Square, London.

4. Annie Raven-Hill

Annie Raven-Hill was born Annie Rogers at 111 Tachbrook Street, Pimlico, London, on 1 July 1864, the youngest of the seven[26] children

---

26 The children were: Mark Junior, Vernon, Martha Maria, Ellen, Edith Emma, Frederick, and Annie. Only Ellen was not involved in the art world: her occupation in the 1881 census is given as dressmaker. The 1871 census lists a son called Frank (but not Mark Jr), but given that "Frank" has apparently the same birth year as Mark Jr (1848) and does not appear in the 1851 census from Derby that lists Mark Sr, Martha, and their children Mark Jr and Vernon, "Frank" is almost certainly a mistake by the census-taker for "Mark".

of Mark Rogers and Martha Maria Rogers. The Rogerses were a family of artworkers who were deeply embedded in the world of Victorian and Edwardian decorative-arts production. Mark Senior was born in Penryn, Cornwall,[27] but by 1847 was living in London, where he married Martha Maria Colello on 6 March. After a spell working as a cabinet-maker in Derby, from where he sent an ornamental lime-wood bracket for display at the Great Exhibition of 1851,[28] he was back in London by the mid-1850s and becoming increasingly well-known as a wood-carver.

His children were, artistically, chips off the old block, with all three of his sons, Mark Junior, Vernon, and Frederick, becoming wood-carvers and sculptors, while two of the couple's four daughters, Martha Maria and Edith Emma,[29] were skilled pottery-artists, who worked for a time as senior artists at Doulton's Lambeth Art Pottery.[30] We know that Mark Junior, Martha, Edith, and Annie, at least, attended Lambeth School of Art. Under its energetic headmaster, John Sparkes, the School had established a relationship with Doulton's, and the company's mainly female pottery-decorators were trained at the School. Mark Junior went on to become a highly regarded wood-carver and modeller in terracotta and plaster and teacher of modelling and carving, who exhibited regularly at the Royal Academy of Arts.[31]

27　Not Penzance, as stated in at least one source.

28　Yapp, *Class 28. Manufactures from Animal and Vegetable Substances*, 142, no. 179.

29　Several sources mistakenly claim that Edith was the daughter of another wood-carver named Rogers – William Gibbs Rogers or his son, George Alfred Rogers. However, our research has established that she was actually the daughter of Mark Rogers Sr and the sister of Martha Maria Rogers.

30　The catalogue of the work of students from schools of art at the International Health Exhibition, 1884, records that both Martha M. and Edith E. Rogers produced work for Doulton and studied at Lambeth 1879–1884 and at Westminster School of Art (Wallis, 146–147); the 1881 census describes the sisters as "pottery artists". Both appear in the two extraordinary and beautifully illustrated presentation-volumes prepared by the then 229 "Lady Artists" and their female assistants who painted art-pottery at Doulton's Lambeth Works. The volumes were presented to Henry Doulton on 26 April 1882 in appreciation for his originating "an occupation at once interesting and elevating to so large a number of our sex". Volume I lists the female artists and assistants with their signatures and pottery-marks; Martha and Edith are in the first group of senior Doulton Ware Artists (marks MMR and EEM), alongside such well-known decorators as Hannah Barlow and Elizabeth Simmance. Volume II contains photographs of all the female artists and assistants listed in Volume I. The volumes, a remarkable record of highly skilled female artists working in the late nineteenth century, are now in the Lambeth Archives (Doulton Presentation Volumes, 12/369).

31　An example of Mark Rogers Jr's work is in the Victoria and Albert Museum. See: "Mark Rogers Junior", *Mapping the Practice and Profession of Sculpture in Britain*

It was while attending Lambeth School of Art that Annie met her future husband, Leonard Raven-Hill.[32] The son of William Hill, a manufacturer and retailer of patent lock-rib umbrellas,[33] Leonard was born in Bath on 10 March 1867 and so was more than two years younger than Annie. He had been only fourteen when, on 1 January 1882, he joined an engraving class at the City of London Technical Schools at Kennington, where two of his classmates were Charles Ricketts and Charles Shannon. Leonard called them and him "The Three Woodpeckers". The trio soon continued their studies at the Lambeth School of Art. Another art-school friend was Frederick Henry Townsend, who later cartooned for *Punch* and became its first art-director in 1905.

Leonard remained at Lambeth until late 1885, when he moved to Paris to study at Académie Colarossi and Académie Julian where his most influential teachers were William-Adolphe Bouguereau and Aimé Morot. By the beginning of 1888 he was back in London, ready to begin his artistic career.

Leonard and Annie were married the following year at the parish church of St Saviour, Pimlico, on 16 April 1889. The address of both bride and groom is given on the marriage-certificate as 146 Tachbrook Street, the Rogers family home. However the young couple were soon moving around different addresses in the Bohemian and artistic environs of Chelsea.

According to Clive's memoir, Annie had once lived in Paris, "… in the *quartier latin*, before her husband had become famous enough to sink ambition and take to *Punch*". But we have discovered no evidence that Leonard lived in Paris after their marriage, with or without Annie. So, if she lived there at all, it was almost certainly as a single woman. Perhaps she followed her future husband to Paris after meeting him at Lambeth School of Art – Clive certainly implies that her sojourn in Paris was with Leonard, presumably because Annie told him so. If she wanted to continue her own study of art, there would have been no problem, for both Académie Julian and Académie Colarossi accepted female students, usually catering for them in separate studios, and they were not alone in doing that.[34]

and Ireland 1851–1951, University of Glasgow History of Art and HATII, online database 2011 http://sculpture.gla.ac.uk/view/person.php?id=msib2_1208257662.

32 Raven-Hill, *Rosemary*.
33 William Hill is called a stockbroker on Leonard and Annie's marriage certificate, but described in a newspaper article after his death in 1928 as "head of William Hill and Sons, umbrella manufacturers". See "Other People's Money", *Daily Mail*, 1 October 1928, 7.
34 See Fehrer.

Annie's elder daughter, Sylvia, who stayed in Paris in 1910–1911 to study French and art after completing her schooling at Roedean,[35] records that both parents travelled with her to Paris to settle her in with her French hosts. But she does not mention that her mother ever lived there, though she does say that the instructor of her life-class at Les Invalides had been trained by the same professor who had taught her father.[36] A possibility is that knowledge of Annie's stay in Paris (which would have been *before* her parents' marriage) was kept by both Raven-Hills from their gently-reared daughter, as Clive describes in some detail the lengths to which Annie went to be discreet and appear respectable.

Despite her time at Lambeth School of Art, Annie seems to have had less artistic talent than her siblings. Sylvia, after mentioning that her mother had studied art as a young woman, writes that she never saw her painting "and she couldn't draw for toffee", but that "she had good taste in dress and in the home".[37] Annie's good (and expensive!) taste in dress and her alluring deportment are abundantly attested by Clive in his memoir. While Clive found her lacking in culture and intellect, he allows that she had what he rather snobbishly calls "a genuine vulgar feeling for the more obvious in art". When the two met up in London one fine day in May for a love-making marathon in his rooms in King's Bench Walk in The Temple, they went first to view the pictures in the nearby Guildhall Art Gallery. According to Spalding, it was Clive who took Annie to the Guildhall.[38] But he does not say whose suggestion it was: it could as easily have been hers, since he begins rather more mundanely, saying that they spent the morning sightseeing.

If, as is most likely, the meeting was in May 1903,[39] Annie, up from rural Wiltshire, may well have wanted to catch the exhibition of paintings of the Dutch School, then on at the Guildhall Art Gallery (28 April–25 July). It included works by Rembrandt and other Dutch Old Masters. Also on view there was the fine collection of English paintings recently acquired by the Corporation of London under the will of Charles Gassiot. Another exhibition in May 1903 was of Leonard's Indian drawings at the Fine Art Society in New Bond Street, and viewing this was perhaps Annie's "official" reason for visiting London.[40]

35 Needham.
36 Needham.
37 Needham.
38 Spalding, 52.
39 On the year probably being 1903, see n. 111 below.
40 *Catalogue of an Exhibition of Drawings Illustrating the Durbar and Indian Life, by L. Raven-Hill and Inglis Sheldon-Williams: with a Prefatory Note: Held in the Rooms of the Fine Art Society, 148 New Bond Street, May, 1903.* On Leonard's visit to India for the Durbar, see below and n. 53.

If Quentin Bell is right, Annie may have made a significant contribution to her young lover's artistic experience and development. He speculates that the reproduction of a Degas which Clive had in his rooms in Trinity College, Cambridge, in his student days, and which Quentin believes he brought to Cambridge with him in the autumn of 1899, is very likely to have been a gift from her, Degas being little known in England at this time.[41] The suggestion is made in the awareness that the Raven-Hills were at the time near-neighbours of the Bell family in rural Wiltshire and moved in their social circles.

Although Leonard was well-regarded as a painter, exhibiting at the Salon in Paris, the Royal Academy of Arts, the Royal Institute of Oil Painters, the Royal Institute of Painters in Water Colours, the New English Art Club, and elsewhere, it became increasingly clear on his return from Paris that his special talent was drawing. He himself wrote: "I wanted to paint but the pen and the pencil were to be my tools, and the palette and brush were soon to be hung upon the wall, for alas! my painting was only coloured drawing, lacking colour, and colour is the soul of painting."[42]

During the 1890s he became much in demand as an illustrator, caricaturist, and cartoonist for publications that included *Black & White*, *The Art Journal*, *The Idler*, *The Pall Mall Magazine*, and *The Windsor Magazine*. In 1890 he was appointed art editor of *Pick-Me-Up* and from 1893 was a founding editor of the highly-regarded but short-lived art periodical *Butterfly*. He went on to illustrate novels by Rudyard Kipling and H. G. Wells, but was best known for his contributions, over a period of forty years, to *Punch*, to which he began to contribute on 28 December 1895. It is worth noting that the period over which Clive and Annie conducted their affair coincided with what was probably the peak of Leonard's fame. There were scores of articles on him and his work in both the popular and the art press. He was nationally known and often photographed, occasionally with Annie as well. Increasing fame brought Leonard and Annie increasing material prosperity at a time when they were starting a family. And Leonard was longing to get away from Chelsea, where "there were too many artists, groups, movements, and *dernier cri's* ... and it is difficult to be oneself".[43] The couple's first child, Sylvia Colello Raven-Hill, was born on 3 May 1893, at 20 North Side, Clapham Common, a house of which the Raven-Hills had taken the lease early the previous year. Leonard had been alerted to its availability by the engraver Edgar Wilson, a Lambeth Art School friend and a contributor to *Butterfly*, who lived nearby.

41 Quentin Bell, 28–29.
42 Raven-Hill, *Rosemary*.
43 Raven-Hill, *Rosemary*.

The terrace of tall red brick early Georgian houses facing the Common, known locally as Church Buildings, was a survivor of the time when Clapham was a fashionable rural retreat from the smoke and noise of London. Annie befriended her next door but one neighbour, Caroline ("Carrie") Nicholls. Carrie was about the same age as her, and the daughter and sister of architectural sculptors – artistic craftworkers like Annie's father and brothers. Carrie lived with her widowed mother and siblings at number 18. Both the house and Carrie were to figure in Clive's memoir: when, visiting London from Wiltshire in the early 1900s, Annie would stay at number 18 and be escorted back there in a hansom cab by Clive after their trysts. Clive remembered "at least a dozen" of the "long jingling drives – there and back – especially back" when he would contemplatively smoke a cigar.

The Raven-Hills' next two children were boys – Lucien Ennar, born at 16 Adamson Road, Belsize Park, Hampstead, on 15 May 1896, and Arthur Leonard, born at the large and historic Battle House in the Wiltshire village of Bromham on 24 October 1898. Battle House was to be the Raven-Hills' home until 1912 (Plate 23). Before occupying it, they briefly rented a cottage at Stert near Etchilhampton, about three miles east of Devizes.[44]

Even in Clapham, Leonard had been enthusiastic about growing vegetables, and Annie was to revel in country-life at least as much as he. They maintained a productive kitchen-garden and orchard, kept pigs, dairy-cows, and hens, and bred geese and turkeys. Leonard's role in the running of the farm was mainly supervisory,[45] whereas Annie's was more "hands on".[46] But Leonard threw himself into local activities: as he wrote, "the life of the country interested me as nothing had ever interested me before", and he held a series of posts including those of parish councillor, overseer of rates, head of the British school council, and chairman of a small-holding scheme.[47]

Five years after Leonard's first contribution to *Punch*, he was invited, in November 1900, to become a member of the fabled *Punch* Table and one of the magazine's few staff-members.[48] Despite Clive's disparaging

---

44 In his memoir Leonard gives the name of his house in Stert as Royal Cottage, but his address at Stert is listed as Hillside Cottage in *Gillman's Devizes Public Register* for 1898. Leonard's memoir dates his "Wiltshire Days" from 1894 to 1912.

45 Lawrence, 534.

46 Needham.

47 Raven-Hill, *Rosemary*.

48 One could be a *Punch* staff-member without being invited to become a member of the *Punch* Table. For example, the young A. A. Milne began working for *Punch* as its Assistant Editor in 1906, but was not invited to join the Table until 1910 – a delay he attributed to his left-leaning politics.

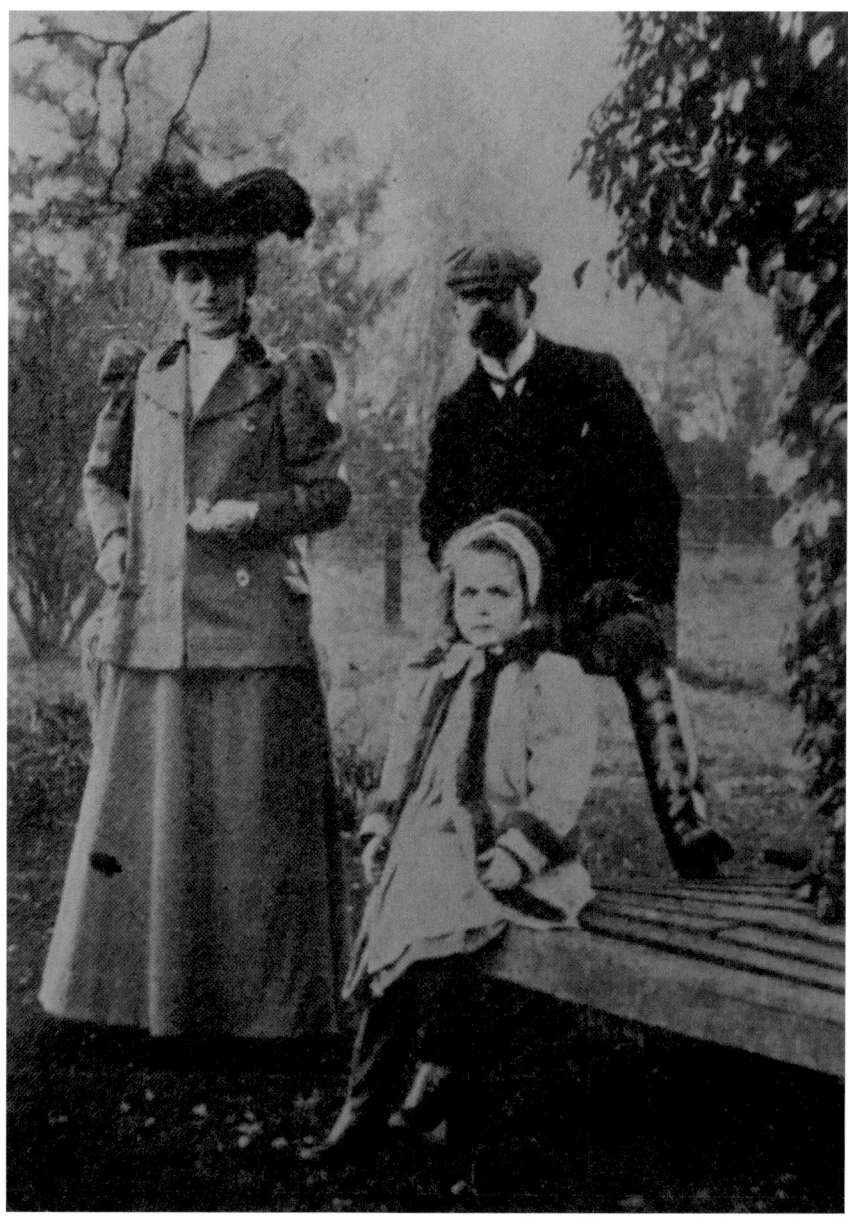

23 Annie and Leonard Raven-Hill with daughter Sylvia at Battle House, Bromham, Wiltshire, 1898–1899.

remark about *Punch*, to be on its staff and a member of the Table was a highly-sought prize among artists and writers, and remained so well into the twentieth century.

Leonard's first dinner at the Table, on 2 January 1901, was also the last for *Punch*'s legendary political cartoonist, Sir John Tenniel (illustrator of Lewis Carroll's "Alice" books), who was retiring. Leonard went on to be *Punch*'s second political cartoonist in 1910 on the death of Linley Sambourne. He was now "Raven-Hill of *Punch*" and Annie shared in his prestige, attending formal dinners in London with *Punch*'s proprietors (including the renowned art-dealer Sir William Agnew)[49] and staff, receiving invitations to artists' balls as "the wife of the well-known 'Punch' artist" (Plate 24), and occasionally appearing in print in the course of interviews with Leonard.[50]

Leonard's friend the artist George Denholm Armour and his wife, Mary Emma Robb, had moved near to the Raven-Hills when George acquired the tenancy of Etchilhampton House. George, a Scot, and close friend of "Glasgow Boy" artist Joseph Crawhall III, was an expert horseman – a breeder as well as a rider – and an enthusiastic all-round sportsman, who was in much demand for his drawings and paintings of hunting scenes. At the time, like Leonard, he was one of *Punch*'s regular and most prolific contributors. One of Armour's paintings hung in Cleeve House, the Bell family home in Seend. In the words of Quentin Bell he "had immortalized grandfather Bell mounted and wearing a pink coat".[51] Quentin also mentions that "in the morning room a series of pictures by a *Punch* artist explored the funny possibilities of a game of bridge, or it may have been whist". This other *Punch* artist was undoubtedly Leonard, who had drawn a series of five cartoons titled "Bridge Problems" for *Punch* in 1905, four of which were later sold as colour prints.[52]

49 Linley Sambourne diary for 1901, entry Tuesday, 18 June. Sambourne's diaries are in the Archive of his former home, 18 Stafford Terrace, Kensington, London, now a museum operated by the Royal Borough of Kensington and Chelsea.

50 We reproduce (Plate 24) a photograph from *The Tatler and Bystander* from 1910 of Annie at an artists' ball, appropriately costumed as another *femme fatale*, Cleopatra. She is quoted in the article "An Accidental Interview" in *The Sketch*, 29 March 1899, 422.

51 Quentin Bell, 24.

52 The series of five half-tone cartoons, published in *Punch* over May and June 1905, had "excited a good deal of interest and amusement" (*Daily Mail*, 19 January 1907). Four were subsequently redrawn by Leonard in colour and reproduced to be sold as exclusive prints by Lawrence & Jellicoe Ltd. Leonard may well have given (or sold) the original colour watercolours to his Bell neighbours – or they may have bought the set of prints.

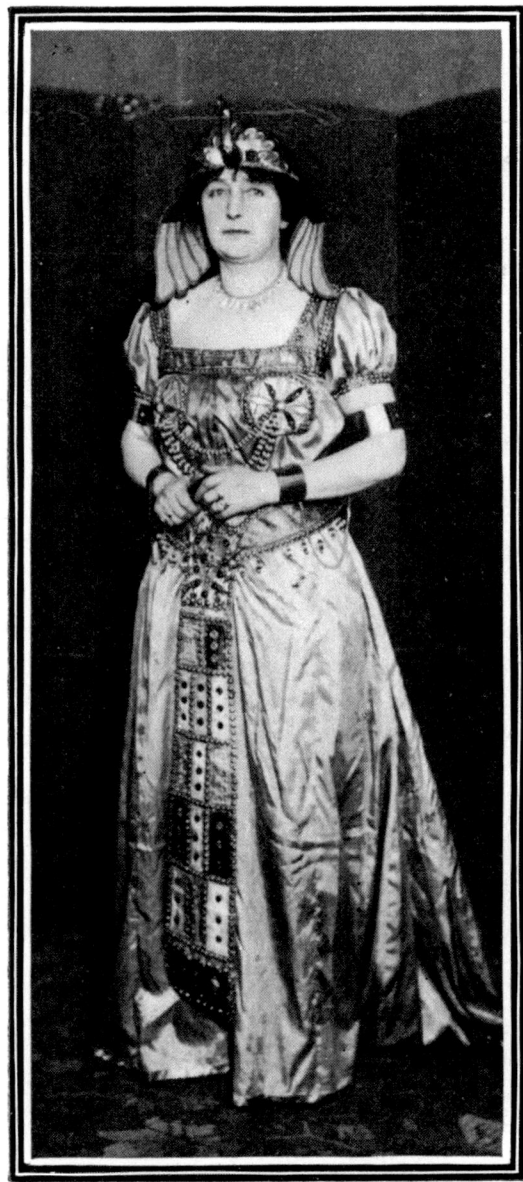

MRS. RAVEN HILL

The wife of the well-known " Punch " artist,
who appeared as Cleopatra

24 Annie Raven-Hill as Cleopatra at the Artists' Ball, Grafton Galleries,
London, May 1910.

Leonard and Annie, like George and Mary Armour, lived just a few miles from Cleeve House, and the Bells, Raven-Hills, and Armours moved in the same moneyed upper- and middle-class social circles. It was at a garden-party hosted by the Bells in August 1899 that the young Clive's possibilities as a potential lover first drew Annie's attention (for they must surely have met before), and the socialising certainly did not end after the affair started. We shall see that Vanessa Bell sometimes joined in the socialising and enjoyed it. Clive describes in detail his encounter with Annie beside the tennis-court at Cleeve House during his game of mixed doubles with three teenage friends. The exchange with her was a brief one, and "exchange" is not perhaps the right word, for she made all the running. The incident might have led to nothing if she had not closed it with the words "I suppose you know that your curls are lovely". When Clive rode to Battle House the following day, nothing happened, but it was not long before it did "on the immense sofa in the studio", with a bottle of sparkling Moselle thoughtfully provided by Annie on the first occasion to give him Dutch courage. He needed that because of his inexperience and also for fear of making her pregnant, or, as he puts it, "of doing what the adjutant had done", in reference to an officer in the Wiltshire Regiment who took inadequate precautions when making love to her and landed her with her fourth child, Betty Margaret – a child whom Leonard gallantly accepted as his own – or perhaps believed was his own.

But when Clive first committed adultery with Annie, he knew nothing of the adjutant, whose transgression was still nearly three years in the future, as Betty was not born until 22 February 1903. What he did know was that Annie's company was very much sought after – not only by men, who found her exceptionally attractive, but also, more surprisingly, by her upper-class neighbours' wives as well. Given that Clive was still not quite eighteen when this admired, beautiful, and mature woman of thirty-five gave him the come-hither signal, it is no wonder that he was enormously pleased. Predictably, that first engagement on the sofa was less than satisfactory, but she was extraordinarily nice about it all and made him feel good, and not a failure.

It seems that the two had several more meetings, including at least one in London, before he went up to Cambridge for the start of his first term there. So far as meetings at Battle House were concerned, it was a great advantage that Leonard needed to be in London for two or three days a week for the sake of his work for *Punch*. How much he knew of Annie's infidelities, we cannot tell. She exercised much caution, as Clive relates, but he was not her only lover: he mentions two others – the adjutant and John Fisher, a well-heeled elderly near-neighbour of the Raven-Hills, who settled her substantial millinery accounts. However discreet she may have been for most of the time, the arrival of Betty must have taken some explaining – unless of course Leonard believed that he was her biological father. When Betty's birth was registered by Leonard on 26 March 1903, he was not long back from a visit to India where he had been sent by *Punch* to record the extravagant Delhi Durbar, which took place on New Year's Day 1903, and where he had also travelled about on his own account and sketched other scenes.[53] But he did not set sail for India before autumn 1902, some months after Betty would have been conceived.

The writer E. V. Knox ("Evoe"), who knew Raven-Hill as a member of the *Punch* Table from 1920 and as the magazine's editor from 1932, describes him as "irascible",[54] and one might think that his wife's conduct gave him good reason to be angry with her from time to time. We do not know if he ever took advantage of his weekly visits to town to see other women. We do know that in October 1923, just over a year and a half after Annie died, he married a much younger (though mature) woman, the formidable Scot Marion Jean Lyon, *Punch*'s advertising manager.[55] But there is no evidence that he had a "relationship" with her or any other woman during Annie's lifetime.

A period of fifteen years separated the beginning of Clive's affair with Annie and its end in October 1914. They did not see one another at regular intervals all this time. Opportunities would have been limited during term-time at Cambridge, and he spent most of 1904 in France. From 1905 his main interest was focused on Vanessa Bell, to whom he became engaged in 1906 and whom he married in 1907.

But within a year or so of the birth of the Bells' elder son, Julian, in February 1908, Clive and Annie resumed their affair. Vanessa first met Annie at Cleeve House in August 1907 and found her a breath of fresh air, writing to her sister Virginia: "We went to tea with the Raven Hills yesterday as it cleared up. I like her and it is a relief occasionally to see people who do understand what you say and have some feeling for other things

53 The result was his *An Indian Sketch-book. Impressions of the East and the Great Durbar*, London: Punch Office, 26 May 1903, as well as cartoons for a special Delhi Durbar edition of *Punch* on 7 January 1903. Writer Owen Seaman and cartoonist Edward Tennyson Reed had also been sent by *Punch* to cover the Durbar. See also Raven-Hill, "In India", 433–449. On the exhibition of Leonard's Indian drawings in May 1903, see above and note 40.

54 Knox.

55 Marion Jean Lyon, *Punch*'s advertising manager from 1922, was founder president of the Women's Advertising Club of London (WACL) in 1923 and a director of the feminist journal *Time and Tide* whose owner Lady (Margaret) Rhondda was greatly impressed by her abilities. Unusually for the time, Lyon kept her maiden name for professional purposes even after she and Leonard married.

besides the crops."[56] Vanessa again gave a favourable report of Annie when she, Clive, and Julian stayed at Cleeve House in the spring of 1908, as she tells Virginia:

> We dined on Friday with the Raven-Hills and I believe Clive gave you some description of the proceedings there. Mrs R. H. is really amusing and also most wildly improper in conversation. Talk of freedom in talk. She stops at nothing. Different methods of stopping children and the joys of married life were freely discussed and notes compared by her, Mrs Armour and myself, and I quite enjoyed myself as you will believe. Also I see that I can get some useful tips from Mrs Raven-Hill as to the best methods of checking one's family and I mean to make use of the dance at Devizes for the purpose, though as she is very deaf I shall probably cause a scandal.
>
> Today we have been lunching with the Armours, who are very nice but not exciting. Still it is a mercy to escape the Sunday dinner here.[57]

Given the "accident" that had occurred when Annie and the adjutant made love a few years earlier, her credentials as an authority on family-planning methods might not have been considered impeccable, but perhaps since that slip-up she had made a study of the subject and become an expert; anyhow, she was to have no more children after Betty. Worth noting is that Vanessa mentions Annie's deafness, as does the latter's daughter Sylvia in her memoirs; but Clive never does.

Clive's letter to Virginia was written the previous day, also from Cleeve House. He writes of the Raven-Hills' dinner-party:

> Have you ever noticed that the atmosphere of the private bar is more perceptible than that of feminine purity? Perhaps it is well – for women. Mrs. Raven Hill, Mrs. Armour, Mrs. Clive Bell; three young or youngish women: mothers, how beautiful do they sit, each in her own shy[58] nursery smiling down Madona-like [*sic*] on a smiling child. Last night they dined with three men; Mr. Raven Hill, Mr. Armour, Mr. Clive Bell; artists, young members of the youngest Bohemian clubs, stained by drink and lust and too warm contact with a sin-be-sodden world. How would they have blushed (they would have blushed, I swear to you they would) these men who sat smoking their cigars and drinking their port and talking of music-halls and dancers and bull-fights, blushed to have heard one sentence of the conversation that was

56 Vanessa Bell to Virginia Stephen, Tuesday [13 August 1907]. Virginia Woolf Collection of Papers, 1882–1984, The Henry W. and Albert A. Berg Collection of English and American Literature, The New York Public Library, Astor, Lenox and Tilden Foundations.

57 Vanessa Bell to Virginia Stephen, Sunday, [19 April 1908], in Vanessa Bell, 61.

58 Misread by Spalding, 71, as "day".

going forward over the way[59] in the ladies' withdrawing room. Your sister will perhaps repeat it to you, though certainly I hope she will not. You will be glad to hear, at any rate, that she is much the better for her half hour's bawdy talk.[60]

At this stage Vanessa apparently had no knowledge of Clive's past relationship with Annie. But by the summer of 1910 she was aware of it. A few days after the birth of their second child, Quentin, in London on 19 August, Clive went to his parents' home at Seend, where their elder son, Julian, was being looked after. In an affectionate letter to Clive there, Vanessa, still confined to bed on medical advice and missing him and Julian ("my blue puppy"), writes: "I hope youll [*sic*] see your whore soon and get some amusing gossip out of her and the truth about Mr. Chesterton and Mr. Dawes."[61] She makes a rather similar comment to Clive in another letter, written early in 1913, when her loving attention, having been focused on Roger Fry since the spring of 1911, was about to change in favour of Duncan Grant: "I imagine you tonight with your Little Lady – Am I right? I think perhaps you ought to seize the opportunity of going to see your Regents Park P. and find out from her the truth of all these reports about Sylvia's young man."[62] Clive's "Little Lady" is most likely to be Molly MacCarthy. Of the identity of his "Regents Park P.", where "P" stands for "Prostitute", there can be no doubt. In 1912 the Raven-Hills had moved back to London from Wiltshire and had taken up residence first at 7 Regent's Court, Park Road, Regent's Park, then nearby at 4 York Terrace. Annie's elder daughter, Sylvia, now aged nineteen and living at the same address, was engaged to Roderic Douglas James ("Tim") Hodgson and was to marry him on 3 June 1913. He turned out to have a severe problem with alcohol, and the marriage was short-lived. It was perhaps reports of Tim's alcohol-addiction that Vanessa suggested Clive should ask Annie about. As Sylvia recalls in her memoir, her father, at least, had an inkling of Tim's (and his mother's) problems with alcohol:

> I remembered my mother-in-law's curious habit of having a large jug of what she called "cold tea for breakfast". I now found out it was whiskey, I also

---

59 Clive first wrote "across the hall".

60 Clive Bell to Virginia Stephen, Saturday, 18 April 1908, Special Collections, The Keep, Brighton, SxMs – 18/1/D/13/1.

61 Vanessa Bell to Clive Bell, Sunday [late August or early September 1910], Tate Gallery Archive 8010/2/46. The matter involving Messrs Chesterton and Dawes is obscure. Vanessa's following (and concluding) remark on it is: "I suspect that the present arrangement suits Mr. D. very well and he is too wise to upset it."

62 Vanessa Bell to Clive Bell, 7 January [1913], Tate Gallery Archive 8010/2/103.

remembered that she often went off to bed with the help of their butler and footman, because she had broken her glasses. I remembered too father's gently warning "I shouldn't encourage him to drink if I were you" which I couldn't understand then, but now it became clear, father had evidently heard that drink was in the family.[63]

In his memoir Clive claims that he "was never in the least in love with Mrs. Raven Hill, and I do not think there was ever anything between us that could be well called affection". One may accept that they were not in love, but question whether there was no affection. The sheer longevity of the relationship makes it unlikely that there was none, and in fact Clive admits to "some liking", which is not quite consistent.

One may question, too, his claim that he was not interested in Annie's life. Surviving letters show that he and Vanessa socialised with the Raven-Hills over a period of seven years, and it is unlikely that the letters tell the full story. A valuable source of information about Clive's activities in 1913 (after the Raven-Hills had returned to live in London) is his engagements' diary for that year – the only surviving diary of his prior to 1925. In this diary alone, for the penultimate year of their long sporadic affair, he records a dozen or so meetings with Annie.

The 1913 diary also has two entries relating to Sylvia: one, for Monday 17 February, is "tea"; the other, for Tuesday 3 June, her wedding-day, gives only her name. Whether he attended Sylvia's wedding or not, the event was clearly of interest. There are certainly indications that both he and Vanessa were interested in Sylvia. One is Vanessa's suggestion that he find out the truth of the reports about her young man. Another is a letter Vanessa wrote a year earlier, in which she commented: "Skin tights hardly sound to me the right clothing for Sylvia, but I suppose they were."[64]

Of his meetings with Annie in 1913, one was two days after tea with Sylvia, another six days before Sylvia's wedding. Some meetings were for dinner, others for lunch. Three dinners were at the Savoy. In other cases the venue is not given. The meetings were always on weekdays, and seven were on a Wednesday, a day when Annie's husband would be fully occupied with his duties at *Punch* and the *Punch* Table – duties that were extra-important now that he was one of the magazine's political cartoonists. On a "Memoranda" page at the back of the diary Annie is mentioned, apparently as one of those to whom he meant to write.[65]

63 Needham.
64 Vanessa Bell to Clive Bell, 15 January [1912], in Vanessa Bell, 114.
65 Clive was in Italy from 15 April until just before his meeting with Annie on 28 May 1913, and in Scotland 10–28 August.

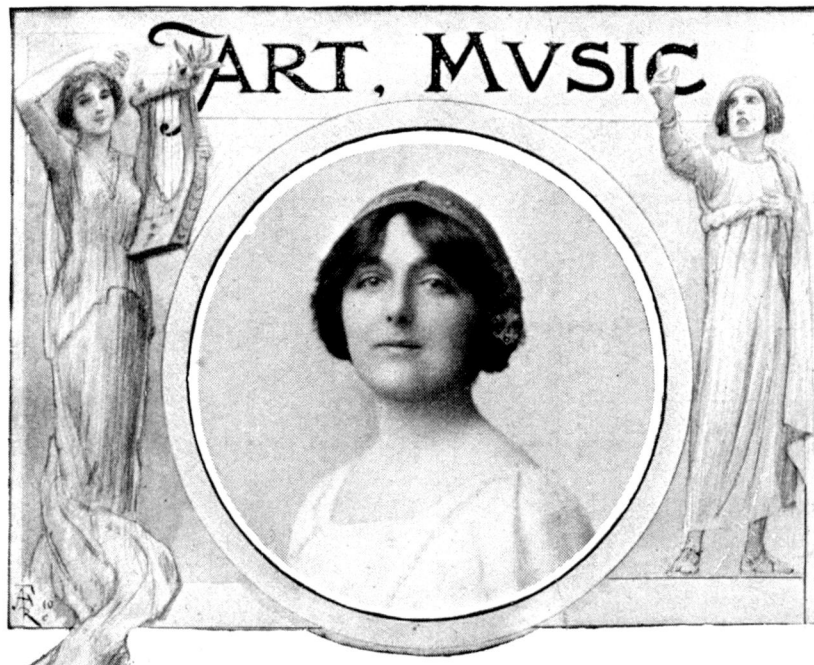

25 Sylvia Raven-Hill featured in "Art, Music and the Drama".

Sylvia, who, prior to her marriage, had been showing promise as an
actress (Plate 25), herself describes meeting Clive and Vanessa, and it is
clear from her memoir that she attended more than one of their social gatherings, apparently brought there by Annie:

Mother took me to meet Clive Bell, a well known art critic: he had a fascinating room, all white including white covered books with only one very red
apple on the mantelpiece. There I met Roger Fry and felt very flattered when
he gave me one of his contemporary hand-painted sunshades. Vanessa Bell,
wife of Clive Bell, fascinated me with her large eyes and deep seductive voice
and her fun! At one of their parties, one of the artistic type young men, having
had some vodka for supper, had his melancholy song of "Down among the

dead men" drowned by a healthy squirt of soda water on his chest directed by Vanessa.[66]

After Sylvia's marriage in June 1913, the Raven-Hills moved from Regent's Park to Richmond in Surrey, where their address was 2 The Paragon, part of a house dating from about 1720. It was in the Richmond house that Annie and Leonard entertained Vanessa and Clive to lunch on Sunday, 1 February 1914. Six years earlier, Annie had astonished and entertained Vanessa with her frank talk about sex and contraception. On this occasion she astonished and entertained her no less with her free behaviour. Vanessa describes what took place in a letter to Duncan Grant:

> Clive and I went to lunch with the Raven Hills at Richmond on Sunday and she gave me a great lecture on dress. She showed me all her clothes and finally tried most of them on. Clive came to her bedroom and she got off her clothes down to her drawers and skipped about with a great deal of coyness – you would have enjoyed it thoroughly but the most extraordinary sight was finally when she wanted to go on the po[67] (Clive had left the room) and her skirt was too tight to do it in the ordinary way and she got into the most extraordinary attitude something like this kneeling on the floor but I don't think I've given the effect very well – only it really would have made a very good thing to paint as her legs somehow made a very good design and her blouse was bright yellow, carried out by the other touches of yellow. With some of the children's chalks I have now managed to make it very realistic.[68] [Plate 26]

At the last of Clive and Annie's meetings, in October 1914, their affair went out with a bang in all senses, as, according to his account: "our encounter was one of the most violent we had ever enjoyed, and quite the most indecent".

Early in the First World War the Raven-Hills moved the short distance from Richmond to a Thames-side house called Waterton at 101 Strawberry Vale, Teddington. While continuing his work for *Punch*, Leonard contributed to the war-effort as Chief Musketry Instructor for the City of London National Guard.[69] Before the end of the war he and Annie were living in a seafront apartment, 10a Brunswick Terrace, in Hove, next door to Brighton.

---

66 Needham.
67 Chamber pot.
68 Vanessa Bell to Duncan Grant, Thursday [5 March 1914], Tate Gallery Archive 20078/1/44/21 (misdated there 6 March 1914).
69 The City of London National Guard was a volunteer corps of men over military age in which Leonard held the rank of captain. His military expertise and organisational skills had been in demand as early as the time of the Boer War, when he was asked to train Bromham men as volunteers.

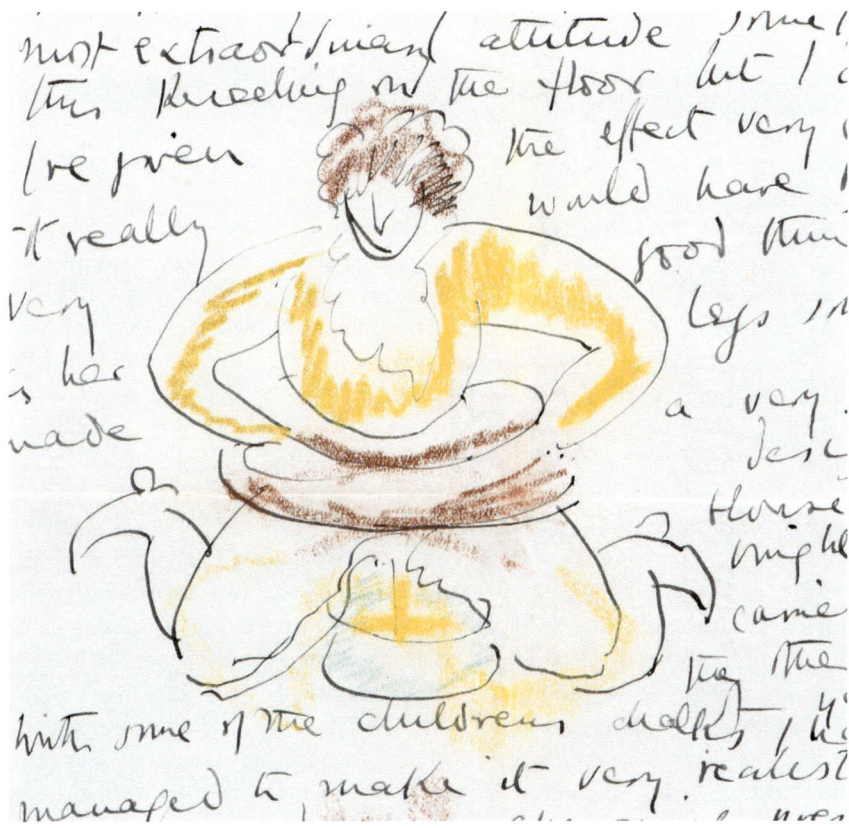

26 Detail from a letter from Vanessa Bell to Duncan Grant, [5 March 1914], with a sketch of Annie Raven-Hill "on the po".

In 1918 Annie's health deteriorated sharply. According to Sylvia,[70] she was recuperating from an appendix operation when her eldest sister (Martha Maria) had a stroke and died and, as she was preparing to go to Martha's funeral, she too suffered a stroke. To make matters worse, soon afterwards another of her sisters (almost certainly Ellen) also had a stroke and died.[71] Annie made a limited recovery, regaining the use of her legs. But she did not recover full use of her hands and speech and was a shadow of her former lively self. She and Leonard moved from Hove to The Duver, a seafront house at St Helen's on the Isle of Wight. There she suffered another stroke, but again survived. Wrote Sylvia:

70 Needham.
71 Ellen, who had married George William Woodward in 1883, died of a cerebral thrombosis on 11 December 1918, aged sixty.

> She was so handicapped poor darling and still could not use her hands very well, and when excited her speech became blurred, but she could take walks if she lead [*sic*] a very quiet life, but a stroke is a stroke and it seemed to me like a living death for such a gay active woman.[72]

Still, this was hardly the almost complete "imbecility" that Clive wrote of in 1921.

In April 1922, a fortnight after Sylvia (who had remarried and had one son) had undergone the trauma of giving birth to a still-born baby girl, Annie had a third stroke, which after a few days proved fatal. She died on 26 April and is buried with Leonard, who died almost twenty years later on 31 March 1942, in St Helen's churchyard beneath a gravestone designed by her eldest brother, Mark Rogers Junior.

Although Clive is disparaging about Annie's intellect, culture, and character, he allows that "she was not stupid". He allows too that she was practical, good-natured, kind, generous, and an extraordinarily skilful lover. It is clear that she was no intellectual, and never pretended to be one, but it is equally clear that she had a mind of her own and was not afraid to speak it, and that her exceptional attractiveness consisted not just in her alluring looks, deportment, and dress, but also in her sparkling personality and sense of fun. How else could one explain the remarkable impact she had on so many of those she encountered – women as well as men?

Despite his disparaging comments, Clive's tone towards Annie throughout his memoir is generally affectionate and admiring. Some readers may find his last words, describing her as "imprisoned, in the depths of the Isle of Wight, a complete, or almost a complete imbecile" and explaining that he has "written of her with some freedom" partly "because she is now beyond the reach of scandal or censure", as jarringly unsympathetic, but they can also be interpreted as sad. Anyhow, they show that, although he and she never had another sexual encounter – or even met – after October 1914, for reasons probably to do with wartime conditions and the start of his affair with Mary Hutchinson, he did not lose track of her altogether, and we can conjecture that it was Sylvia who kept him informed about Annie's health problems and death. Despite its apparent sensationalism, Clive's memoir cannot conceal his affection and regard for Annie, and it may be added that Sylvia's memoir has only good things to say about a loving and much-loved mother.

---

72 Needham.

II. The text of Clive Bell's memoir

I was talking about Jenny – a white pony – before I began to talk about Dorothea[73] and the loves of my nonage;[74] and though I have almost forgotten the points of a horse, and though it is years now since I charged so much as a sheep-hurdle, the moment I begin to dream of those times, horses of all shapes, colours and sizes keep cantering and galloping in and out of my vision.[75] So, perhaps, after all, it is only appropriate that in the first considerable affair of my life one of the principal figures should have been a beautiful, bright bay weight-carrier, – called Huntsman. For I never think of Huntsman without thinking of Mrs. Raven Hill though I do sometimes think of her without thinking of Huntsman. And the best of Huntsman is that he makes me think, not of the Mrs. Raven Hill whom you, Vanessa, knew, but of the Mrs. Raven Hill of the summer of '99 – the summer when I was rising eighteen and about to go up to Trinity as a freshman.

Those who saw her only in her old, fat, demoralized, whorish, raddled days, I will ask to clear their minds of all such recollections.[76]

73 Almost certainly Dorothea Godiva Mann, one of the four children (three daughters and a son) of William John Mann, a wealthy solicitor and prominent public figure in Trowbridge, and his wife Julia Mann, *née* Brown. The family lived until at least 1901 at Rodney House, 5 Roundstone Street, Trowbridge, and later moved to a large nineteenth-century mansion, Highfield, in nearby Hilperton. Dorothea was born on 16 March 1880 and so was over a year older than Clive. She is mentioned again below as Clive's tennis-partner at the time he was approached by Annie Raven-Hill. She married William Harold Montgomery on 7 October 1908. Among the guests invited to the wedding at St Michael's Church, Hilperton, were Clive's parents and sisters and Annie and Leonard Raven-Hill. The Bells gave the couple "an old bureau", the Raven-Hills "an original sketch", very likely the work of Leonard. For a detailed report of the wedding, see *The Wiltshire Times and Trowbridge Advertiser*, Saturday, 10 October 1908. Dorothea had two daughters and a son and died, aged eighty-eight, in Edinburgh on 9 March 1968.

74 Clive refers to the paper he read to the Memoir Club on 7 July 1920. See I.2 above. The paper has not survived.

75 Clive went hunting as a young man, including at Cambridge, where he arrived "with all the apparatus and livestock needed for pursuing the hunt, killing birds, or entertaining actresses" (Quentin Bell, 27) and discussed hunting with Thoby Stephen (Clive Bell, 27).

76 Clive says at the end of the memoir that he did not see Annie after October 1914, so it seems that he is referring here to the way she was in the last years of their affair, even though it is clear that he still found her attractive then. Those in his audience

But Vanessa, who knew her eight years later, can guess, perhaps, what she was like at the time of which I write. She was at once the Aspasia[77] and the Gaby de Lys[78] of North Wilts. At the same time, though, as I discovered much later, her youngest child was in fact illegitimate,[79] she was commonly supposed to be, in the last resort, inaccessible. She was universally courted, and somewhat kissed I presume. Lord Lansdowne himself, the Lord-Lieutenant,[80] has been known to press her foot beneath the bridge-table, and the subalterns from Trowbridge barracks were for ever making shy pilgrimages to Battle House in dog carts, on more or less improbable errands, with flowers and chocolates and other unexceptionable presents. Even my father – steadiest of husbands – has on more than one occasion pinched her leg. And she deserved it. For at that time she was lovely – soft without being fat and fair without being flaxen – rather pale brown over lilies and roses – and sweet as an October pear.

Hers were all the more obvious feminine charms: she knew just how to hold up her skirts – which came from Paris by the way, where once she had lived, in the *quartier latin*, before her husband became famous enough to sink ambition and take to *Punch*: she could strike a rich note of provocation – she could swing adroitly from one trapeze to the other, from mother to mistress, from housewife to whore –: her sensuality emanated from her like a fine scent; and her scent itself was fine – fine as her pocket-handkerchiefs. Her voice was musical though – I must say it – ever so little common;[81] her phrasing was often pretty; and she was not incapable of a bluntish point of irony. She was not stupid. There was something

who met her included Vanessa Bell and Roger Fry (see I.4 above), and it is likely that others at the reading had done so at the Bells' parties, or even elsewhere.

77 The cultivated and influential mistress of the Athenian politician Pericles, whom she survived. Leonard Woolf, a great admirer of Pericles, on falling in love with Virginia Stephen, took to calling her "Aspasia" in his diary. See Glendenning, 134–135.

78 Gaby Deslys, real name Marie-Elise-Gabrielle Caire, famously beautiful French singer, dancer, and actress, at one time lover of King Manuel II of Portugal.

79 See n. 97.

80 Henry Petty-Fitzmaurice, Fifth Marquis of Lansdowne, statesman, at various times Governor-general of Canada, Viceroy of India, Secretary of State for War, and Secretary of State for Foreign Affairs, was Lord Lieutenant of Wiltshire from 1896 to 1920.

81 Here and after "pretty" just below and in several places elsewhere in Clive's typescript, what appears to be a colon is probably actually a semi-colon whose lower element has lost its tail. Likewise there are many places where a comma appears as a full stop.

in her manner which reminds me now of the rich and florid and slightly used contralto of a well-developed Italian prima donna. She was welcoming always, never turned anyone brutally down, and rarely quite gave herself away. She was of those women who remind you at one moment of a plumpish partridge and at another of a just browning gardenia. They never want for lovers, and Mrs. Raven Hill could have had the whole Badminton Hunt[82] had she chosen.

I wish I could describe her as "*une grande amoureuse*": and if I hesitate to pay her that supreme compliment – the highest compliment I can pay a woman – it implies no reflexion on her appearance, her temperament, or her technique. What she lacked was culture and intellect. For, as a glance at history will prove to any doubter, in the wardrobe of "une grande amoureuse", a bluish stocking is the indispensable garment. Only a cultivated and rather intellectual woman can possibly possess that shameless self-consciousness which gives the finest sting of pleasure to our more elaborate encounters. Mrs. Raven Hill was neither cultivated nor quite clever *enough*. It was not that she was *too* much of a whore, but that she was not sufficiently aware of being a fine lady who was making herself one. And so I must not crown her with an unearned title, but only with that which le sieur de Branthôme thought good enough for Madame de Valentinois, dite[83] Diane de Poictiers[84] – "Belle et noble dame, grande Paillarde et bonne putaine, qui entre-tenait gentiment le mestier."[85]

Of course I was thrilled by her, like everyone else – yes, every-one, for it is to be noted that even the ladies – the married ladies of Wiltshire – my mother even – made a pet of her; but though at this time (August 1899), with my bran new Cambridge allowance and the right to drink whisky and smoke cigarettes, I was gaining confidence enough to surmise that I might find more favour in a lady's eyes than a far better hockey-player, I should never have

---

82 A prominent and long-established fox-hunt, maintained by the Dukes of Beaufort and operating in Gloucestershire and Wiltshire. The hunt has always been based at Badminton, the ducal seat, but is now called the Beaufort.

83 "So-called."

84 "Branthôme" and "Poictiers" are misspellings. Pierre de Bourdeille, Seigneur de Brantôme, soldier, biographer, and historian. Diane de Poitiers, Duchesse de Valentinois, official mistress of King Henri II of France.

85 "Beautiful and noble lady, great wanton and good whore, who kept up her craft nicely"; "putaine" and "mestier" are misspellings of "putain" and "metier".

dared to raise mine to such heights as these, and, to be frank, I had never yet cast them, in a spirit of lust, on a married woman. So imagine my feelings when, one afternoon, during a garden party at Cleeve House,[86] something happened which I must now attempt to describe. I was playing a set of lawn-tennis with Dorothea[87] as my partner, against Dora Gardiner[88] and Herbert Thynne[89] – and remember, for it makes the whole thing stranger, that I was a very bad player and Herbert Thynne quite a good one. I had gone to the high net that separated the tennis-courts from the gravel, preventing the balls, which I had gone to collect, from bouncing away into the shrubs and flower-beds, and I was stooping to pick one up, when on the other side – the gravel side – of the net, came towards me Mrs. Raven Hill from a herbaceous border where she was being shown the plants and flirted with by old Sir John Goldney.[90] She was wearing a tight-fitting blue cloth dress, the skirt of which she adorably held up to keep the braid out of the dust and emphasize her delicious contours; and as I was stooping down, she said – "Well, Arthur,[91] you haven't found time to speak to me." Pleased but uncomfortable, I looked up, wondering, no doubt, how exactly to reply, when she added – "But you must go back to your partner now – I suppose you know that your curls are lovely."[92] [Plate 27] I went back to my game, and enjoyed it. But from that moment I quite definitely realised that playing hockey and tennis with maidens, and giving them tea and ices, was not the last word in love-making: more dimly I understood that if I were to call at Battle House I should not be made to feel that I ought to

---

86 The home of Clive's family in the Wiltshire village of Seend.

87 See n. 73 above.

88 Dora Jessie Gardiner, daughter of the Rev. William Gardiner, vicar of St James's Church, Devizes.

89 Herbert Sayer Thynne, elder son of the Rev. Arthur Barugh Thynne, vicar of Seend. He and his brother, Geoffrey Arthur Carlisle Thynne, were educated, like Clive, at Marlborough College. They established H. & G. Thynne Ltd, a decorative tile-manufacturing business in Hereford.

90 Sir John Tankerville Goldney was not all that old at the time. He had recently resigned, at the age of fifty-three, from the office of Chief Justice of Trinidad and Tobago. He was appointed High Sheriff of Wiltshire in 1910.

91 Arthur was Clive's first name, and the one by which he was known in his childhood and youth. Whether Annie called him that throughout their relationship is not known.

92 The "beautiful curls" Clive had in 1899 did not last, but are to be seen in a photograph taken just after he went up to Cambridge (Plate 27).

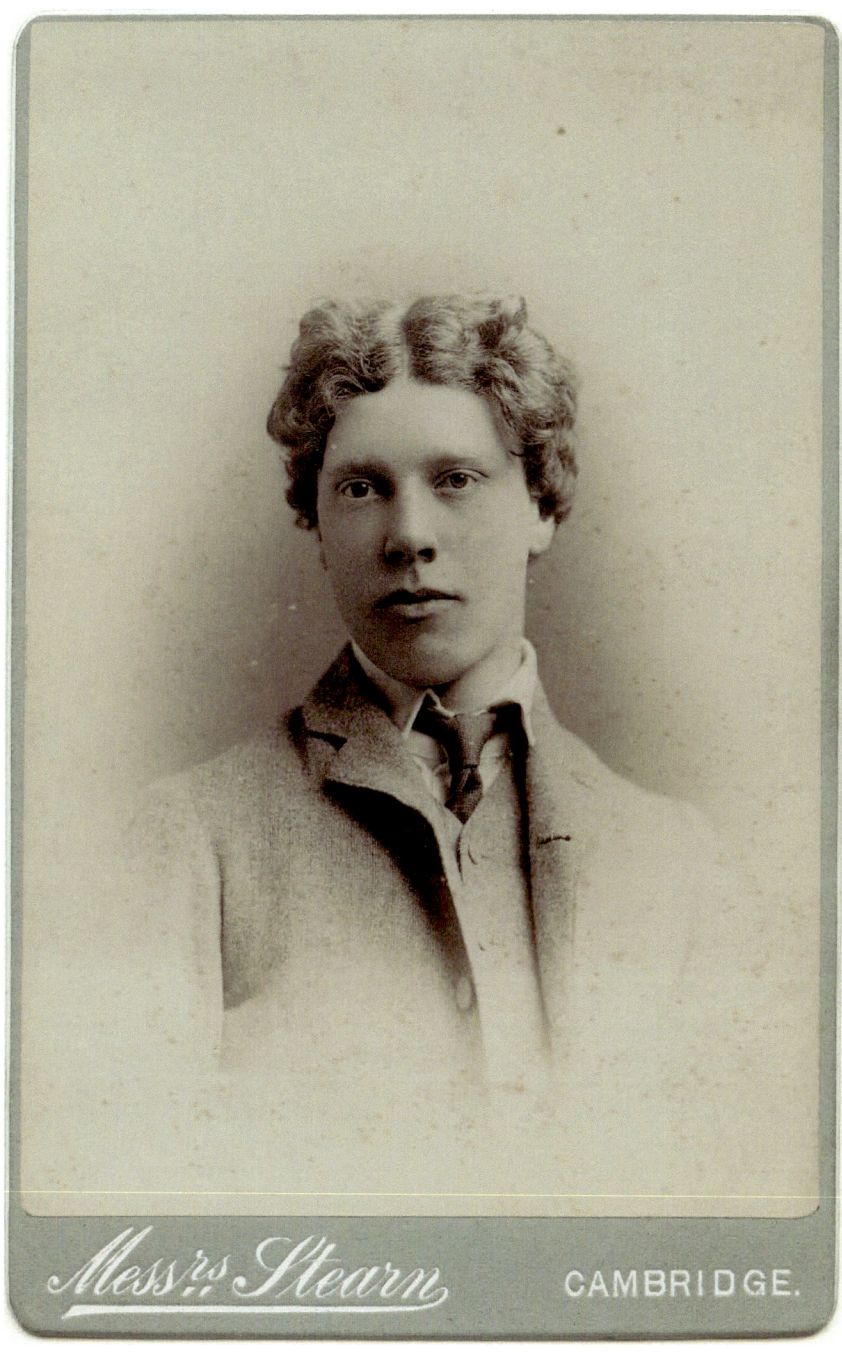

27 Arthur Clive Heward Bell in Cambridge, 1899 or soon after.

be at school: and I can recapture well enough that queer breathless sensation, which I now know to have been a beating heart, with which I decided to ride over the very next day.

And next day, under a blazing sun, over I rode on my bright bay hunter, in my white polo breeches and brown polo boots, with my Panama hat and my beautiful curls – a subject for the pen of George Meredith[93] or the pencil of Charles Furse.[94] A mile by lane and road to Seend station, and then three more across fields without so much as the glimpse of a farm house, over fields that once – in Crimean boom days – had been under plough, but were now running to coarse grass, islands of rest-harrow[95] and shabby overgrown hedges – fields well stocked with rabbits and derelict donkeys, but incapable of supporting a single cow; and so along untidy, hollowing coverts to the iron gate that opens into Sandridge lane; and from Sandridge it is ten minutes trot to Bromham. Wednesday should have been the day; for on Wednesdays Mr. Raven Hill, who was at the *Punch* table,[96] went up to London to discuss with his colleagues the next week's cartoon, and never returned before Thursday night and often not till Friday lunch-time. And so Wednesday afternoon

93 George Meredith, best known for his novel *Diana of the Crossways*. He was a friend of Leslie Stephen, father of Vanessa Bell and Virginia Woolf. Vanessa liked him (letter, dated "Sunday", written in summer 1911 to Clive, Tate Gallery Archive 8010/2/68).

94 Charles Wellington Furse, noted for his portrayals of people engaged in outdoor activities, including people on horseback. Vanessa met him through her parents and was influenced by his work.

95 Grassland plant with pink flowers. In the last three decades of the nineteenth century English agriculture was very seriously affected by steep falls in cereal prices caused by the huge increase of wheat imports from the USA. Hence the comments of Lady Bracknell in Oscar Wilde's *The Importance of Being Earnest* (first performed in 1895): "Land has ceased to be either a profit or a pleasure. It gives one position and prevents one from keeping it up. That's all that can be said about land."

96 The *Punch* Table was both an actual dining-table and an exclusive club which staff and contributors to *Punch* had to be invited to join. The weekly Wednesday dinners (and later lunches) at the *Punch* Table were used to decide collegially on the subject of the full-page political cartoon for the coming week, after which the cartoonist of the day had to draw the subject quickly for delivery to the block makers, usually on a Friday, and for publication on Saturday. New members of the *Punch* Table were expected to carve their initials into the historic table, with proprietors grouped at one end, editors at the other, and contributors along the sides. The *Punch* Table is now owned by the British Library. Annie's husband, Leonard, was not admitted to the Table until Wednesday, 2 January 1901, and this is just one of several places where Clive is unreliable about dates and the order of events.

was the time for a visit, though my first may have been made on any day of the week. Nothing came of it.

You must remember I was barely eighteen at the time; for all that I had a confident feeling that *some* day *something* would come of it. This feeling must have been born, I suppose of something in Mrs. Raven Hill's manner; for I knew nothing of her beyond the fact that everyone was quite obviously after her. I have said that she passed for chaste and that in fact she was not. Already she had dismissed, or thought she had dismissed, her first lover, a wretched infantry officer – the adjutant – who by gross negligence and lack of gumption had landed her with Betty.[97] Also, there was old Mr. Fisher of St. Edith's, who paid her milliners' bills and to whom she was kind – the extent of her wardrobe, I recollect, provoked some comment even amongst her nicest friends, – but old Mr. Fisher was long past serious mischief.[98] However I knew nothing of this; and for a year at least after our first encounter she pretended that ours was her first affair; later she developed as frank a cynicism as ever I knew in a woman. Yet here again her intellect was at fault: her cynicism was too naïf and too impersonal; it lacked the provocation of self-consciousness; and so, very often, was disarming in the worst sense of the word. Yet from her I learnt the best of what I know. You see she had her sense of life, limited and bourgeois no doubt, but real; and so in a world of unreal, unpurposeful country gentry, she was mistress of the event. Why,

97 Betty Margaret Raven-Hill, born on 22 February 1903. Clive calls her "illegitimate", but, although she was sired by the adjutant, her birth certificate shows that Leonard registered her birth and identified himself as her father. The possibility that he believed Betty to be his child cannot be ruled out. We have not identified Betty's biological father with certainty, and would not like to indulge in speculation. It is worth pointing out that at the time Clive wrote his memoir, he, like Leonard, had presented himself to the world as the father of a girl who was his wife's biological daughter but not his – Angelica Vanessa Bell (later Garnett), born on 25 December 1918. Her father was actually Duncan Grant.

98 John Fisher, who lived with his wife (and six indoor servants) at St Edith's, his residence in Bromham. St Edith's is described as "a modern mansion of stone, in the Italian style, standing in its own grounds of about 36 acres, and has lawns, gardens and a conservatory attached" (*Kelly's Directory: Wiltshire*, 45), so he could probably well afford to pay the bills for Annie's hats. However, he did not take up residence in St Edith's until around January 1902. The previous long-term occupant was Capt. G. J. W. Prowse, a member of an old Yeovil family. When Prowse's daughter Ethel was married at Bromham church on 5 September 1900, Sylvia Raven-Hill acted as train-bearer and wore a pearl and turquoise pin that was a gift of the bride (*Bath Chronicle and Weekly Gazette*, 6 September 1900).

Vanessa herself was astonished, I remember, at the way in which she managed Mr. Fisher – a jealous, pompous, testy old fellow – keeping him in his place without snubbing or maltreating him, and so never for a moment jeopardising the two or three hundred a year she must have cost him. Later, she used to give me exact accounts – in bed – of his prowess, and of the *ménagements*[99] necessary on her side. She was infinitely skillful [*sic*] with both fingers and lips. I remember she thought him remarkable for his age.

For *mine* I consider that I was on the whole bold and fore-thoughtful. At any rate, from the first, I took to tipping the groom at Battle House, and giving him to understand in as off-hand a way as I could command, that as sometimes I might be rather late, it was never worth his while to sit up for me: he might feed my horse, I suggested, and leave him to stand on the pillar-rein. And yet, though bold in some ways, I was often horribly frightened when I found myself on the immense sofa in the studio tête-a-tête with Mrs. Raven Hill. However, on the night I first committed adultery she had made me brave with a bottle of sparkling Moselle and her own intolerable seductiveness, for she looked enchanting, I remember well, in a lilac silk frock and stockings, and high-heeled patent leather shoes. And so greatly daring, and miserably uncom-fortable, I kissed her out of shere [*sic*] desperate courage, not lust, as she sat beside me on the sofa. It was a wretched kiss – cold and short and quite unmeaning – on the corner of the mouth. It gave *her* no pleasure, nor me either: and so, no doubt, her first move-ment was one of vexation – "I suppose I ought to say thank you for kissing me" and then, charmingly: "That's not the way to kiss, I'll show you how to kiss." The next thing I clearly remember is my ridiculously clumsy haste pulling up her skirts and petticoats. I remember her sole exclamation – "Oh Arthur!" I remember my riding-breeches were of the kind which button with a broad flap across the front – not ill adapted to the matter in hand. And I think of a duck and drake affair on the pond at Charleston.[100] Certainly it was over in less than a minute, and issue was not properly joined during half that time – so terrified was I of doing what the adjutant had done.[101] Nothing could have been flatter. I can recall

99   "Caution".

100   Farmhouse in East Sussex, the home from 1916 of Vanessa Bell, Duncan Grant, and David Garnett. Clive, who remained married to Vanessa, was a frequent visitor, as were other members of the Bloomsbury Group.

101   The careless act of the adjutant that brought Betty into being occurred more than two years later, around July 1902.

with agonizing precision just what I felt – the blank mournfulness of a complete fiasco, the sense of humiliation, of having made myself ridiculous, of being thought a failure by a woman. I can remember – but unluckily Henri Beyle could remember too, and I have no notion of putting my experiences in competition with those of Julien Sorel.[102]

Mrs. Raven Hill was perfect. What she had just gone through must have been for her a disagreeable and slightly dirty *corvée*;[103] and she was charming. I shall never know why she behaved so well: I never thought of asking her: presumably she had conceived some sort of a *béguin*[104] for me; but I shall never know for certain. At any rate, she did *not* dash off to her room to dry and tidy herself; but half sat, half lay, on a pile of cushions at one end of the sofa in what the XVIIIth century would have called "a charming disorder,"[105] giving me time to collect my wits and button myself up, and making me again feel pleased with myself by talking in a serious flattering way about everything to do with me except what I had just done. Then she told me to smoke a cigarette while she went away for ten minutes and, returned radiant and exquisite, saying, that if I stayed any later it would be scandalous – which was quite untrue but most gratifying to hear. She added, in such a conversation-making tone that for some minutes I did not realise that the remark had any particular import for me, that the week after next she would be in London. And then she said I must go. I remember coming downstairs behind her and out into the warm garden; I remember her delicious movement as she walked over the gravel and the pretty way she held up her skirts to show her feet and ankles and a little lilac leg. I remember catching her in the cobbled stable-yard, close to the stable door, and kissing her lasciviously on the mouth. And for the first time in my life I had the best of it with a woman: I gave more than I got.

But it was riding home, through the dim, flattering night, that my real pleasure began. Then, at last, I was *safely* happy because I was alone, – no danger of a *bêtise*[106] now, – no question of doing

---

102 *Le rouge et le noir*, one of the best-known novels of Stendhal, pseudonym of Marie-Henri Beyle, follows the rise and fall of Julien Sorel.

103 "Chore."

104 "Fancy", "infatuation".

105 One might think also of the seventeenth century, and specifically of Robert Herrick, "Delight in Disorder": "A sweet disorder in the dresse / Kindles in cloathes a wantonnesse".

106 "Blunder."

the wrong thing or leaving the right undone. Truly I was still a stranger to the ecstasy of the senses, but at least I now knew, for the first time, the delirious extasy [*sic*][107] of vanity gratified. I had a mistress – a charming and much desired lady – a prize. I was a match for Meredith's young gentlemen,[108] I was more real than Pendennis,[109] I shook hands with Lord Byron; as for the black and blue hockey players, they had ceased to exist. Putting my hand in my pocket for a match I pressed my shirt to my skin: it was wet. Yes, I had done it: I had had Mrs. Raven Hill.

I was gloriously happy, and I had reason to be, – far more reason than I could then possibly know. In fact I was at the beginning of a liaison which was to last, off and on, by fits and starts, till October 1914, – a liaison in which I can honestly say there was not – on my side at any rate – one moment of pain to set against long evenings and afternoons of sweet and deliberate pleasure. *That* I could not forsee [*sic*]: indeed, I lacked the experience to forsee [*sic*] anything. Yet I did surmise, I think, that the best was to come: I did not surmise – neither I suppose did she – that the best – the very best – was not to come for several years. For instance it was not I should think till *five years* later that I knew what the French novelists mean by "la grande volupté."[110] I had just got into my rooms in King's Bench Walk: it was the month of May, and Mrs. Raven Hill was in town.[111] We had gone in the morning sight-seeing – to pictures at the Guildhall[112] I think – and she was wearing a rather ample apricot-coloured silk dress with a large, high straw hat which became her marvellously. We fell akissing after lunch, and there we lay in my little long, white bed-room, overlooking the Northcliffe factory

---

107 Clive also wrote "extasy" just above, but corrected it there by hand.

108 For example, Percy Dacier in *Diana of the Crossways*.

109 Arthur Pendennis in Thackeray's novel *The History of Pendennis*.

110 "Exquisite pleasure."

111 If Clive were right about "five years later", the date would be May 1904 or 1905, but Mark Hussey advises us that Clive almost certainly moved into rooms at 6 King's Bench Walk at the end of 1902 or at the beginning of 1903, in which case the memorable day with Annie will have been in May 1903. She had given birth to her younger daughter, Betty, on 22 February 1903, but that is not an objection if Betty was in the care of a nurse. King's Bench Walk is in The Temple, between Fleet Street and the Thames. The Guildhall was just a few minutes' walk away, and the Savoy Hotel in the Strand, where Annie and Clive had supper, very near.

112 On the pictures they are likely to have seen, see I.4 above.

in Bouverie Street,[113] and the sun shone and the hours ticked by, and Thoby and Saxon[114] came hammering on my sported[115] door for tea, and went away grumbling I suppose. It was at half-past nine we got up and dressed and had supper at the Savoy, and then drove in a Hansom to Clapham Common – a pretty Georgian house on the north side – where she used often to stay with her friend Carrie Nickalls.[116] I remember a dozen at least of these long jingling drives – there and back – especially back – for it was then I used to enjoy that moment when, as Catulle Mendès says, "on a une besoin absolu de fumer une [*sic*] cigare."[117] But on that night it was different: my head was too full of a new experience – and at last I knew what was meant by "la grande volupté." It was not the frantic thrill of three or four distinct orgasms – though that

113 Newspaper factory. Lord Northcliffe owned and published the *Daily Mail* and *Daily Mirror*. Clive does not mention that at 10 Bouverie Street were the offices of *Punch* and its proprietors, Bradbury, Agnew & Co, for which Annie's husband worked, and this may have added a certain frisson to the couple's love-making.

114 Thoby Stephen, brother of Vanessa and Virginia Stephen, and Saxon Sydney-Turner had entered Trinity College, Cambridge, at the same time as Clive, as had Lytton Strachey and Leonard Woolf.

115 Closed from the inside.

116 "Nickalls" is a misspelling. Clive means Caroline Nicholls, who lived at 18 North Side, Clapham Common, from at least 1901 until 1915, when she moved to 81 Larkhill Rise, Clapham. The house still stands and well fits Clive's description of "a pretty Georgian house on the north side [of Clapham Common]". Rosenbaum, 82, summarising the memoir, says that among the places where Clive and Annie made love was "a house on, of all places, Clapham Common". But Clive does not say that they made love there, and in any case "of all places" is inappropriate, as is Frances Spalding's location of the house in "insalubrious Clapham" (Spalding, 51). The area was in fact considered much more salubrious than many inner-city parts, and, when the Raven-Hills moved into 20 North Side from Chelsea in February 1892, Leonard remarked to his father that "the air is very much fresher and cleaner" (Raven-Hill). Caroline shared 18 North Side with her widowed mother and her brothers and sisters. Her brothers, Thomas and Edward Nicholls, followed their father, Thomas Nicholls (c. 1825–1896), in becoming sculptors.

117 "One positively needs to smoke a cigar." Clive's "une" is a mistake for "un". The quotation of Catulle Mendès, French poet, novelist, and dramatist is not exact, but Clive is recalling a passage of *Le fin du fin, ou Conseils à un jeune homme qui se destine à l'amour*, ch. IX: "C'est en vain que tu voudrais être loin de celle qui t'est chère, et que tu sens, comme l'a dit un auteur dramatique, 'le besoin de fumer un cigare'" ("It is in vain that you would like to be far from your beloved, and that you feel, in a dramatist's words, 'the need to smoke a cigar'"). The dramatist has not been identified, and Mendès, who wrote plays and was a habitual cigar-smoker, may not mean anyone but himself.

was in it –: it was a long chain of golden and inseparable moments: a summer's day with its peculiar pleasures of morning, afternoon and evening; a spell – six hours perhaps – of palpable, unflagging, reciprocated sensuality. She had given me "la grande volupté" and with that odd self-consciousness of mine, which gives me often a sense of Life flowing through me and of myself[118] converting it into experience, I felt to myself as I drove home, "I have had it, I have *almost* got it now, the thing we all desire."

We did not meet very often. I was never in the least in love; neither I think was she. But I speak only of myself because it would be mere impertinence to pretend that a boy of twenty – or five-and-twenty – can possibly know anything about the feelings of a mature woman of the world. Certainly I was never in the least in love with Mrs. Raven Hill, and I do not think there was ever anything between us that could be well called affection; on the other hand, our liaison was never defiled by the slightest tinge of cammerard-erie [*sic*].[119] It was always a lover and mistress affair: we never met save when we were in lust. Except to make rendez-vous we rarely wrote letters; though after a love-making she always expected a few words – a Collins[120] as it were. She was not exacting; and if she had to upbraid she contrived to do it in some way that was partly flattering. Occasionally she gave me a lesson by dropping a hint, but she was infinitely wary. Once I remember her saying in the winter-garden of the Metropole at Brighton[121] – "You are very nice about never[122] showing how bored you are next morning." And I was bored a little sometimes, because, though clever enough, she was uncultivated and ignorant,[123] – lacking the variety to keep me interested, or the distinction to keep me at her feet. In conversation I never encouraged her to take the initiative because that

118 The words "of myself" have been added by Clive in manuscript, replacing his original "I".
119 A misspelling of "camaraderie".
120 A letter of thanks for hospitality sent by a departed guest, so called after William Collins in Jane Austen's *Pride and Prejudice*.
121 The Metropole Hotel on the seafront at Brighton was built in 1890. Annie's two daughters were educated at Roedean School, on the outskirts of Brighton, and it is possible that she sometimes combined visiting her elder daughter, Sylvia, with seeing Clive. A number of Leonard Raven-Hill's cartoons feature Roedean and its pupils.
122 Clive has added "never" in manuscript.
123 Clive has substituted, in manuscript, "uncultivated and ignorant" for "ill-educated and deficient in culture".

might have ended distressingly. I was not interested in her mind or her character or her life; and at any moment she might show something alarmingly plebeian – and almost *bourgeois*. But I was never badly bored, never so bored that I forgot to be grateful – and then, as I have said, she was wary, and always insisted on taking the first possible train next day, and on travelling *back* alone. No, we were never in love; but we had lust and some liking, and on *her* side consummate strategy and technique and discretion, and that, perhaps, is more than most people are likely to get in their lives. Never, for one moment, was I jealous. I can say honestly that I listened without a twinge, with interest and amusement only, to her exact accounts, with their picturesque details, of doings with old Mr. Fisher and passionate junketings with the father of Betty. She had the art to make me always believe that I was her most attractive and amusing lover. "You are my luxury" she would say; or after she had been curiously kind, "No-one else has ever had that" – which I am now sure was a lie. She had a perfect temper and pretty underclothes, – which were sometimes a little over fussy. Some part of her fringe was false. She had a soft, laughing sense of fun, a respect for, but no understanding of, the things of the intellect, a genuine vulgar feeling for the more obvious in art, strong practical sense, a weak character, a resolute taste for pleasure, a determination to keep respectable at all costs, and, for my taste, rather too large a bottom.

She was never entirely whorish in her relations with me – I am not of course talking about the actual moment of copulation when it is a question of temperament not of whorishness: she was never quite abandoned even, at any rate till near the end, and *so* she remained mistress of the situation, making me feel always that I wanted her more than she wanted me. She was generous and ingenious; and, in spite of considerable difficulties, I think she never failed me once. In her heart she was a little cross when I married, because I did not come back to her – for a couple of years I think. After that everything went charmingly again, and we made love periodically, in her flat, when she came to live in London,[124] at Brighton and at Bournemouth, in a sea-side cottage of hers near Colchester, in my study at Gordon Square and even in the blue

---

124 In 1912 she and Leonard moved from Battle House, Bromham, to 7 Regent's Court, Park Road, Regent's Park, London NW, then in 1913 the short distance to 4 York Terrace, before moving again to Richmond.

spare-room at Cleeve House. Our last meeting was at 46[125] in the October of 1914. The war had begun and the world was being turned topsy-turvey, but I do not suppose that that had anything to do with the fact that our encounter was one of the most violent we had ever enjoyed, and quite the most indecent. This seems to me remarkable: for we had been learning each other's[126] secrets during fifteen years and she must have been at least forty-three.[127] I can offer no explanation. I have not seen her since. She has had two strokes; and if I have written of her with some freedom that may be partly because she is now beyond the reach of scandal or censure. Not that she is dead; but she is imprisoned, in the depths of the Isle of Wight, a complete, or almost a complete imbecile.*[128]

    Written in January 1921[129]

    *She has now been dead some years 1930[130]

Acknowledgements

We warmly thank the following: Julian Bell and the Society of Authors for permission to publish Clive Bell's memoir of Annie Raven-Hill and to quote other writings of his; Henrietta Garnett for permission to quote writings of Vanessa Bell and to reproduce her painting of the Memoir Club in the National Portrait Gallery; Paul Raven-Hill for permission to make use of the unpublished memoirs of Leonard Raven-Hill and Sylvia Colello Needham (*née* Raven-Hill), Annie Raven-Hill's husband and elder daughter respectively; Michael Bond, who transcribed the memoirs and alerted us to their existence; Peter Stowell who discovered the memoirs and realised their importance; The Henry W. and Albert A. Berg Collection of English and American Literature, The New York Public Library, and Carolyn Vega, Curator; Mark Hussey, author of a forthcoming biography of Clive Bell,

---

125 The words "and even in the blue spare-room at Cleeve House. Our last meeting was at 46" are a manuscript addition by Clive, who also adds a note on "46": "46, Gordon Square where I lived till 1923".

126 Corrected from "other" by Clive in manuscript.

127 In October 1914, Annie was actually fifty.

128 Annie died at home at St Helen's, Isle of Wight, on 26 April 1922. The cause of her death is given as "1. Cerebral Haemorrhage 8 days, 2. Asthenia".

129 On this manuscript note, added by Clive after the end of the typescript, see I.2 above.

130 Manuscript note by Clive, presumably added in 1930. Misinterpreting it, Anne Olivier Bell and Andrew McNeillie, editors of Virginia Woolf 2, 89, n. 1, say that Annie died in 1930.

who kindly commented on a draft of our work and was most generous with advice and information all along the line; The British Library, London; José Kany-Turpin, Paris; King's College Cambridge Archive Centre and Patricia McGuire, Archivist; The Keep, Brighton, Special Collections; Marlborough College and Gráinne Lenehan, Archivist; National Portrait Gallery, London; Len Reilly, Archives and Library Manager, London Borough of Lambeth; Tate Gallery Archive; Jon Richardson; Trinity College Cambridge Library and Jonathan Smith, Archivist and Modern Manuscript Cataloguer; Washington State University Libraries, Manuscripts, Archives, and Special Collections, and Greg Matthews, Special Collections Librarian.

References

Austen, Jane. *Pride and Prejudice*. London: Thomas Egerton, 1813.

Bell, Clive. *Old Friends: Personal Recollections*. London: Chatto & Windus, 1956.

Bell, Quentin. *Elders and Betters*. London: Pimlico, 1997 (first published by John Murray, 1995).

Bell, Vanessa. *Selected Letters of Vanessa Bell*. Edited by Regina Marler, Introduction by Quentin Bell. London: Bloomsbury, 1994 (first published 1993).

Cecil, Hugh, and Mirabel Cecil. *Clever Hearts: Desmond and Molly MacCarthy: A Biography*. London: Victor Gollanz, 1991.

Eighteen Stafford Terrace, Kensington, London, Archives: Linley Sambourne Diaries.

Fehrer, Catherine. "Women at the Académie Julian in Paris." *The Burlington Magazine* 136, no. 1100 (November 1994), 752–757.

Forster, Edward Morgan. *Diary*. Among his papers in King's College Cambridge Archive Centre (EMF/12/8).

Fry, Roger Eliot. *Diary 1921*. Among his papers in King's College Cambridge Archive Centre (REF/ 5).

———. *Letters of Roger Fry*. Edited and with an Introduction by Denys Sutton. London: Chatto & Windus, 1972.

Glendenning, Victoria. *Leonard Woolf*. London: Simon & Schuster, 2006.

Herrick, Robert. "Delight in Disorder." In *Hesperides; or, The Works both Humane and Divine of Robert Herrick Esq*. London: John Williams & Francis Eglesfield, 1648, 28 (misprinted 29).

Kelly's Directory of Hampshire, Wiltshire, Dorsetshire, the Isle of Wight and the Channel Islands, 1903. London: Kelly, 1903.

King's College Cambridge Archive Centre, Cambridge. Diaries of Edward Morgan Forster and Roger Eliot Fry.

Knox, E. V. "Raven-Hill, Leonard." In *Dictionary of National Biography 1941–1950*. Oxford: Oxford University Press, 1959, 713.

Lawrence, Arthur. "Art and Agriculture: An Interview with Mr. L. Raven-Hill." *The Idler* 15 (July 1899), 484, 525–536.

Mendès, Catulle. *Le fin du fin, ou Conseils à un jeune homme qui se destine à l'amour*. Paris: Marpon et Flammarion, 1885.

Meredith, George. *Diana of the Crossways*. London: Chapman & Hall, 1885.

Monks House Papers (Virginia Woolf). Special Collections, The Keep, Brighton, UK. Letters from Vanessa Bell to Virginia Stephen.

Needham, Sylvia Colello. *Between You and Me*. Unpublished memoir, written in 1958–1959, with editorial notes added by the author's brother Lucien Ennar Raven-Hill in 1972. In the possession of the Raven-Hill family. No page-numbers.

Partridge, Frances. *Everything to Lose: Diaries 1945–1960*. London: Gollancz, 1985.

Raven-Hill, Leonard. *Rosemary: The Flower of Remembrance: Reminiscences and Observations of a "Black and White" Man (Leonard Raven-Hill of Punch)*. Unpublished memoir in the possession of the writer's descendants. No page-numbers.

———. "To India with a Sketch-Book." *The Pall Mall Magazine* 29 (April 1903), 433–449.

Rosenbaum, S. P. *The Bloomsbury Group Memoir Club*. Edited with an Introduction and Afterword by James M. Haule. Basingstoke and New York: Palgrave Macmillan, 2014.

Spalding, Frances. *Vanessa Bell*. London: Weidenfeld & Nicolson, 1983.

Stendhal (pseudonym of Marie-Henri Beyle). *Le rouge et le noir*. Paris: A. Levavasseur, 1830.

Tate Gallery Archive, London, UK. Correspondence of Vanessa Bell. Letters from Vanessa Bell to Clive Bell and Duncan Grant.

Thackeray, William Makepeace. *The History of Pendennis, His Fortunes and Misfortunes, His Friends and His Greatest Enemy*. London: Bradbury & Evans, 1849–1850.

Trinity College Cambridge Library, Cambridge. Papers of Arthur Clive Heward Bell.

Wallis, George. *A Catalogue of Manufactures, Decorations, And Designs, Section II – Education. The Work of the Students of the Schools of Art in Great Britain and Ireland, in Connection with the Science and Art Department, South Kensington, International Health Exhibition*. London: William Clowes & Sons Ltd, 1884.

Washington State University, Pullman, WA, Manuscripts, Archives, and Special Collections. Clive and Vanessa Bell Papers 1907–1957. Letter from Lyn Lloyd Irvine to Clive Bell.

Wilde, Oscar. *The Importance of Being Earnest: A Trivial Comedy for Serious People*. London: Leonard Smithers, 1899, but first performed 14 February 1895.

Woolf, Leonard. *Downhill All the Way: An Autobiography of the Years 1919 to 1939*. London: The Hogarth Press, 1968.

Woolf, Virginia. *The Diary of Virginia Woolf*. Edited by Anne Olivier Bell, assisted in vols 2–5 by Andrew McNeillie. 5 vols. London: The Hogarth Press, 1977–1984.

Yapp, George Wagstaffe. *Official Catalogue of the Great Exhibition of the Works of Industry of All Nations, 1851, Second Corrected and Improved Edition*. London: Spicer Brothers, 1 July 1851.

4

"Far the best holiday for years": Virginia Woolf's second visit to Greece

1. Introduction

In the spring of 1932 Virginia and Leonard Woolf visited Greece in the company of Roger Fry and his sister Margery Fry. For Leonard and the Frys it was a first visit. For Virginia, who had just turned fifty (25 January), it was a return to the country. She had been there in the autumn of 1906 with her sister, Vanessa, their brothers, Thoby and Adrian, and Violet Dickinson. That visit was followed by a death: Thoby contracted typhoid and died a few weeks after his return to England. The second visit was preceded by the death of another person who was important to Virginia, Lytton Strachey. He lost his battle with stomach cancer on 21 January 1932, and his death, at the age of fifty-one, triggered (the metaphor is grimly appropriate, for she used a gun) the suicide of Dora Carrington, the wife of Ralph Partridge, on 11 March, the day after she had been visited by Virginia and Leonard. Less than a week later, on 17 March, Virginia wrote in her diary that she and Leonard would go "– perhaps – to Greece with Roger and Ha" (Margery), adding: "A venture that would be: and I think we're both in the mood for ventures after this morbid time; so much talk of death; and there death is of course."[1] Roger had had dinner with the Woolfs on 9 March, and they had stayed the night of 14 March at Rodwell House, the home Roger shared with his partner, Helen Anrep, at Baylham in Suffolk, and it is likely that the plan was discussed on one or both of those occasions.

It was not a new plan, however. Five years earlier Virginia had written to Vita Sackville-West: "I think we shall go to Greece with Roger."[2] But three weeks later she told Vita that she doubted that the Greek visit would take place,[3] and after another week said that it would not happen.[4] Vanessa,

---

1 Woolf, *Diary* 4, 83–84.
2 Woolf, *Letters* 3, 326, 7 February 1927.
3 Woolf, *Letters* 3, 338, 28 February 1927.
4 Woolf, *Letters* 3, 342, 6 March 1927; 3, 341, 5 March 1927, to Vanessa Bell.

writing to Helen Anrep from Cassis on 9 March 1927 and not yet aware that the Greek plan was not going ahead, expressed reservations about it:

> For one thing I hoped he [Roger] might wait till next year when there might be just a chance of my going too. Then I feel very doubtful as to how he and the Woolves will get on as travelling companions, having had experience myself of both him and Virginia in that capacity.[5]

But Vanessa was mistaken in thinking that Virginia and Roger might not get on. In her first letter to her sister Virginia reported: "So far, the Frys and Wolves have been as sweet as nuts and soft as silk",[6] and they continued to enjoy one another's company. Virginia's experience of Roger in (and on the way to) Greece in 1932 was to be very much like that of Vanessa in Turkey in 1911, as described by Regina Marler: "She had already discovered his unique empathy and openmindedness, and now she learned what a delightful and adventurous companion he made. His energy astonished her."[7] Virginia found him "sweet, rich, accommodating, infinitely porous"[8] and "far and away the best admirer of life and art I've ever travelled with; so humane; so sympathetic, so indomitable".[9] In a letter to John Lehmann on the eve of her and Leonard's departure from Athens and their parting from the Frys, who were staying in Greece for a few more days, she writes:

> Roger is the greatest fun – as mild as milk, and if you've ever seen milk that is also quicksilver you'll know what I mean. He disposes of whole museums with one brush of his tail. He plays chess when the dust is sweeping the pawns from the board. He writes articles with one hand, and carries on violent arguments with the other.[10]

His mental energy, interest in everything, and sense of fun were the more remarkable because of the physical discomfort he was in throughout the trip: he was suffering badly from haemorrhoids, which prevented him from walking far and necessitated his "going behind a hedge now and then with a buttonhook".[11] In Roger's letters from Greece there is nothing to contradict

  5 Bell, 310.
  6 Woolf, *Letters* 5, 49, 19 April [1932].
  7 Bell, 97.
  8 Woolf, *Diary* 4, 90, 18 April 1932. On my correction of the editors' disastrous mis-reading of Virginia's handwriting here, see Section 4 below, on 90.6.
  9 Woolf, *Letters* 5, 59, 4 May 1932.
 10 Woolf, *Letters* 5, 63, 8 May [1932].
 11 Woolf, *Letters* 5, 54, 1 May 1932. It was presumably to have this problem dealt with that Roger went into a clinic on 22 July 1932, coming out the same day. See his letter of that date to Vanessa Bell (Tate Gallery Archive 8010/5/1082 = RFVB451).

the picture of agreeable companionship, although he has much less to say about Virginia than she has to say about him, partly perhaps because he did not wish to arouse any feeling of jealousy in his letters to Helen Anrep, partly perhaps because she was apparently the least talkative member of the party, at least when travelling and sightseeing: "Virginia in particular doesn't seem to want to talk as well. I think she gets immense pleasure from just having experiences."[12] In the same place he remarks that, despite her sunburn, "she always looks incredibly lovely and more distinguished than the goddesses" – a comment unlikely to have pleased Helen as much as it would have pleased Virginia if she had read or heard it. The already strong friendship between Virginia and Roger was further strengthened during the holiday, which she recalls in *Roger Fry*,[13] her only biography, published six years after his death and eight months before her own. His death, on 9 September 1934, was to come as a heavy blow to her. As she put it the following summer: "I never minded any death of a friend half as much: its [*sic*] like coming into a room and expecting all the violins and trumpets and hearing a mouse squeak."[14]

In general, Roger and Leonard got on well, although their frequent games of chess were not completely harmonious: Leonard played better than Roger, but also more slowly, and his slowness irritated Roger, who complained that it put him off his game. They practised Modern Greek together too, seemingly with limited success, partly because "Roger learnt … out of the wrong book"; in fact, none of the party managed the language well, and in Delphi they "were almost landed with two black kids and a pail full of sour milk, owing to a misunderstanding between Margery and a shepherd".[15]

Margery was much less on Virginia's wavelength than her brother. Virginia thinks that she "was probably a good deal chastened by Roger's infatuation with Bloomsbury, and suspects me of being in conspiracy against her" and "of being an intellectual and moral and social snob".[16] She comments also: "she has no foothold among us; and will slip off this rock into her obscure waters when we go back – not that she needs us".[17] But both women made a real effort to be pleasant to one another, and cordial relations were maintained throughout the holiday. Like Roger, Margery talked incessantly and painted. Virginia acknowledges, although without

---

12 Fry, *Letters* 2, 670, 4 May 1932, to Helen Anrep.
13 Woolf, *Roger Fry*, 280–281.
14 Woolf, *Letters* 5, 399, [6 June 1935], to Ethel Smyth.
15 Woolf, *Letters* 5, 54, 1 May 1932.
16 Woolf, *Letters* 5, 50, 19 April [1932].
17 Woolf, *Diary* 4, 93, 24 April 1932.

warm admiration, her knowledge of plants, birds, and myriad other subjects. She acknowledges too that Margery "has sympathy far more widely
than I have for beggars, children, state of the people", but finds her lacking
in "charm".[18] Margery and Leonard "talk[ed] a good deal of administration and quasi politics";[19] they also discussed prison reform.[20]

Virginia enjoyed her second visit to Greece so much that, writing to John
Lehmann the day before she and Leonard began their journey home, she
described it as "far the best holiday we've had for years".[21] It was the only
bright period in an otherwise dark year for her. She even fantasised "how
yearly we shall come here, with a tent, escaping England, and sloughing the
respectable skin; and all the tightness and formality of London; and fame,
and wealth; and go back and become irresponsible, livers, existing on bread
yaot, butter, eggs, say in Crete".[22] She told Vanessa "I cant think why we
dont live in Greece"[23] and John Lehmann "I'm setting on foot a plan to
remove the Hogarth Press to Crete".[24] But, although she was genuinely
attracted by the unspoiled beauty of Greece, by the warmth of its climate
(when it was not wet and/or cold, as it was at times during the visit), and
by the friendliness of its people ("even though we can't understand a word
they say"),[25] it would be a mistake to think that the vision she says she
had in Aigina of living a simple life in Greece for part of each year was
anything more substantial and serious than a daydream. The dream quickly
evaporated: only three days after her return home, she wrote: "Greece is
perceptibly melting" and "its force is waning".[26] She never returned to the
country.

For Roger the visit to Greece was not only personally pleasurable, but
also professionally significant for an art-critic and art-historian, who,
although he had much knowledge of Greek art from museum collections
outside Greece and had seen the famous Greek temples at Paestum in southern Italy, had not set foot on Greek soil before. The visit confirmed him in
his unorthodox view that, while some classical Greek temples, notably the

18 Woolf, *Diary* 4, 97, 8 May [1932].
19 Fry, *Letters* 2, 670, 4 May 1932, to Helen Anrep.
20 Woolf, *Diary* 4, 96, 8 May 1932.
21 Woolf, *Letters* 5, 63, 8 May [1932]. See also Woolf, *Diary* 4, 95, 8 May 1932:
    "… the best holiday these many years".
22 Woolf, *Diary* 4, 97, 8 May 1932. Yaot = Yog(h)urt. Virginia's spelling is not as
    eccentric as it looks, there being no pronounced *g* in the middle of the Turkish,
    Greek, and French forms.
23 Woolf, *Letters* 5, 58, 2 May [1932].
24 Woolf, *Letters* 5, 62, 8 May [1932].
25 Woolf, *Letters* 5, 62, 8 May [1932].
26 Woolf, *Diary* 4, 100, [15 May 1932].

Parthenon and the temple of Aphaia on the island of Aigina, were "awfully swell" (his favourite laudatory expression on the Greek trip), much of classical Greek art was overrated. On the whole he regarded Byzantine art as superior. In March 1933 he was elected Slade Professor of Fine Art in the University of Cambridge, a post for which he had applied unsuccessfully in 1904, and delivered lectures on Greek art as well as on the art of other civilisations.[27] His always entertaining and often iconoclastic views about art and architecture manifested themselves not only in Greece, but also, on the journey out, in Venice:

> The palaces, says R[oger] pretty frauds, examples of inlay and carpentry. That old fraud Ruskin – we were now in St Marks Square, looking at Adam and Eve. There are chapters about that. He was too virtuous. That's a great pity. Everything had to be squared – even these finicking palaces must be morally Good – which theyre not – oh no – merely slices of coloured stone.[28]

This is Virginia's report, but any doubt that she is reporting Roger's opinions rather than giving her own is dispelled by her account in *Roger Fry*.[29]

Most of our knowledge of the Greek "venture" is derived from the accounts Virginia gives in her diary, in letters, and briefly in *Roger Fry*, and from Roger's letters, some published, some unpublished.[30] An unpublished source of information is Leonard's pocket diary, which contains a very brief and incomplete but useful record of the travels. These written accounts are supplemented and enlivened by the photographs taken by Virginia and Leonard.

The scope and purpose of this essay are limited. It does not provide a full description and discussion of the trip. It is much better that readers unfamiliar with Virginia's accounts of it should read those. The aim is rather to put the record straight or straighter in four areas that are the subject of Sections 2–5 below. In Section 2 the above-mentioned written and photographic records, together with other sources, including railway timetables, are used to draw up the party's exact itinerary and timetable. Section 3 deals with

27 Fry, *Last Lectures*. Published five years after Roger's death, the lectures required much editing, only the first, the inaugural lecture, having been revised by him for publication.

28 Woolf, *Diary* 4, 90, 18 April 1932.

29 Woolf, *Roger Fry*, 280.

30 I know of only one letter written by Margery during the trip. Written on 4 May 1932 from Athens to her sister Isabel (Somerville College, Oxford, Margery Fry Papers, Box 13.1), it is disappointing, for, apart from mentioning that "we got back from Delphi last night", it contains no news at all about the trip.

the photographs. Wherever possible, the scenes are identified and the exact dates given. Sections 4 and 5 are concerned with the accounts of the trip in Virginia's diary and letters respectively. Based on scrutiny of copies of the manuscripts, they contain corrections of the published versions.

2. Itinerary and timetable

All times in this section are given in accordance with 24-hour-clock notation.

Friday 15 April

The Woolfs and Frys departed London, Victoria Station, at 10.00. Roger's partner, Helen Anrep, saw them off. They travelled to Paris via Dover and Calais, arriving at Gare du Nord at 18.10. Virginia reports that they dined at "a little place where Roger took his wife 36 years ago".[31] She does not name the restaurant, but Leonard's diary reveals that it was Michaud, which was at 29 rue des Saints-Pères, on the corner of that street and rue Jacob. The establishment, now called Le Comptoir des Saints-Pères, was favoured by publishers and writers. It was here that James Joyce liked to dine with his family, and it was here that Scott Fitzgerald confided in Ernest Hemingway that he was concerned about the small size of his penis, about which his wife, Zelda, had complained: after inspecting Fitzgerald's organ in the restaurant's washroom, Hemingway tried to reassure his friend that all was normal and, when he did not succeed, took him to the nearby Louvre, so that they could compare his size with that of the nude male statues there.[32] The Woolfs and Frys departed Paris on the Simplon-Orient Express from Gare de Lyon at 20.40.

Saturday 16 April

They were scheduled to arrive in Venice at 15.50. Leonard's diary gives 16.00. They stayed at Casa Petrarca, a *pensione* on the west side of the

---

31　This was on Roger's honeymoon. He married the artist Helen Coombe on 3 December 1896. The two were deeply in love, but their happiness was to be short-lived, for Helen soon developed signs of a serious mental illness. For much information and discussion, see Essays 1, 5, and 6.

32　Hemingway, *A Moveable Feast*, ch. 6 (Joyce), 19 (Fitzgerald). In *A Moveable Feast: The Restored Edition*, Joyce is in chapter 5. Ernest Hemingway had earlier related the incident to Fitzgerald's first biographer, Arthur Mizener, in a letter of 22 April 1950. See Hemingway, *Ernest Hemingway*, 689–690. Mizener did not mention it in his book, presumably because it was not the sort of thing one could easily mention

Grand Canal. Roger and Margery had stayed there in late August and early September 1929, and Roger was to stay there again on the way back from Greece, when he met up with Helen Anrep in Venice. At the Molo they hired a gondola for an hour, to take them across to the church of San Giorgio Maggiore and back. Virginia mentions dinner at "the Cavallo", but probably means the Hotel Cavalletto just off Piazza San Marco. After dinner the party saw a play "in the theatre slung with green glass beads". She does not name either the play or the venue. *La Gazzetta di Venezia* reveals that there were plays in two theatres in Venice that evening – Teatro Malibran and Teatro Goldoni. The latter is topographically far more plausible, being much nearer to Piazza San Marco than the Malibran, and convenient for the ferry that took the party after the performance "onto the black tossing water, so silent, so swaying", across the Grand Canal to Casa Petrarca. What makes the identification certain is "slung with green glass beads". Such beads are still a decorative feature of the Goldoni, suspended from the hangings of each of the four galleries that contain the boxes.[33] Often, especially in photographs, the beads look white, but they are in fact light green. The play was *Cento all'ora*, the Italian version of *Tempo über Hundert*, an upper-class comedy, set in contemporary Paris and involving shady business dealings, by the Austrian dramatist Franz Cammerlohr. It is not clear whether the Woolfs and Frys saw the whole performance or only the closing scenes.

Sunday 17 April

The party visited the Accademia di Belle Arti di Venezia and Caffè Florian in the morning. Virginia and Roger also visited the church of the Gesuati (Santa Maria del Rosario), with its ceiling painted in fresco by Tiepolo, on the Zattere. They sailed from Venice for Piraeus aboard the 8,848 ton Lloyd Triestino S.S. *Tevere* at 12.30. The Woolfs travelled in first class, the Frys in second, which meant that any Woolf–Fry communication, whether conversation or chess, was conducted in second class. There was a cinema for the evening entertainment of first-class passengers, and Virginia describes "a

in a biography published in 1951. In *A Moveable Feast*, chapter 19, first sentence, Hemingway says that it occurred "in the time after Zelda had what was then called her first nervous breakdown". Zelda's first breakdown was in Paris in April 1930, so the unusual lunchtime meeting at Michaud's will have taken place between then and September 1931, when Zelda was discharged from a clinic in Geneva and the Fitzgeralds returned to the USA, where Zelda had her second and third breakdowns in February 1932 and May 1934 respectively. Certainly it predated the visit of the Woolfs and Frys, who of course would not have heard of it.

33 In identifying the theatre as the Goldoni, I have been much helped by Paola Margarito.

lighthouse suddenly opening as we sat at a movie with Venizelos",[34] referring to Eleutherios Venizelos, the Greek prime minister.

Monday 18 April

As the ship sailed down Italy's Adriatic coast, Virginia wrote her diary for
the first time since leaving England. During a call at Brindisi the party went
ashore for a drive around the town, looking for a building whose dome
Roger had seen from the ship, but succeeded only in finding the railway
station and a locked church. The dome is most likely to have been that of
the Cathedral, specifically that of its Oratory of San Teodoro. It is easily
visible to those who approach Brindisi by sea. The only other possibility is
the dome of the Church of the Scuole Pie (San Michele Arcangelo), which is
sometimes visible, sometimes not, depending on what manoeuvres a vessel
makes as it approaches its berth in the inner harbour.

Tuesday 19 April

At sea. Virginia took her sponge-bag with her to breakfast – an action
which, like her having wandered into the barber's shop in her dressing-
gown, she attributes to having dreamt of Duncan Grant all night. As the
ship sailed past the Ionian Islands and Leonard and Roger played chess,
she retreated to the first-class writing-room, where, with "only bald headed
merchants" for company, she penned her first letter of the trip, to Vanessa
Bell. They had been scheduled to arrive at Piraeus in the evening, but the
Corinth Canal (not, as Virginia keeps saying, the Gulf of Corinth) had been
closed by a rock-fall, making it necessary to sail around the Peloponnese.
Writing to Ethel Smyth on 4 May, Virginia says that the clearance of the
fallen rocks "will take 6 months or year", but the Canal was to be reopened
on 17 June 1932.

Wednesday 20 April

Arrived Piraeus 05.30. Met by travel agent and transferred to Hôtel
Majestic, Athens, at 71 University Avenue (Panepistimiou). This second-
category hotel was where they were to spend all twelve of their nights in
the city. In the morning they visited the National Archaeological Museum,
where Roger made some critical remarks about Greek art: "They dont
compose. ... Look at the thinness of the lines: and no background."
Virginia wrote to Ethel Smyth. Lunch at Averov Restaurant at 6 Stadium
Street (Stadiou). Afterwards drove to the Acropolis. Virginia found the

---

34 Woolf, *Letters 5*, 51–52, to Ethel Smyth.

Parthenon ("where my own ghost met me, the girl of 23, with all her life to come")[35] more impressive than she had remembered. Clear weather was interrupted by a sudden rainstorm, whereupon "10 million German tourists rushed across the temple precisely like suppliants in their grey and purple mackintoshes".[36] Walked back to hotel. Dinner at Pantheon Restaurant, 73 University Avenue.

Thursday 21 April

In the morning the party walked to the travel agency of Ghiolman Bros. (founded in 1885 and still in existence) in Constitution (Sintagma) Square to arrange day-excursions and more extensive expeditions. Lunch at Averov. In the afternoon walked to the Acropolis to pick up a taxi. Drove to Daphni to see the famous Byzantine church, arriving there at about 15.30. Drove on for about two miles to the point where the road arrives at the shore of the Bay of Eleusis before returning to Athens. After dinner at Averov Virginia wrote her diary.

Friday 22 April

After breakfast they went by car, a chauffeur-driven Hupmobile provided by Ghiolman, from Athens to the temple of Poseidon at Cape Sounion. Lunch in the sunshine beside "the chalk white pillars set high like a light-house" and a carpet of wild flowers. Back to Athens via Marathon, where they saw the *sōros*, "mound", raised over the cremated remains of the Athenians who died in the famous battle against the Persians in 490 BC. The Hupmobile was open-sided, and the Woolfs were perished with cold. After the excursion Virginia described it in her diary.

Saturday 23 April

Day-trip to the island of Aigina with an American archaeological group,[37] landing on the part of the coast nearest the temple of Aphaia, that is to say at Aghia Marina. Roger and Margery went up on mules, Virginia and

---

35 Woolf, *Diary* 4, 90. Also Woolf, *Letters* 5, 62, to Vita Sackville-West, 8 May [1932]: "There was my own ghost coming down from the Acropolis, aged 23: and how I pitied her!" For the record, Virginia was actually aged twenty-four and not far off twenty-five in the autumn of 1906.

36 Woolf, *Letters* 5, 53, to Vita Sackville-West.

37 The trip is misdated 24 April by Fry, *Letters* 2, 667. There appears to be no mention of it in the records of the American School of Classical Studies at Athens, the reason being that there was a change of directors at that time and the events of April were not reported on either by the outgoing director or by the incoming one. But interestingly a visit to Aigina is still part of the School's spring programme.

Leonard on foot. The weather, cold and grey when they disembarked, deteriorated during the ascent to the temple, with heavy rain setting in. Lunch
was taken "under a very leaky fir tree".[38] Nevertheless they thought both
temple and island most attractive, and they were to return in fine weather
on 6 May.

Sunday 24 April

Athens. To the Byzantine Museum in the morning, when the weather was
again wet. After lunch Virginia wrote to Vita Sackville-West. Then the
party drove to Kaisariani, "the little round Byzantine Church on the slopes
of Hymettus".[39] Roger (see Plate 29 below) and Margery sat in the courtyard painting. Virginia picked wild anemones and orchids and felt content
("how happy today was"). Dinner at Costi, 2 Korai Street. Virginia wrote
her diary, describing the activities of the weekend.

Monday 25 April

Left Athens early morning in a chauffeur-driven car. Visited Eleusis,
Corinth, Acrocorinth, and Mycenae. At Mycenae took tea in Hôtel de la
Belle Hélène et du Roi Ménélas and signed the visitors' book. Stayed over-
night in the New Hotel at Nauplion, "the most sympathetic town we've
seen, a little like St Tropez, but with a great citadel up above ...".[40] The
weather was fine and remained so for the rest of Virginia and Leonard's
time in Greece.

Tuesday 26 April

Over breakfast in Nauplion, "on a quay, red and blue boats mountains,
sun, incredibly lovely", Virginia wrote a picture postcard, showing the
so-called Tomb of Agamemnon at Mycenae, to Ethel Smyth. After breakfast they drove east to Epidauros, famous for its very well preserved
ancient theatre and for its sanctuary of Asclepius, god of healing. Roger
describes it as "a grand sort of Vichy only the cures were religious".[41] In
the afternoon they travelled the mountainous and, at that time, poorly
maintained and hair-raising road to Tripolis, the chief town of the central
Peloponnese, arriving at the Hotel Arcadia just before 19.00 for a two-night
stay.

38 Fry, *Letters* 2, 667.
39 Woolf, *Diary* 2, 93.
40 Fry, *Letters* 2, 667, 26 April 1932, to Helen Anrep.
41 Fry, *Letters* 2, 667, 26 April 1932, to Helen Anrep.

Wednesday 27 April

Drove south from Tripolis to Sparta and Byzantine Mistra, then back to Tripolis for the night.

Thursday 28 April

Returned to Athens and to Hôtel Majestic.

Friday 29 April

Athens. Good Friday in the Greek Orthodox Church. In the afternoon visited the so-called Theseion (temple of Theseus), actually the Hephaisteion (temple of Hephaestus), the best-preserved specimen of a fifth-century BC Doric temple. In the evening from the balcony of the hotel they watched a candlelit religious procession pass by. Virginia was moved by the sight and sound of it, telling Ethel Smyth: "I can assure you all that is in me of stunted and deformed religion flowered under this hot sensuality, so thick, so yellow, so waxen; and I thought of the lights of the herring fleet at sea."[42]

Saturday 30 April

Left Athens before 07.00 for Delphi, travelling via Thebes, Livadhia, and then Amphissa, the much more direct road from Livadhia to Delphi being in such a state of disrepair as to be impassable. A plan for a diversion to Hosios Loukas had to be abandoned, for lack of time, but was to be fulfilled on 3 May. Lunched at Chaironeia (Chaeronea), the scene of two famous battles in antiquity. In 338 BC Philip II of Macedon heavily defeated the Athenians and Spartans and their allies, and in 86 BC the Roman general Sulla was victorious over the army of Mithradates VI of Pontus. The battlefield is marked by a colossal statue of a seated lion on a pedestal.[43] The monument, commemorating the Thebans who died in 338 BC and specifically (probably) the fallen members of the élite Sacred Band, was set up in the late fourth or early third century BC, and the statue was reconstructed from fragments of the original at the beginning of the twentieth century. Roger Fry calls the lion "a most comic beast", adding that what made it more comic still was that "a stork had built its nest on its head and made it a rather rakish elderly ladies' hat".[44] One of the Woolfs' photographs (see Section 3 below) shows lion and nest, and another shows lion, nest, and stork. During the stop at

---

42 Woolf, *Letters 5*, 59.

43 Measurements or estimates of the lion's height vary widely, from 4 m to 6 m, which is remarkable, given that the monument is so well known. The figure of 6 m is given by Ma, 86.

44 Fry, *Letters 2*, 670, 1 May 1932, to Helen Anrep.

Chaironeia Leonard read an account of the 338 BC battle in Greek. Virginia, who reports this, probably means that he read it aloud rather than silently to himself. The only significant ancient account is that of the first-century BC historian Diodorus Siculus,[45] so presumably Leonard read part or all of that. On arrival in Delphi the party checked into the Hotel Castalia for a three-night stay. The day before they arrived, according to Virginia, the skeleton of an Oxford undergraduate, David Cochrane, who had disappeared on 18 April 1931, was discovered in the branches of a tree in a ravine near Delphi. Virginia knew his mother, Margaret ("Mora") Cochrane, *née* Ilbert, Mora's sister Lettice being the wife of Herbert Albert Laurens Fisher, a first cousin of hers. She is not accurate about the date of the discovery, for it had already been reported in *The Times* on 26 April 1932, 15, in a despatch of 25 April from its Athens correspondent.[46]

Sunday 1 May

Delphi. Greek Orthodox Easter Day. Explored the ancient site. In the evening sat on hillside above the modern village and attempted conversation with a young shepherdess and her brother (see Section 4 below, notes on 95.9–10, 13–15). After dinner watched young men dancing. Virginia wrote to Quentin Bell.

Monday 2 May

Delphi. At 09.55 Virginia, sitting shoeless on the ground among white daisies in the shade of an olive tree at the bottom of the hill on which Delphi is built, began writing her diary for the first time for eight days. One of three thoughts she jotted down at the end of the entry, when halfway back up

---

45 Diodorus Siculus, *Bibliotheca* 16.85–86.

46 In June 1931 several letters about Cochrane's disappearance were published in *The Times*. The first was from Sir George Young, an uncle of the young man, who said that "the only possible explanation" was that his nephew had been murdered and the crime concealed (8 June 1931, 13). His letter drew a polite but robust response from D. Caclamanos, Minister at the Greek Legation in London (12 June 1931, 12): he pointed out that the theory of a concealed murder was not supported by any evidence, and suggested: "If Sir George Young thinks inexplicable the fact that the body of the unfortunate young man has not been discovered, such a fact may be reasonably explained by the existence of inaccessible wooded ravines in the mountain." Another correspondent, Arthur Reade, independently made the same suggestion, though he thought it not impossible that Cochrane had "vanished ... to reside ... in the rude habitation of some friendly shepherd", saying that "there is something in the atmosphere and the scene above Delphi, added to the tradition with which it is associated, that induces an ecstasy almost hysterical in those who come there from afar" (13 June 1931, 8).

the slope, was "that [D. H.] Lawrence writes his books as I write this diary in gulps and jerks: and has not the strength to come down in one blow: no welding, no shaping – the result of a false anti-literariness perhaps". The other thoughts were "that the ridge seen from the top is like a badly peeled pear, when lines of peel are left along the edges", and "that the male virtues are never for themselves, but to be paid for".[47] The third thought, like the first, arose from her reading of one of the books she had brought with her, J. Middleton Murry's *Son of Woman: The Story of D. H. Lawrence*.[48] While she wrote under the olive tree, Leonard was sitting beside her, studying his Greek grammar-book. Roger and Margery were sketching. On one of the two days in Delphi, Virginia washed her feet in the waters of the Castalian spring. She suffered badly from sunburn contracted during long journeys in an open car. Leonard and Margery were also affected, though less badly. Virginia wrote the first half of a long letter to Vanessa Bell.

Tuesday 3 May

Got up 05.00. Departed Delphi for Athens 06.00. The reason for the early start was the party's wish to visit the Byzantine monastery of Hosios Loukas, particularly famous for the mosaics in the larger of its two churches. Roger had persuaded their driver to take the direct road that runs east from Delphi, despite the man's protestation that it was impassable, but just before their departure "news came that a car had rolled over the precipice owing to the bad road, and the driver absolutely refused to go".[49] Roger reports that a bridge broke under the weight of the vehicle, which fell 80 metres into a ravine, although nobody was hurt.[50] So they had to go the long way round after all. The car took them to Stiris, from which, after a hurried lunch at about 11.00, they rode or walked to the monastery. (Roger mentions riding on mules; Virginia says "rode"; Leonard records "walked" and seems to have been the only one of the four to have done so.) The visit, which they made such a determined effort to achieve, was disappointing. Virginia says: "the mosaics were very inferior and the Monks were very annoying";[51] Roger, although reporting that "the church itself is rather splendid", calls the mosaics "rather dull".[52] They left Stiris about 14.00.

---

47 Woolf, *Diary* 4, 95.
48 Murry.
49 Woolf, *Letters* 5, 57, 2 and 4 May, to Vanessa Bell.
50 Unpublished letter, 6 May, to Helen Anrep. Photocopy in King's College Cambridge Archive Centre, REF/11/g.
51 Woolf, *Letters* 5, 57.
52 Letter, 6 May 1932, to Helen Anrep. Photocopy in King's College Cambridge Archive Centre, REF/11/g.

The car broke a spring and a tyre was punctured. With its steering damaged by the broken spring, the vehicle at one point nearly veered into a deep ditch, and the tired travellers were relieved to be safely back in Athens at Hôtel Majestic between 20.15 and 20.30. "A very good dinner" in an unnamed restaurant.

Wednesday 4 May

Athens. The party took it easy after the long and tiring journey the previous day. In the morning Roger and Margery painted the Parthenon, while Virginia, happy to keep her sunburn-sores out of the "blazing hot" sun, sat on her bed, writing a letter to Ethel Smyth and completing the letter she began writing to Vanessa on 2 May.[53] Margery wrote to her sister Isabel, without giving any account of her time in Greece. Roger and Margery suggested a trip to Olympia, leaving Athens on Friday 6 May and returning on Sunday 8 May, but this did not take place. Before dinner Roger wrote to Helen Anrep.

Thursday 5 May

Athens. In the morning drove to Omorphi Ekklesia or Omorfoklissia ("Beautiful Church"), an eleventh- or twelfth-century Byzantine church, famous for its wall-paintings, in Galatsi, which was a rural area northeast of Athens in 1932, but is now a suburb of the vastly expanded city. Virginia wrote a postcard, showing, like the two one-drachma stamps which it carries, the Hephaisteion (see above, under 29 April), to Julian Bell, mentioning that they were "just off to a monastery", referring to Daou Pendeli, which they visited in the afternoon. Daou Pendeli is about ten miles north-east of Athens, and, since Omorphi Ekklesia is virtually on the way, it may be assumed that they went straight from there to the monastery, which is on the western slope of Mount Pentelikon, below the quarries from which the Athenians extracted the famous Pentelic marble for the building of the Parthenon and other major buildings in the second half of the fifth century BC.

---

53 The letter to Ethel, begun (she says) at 11.35, is four sides long and was longer than that, for it breaks off in mid-sentence. After writing four sides to Vanessa, to add to the four she had written two days earlier, she says that she must stop because it is nearly 12.00 (midday). Virginia could write quickly, but even she is unlikely to have managed over eight sides in under twenty-five minutes. Maybe she broke off her letter to Ethel to write to Vanessa and completed the letter to Ethel later, or, after writing the bulk of her letter to Vanessa, broke off to write to Ethel before finishing the letter to her sister.

Friday 6 May

The party made a second day-trip from Athens to Aigina, but in much better weather than the first, "sun and blue gradually rolling up the mist".[54] Revisited the Temple of Aphaia. As on 23 April, the Frys rode up to it, the Woolfs walked. Later, probably while the Frys were painting or sketching, the Woolfs found "a desert bay", where Virginia paddled and Leonard swam. Back in Athens, Roger wrote to Helen Anrep and enclosed a cheque for £25 to cover the cost of her travel to Venice for their meeting there.

Saturday 7 May

Athens. Shopping in the morning. To the Acropolis in the afternoon. Drove to see the Monument of Philopappos, but found it "wired off". Visited the Theatre of Dionysus. Virginia wrote a postcard to Lady Ottoline Morrell. The postcard carries a view, in black and white, of the Propylaea of the Acropolis, including the Temple of Athena Nike and part of the western end of the Parthenon, and Virginia comments: "This is where we are, not much like Gower Street."[55]

Sunday 8 May

Athens. After a breakfast of plain rolls and honey and a visit to the post office, where Virginia collected a letter from Vita Sackville-West,[56] they made a second visit, by car, to Kaisariani. It was probably after lunch that Virginia wrote to Vita and to John Lehmann.[57] With her letter to Vita she sent the "decaying petals" of a yellow sea-poppy picked on Aigina two days earlier. In the afternoon the party walked to the Zappeion and National Garden. They visited the Temple of Olympian Zeus (as Plate 28 shows)

---

54 Woolf, *Diary* 4, 96.

55 Lady Ottoline lived at 10 Gower Street, London, from 1924 until her death in 1938. The postcard is in the Ottoline Morrell Collection of the Harry Ransom Center, University of Texas, Box 34, Folder 6. The editors of *Letters* give no indication of what the view on the postcard is, which, in view of Virginia's reference to it, seems rather neglectful.

56 For Vita's letter, dated "Sunday 25 April", but presumably written on Sunday, 24 April, see Sackville-West, 381–382.

57 Virginia (Woolf, *Letters* 5, 62) tells Vita that they are "about to go out for the last time in Athens", which probably refers to the afternoon's programme rather than to going out to dinner in a nearby restaurant. When she writes to John Lehmann, she is "balanced on the edge of a hotel bed with Marjorie [*sic*] and Roger popping in and out to suggest excursions, and Leonard ranging the sponge bags with a view to packing". Presumably she is writing before the afternoon programme had been agreed, and perhaps before the morning excursion, although in that case Leonard's ranging of the sponge bags seems improbably premature!

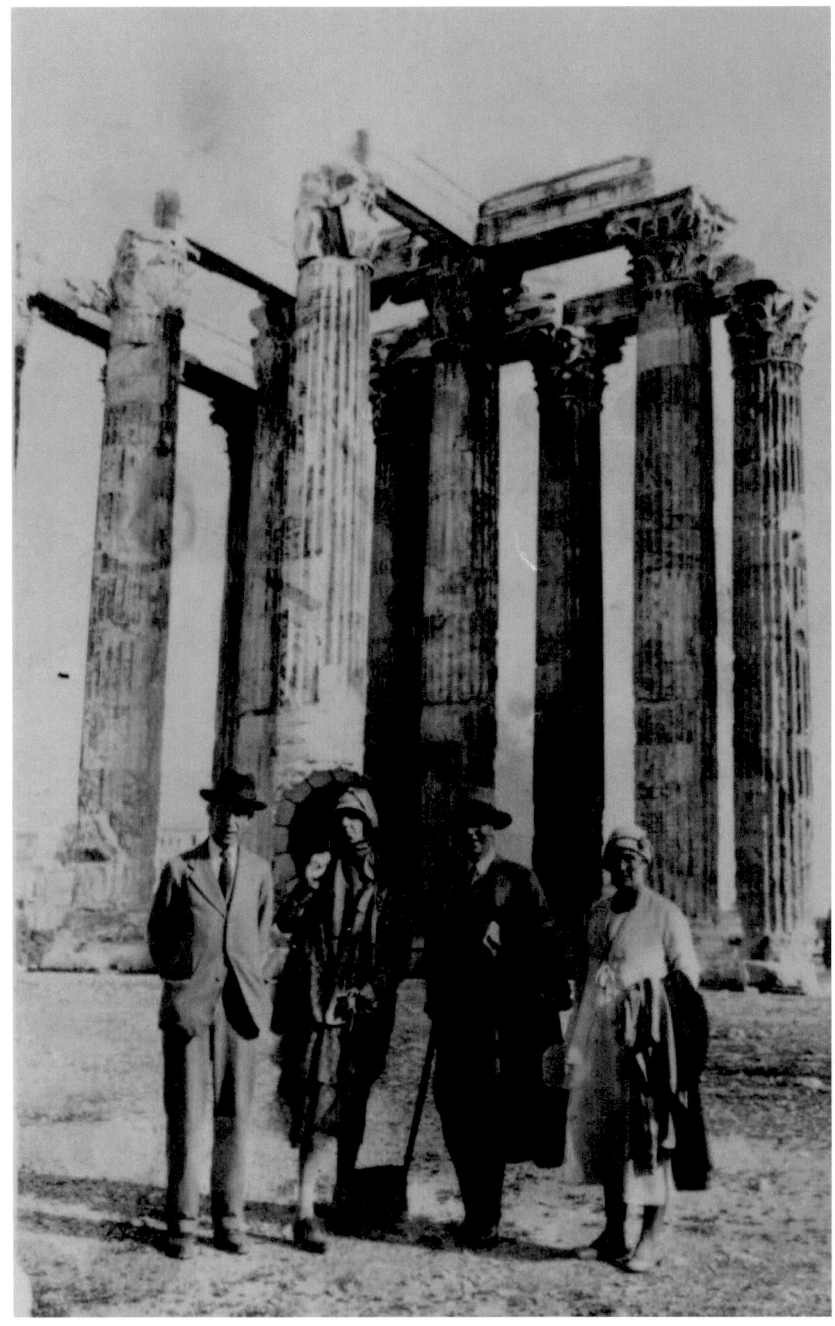

28 Leonard Woolf, Virginia Woolf, Roger Fry, and Margery Fry at the Temple of Olympian Zeus, Athens, 8 May 1932.

and the Arch of Hadrian as well: the temple is next to the National Garden, and the Arch of Hadrian, which is beside the temple, must be the "marble ruined arch" at which Virginia saw Greek boys throwing stones.[58] At 18.58, with "L[eonard] reading, not with sympathy, Ethel Smyth",[59] she began writing her diary for the last time in Greece. She was going to have to stop at 19.30, but she resumed writing after dinner, perhaps taken at Costi,[60] while Leonard and Roger played chess. It was nearly midnight when she stopped.

Monday 9 May

To the Acropolis in the morning. The Woolfs left Athens (Larissa Station) for Paris by train at 13.50. The Frys remained in Greece for a few more days, probably until 12 or 13 May.

Tuesday 10 May

The first of the Woolfs' three nights in the train was a bad one: their sleeping compartment was too hot, and they were disturbed first by Greek officials at Salonika (dep. 02.00), later by Yugoslav officials, all wanting to know what money they had with them. As advised by someone, they hid most of their money, although not, as he had suggested, in the electric-light bell. Yugoslav time being (an hour) behind Greek time, they rose in the morning to find that coffee would not be served for another two hours. At 10.30 Virginia started writing her diary, describing the homeward journey so far. The entry ends: "Now for Rousseau". At Nisch (arr. 12.10, dep. 13.44) the Woolfs' carriage joined the carriages of the Istanbul–Paris Orient–Simplon Express. During the stop in Belgrade (dep. 18.34) they had a wet walk in the streets near the station.

Wednesday 11 May

In train. During the stop in Trieste (dep. 09.30) the Woolfs had a sunny walk and "attached [them]selves to England by buying The Times". "The paper", Virginia comments, "reads empty and provincial – these good Englishmen making such a bother about the Academy and motor cars when all the time there is Athens and the Greek islands".[61] The issue of *The Times* bought by Virginia and Leonard was that of Monday 9 May, which describes the visit of the King and Queen to the Summer Exhibition of the Royal Academy of

58 Woolf, *Diary* 4, 99.
59 Smyth. Ethel made the tour in 1925 with her great-niece Elizabeth Williamson. For Virginia's remark, see Woolf, *Diary* 4, 95.
60 Woolf, *Diary* 4, 98.
61 Woolf, *Diary* 4, 100, 11 May.

Arts at Burlington House and contains four letters on road accidents. Also in Trieste they wrote a postcard, with a message for Roger and Margery, for him or them to pick up in Venice.[62] Their train went on via Venice (dep. 12.40) and Milan (dep. 17.02). At 18.00, as it made its way towards the Simplon Tunnel and Switzerland, Virginia, "tired of reading Rousseau", began her last diary entry before returning to England.

Thursday 12 May

The Woolfs arrived Paris Gare de Lyon 08.40. Departed Paris Gare St Lazare 10.36 for Dieppe Maritime (arr. 13.09, dep. 13.30). Arrived Newhaven 17.00 (Leonard's diary; scheduled arrival 16.40) and went to Monk's House, their home at Rodmell, between Newhaven and Lewes.

Whit Sunday 15 May

At 14.30 the Woolfs departed Monk's House by car for their Bloomsbury home, 52 Tavistock Square. Before that, Virginia wrote the last entry in her "Greek" diary, describing her and Leonard's reactions to the scenery when they landed back in England, and the way Greece's grip on her was weakening rapidly. The previous evening they had had dinner at Charleston (Vanessa's Sussex home), and the gossip there had "further strewn sand over Greece".[63] Roger expected that Margery and he would reach Venice from Greece on 15 May or perhaps on 14 May, and that Helen Anrep, coming from England, would meet him there on the 15th or 16th. If the Frys reached Venice on the 14th, Margery probably stayed a night there; if on the 15th, it is likely that she went straight on home.

Monday 16 May and after

Margery was expected back in England.[64] Roger and Helen Anrep stayed in Venice for several days and also visited other places in northern Italy, including Castelfranco, Padua, Mantua, Verona, Brescia, and Milan, before reaching the small farmhouse he shared with Charles and Marie Mauron at Saint-Rémy-de-Provence, on or about 28 May.

---

62 For the error of the editors (Woolf, *Letters*) in identifying the addressee as Roger's daughter, Pamela Diamand, see Section 5 below, under 11 May.

63 Woolf, *Diary* 4, 100.

64 In a letter of 4 May 1932 to her sister Isabel, Margery had said that she planned to return on 18 May, but in a marginal note Isabel has written: "I hear now, it's to be <u>16th</u>. I.F" (Somerville College, Oxford, Archives. Margery Fry Collection, Box 13.1).

3. Photographs taken during the Greek holiday

UL = Upper Left
UR = Upper Right
LL = Lower Left
LR = Lower Right

The research for this section and indeed for the present essay was sparked by a reading of the caption to a photograph (no. 72) in Hermione Lee's *Virginia Woolf*: "The Woolfs, Roger Fry and Margery Fry on the Acropolis, 1932". In the photograph, reproduced here as Plate 28, the four are standing inside a ruinous ancient building with columns. Lee's location of the scene on the Acropolis of Athens betrays a breath-taking ignorance of the architecture of one of the most celebrated groups of ancient monuments in the world:[65] the clearly visible Corinthian capitals rule out the

---

65 Although Hermione Lee's biography has many merits, it is too often factually unreliable. Consider, for example, the pages about events in January–May 1932. In discussing the Frys (632), she says that in 1932 Margery (whom she indexes as "Margaret") was Principal of Somerville College, Oxford, when she had retired from that position the previous year, and she gets Roger's age wrong. She is wrong too about Lytton Strachey's age when he died (626) and about the date of his death (628). Because she thinks Strachey died on 22 January 1932, instead of on 21 January, she makes the further mistake of saying that, when the Woolfs visited Dora Carrington on 10 March, it was "nearly seven weeks after Lytton's death" (629). In fact, *exactly* seven weeks had passed. The period between Virginia learning of Strachey's fatal illness (15 December 1931) and his death was not "two months" (627), but five weeks and two days. Strachey's *Portraits in Miniature* appeared not, as Lee says (627) in June 1929, but in May 1931. When she writes that the German National Socialist Party "had had a big victory in the elections of September 1930" (631), she makes it sound as though the National Socialists took more seats than any other party. In fact, they took 107, which was 36 fewer than the Social Democrats. In the next sentence she gives us to understand that Metaxas became prime minister of Greece in 1935. The correct date is April 1936. That makes nine mistakes in just seven pages (626–632), and this is not an isolated bad patch. In fact, there is a damaging mistake on the very next page (633), where, referring to a spirited exchange of letters Virginia had with Logan Pearsall Smith in the autumn of 1932 about relations between Bloomsbury and Chelsea, Lee writes: "He told her that mockery was her favourite pastime." But he never made that uncomplimentary remark to her. What he actually wrote was: "I may have mocked at Bloomsbury, because mockery is my favorite pastime, …" (letter of 2 November [1932]); and in her reply (6 November 1932) she wrote: "But much though I admire Chelsea, I freely admit that I have mocked at you all because mockery is 'my favourite pastime', just as it is yours." See Smith, 59, and, for Virginia's reply, Woolf, *Letters 5*, 119.

Acropolis straight away, and the columns are actually those of the temple of Olympian Zeus in Athens.

On investigation, I found that Lee is not alone in having failed to identify the scene correctly. In fact, in a conscientious though not exhaustive search, I did not find that anyone had identified it correctly. Elizabeth P. Richardson[66] and Maggie Humm[67] also say that it is the Acropolis. Monique Nathan's description "en Grèce"[68] or "in a Grecian setting"[69] avoids the blunder committed by the others, but suggests that she does not know where the photograph was taken, and the caption in the translation of her book identifies Margery as Roger's wife.[70]

Humm's catalogue of the Woolfs' photographs has been described by a reviewer as "meticulous",[71] but, so far as the photographs taken in Greece are concerned,[72] it is slapdash. No fewer than six, *excluding* the one already mentioned, are identified as "Acropolis", and each time the identification is incorrect. Where Humm's descriptions are not plain wrong, they tend to be unhelpfully vague, like "A Greek theater", "Three photographs of Greek buildings and churches", "Four views of Greece", and "Three views of Greek exteriors".

The "Greek" photographs are, with one exception, in Virginia Woolf Monk's House Photograph Album no. 3.[73] The exception is a photograph that has undoubtedly been removed from the album. See below on Album 3, page 20 LR. The Monk's House photographs were the gift of Frederick R. Koch in 1982.

The mistaken identification of the Acropolis by Bloomsbury scholars is not a trivial matter. During their days in Athens the Woolfs visited it at least

66 Richardson, 16.
67 Humm, 32, 135, 199.
68 Nathan, *Virginia Woolf par elle-même*, 25.
69 Nathan, *Virginia Woolf*, 25.
70 The French original calls Roger and Margery "les Frys". The translator's mistake prompts one to note that Virginia, writing to Vanessa Bell about Margery, says: "I daresay it would be better if she married Roger as you suggest" (Woolf, *Letters 5*, 56, 2 May [1932]). Cf. Woolf, *Diary* 4, 285, 4 March 1935, where, referring to a conversation with Vanessa and Julian Bell, Virginia reports that "we talked about Roger and Margery's incestuous love".
71 Duguid, 11.
72 Humm, 199.
73 Virginia Woolf Monk's House Photograph Album no. 3 (MS Thr 560), Harvard Theatre Collection, Houghton Library, Harvard University. At the time the original version of this essay was written (April 2010), the photographs were being catalogued and conserved. That work was completed, and the whole collection has been digitised and made available online. See Essay 5, n. 49.

three times, and Virginia makes prominent mention of it and the Parthenon in her diary and letters. And yet there is no photograph of it in the Monk's House collection, and the photograph taken in the temple of Olympian Zeus is the only photograph taken in Athens. Why is this? And why is there not a single photograph of either Mycenae or Delphi, even though there are photographs of other places visited during the party's excursions into the Peloponnese and to Delphi? I am in no position to answer these questions. Perhaps the Woolfs tended not to take photographs of places if picture postcards of them were available.

Roger (and Margery?) too took photographs in Greece. Writing to Margery from France on 10 June 1932,[74] Roger says that he has had eleven of them enlarged, and that he is thinking of having some enlargements made for her. If any of the Fry photographs survive, I have not traced them.

Below I try to identify the Woolfs' photographs accurately, and, where possible, give the date on which each was taken. There remain several whose location is unknown or uncertain, but in most cases identification has been achieved. Sometimes help is provided by brief descriptions written either below or beside the photos or on the back, although these are very brief. The page numbers below are those of Monk's House Album 3.

Page 19 (see Plate 28)

Athens: temple of Olympian Zeus, from NW. Group (left to right): Leonard Woolf, Virginia Woolf, Roger Fry, Margery Fry. 8 May.

"Postcard from the Acropolis," says Humm,[75] as if it had been bought at a tourist kiosk! In the album, under the photograph, Virginia has written in ink "Athens. May 1932" and below that in pencil "LW. V.W. Roger Fry. Margery Fry", and on the back of the photograph Leonard has identified the four members of the group in the same manner. On the page of the album, behind the photograph, Leonard has written "War trophy", which suggests that he had originally intended to place here one of the photographs of the lion monument at Chaironeia (see below under page 21 LR, page 22 LR).

Page 20

UL. Aigina (?): Roger mounted on a donkey and reading a book. 23 April or 6 May (if Aigina).

UR. Margery, seated and painting (not, as Humm says, "reading"), in a courtyard, almost certainly (see page 20 LR) at Kaisariani. 24 April.

---

74 Photocopy in King's College Cambridge Archive Centre, REF/11/19.
75 Humm, 199.

LL. Virginia and Roger sitting with their backs to a piece of fallen column, with part of Margery visible on the right. The scene is almost certainly the temple of Poseidon at Sounion. The main indication of this is the large size of the column's grooves: at Sounion each column had just sixteen instead of the usual twenty. It may be assumed that the photograph was taken by Leonard. 22 April (if Sounion).

LR. The photograph has been removed, but below its place Virginia has written "Roger", and it can be regarded as practically certain that it is the photograph, reproduced in Plate 29, that shows Roger seated and painting in what is almost certainly the same courtyard as that in which Margery is seen in page 20 UR, at Kaisariani. It is very natural that the photographs should be neighbours in the album. The photograph of Roger, which shows him using what looks comically like a laptop computer, but is actually his pochade-box (see Section 4 below, on 91.33), was located by Micah Hoggatt in Box 4, one of four boxes of photographs that belong with the Monk's House Albums. The negative of the photograph is in an envelope marked "<u>FRY</u>, Roger, in Greece, 1932" and "MH [Monk's House] neg". A print of the photograph is attached to the outside of the envelope. Kaisariani. 24 April.

Page 21

UL. Margery striding out of a doorway.

UR. Aigina, Aghia Marina: group of about twenty people in the foreground with the sea and two boats beyond. 23 April or 6 May.

LL. Aigina: Virginia on rocks by sea. 6 May.

LR. Chaironeia: lion monument, with stork's nest on the lion's head. 30 April.

Page 22

UL. Corinth: temple of Apollo, SW corner, from NE. 25 April.

UR. Corinth: temple of Apollo, SW corner, from SE. 25 April.

LL. Aigina: temple of Aphaia, from SE. 6 May.

LR. Chaironeia: lion monument, with stork and stork's nest on the lion's head. 30 April. Humm wrongly calls this photograph "a duplicate" of the one on page 21 LR.

Page 23

Upper. Sounion: temple of Poseidon, pronaos façade and S colonnade, from W. 22 April.

Lower. Sounion: temple of Poseidon, S colonnade with pronaos behind, from S. 22 April.

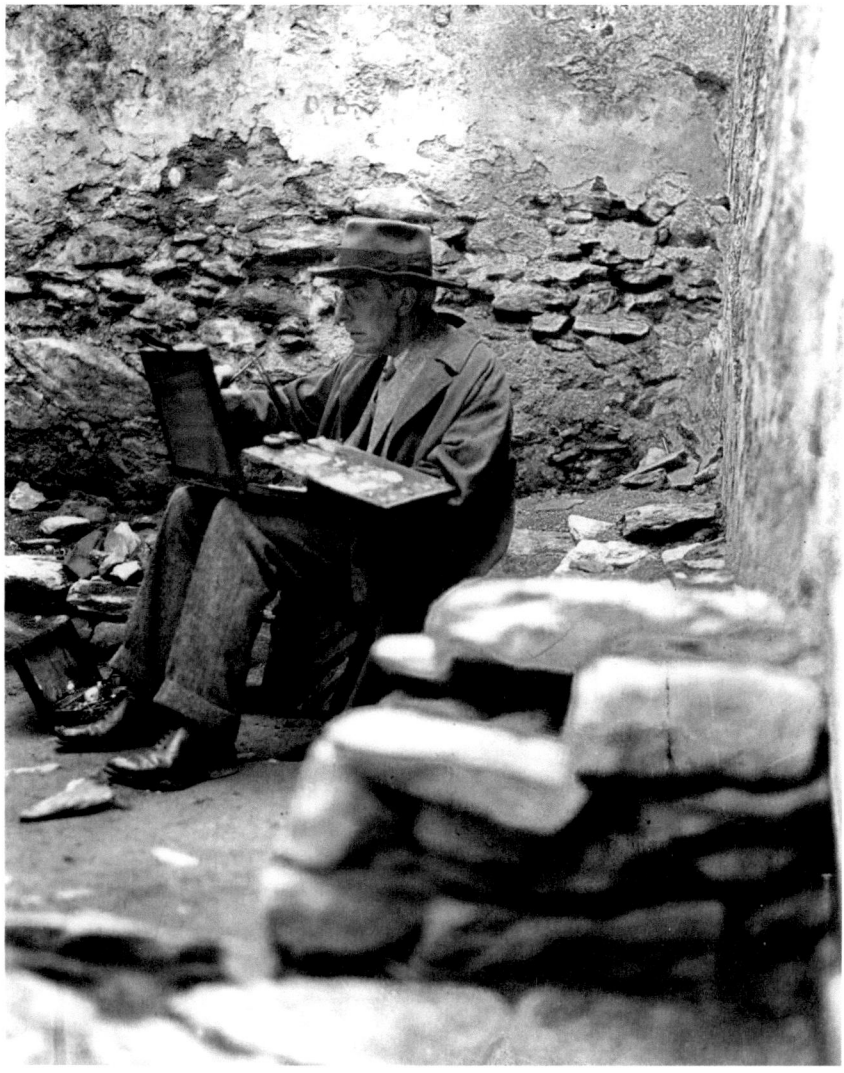

29 Roger Fry painting at Kaisariani, near Athens, 24 April 1932.

Page 24

UL. Near Nauplion: view across a field to a belt of trees and a low hill with buildings on the summit. 25/26 April.

UR. Aigina: temple of Aphaia, cella, from W. 6 May.

LL. Epidauros: theatre: upper parts of E side of cavea, from W. 26 April.

LR. Epidauros: theatre: orchestra and central part of cavea, from NW. 26 April.

Page 25

UL. Acrocorinth: second gate of the fortress, from WNW. 25 April.

UR. Acrocorinth: view from the fortress, looking N. 25 April.

LL. Mistra: courtyard of the Metropolitan Church of St Demetrios, from E. 27 April.

LR. Mistra: Pantanassa, from NNW. 27 April.

Page 26

UL. Mistra: fountain of Marmara, with carved sarcophagus at base on right. 27 April.

UR. Galatsi, near Athens: Omorphi Ekklesia (Omorfoklissia), Byzantine Church of St George, from SE. 5 May.

Lower. Daphni: entrance of the Byzantine church, from SW. 21 April.

Page 27

UL. Daou Pendeli: tower, and church beyond. 5 May.

UR. Unidentified post-Byzantine church.

LL. Wooded slope, with mule or donkey, perhaps on Pentelikon. 5 May (?).

LR. Daou Pendeli: cloister with archway and upper gallery. 5 May.

Page 28

UL. Daphni: the church, from SE. 21 April.

UR. Kaisariani: the monastery church. 24 April or 8 May.

Lower. Daphni: courtyard, from E. 21 April.

Page 47

Near Nauplion, the same view as that on page 24 UL. 25/26 April.

4. Virginia Woolf's diary of the holiday: Corrections of the published version

Virginia's account of the holiday occupies a twenty-eight-page manuscript inserted into her diary for 1932. The published version is in *The Diary of Virginia Woolf*.[76] As the editors, Anne Olivier Bell and Andrew McNeillie (B-M) say, the handwriting "is at places very difficult to decipher", the circumstances in which the diary was written – now on board ship, now in a

---

76 Woolf, *Diary* 4, 89–100.

hotel bedroom, now in an olive grove, now in a train, sometimes when tired and/or in hurry – not exactly assisting its legibility. Nevertheless, comparison of the editors' text with a copy of the manuscript reveals a surprising number of mistakes. Most of these are minor, involving punctuation and the use of capital or small letters, and I shall ignore these, but others are more significant. I refer to the page- and line-numbers in Woolf's *The Diary of Virginia Woolf*, volume 4.

90.6. B-M make Virginia describe Roger as "sweet, rich, accommodating, infinitely serious", but "serious" is a misreading of "porous". This is by far the most unfortunate and damaging of B-M's mistakes, for it attributes to Roger, the subject of Virginia's only biography, a characteristic he did not possess and she would not have admired, and deprives him of a characteristic he did possess and she did admire. Of course he could be and often was "serious", but "infinitely serious" does not at all suit a man whom she describes as "a saint who laughed; a saint who enjoyed life to the uttermost".[77] On the other hand, "porous" perfectly suits someone who used "to deplore the natural imperviousness of the human mind to reason" and "detested fixed attitudes".[78] Virginia connects porousness, which enables both giving and receiving, with creativity. She does this in *A Room of One's Own*, chapter 6, when discussing Coleridge's view that a great mind is androgynous: "He meant, perhaps, that the androgynous mind is resonant and porous; that it transmits emotion without impediment; that it is naturally creative, incandescent and undivided."[79]

90.15. B-M's "finicking palaces" is right, although Virginia, quoting her diary in Woolf, *Roger Fry*, 290, has "finicky."

91.20. B-M read "mantlepiece", but the misspelling is theirs, not Virginia's.

91.24. "Margery" (B-M), in reference to Margery Fry, but Virginia here calls her "Marjorie", and this seems not to be a case of the editors tacitly correcting the diarist's spelling, for on page 96, last line, they retain "Marjorie". Virginia misspells the name also in *The Letters of Virginia Woolf*.[80]

---

77 Woolf, *Roger Fry*, 297.
78 Woolf, *Roger Fry*, 291.
79 Porousness is connected with creativity in a very different context in Woolf, *The Waves*, where Rhoda engages in an erotically expressed flight of her imagination: "To whom shall I give all that now flows through me, from my warm, my porous body? I will gather my flowers and present them—Oh! to whom?" (60–61).
80 Woolf, *Letters* 5, 62.

91.33. B-M rightly read "pochard", but do not point out Virginia's mistake. The party enters the Byzantine church at Daphni: "'Oh awfully swell – better than I'd any notion of' said Roger depositing his hat stick pochard and two or three guides and dictionaries on a pillar." Roger did not carry a duck around with him, but he did carry a pochade-box, a portable container for artist's materials with a hinged lid that, when raised, served as an easel. One of the Woolfs' photographs (Plate 29) shows Roger using it. What Roger was calling "awfully swell" was the late eleventh-century mosaic of Christ Pantocrator in the dome. Virginia says: "we all stared up at the white vindictive Christ, larger than a nightmare". Apparently Christ's appearance was made more vindictive by those who restored the mosaic in the late nineteenth century.

91.21–24. B-M read: "I like Athens about 7, when the streets are hurrying clamouring, flitted across by all those black whitefaced women, and shawled women, and dapper little men who come with the bats and the evening primroses in Southern towns, ari lalagos". In a footnote they explain *ari lalagos* as "chattering, babbling, garrulous". That just about gets the intended meaning, but there are no words *ari* or *lalagos* in Greek, Modern or Ancient. Virginia, who seems to be attempting Ancient Greek here, has written not *ari*, but *aei*, "always", and *lalagos* is perhaps to be explained as an erroneous conflation of the adjective *lalos*, "babbling", and the participle of the verb *lalageo*, with the same meaning. A minor point is that -*os* is a singular ending and therefore inappropriate in this context. To be correct, Virginia would have written *aei laloi* (either as two words or as one) or *aei lalagountes*. In any case, her intended meaning is "always chattering".

92.11. For "Suniun" (B-M) read "Sunium", as at 92.20, 34.

92.18. Although it is not impossible that Virginia referred to "the patiently amenable flat land", B-M's "patiently" is probably "perfectly", a word that occurs several times in the "Greek" section of the diary and is written in almost exactly the same way here.

92.23–25. B-M give: "At Salamis the Greek Army were carrying little sacks of earth to the top of the Tomb of the dead soldiers to make it [*word illegible*]. A tuft of flowers was on the top." The "illegible" word is "soily". The editors rightly note that "Salamis" is a mistake for "Marathon".

92.30. Virginia aptly compares the remains of the columned temple on the island of Aigina to a skeleton. B-M print "skeletal", but the word looks more like "skeletic".

92.34–36. B-M read: "Marvellous what genius can do in a little space – heres the perfectly moving proportions." The true reading, rescuing Virginia from a charge of bad English, is: "here, the perfectly moving proportions".

93.7. B-M misread Virginia's Greek for "far distant". It is *polu makria*, not *polie makria*.

94.30. For "summer days" (B-M) read "summers days", with, as usual, no apostrophe.

95.9–10. The most curious, though not the most harmful, of B-M's mistakes occurs here. They make Virginia say: "the goat girl came bounding up as if to rick her sheep". One wonders what they think ricking sheep would involve. Making them into a stack? The reading makes no sense. Virginia actually wrote: "as if to seek her sheep".

95.13–15. B-M read: "Then she told us words for things. Skotos her rough thick coat, ouranos the sky, a flower lullulin (?) [*luludi*] my watch orologe [*orologiou*], the car – I've forgotten." The bracketed question-mark is Virginia's. *Skotos* is a puzzle, because the word means "darkness". It seems that Virginia misheard and/or misunderstood what was said. One possibility is that the girl pointed to herself and said *skopos*, "watcher". She is most likely to have called Virginia's watch *rolo(g)i*. For "car" read "cars", as in 95.8.

98.1. For "stop" (B-M) read "stops".

100.7. For "towards" (B-M) read "toward".

100.12–13. Just above, Virginia has described a wet walk she and Leonard had when their train stopped in Belgrade the previous day. She continues, according to B-M: "We saw Trieste in the same way this morning, but hot sunny [?], with its sea spread silky & boats ..." There is an interesting sort of dittography here: it seems that the editors debated as to whether the word before "sunny" is "but" or "hot", noted both possibilities, and, instead of making a choice between them, included both words. Undoubtedly "hot" is right, but the queried "sunny" is incorrect. What Virginia wrote is: "We saw Trieste in the same way this morning, hot going, with its sea ..."

5. Virginia Woolf's letters written during and just before the holiday: Corrections of the published versions

Except in two cases, I have compared the published versions of the letters with copies of the manuscripts. One exception is the letter Virginia wrote to John Lehmann on 8 May. I have been unable to trace the present location of the original, and, although there is a photocopy in Princeton University Library, a request for a copy of this was declined. The other exception is the postcard the Woolfs wrote from Trieste on 11 May.

With respect to what Virginia wrote just before and during the Greek holiday, the editors of *The Letters of Virginia Woolf*, Nigel Nicolson and Joanne Trautmann (N-T), are more accurate than the editors of *The Diary of Virginia Woolf*[81] in their reading of her handwriting, but below I mention some corrections and queries. I give the page- and line-numbers of Woolf's *The Letters of Virginia Woolf*, volume 5.

11 April, from London, to Vanessa Bell

46. In the last paragraph N-T make Virginia write: "We shall be in Greece about a fortnight – from April 19th to May 14th: and stay perhaps in Italy on the way back and be home on the 4th." This would be nonsense, and in fact Virginia says: "… from April 19th to May 4th … and be home on the 14th".

19 April, from S.S. Tevere in the Ionian Sea, to Vanessa Bell

50.1–4. Describing the party's brief visit to Venice, Virginia says, according to N-T: "We only had time for 3 churches and part of the Academia – and Florias Ha – [Margery Fry] – (I've once called her so, by mistake) dressed like an elderly yak in a white pelt constrained by a girdle, is admirable in bearing the brunt of aesthetic criticism." This is likely to puzzle readers, some of whom may suppose that Virginia is calling Margery not just "Ha", but "Florias Ha". But "Florias" is the editors' mistaken reading of "Florian", which is the famous café, established in 1720, on Piazza San Marco, and it is perversely "correct" not to have printed after it, even inside square brackets, the stop omitted by Virginia but required by the sense. The parenthetic dash immediately after "Ha" is unwanted. Joanne Trautmann Banks includes this letter in *Congenial Spirits*. There she still reads "Florias", even though she glosses it "Florians café", but she does place a full stop after it.[82]

81 Woolf, *Letters*; Woolf, *Diary*.
82 Woolf, *Congenial Spirits*, 309.

20 April, from Athens, to Ethel Smyth

51. In the first paragraph, line 7, where Virginia is describing the voyage from Venice to Piraeus, N-T print: "Roger and his sister went 2nd; hes coagulated various greeks and Jews – its their way – Rogers and M's I mean; so have a thousand pieces of good advice." For "hes" read "we", for "greeks" read "Greeks".

24 April, from Athens, to Vita Sackville-West

52. In line 2 Virginia abbreviates Sissinghurst (the Kent mansion of Vita and Harold Nicolson) to "Sissingt.", not to "Sissigt.". In the fifth last line it is not clear that she has misspelt "Peloponnese" with one "n", despite her having stumbled over the writing of it and confessed "(cant spell)".

2 May, from Delphi, to Vanessa Bell

56.29. N-T read: "As for his [Roger Fry's] amiability and indeed docility its astonishing as he cant walk and cant sit our doings have to be very mild." This makes difficult reading, but there is no difficulty in what Virginia actually writes "… its astonishing. As he cant …"

4 May, from Athens, to Ethel Smyth

59. In line 2 it is "in the cypress" that the nightingales were singing, not "in the cypresses". In line 12 Virginia writes "so to Nauplia in the evening", not "in the evenings": she and her party spent only one night there. She continues: "oh and then next day up the most nerve wracking pass, shooting like an arrow along a razor with caverns of rock in abysses a million feet deep under one's left eye, and donkeys emerging round the corners to Mitrovitza". Mitrovitza (Mitrovica) is not in Greece and is mentioned in error for Tripolitza or Tripolis, the town in the Peloponnese in which the Woolfs and Frys stayed the night before and the night after their visit to Mistra. It is surprising that Virginia's mistake is not noted either by N-T or by Joanne Trautmann Banks in *Congenial Spirits*.[83] Virginia gives the town its correct name in *The Diary*.[84]

7 May, from Athens, to Lady Ottoline Morrell

See n. 55.

83 Woolf, *Congenial Spirits*.
84 Woolf, *Diary* 4, 94.

8 May, from Athens, to Vita Sackville-West

61.9. Virginia's spelling is "sestet", not "sextet".
62.13. N-T give the end of the letter as "forgive scrawling scribbles", but the last word may well be "scribbling".

11 May, from Trieste, to Roger and/or Margery Fry

63. According to N-T, this postcard was written to Roger's daughter, Pamela Diamand, in whose ownership they record that it was at the time of their editing. They are right about Pamela's ownership, but wrong about her being the addressee. The message on the card is:

> The Wolves have missed the Frys greatly. Otherwise a comfortable dull journey: rain yesterday and cold. Threw most of our lunch to beggars in memory of you. V. is being taught chess. Love from both. O to stay in Venice!
> Leonard and Virginia

In a footnote N-T explain: "Roger and Margery Fry remained in Greece while Virginia and Leonard returned to England by Orient Express. Pamela Diamand, Roger's daughter, was then staying in Venice, and the Woolfs had met her there on the way back." Immediately I read this note, I suspected that N-T must be wrong. In the first place, the Woolfs' message is very obviously intended for Margery and/or Roger, not for Roger's daughter. Secondly, "*had* met her" would be very odd, given that Trieste, where the postcard was written, is *before* Venice for those travelling from east to west. Thirdly, the Woolfs did not break their journey in Venice on their homeward journey. Their train was scheduled to stop there for just seven minutes, arriving at 12.33, departing at 12.40, so any meeting could only have been a fleeting one on the platform at the railway station. Fourthly, writing her diary entry for 11 May at 18.00, just over five hours after the train's departure from Venice, Virginia makes no mention of such a meeting, although she does say what happened during the train's stops in Belgrade and Trieste. Nor does Leonard mention a meeting with Pamela in his pocket diary, even though he records that the train called at Venice.

I was (and still am) unable to locate the original postcard or a photocopy or microfilm copy of it, but Pamela's daughter Annabel Cole told me that neither she nor her sister, Betty Taber, believed that their mother could have stayed in Venice at this time. As I soon discovered after that, confirmation of N-T's mistake and the explanation of the circumstances that gave rise to it are revealed in correspondence between Pamela and Nigel Nicolson (NN) among the latter's papers in Special Collections in University of Sussex Library. In a letter of 8 January 1980 Pamela draws NN's attention to several mistakes in Woolf's *Letters*, volume 5. Referring to the postcard said by N-T to have been addressed to her, she writes: "I wish I had had the holiday in Venice with the 'Woolves' which you ascribe to me. It must have been Margery." Replying on 9 January 1980, NN writes: "As for the postcard dated 11 May 1932. You did send me a xerox of this (and I enclose it). The initial before 'Fry' is obscured by the postmark, but I took it to be 'P.' and not 'M.' because Roger and Margery were still in Greece at the time, and why should Virginia send the postcard to Venice?" If Pamela had replied to this, she might well have pointed out that one would expect the Woolfs to have addressed her as "P. Diamand", not as "P. Fry". As for NN's question about why the card should have been sent to Venice, the answer is that the Woolfs knew that Roger at any rate was going to stay there on the way back from Greece. He was hoping that Margery and he would arrive there on Saturday 14 or Sunday 15 May and meet up with Helen Anrep.[85] His meeting with Helen certainly took place. He and she stayed in Venice for about a week before moving on to other places in northern Italy. They lodged in Casa Petrarca, to which the Woolfs' card was probably addressed. It is not clear whether Margery also stopped off in Venice. If she did, it was probably only for one night, because she was expected back in England on 16 May.

Since the card's message is clearly intended for both Margery and Roger, the question of whether the name in the address was hers or his or theirs is unimportant. It would appear, from what NN says in his letter to Pamela, that there was only one initial, and that it was not completely obliterated. Since he thought that the letter looked more like P than M, it is likely that it was actually R. Moreover, it would have been natural to make Roger the addressee, since he was going to stay in Venice for a week, whereas Margery was hurrying back to England.

Acknowledgements

I warmly thank the following: The Society of Authors for permission to receive copies of the manuscripts of that part of Virginia Woolf's diary and those of her letters that relate to her visit to Greece in 1932, to make quotations from her writings, and to publish two of her and Leonard Woolf's photographs; The Berg Collection, New York Public Library, for supplying copies of Virginia's diary account and of her letters to Vanessa Bell, Vita Sackville-West, and Ethel Smyth, with special thanks to Isaac Gewirtz (Curator) and Anne Garner; The British Library, Manuscripts Department,

85 See Roger Fry's letters of 4 and 6 May 1932. Photocopies in King's College Cambridge Archive Centre, REF/11/9.

and especially Michael Boggan, for enabling me to read microfilm copies of her letter to Quentin Bell and postcard to Julian Bell; The Harry Ransom Center, University of Texas, for supplying images of her postcard to Lady Ottoline Morrell; Charles Green of Rare Books and Special Collections, Princeton University Library, for checking on my behalf the Library's photocopy of her letter to John Lehmann; Random House for permission to quote the editions of her diary and letters published by The Hogarth Press; Adam Nicolson of Sissinghurst for permission to quote from Nigel Nicolson's edition of her letters and from an unpublished letter NN wrote to Pamela Diamand; Special Collections, University of Sussex Library, especially Catrina Hey, for providing images of the relevant pages of Leonard Woolf's pocket diary for 1932 and of the correspondence between Nigel Nicolson and Pamela Diamand (Nigel Nicolson Papers); The Houghton Library, Harvard University, for supplying scans and prints of photographs, taken by Virginia and Leonard, in The Harvard Theatre Collection, with very special thanks to Micah Jared Hoggatt for his extraordinary kindness and helpfulness; Annabel Cole for permission to quote from the letters of Roger Fry, Margery Fry, and Pamela Diamand, and her and her sister, Betty Taber, for information about the Fry family; The Tate Gallery Archive for allowing me to read correspondence between Roger Fry and Vanessa Bell, and The Archive Centre, King's College, Cambridge, for enabling me to study photocopies of letters of Roger Fry, with particular thanks to Patricia McGuire (Archivist) and Tracy Wilkinson (Assistant Archivist); Somerville College, Oxford, and its Librarian and Archivist, Anne Manuel, for giving me access to the Margery Fry Papers. For information, advice, and other assistance, I am much indebted also to the following: Anthony Bryer (Birmingham); David Butterfield (Cambridge); Giacomo Carito (Brindisi); Stuart Clarke (Virginia Woolf Society of Great Britain); Lyndsay Coo (Cambridge); James and Mary Coulton (Athens); Celia Denney (Paris); Marina Dorigo (Archivio Storico del Teatro La Fenice, Venice); John Ellis Jones (Bangor); Haris Kalligas (Monemvasia); John Ma (Oxford); Paola Margarito (Biblioteca Nazionale Marciana, Venice); Jan Morris (Llanystumdwy); Peter Rhodes (Durham); Thomas Sessler Verlag (Vienna); Barbara Thomas (Rottenburg am Neckar); Natalia Vogeikoff-Brogan (Head Archivist, American School of Classical Studies at Athens); Katherine Webb (Archivist, The Borthwick Institute, University of York); Joan Winterkorn (Bernard Quaritch Ltd, London).

References

Bell, Vanessa. *Selected Letters of Vanessa Bell*. Edited by Regina Marler. London: Bloomsbury, 1993.

Caclamanos, D. [Response to letter by Young]. *The Times*, 12 June 1931, 12.

Diodorus Siculus, *Bibliotheca Historica*. Completed c. 30 BC.

Duguid, Lindsay. "My Legs Show." Review of *Snapshots of Bloomsbury: The Private Lives of Virginia Woolf and Vanessa Bell*, by Maggie Humm. *The Times Literary Supplement* 5372 (17 March 2006), 11.

Fry, Roger. *Last Lectures*. Introduced by Kenneth Clark. Cambridge: Cambridge University Press, 1939.

———. *Letters of Roger Fry*. Edited by Denys Sutton. 2 vols. London: Chatto & Windus, 1972.

Hemingway, Ernest. *Ernest Hemingway: Selected Letters 1917–1961*. Edited by Carlos Baker. New York: Scribner, 2003.

———. *A Moveable Feast*. London: Jonathan Cape, 1964.

———. *A Moveable Feast: The Restored Edition*. Edited by Seán Hemingway. New York: Scribner, 2009.

Humm, Maggie. *Snapshots of Bloomsbury: The Private Lives of Virginia Woolf and Vanessa Bell*. London: Tate Publishing, 2006.

Lee, Hermione. *Virginia Woolf*. London: Chatto & Windus, 1996.

Ma, John. "Chaironeia 338: Topographies of Commemoration." *Journal of Hellenic Studies* 128 (2008), 72–91.

Murry, J. Middleton. *Son of Woman: The Story of D. H. Lawrence*. London: Jonathan Cape, 1931.

Nathan, Monique. *Virginia Woolf par elle-même*. Paris: Seuil, 1956.

———. *Virginia Woolf*. Translated by Herma Briffault. New York: Evergreen Books; London: Grove Press, 1961.

Reade, Arthur. [Letter concerning Cochrane's disappearance]. *The Times*, 13 June 1931, 8.

Richardson, Elizabeth P. *A Bloomsbury Iconography*. Winchester: St Paul's Bibliographies, 1989.

Sackville-West, Vita. *The Letters of Vita Sackville-West to Virginia Woolf*. Edited by Louise DeSalvo and Mitchell A. Leaska. London: Hutchinson, 1984.

Smith, Logan Pearsall. *A Chime of Words: The Letters of Logan Pearsall Smith*. Edited by Edwina Tribble. New York: Tickner & Fields, 1984.

Smyth, Ethel. *A Three-Legged Tour in Greece [March 24–May 4, 1925]*. London: Heinemann, 1927.

Woolf, Virginia. *Congenial Spirits: The Selected Letters of Virginia Woolf*. Edited by Joanne Trautmann Banks. London: Hogarth Press, 1989.

———. *The Diary of Virginia Woolf*. Edited by Anne Olivier Bell, assisted in vols 2–5 by Andrew McNeillie. 5 vols. London: Hogarth Press, 1977–1984.

———. *The Letters of Virginia Woolf*. Edited by Nigel Nicolson, assisted by Joanne Trautmann. 6 vols. London: Hogarth Press, 1975–1980.

———. *Roger Fry: A Biography*. London: Hogarth Press, 1940.

———. *A Room of One's Own*. London: Hogarth Press, 1929.

———. *The Waves*. London: Hogarth Press, 1931.

Young, George. [Letter concerning Cochrane's disappearance]. *The Times*, 8 June 1931, 13.

5

"Suicidal mania" and flawed psychobiography:
Two discussions of Virginia Woolf

1. "Suicidal mania"

In the summer of 1913, about a year after her marriage to Leonard Woolf (10 August 1912), Virginia Woolf suffered a serious nervous breakdown. It was by no means the first such episode, and it was not to be the last. Her mental instability is likely to have had a genetic origin,[1] but to have been aggravated by events in her childhood and young adulthood, including the deaths of her mother, Julia Stephen, in 1895, her half-sister Stella Hills *née* Duckworth in 1897, and her brother Thoby Stephen in 1906, and sexual interference from her two half-brothers – first from Gerald Duckworth,[2] the younger of the two, later from George Duckworth.[3]

About the prospect of marriage she had been ambivalent. She delayed for over four months (11 January–29 May 1912) before accepting Leonard's proposal. In an extraordinarily frank and revealing letter to him just four weeks before they became engaged, she described her doubts and fears, as well as her hopes and desires, about marriage:

> Again, I want everything – love, children, adventure, intimacy, work. … So I go from being half in love with you, and wanting you to be with me always, and know everything about me, to the extreme of wildness and aloofness. I sometimes think that if I married you, I could have everything – and then – is it the sexual side of it that comes between us? As I told you brutally the other day, I feel no sexual attraction in you. There are moments – when you kissed me the other day was one – when I feel no more than a rock.[4]

Not only did getting married involve surrendering her independence, but her wish to have children was to be thwarted: the decision about that

---

1 See especially Caramagno, 97–113.
2 Virginia Woolf, *Moments*, 69.
3 Virginia Woolf, *Moments*, 177.
4 Virginia Woolf, *Letters* 1, 496, 1 May [1912].

was made prior to the wedding by Leonard and the "experts" whom he consulted, on the ground that her mental instability made her unsuited for motherhood. He began his medical consultations about her even before they became engaged. In the circumstances, it is unlikely that her anxiety about her long-digested and much-rewritten first novel, *The Voyage Out*, completed at the beginning of March 1913 but not published until 26 March 1915, was the only cause of the sleeplessness, headaches, and eating problems that followed the book's acceptance on 12 April 1913.[5]

As the summer progressed, her problems worsened, and from 25 July until 11 August, the day after her first wedding anniversary, she was a patient at Burley, a small private nursing home for women with mental-health difficulties in Cambridge Park, Twickenham, run by Jean Mary Grove Thomas. She had been there on two earlier occasions – in July–August 1910 and in the second half of February 1912.[6] That second occasion was just over a month after Leonard proposed to her, and the two happenings may not have been unconnected. Her third spell at Burley did little good. Leonard's diary reveals that in the following days she was often "worried" and not sleeping well. A sixteen-day holiday (23 August–8 September) at the Plough Inn, Holford, on the northeast edge of the Quantock Hills in Somerset, where the Woolfs had stayed near the start of their honeymoon, had a decidedly negative effect. From 2 September they had the company of Rupert Brooke's former girlfriend Katherine ("Ka") Cox, whom Leonard had summoned to help him look after Virginia in a deteriorating situation.

The day after the three (Virginia, Leonard, and Ka) returned to London, Virginia was seen first by one psychological doctor, then by another. The second, Henry Head, recommended return to a nursing home. The Woolfs and Ka were staying at 38 Brunswick Square, Bloomsbury, and it was there in the late afternoon or early evening of the same day (9 September) that Virginia attempted, and only narrowly failed, to commit suicide by taking an overdose of barbitone (barbital in the USA), a hypnotic drug introduced in 1903 and marketed under the brand name Veronal. She is said to have taken 100 grains or nearly 6.5 grams. A lethal dose is 3.5–4.4 grams.

---

5 In a letter to Roger Fry on Saturday [26 July 1913], Vanessa Bell writes: "Please be *very* careful not to say a word to *anyone* about her [Virginia] worrying over what people will think of her novel, which seems really to be the entire cause of her break-down" (TGA [Tate Gallery Archive] 8010/8/100). Cf. Jean Thomas's letter to Violet Dickinson, 14 September 1913, quoted by Quentin Bell, 2, 16, footnote: "It is the novel which has broken her up."

6 Virginia was to return to Jean Thomas's establishment for the fourth and last time on 25 March 1915, the day before the publication of *The Voyage Out*. That stay lasted six days, until 1 April 1915.

Leonard had gone out and forgotten to lock the case containing the drug. Ka raised the alarm at 6.30 p.m. after discovering Virginia unconscious on her bed. For twelve hours Virginia's life was in the balance, and it was saved only because the summoned doctors and nurses did vigorous and effective work on her with a stomach- pump obtained from St Bartholomew's Hospital by Geoffrey Keynes (younger brother of John Maynard Keynes), who was a trainee surgeon there and lodging at 38 Brunswick Square.

Until 3 August 1961, when the Suicide Act 1961 became law, taking one's own life was a crime in England and Wales, and, at the time Virginia overdosed herself with barbitone, persons who attempted suicide could be sent to prison or sectioned under the Lunacy Act 1890. Leonard inspected two or three asylums licensed to admit certified patients, but found them grim, and the doctors agreed to his request that, instead of her being certified, she should stay with him in a quiet place in the country, where he would employ nurses to help him give her round-the-clock supervision and care.

But where would they go? Asheham (or "Asham") House, Beddingham, at the foot of the South Downs, which Virginia and her sister, Vanessa Bell, had rented since New Year 1912, was reckoned unsuitable at this stage, partly because of its remote location, partly because up to four nurses were to be employed – two to provide care during the day and two to do so at night – and the house was not large enough to accommodate them as well as the Woolfs, who henceforth slept in separate bedrooms, and supportive friends like Ka Cox. George Duckworth relieved a potentially difficult situation by offering the use of his country home, Dalingridge Place, at Sharpthorne near East Grinstead. An entry in Leonard's diary for 10 September suggests that the offer was made with extraordinary promptness, before Virginia had fully recovered consciousness: "I went to see George at his office morn re Dalingridge."[7] But the arrangement had to be approved by the doctors, and this did not happen until 15 September.

To Virginia, for whose psychological problems the sexual abuse to which George had subjected her was partly responsible, the offer can hardly have seemed ideal, but the alternative of an asylum was much worse. To Leonard, who apparently knew nothing about George's mistreatment of Virginia,[8] the offer was a godsend. They went to Dalingridge Place on 20 September and remained there for two months.[9] Ka stayed until 26 September. She was to return on 22 October for at least four nights and on

---

7 Monks House Papers.
8 See Poole, 145.
9 Hermione Lee misnames the property "Dalingridge Hall" (Lee, 330, 878) and refers to George's "house in Dalingridge" (Lee, 157), as if this were the name of a village

15 November for two nights. In her absence, Leonard soldiered on with two and at one stage four nurses. Virginia was reluctant to eat, slept very badly, and sometimes experienced delusions,[10] but she put on some weight,[11] and by 18 November her condition had improved sufficiently to allow her and Leonard to move to Asheham House. Among those whose advice about Virginia was sought and given both before and after she attempted suicide was Roger Fry. It is natural that it should have been, for two reasons.

In the first place, Roger was intimately involved with Vanessa Bell. Although she had now fallen in love with Duncan Grant, Roger was still very much in love with her, and a close friendship continued. Their relationship was tied up, all along the line, with their passion for art, and both Vanessa and Duncan were co-directors with Roger of Omega Workshops Ltd, a decorative-art enterprise that had opened at 33 Fitzroy Square on 8 July 1913. Roger's friendship with Vanessa and her husband Clive Bell had naturally brought him into close contact with Virginia and Leonard as well, and Leonard, on his return from honeymoon, assisted him with the Second Post-Impressionist Exhibition at the Grafton Galleries. The exhibition, in which Vanessa and Duncan were among the artists represented, opened on 5 October 1912, two days after the Woolfs got back.[12] It was scheduled to close on 31 December, but ran on into January 1913, when many new pictures, including about thirty Cézanne watercolours, were added.

The second reason why Roger's opinion was sought is that his wife, the talented artist Helen Fry, had a long and sad history of mental unbalance.[13] The attacks of paranoid schizophrenia she suffered in 1898, 1903, and 1907–1908 were so severe that she had to be hospitalised. In November 1910 she was admitted to The Retreat, the old-established and renowned Quaker mental hospital in York, and it was there that she spent the last twenty-seven years of her life.[14] Obviously, therefore, Roger had all too much experience of mental physicians, nurses, and institutions.

---

or town. She also says that the Woolfs went there "in August" (Lee, 330), which is a strange error, given that she is describing what happened after the crisis of 9–10 September.

10 Leonard's diary, 4 October 1913, Monks House Papers.

11 Writing to Roger Fry on 16 October [1913], Vanessa Bell reports that "Virginia has gone up 11 lbs in the last fortnight" (TGA 8010/8/113).

12 Leonard Woolf (*Beginning Again*, 83) states that they returned "at the end of November", but this is incorrect: writing from Venice on 28 September 1912, he tells Molly MacCarthy that Virginia and he have "got to be back in London next Thursday", i.e. on 3 October (Virginia Woolf, *Letters* 2, 9).

13 See especially Essay 6.

14 Virginia's half-sister Laura Makepeace Stephen (1870–1945), her father's daughter by his first marriage, who just before her sixteenth birthday was sent away from

Although there are very significant differences between Virginia's and Helen's psychological illnesses and the circumstances that may have triggered them, there are also some significant similarities. I have already mentioned that Virginia's proneness to mental illness was probably partly due to hereditary factors. In Helen's case there is, as I shall reveal in a book I am writing about her, overwhelming evidence that the cause of her illness was to a significant degree genetic.[15] Her father, Joseph Coombe, who died in his mid-fifties, is described as having been a "nervous invalid" for the last eight years of his life. Of her nine siblings who were still living at the time of her marriage, four developed serious mental-health problems: two brothers and a sister were sectioned under the 1890 Lunacy Act, and one of these brothers and another brother committed suicide.

Virginia lost her neurotic father, Leslie Stephen, in 1904, when she was twenty-two, Helen lost hers in 1883, just before her nineteenth birthday. Virginia's brother Thoby Stephen died in 1906 when she was twenty-four, Helen's brother Harold Coombe in 1891 when she was twenty-seven.

Both women valued their independence and were concerned about losing it. In each case the men they married had to work hard to win them. Virginia's reluctance to marry has been remarked on. Roger was made to work even harder than Leonard. He fell in love with Helen on their first meeting, in late May 1895, and she did not agree to marry him until late July 1896. The daughter of a man who on account of the decline of his business as a wharfinger left his large family little or no money when he died, she had not travelled an easy road on her way to becoming a professional artist,

home to be looked after by a family named Searle, and who from 1893 spent her whole life in the care of mental doctors and nurses, is said by Quentin Bell (1, 22 and footnote) to have been sent, at an unspecified date, to an asylum in York and to have died there. He is not alone in thinking that she spent time in a mental hospital in York (Garnett, 256, footnote). But if this ever happened, the institution was not The Retreat: Katherine Webb, Archivist of the Borthwick Institute for Archives, University of York, who has very kindly checked The Retreat's records, reports that they contain no mention of her. Hilary Newman, who has thrown much light on Laura's life, questions (rightly, in my opinion) whether Laura was ever in an institution in York (Newman, *Laura Stephen*, 46 n. 41). It is certainly not the case that she died there: she was to die in The Priory, Roehampton, a mental hospital in which Helen was a patient in 1898 and 1907–1908. (Thomas C. Caramagno misidentifies the place of her death as "The Priory Hospital, Southgate" [108].)

15 Virginia Woolf (*Roger Fry*, 148 n. 1) asserts: "After her [Helen's] death the cause of her illness was found to be an incurable thickening of the bone of the skull". This is pure fiction, as is the explanation, reported by Frances Spalding, "that Helen was the victim of inherited syphilis" (xiii–xiv). It is remarkable that the source of both fables is said to have been Helen's sister-in-law Margery Fry.

and she was well used to looking after herself in an environment dominated by men. Moreover, at the time she started seeing Roger regularly, she had completed one significant commission and was about to undertake another. So her artistic career was taking off in a very promising way. What eventually nudged her into agreeing to marry Roger was his assistance with suggestions for her decoration of Arnold Dolmetsch's "Green Harpsichord", one of the most admired exhibits at the Fifth Exhibition of the Arts and Crafts Exhibition Society in October–December 1896.

The psychological problems that both women experienced during the early months and years of marriage were not helped by their loss of independence, and were perhaps aggravated by it. This appears to be true of Virginia, although with time and the growth of affection and understanding between her and Leonard, marriage became a stabilising factor. As for Helen, there is no firm evidence that she suffered any significant attack of mental illness before her marriage. The first documented sign of significant trouble occurred in the autumn of 1897, and, when she had her first full-blown attack of illness eighteen months after the wedding, in the early summer of 1898, she became hostile to her husband. Hostility to him also manifested itself during later attacks, although he was not the only target, and she could be violent both to nurses and to fellow patients. After her suicide attempt in 1913 and again during a prolonged attack of mental illness in 1915, Virginia too was sometimes violent to her nurses,[16] and during her 1915 breakdown she displayed marked hostility to Leonard. Two of the doctors who were consulted about Virginia were also consulted about Helen. One was George Henry Savage, a psychiatrist whose advice Virginia's family had sought over many years, and not only about her: he had treated her first cousin James ("Jem") Kenneth Stephen, who in 1892 died in an asylum in Northampton after refusing food for nearly three weeks.[17] He was consulted about Helen at the time of her first major attack in 1898 and later. The other doctor was the neurologist Henry Head, whom Roger first consulted about Helen in 1908.

16 See Leonard's diary for 27, 28, 30 September 1913, Monks House Papers. For Virginia's violence towards her nurses in 1915, see Leonard Woolf, *Beginning Again*, 172; for her hostility to Leonard in 1915, see Quentin Bell, 2, 26; and Glendinning, 193–194.

17 On Jem, see especially Newman, *James Kenneth Stephen*; also Caramagno, 101–103. Savage may also have given advice about Laura Stephen. Among the mental institutions with which he became closely associated was Earlswood Asylum, near Redhill, Surrey, in which Laura was an inmate from 14 July 1893 until 14 January 1897 (Surrey History Centre; Newman, *Laura Stephen*, 29, gives the year of her departure as 1893 – a clearly unintended but unfortunate slip).

It was on Roger's recommendation that Head's opinion was sought just before the Woolfs' unsuccessful stay in Somerset in late August and early September 1913, and Head was consulted again immediately after they returned from it. The consultation of Head without the prior approval of Savage nearly led to Virginia's death, for it was when, at Head's request, Leonard was seeing Savage to put him in the picture that she overdosed herself with Veronal.

On the question of whether it would be a good idea to have children, Savage's advice to Helen and Roger was positive. This is known from "a copy of essentials" of an angry letter Roger wrote to his outspoken friend Cecilia Widdrington on 3 September 1904.[18] Helen and he had a son, Julian, in 1901 and a daughter, Pamela, in 1902, and in July 1904 Helen, pregnant with an unplanned third child, suffered a miscarriage. Widdrington had strongly criticised the couple for having children and gone so far as to call them "criminal". Roger responded robustly and pointed out:

> With regard to the birth of Julian and Pamela we went entirely by the directions of Dr. Savage who I suppose if anyone may be supposed to know what is right in such things and if you could see the children I don't think you would doubt that it was right.[19]

Savage's advice to Leonard concerning Virginia having children was also positive: "Do her a world of good, my dear fellow; do her a world of good!"[20] But Leonard did not agree and went off to consult two other mental physicians, Maurice Craig[21] and Theophilus Bulkeley Hyslop, and Jean Thomas, who advised against her having children.[22] Motherhood was no cure for Helen's illness, and it is arguable that it became a complication and a cause of extra pain for her, because she loved her children and her irrationality and proneness to violence meant that she saw less and less of them, and after 1910 nothing of them at all. How motherhood would have affected Virginia is of course unknown. What is certain is that she always regretted not having had children.

When Helen's mental illness erupted in acute attacks, there was no option but to have her cared for in an asylum. But it is to Roger's credit

---

18 King's College Cambridge Archive Centre, REF/3/184.
19 King's College Cambridge Archive Centre, REF/3/184.
20 Leonard Woolf, *Beginning Again*, 82.
21 Craig, an eminent practitioner of psychological medicine, was a contemporary of Roger Fry at Cambridge and, like him, read Natural Sciences. Leonard had come to value his opinion more than that of George Savage (Leonard Woolf, *Beginning Again*, 159–160).
22 Leonard Woolf, *Beginning Again*, 82.

that at other times, when her illness was present but less acute, he went to great trouble and expense to keep her out of institutions, sometimes looking after her at home with help from nurses and his and Helen's sisters, sometimes taking her away into the country, and sometimes arranging for her to stay away somewhere without him but with a nurse. It was with great reluctance that he eventually conceded defeat and saw her enter The Retreat in York on 7 November 1910. Even after her admission there, he continued to hope for a while that she might make some sort of recovery, but it was not to be. Although no doubt Leonard was capable of making up his own mind in the matter, his wish to keep Virginia out of an asylum after her attempted suicide in September 1913 shows that his thinking was in line with Roger's. The seriousness of her illness must have given rise to hesitation, but her horror of asylums was a powerful consideration, and the absence of children made it easier to go for the private-nursing option, even though, ironically, the decision that she should not have children may well have aggravated her illness. At the stage when George Duckworth's offer of Dalingridge Place had been made, but not yet approved by the doctors, Vanessa Bell reported to Leonard:

> Roger tells me that he had no trouble with the Commissioners and managed them quite easily alone. He says that if they see that you are doing all you can and have good advice they are anxious not to interfere. So if Savage *should* be difficult I should simply write to Craig who was we know in favour of nurses and not complete isolation – and as Head is also strongly against any kind of asylum I dont see what else can be suggested but a house with you and nurses.[23]

By "the Commissioners" Vanessa means "the Commissioners in Lunacy", and what Roger recalled was the arrangements that were negotiated for Helen to be nursed outside of an asylum.

A significant difference between Helen and Virginia concerns the influence their mental-health problems had on their creativity. Although neither was able to work during acute attacks, Virginia was able to make much creative use of her experiences in her writing, as she herself recognised:

> And then I married, and then my brains went up in a shower of fireworks. As an experience, madness is terrific I can assure you, and not to be sniffed at; and in its lava I still find most of the things I write about. It shoots out of one everything shaped, final, not as mere driblets, as sanity does. And the six months – not three – that I lay in bed taught me a good deal about what is called oneself.[24]

23 Letter of Saturday [13 September 1913], Monks House Papers.
24 Virginia Woolf, *Letters* 4, 180, to Ethel Smyth, 22 June [1930].

In contrast, Helen's illness was purely an obstacle: it ruined her career as an artist, and there is no evidence that it ever provided any inspiration for any of her work. In the all-too-few good years after her marriage, she continued to produce fine work, but a commission to design a stained-glass window for a school chapel in December 1906 marked the end of her professional career. However, although her illness destroyed her artistic career, it never entirely destroyed her artistic ability, for in April 1926, when she had already been a patient in The Retreat for over fifteen years, Dr Mildred Creak, the Assistant Physician there, sent Roger a picture which Helen had just produced. Roger replied:

> It was good of you to send me Helen's pastel. What an extraordinary thing. It is far more logical and coherent than anything she has done since first she went to the asylum. It is not only logical and restrained – essentially sane – but it has still so much of her special gift for colour. I am simply amazed at it.[25]

The sanity of the picture raised Roger's hopes for an improvement in Helen's mental condition, but Creak advised him not to entertain any such hopes, and, sadly, she was right. The improvement in Virginia's condition that made possible the move from Dalingridge Place to Asheham on 18 November 1913 also enabled the level of nursing care for her to be reviewed. In an undated letter,[26] probably written shortly after (but possibly shortly before) the move, Vanessa told Leonard that she had just seen Dr Craig, who had advised her that it was no longer necessary to have two nurses, although it remained important for her to have someone with her at night as well as during the day. So the proposal was still to have two people to care for her, but to replace one of the two full-load nurses with one who would undertake lighter work, that is to say the night duty, at a much lower salary. In late November 1913 Vanessa placed an advertisement and approached several employment agencies in search of someone who would be suitable in the new circumstances. On 1 December she wrote to Leonard to report that she had had many replies to the advertisement, but, "though ... strongly tempted by one quite illiterate Nurse Budkin who has nursed an Admiral and a member of the Royal Family", she had not yet identified a satisfactory person in the London area.[27]

A previously unpublished letter in the Borthwick Institute for Archives, University of York, reveals that Roger Fry assisted in the search. The letter,

25 Unpublished letter of 20 April 1926, Borthwick Institute for Archives, Ret 6/20/2/2/14.
26 Monks House Papers.
27 Monks House Papers; Vanessa Bell, 151–152.

written exactly a week after Vanessa's letter to Leonard, is addressed to Dr Bedford Pierce, Medical Superintendent of The Retreat.[28]

Dec.8.13.

Dear Dr. Pierce

I forgot when writing to-day to ask whether you might perhaps know of a nurse who would be suitable to take charge of a case in the country. It is the [*sic*] ~~w~~ for the wife[29] of a friend of mine who has had an attack of suicidal mania but is much better only that for some months the doctor[30] thinks she ought to have a kind of nurse companion. The work would be very light and my friend is looking for someone who might be willing to take the place at a lower rate than the £2.2 a week which he has been paying while the illness was acute. I thought you might perhaps know of someone who was not up to hard work but who would be willing to take such a place at £1.1 a week. Please do not trouble about this if you do not happen to know of anyone likely to take it but I thought that as you were continually in touch with nurses you might perhaps know of one. It would be I think pleasant and easy work in a very beautiful country place near Lewes.

Yrs. sincerely

Roger Fry.

Bedford Pierce, aged fifty-two at this time, had already been Superintendent of The Retreat for twenty-one years, and he was to remain in this position until 1922. His appointment in 1892, at the age of thirty-one, had been an unusual and controversial one, not so much because of his youth as because of his inexperience.[31] The son of Quaker parents, he lost his father when he was only a few months old, left school at the age of fourteen, and was apprenticed to a homoeopathic chemist for eight years before starting his formal medical training at St Bartholomew's Hospital, London. He was an outstandingly good medical student, but, when he was appointed

---

28 The reference for all four letters between Roger Fry and Bedford Pierce quoted in this essay is Borthwick Institute for Archives, Ret 6/20/1/6, correspondence 1910–14.

29 Roger was originally going to say "It is the wife ..." and, when he changed his mind and decided to say "It is for the wife ...," omitted to complete the correction by deleting "the" after "It is".

30 Maurice Craig.

31 In respect of the appointee's youth and inexperience, the case of Bedford Pierce is very similar to that of John Langdon (Haydon) Down, later John Langdon Haydon Langdon-Down, the physician after whom Down's syndrome is called. Down was not quite thirty when in 1858 he was appointed Medical Superintendent at Earlswood Asylum, a post he occupied with distinction until 1868, when he established his own institution at Normansfield. He was one of those whom Leslie Stephen consulted about Laura. That was in 1885. Eight years later she was admitted to Earlswood (see n. 17 above).

Superintendent, he had been a qualified doctor for only four years and, as the Lunacy Commissioners complained to the Committee of The Retreat, had virtually no experience of psychological medicine.[32] The Commissioners' advice to appoint instead "a gentleman with considerable experience in lunacy"[33] was understandable, and they were displeased that it was rejected. But arrangements were made for Pierce to spend nine months working in other mental institutions before he took up his appointment, and the Committee's decision turned out to be a very wise one, for the three decades of his superintendentship, while continuing the enlightened treatment of the mentally ill that had marked The Retreat since its foundation in 1792, developed and strengthened it. One of his notable achievements was to improve nursing standards, converting "attendants" into properly trained mental nurses. As well as producing enough nurses to staff its resident patients, The Retreat supplied nurses to those who required care in their own homes for a maximum of three months. Roger Fry will have been well aware that, in asking Pierce if he could recommend a nurse for Virginia, he was seeking the help of someone with a remarkable knowledge of the nursing field.

Roger had established an excellent rapport with the Superintendent. This is not surprising, for Pierce, as well as being in charge of the good care of his wife and "a man of genial and energetic personality",[34] was keen on culture in general and on art in particular. Although he modestly refused to call himself "an artist", he was a competent painter of watercolours and showed good taste both when selecting pictures for The Retreat and when deciding on the decoration of its rooms and corridors.[35] About four months before asking Pierce about a nurse, Roger raised with him the possible therapeutic effect of colour schemes on the mentally ill:

Aug. 15. 13.

Dear Dr. Pierce

[…]

I hope when next you are in town you will call on me here. I have recently started this workshop for artists to do designs and decorations for ordinary life[36] and I believe you might be interested even from a professional point of view. I have long thought that enough attention was not paid to the psychological effect of colour on the mind. Again and again I have heard people who came to our showroom say (even when they didn't altogether approve) "at least one couldn't have the blues here" or "it's like coming into sunshine". I

32 Hunt, 109; Digby, 117, 119.
33 Hunt, 109.
34 Hunt, 81.
35 Hunt, 84.
36 On Omega Workshops, opened a month earlier, see above.

wonder therefore whether you mightn't try in one or two rooms the effect of our gay and exhilarating colour effects. It's always been a vague desire of mine to use my powers in this direction in asylums ever since I saw how depressing the effect of modern ugliness and dreariness was upon my wife. I think now she is beyond such feelings. I think she has lost her aesthetic sense almost entirely but there are stages of mental illness where these accessory influences are not to be despised.

Yrs. sincerely
Roger Fry.

Pierce replied on 6 September:

Dear Mr. Fry,

Your letter of Aug 15th has awaited my return home. It raises many interesting points, and in a sort of way we have always felt that the surroundings of the patients undoubtedly affected them, though possibly unconsciously. Thus, we have always been careful in relation to such things as wood mouldings, decorations and furniture; and though reasons of expense have prevented us from doing all we should like, yet I hope we have succeeded in giving a comfortable, domestic feeling to the Retreat. I should like to write again after the next meeting of the Committee, which will be in about ten days. I myself should be glad to make further experiments in the direction you indicate, but must consult the Committee on a matter of this kind.

Yours very truly,
[Unsigned]

If Pierce did write to Roger after the September Committee meeting, The Retreat's copy of his letter is not among the papers relating to Helen; and if the Committee did discuss the matter, there is no mention of the discussion in the minutes. One may conjecture that members would have taken the view that they had already done much to brighten up the rooms and passages, and perhaps that some patients might find bold colour effects more disturbing than soothing.

In writing to Pierce about the importance of colour in mental institutions, Roger was, as he makes clear, drawing on his own experience of them as places in which his wife had been confined. But it is also to be noted that Virginia, during her "rest cure"[37] stay at Jean Thomas's nursing home in the summer of 1910, complained about the décor: "However, what I mean is that I shall soon have to jump out of a window. The ugliness of the house is almost inexplicable – having white, and mottled green and red."[38] In response to Roger's enquiry about a nurse, Pierce wrote on 11 December:

37 The term was used by Virginia of her stay at Burley in the summer of 1910. See Virginia Woolf, *Letters* 1, 430, [28 June 1910], to Violet Dickinson.
38 Woolf, *Letters* 1, 431, 28 July [1910], to Vanessa Bell.

I am sorry to say I cannot think of any likely person to act as a nurse-companion for the lady about whom you write. ... I hardly think it likely you will get a suitable lady for the sum you name, unless perchance you should hear of somebody just out of a situation. Trained nurses of any calibre have no difficulty in joining associations and getting higher remuneration.

One guinea (one pound and one shilling) in 1913 equates to £120 in 2019, and a weekly payment of this sum would make an annual salary equivalent to £6,240. Two guineas in 1913 would have been equivalent to a weekly payment of £240 in 2019 and an annual salary of £12,480. Of course board and lodging would have been included, and even the lower salary (£1.1s a week = £54.12s per annum) compares not unfavourably with the remuneration, in 1913, of private staff of the London Hospital, whose nurses started on an annual salary of £30, which rose by annual increments of £5 to £50, with a further increase, after twelve years of service, to £55.[39] Perusal of the classified advertisements in *The Times* in 1913 reveals that it was not unusual for a live-in nurse in London to be offered a salary of £35 per annum. One guinea a week for the light-duty nurse was the salary suggested by Dr Craig in his conversation with Vanessa in November, but, as we shall see, Dr Pierce was right in thinking that it would be difficult to recruit a qualified nurse at that rate.

Although at the time of her engagement Virginia told people that she was marrying "a penniless Jew",[40] she and Leonard were not exactly paupers. Her inherited capital, invested in stocks and shares, amounted to just over £9,000, about £1,000,000 in today's money, and yielded an annual income of nearly £400, the equivalent of about £46,000 in 2019. But the doctors' fees and nurses' wages meant that they were spending more than that amount, and their earnings were small. Hence the wish for economy. It is a wish with which Roger would have fully sympathised: despite welcome assistance from his father, Sir Edward Fry, the bills that streamed in from those who were involved with the care of Helen's health were a huge burden on his modest financial resources, and the correspondence with The Retreat reveals that, while he was always anxious for her to be as comfortable as possible, he was concerned not to incur unnecessary expenses, and The Retreat on more than one occasion agreed to reduce its fees in response to pleading from him.

In a letter written on Monday [8 December 1913],[41] the same day on which Roger Fry approached Dr Pierce, Vanessa wrote to tell Leonard that

---

39 Holland.
40 Letters of [4 June 1912] to Violet Dickinson and [June 1912] to Janet Case, in Virginia Woolf, *Letters* 1, 500–501.
41 Monks House Papers.

she had interviewed a London woman who seemed likely to be suitable as a night-carer for Virginia – a Mrs Rose Allen of 119 Antill Road, North Bow. Although not a trained nurse, she had done plenty of nursing and was "quiet and seemed sensible". She would take her instructions from the qualified nurse, Nurse Read, who would look after Virginia in the daytime. Two days later Vanessa wrote to tell Leonard that Allen's references were good, and that she had engaged her to start work on 15 December.[42] But it then emerged that Read was not very happy about working with an unqualified nurse,[43] and there was a delay while her concern was addressed. Allen arrived at Asheham House on 19 December, replacing Nurse Kingsford. She was to stay until 12 January, when her departure left Read as the only paid carer. Virginia's improvement is indicated not only by the reduction of the nursing care for her, but also by her letter-writing. A letter she wrote to Leonard on 4 December 1913 was the first she is known to have written to anyone for four months. It is sane and positive, ending: "Dearest Mongoose, I wish you would believe how much I am grateful and repentant. You have made me so happy."[44] There were to be some more problems in the weeks that followed, but they became less frequent and serious. Visits from Ka (3–8 January 1914) and another friend, Janet Case, her former Greek tutor, who stayed three times in January and February, were helpful. Virginia did some reading and offered to do typing for Lytton Strachey. On 11 February 1914 she told Violet Dickinson: "It will be such a mercy to get rid of nurses and all this ridiculous nonsense."[45] Her wish was soon to be granted. In a letter of 5 February her general practitioner, Dr Belfrage, told Leonard: "I quite agree that the time has come to place reliance on your wife's self-control."[46]

42 Wednesday [10 December 1913], Monks House Papers.
43 Vanessa Bell to Leonard Woolf, Sunday [14 December 1913], Monks House Papers.
44 Virginia Woolf, *Letters* 2, 35.
45 Woolf, *Letters* 2, 39. The editors put a query against the date of the letter, but there is no uncertainty, because Virginia says that Leonard is in London seeing his publisher, Edward Arnold, and Leonard's diary shows that he went up to London for that meeting on 11 February (Monks House Papers), returning in the evening.
46 Monks House Papers. Sydney Henning Belfrage was nothing if not versatile and industrious – obstetrician, anaesthetist, general practitioner, medical inspector of the Divorce Registry (while at the same time a GP), and author of works on diet and medical aspects of the law. The bill he sent Leonard for his attendance on Virginia between September 1913 and January 1914 was a shocking £88.19s.11d., which Vanessa remarked "seems a curious sum" (letter to Leonard, 23 January [1914], Monks House Papers) – curious, she meant, because why not £89? The equivalent figure in 2019 would be about £10,000.

On 16 February Read, who had been at Asheham since 3 November 1913, departed. Virginia was better, but her recovery was fragile and incomplete, and twelve months later (February 1915) severe trouble erupted again. When that happened, it seemed very much on the cards that, as in the case of Helen Fry, the recurrent attacks of mental illness would continue and make a return to normal life and creative work impossible. Fortunately, Virginia's story was to be a very different one from Helen's.

2. Flawed psychobiography

In Essay 4, a slightly altered version of an article published in 2011,[47] I discuss Virginia Woolf's holiday in Greece with Leonard Woolf, Roger Fry, and Margery Fry in April–May 1932. In it, as well as setting out the exact itinerary and correcting erroneous readings in the published editions of Virginia's diary and letters, I identify the Woolfs' photographs.

All but one of the "Greek" photographs are in Virginia Woolf's Monk's House Photograph Album no. 3 (MH-3; MS Thr 560) in the Harvard Theatre Collection, Houghton Library, Harvard University, the only exception being a photograph that was originally in the album but has been removed from it.[48] Most of them are correctly and precisely identified for the first time in the 2011 article. The earlier catalogue of them in Maggie Humm's *Snapshots of Bloomsbury* is unsatisfactory: most of the identifications are either unacceptably vague or wrong. Her most serious mistakes concern the seven photographs that show Greek temples: she misidentifies each scene as the Acropolis, meaning the Acropolis at Athens. In fact, not one of the seven photographs is of a temple on the Acropolis, and only one is of a temple in Athens, the others being of the temple of Poseidon at Sounion, the temple of Apollo at Corinth, and the temple of Aphaia on the island of Aigina.[49]

---

47 Smith.
48 See Essay 4, 112.
49 The relevant entries in the Houghton Library's catalogue of the Virginia Woolf Monk's House Album 3 published online at http://nrs.harvard.edu/urn-3:FHCL. Hough:hou02070 have been revised to take account of my article, although the descriptions of the scenes are often less detailed and precise than mine. A valuable feature of the catalogue is that it includes a digitised image of each photograph. Album 3 is digitised by page at http://nrs.harvard.edu/urn-3:FHCL.HOUGH:4394410. It must be pointed out that the cataloguers' pagination of Album 3 does not agree with that of Humm (*Snapshots*), whom, not knowing better, because I had not had the opportunity to examine the album itself, I followed in Smith. It turns out that Maggie

Humm returned to the photographs taken by the Woolfs in Greece, and to one photograph in particular, in a paper contributed to an international conference in June 2012 and since published.[50] I regret finding myself being critical of her again in this response, but I feel obliged to point out that her discussion is unsound and involves a serious misrepresentation of Virginia Woolf.

I quote the whole of the first paragraph of the "Greek" passage and most of the second:

> In the 1930s, the Woolfs increasingly reproduced their photographs as postcard reproductions. Photographs of friends, including a photograph of E. M. Forster, taken in the late 1930s, are on postcards. An earlier photograph, taken in 1932, is also on a postcard. As Woolf said in a letter to Ottoline Morrell "this is where we are, not much like Gower Street" (*L5* 61). Martin Ferguson Smith, a classics scholar, in a detailed scholarly account has very helpfully corrected Virginia's misattribution of the Acropolis in the image (and following Woolf, misattributions by critics including Hermione Lee, Elizabeth Richardson, and myself). The building in the photograph is the temple of Olympian Zeus not the Acropolis (although the temple is only five hundred metres away from the Acropolis). But, although mentioning Woolf's memory of her earlier 1906 visit, Smith downplays the more significant issue of multidisciplines: of psychobiography, visual grammar and syntax, and the cultural moment (Smith 62). For example, as important as what is *behind* the four figures, is what, or rather who is *in front*? Who took the photograph? Why did the Woolfs choose a postcard format for this image and then increasingly for images of their friends, for Monk's House, for the garden, and even for the Monk's House *pond* (there are over thirty images reproduced on postcards in the albums)? And, the most significant question, why the misattribution by Woolf?
>
> As Virginia had said in a letter to Vita, she had been reminded of "my own ghost coming down from the Acropolis" and of her 1906 visit (*L5* 62). For Virginia the photographic representation had to be the Acropolis for the memory to have affect. Psycho-biographic indices then are crucial and not only for Virginia. The visit was Leonard's first to Greece. Leonard was obsessed with Greek writing throughout his life and with Athens in particular. … Leonard also associated the Acropolis with photography. There he had met a photographer whose "intelligence, knowledge, humanity of this man were

Humm did not count page 2, which displays slots for a photograph that is no longer there. The Houghton Library's cataloguers are quite right to number this page, but the unfortunate consequence is that their page numbers for the "Greek" photographs are in every case one ahead of Humm's and mine. To avoid further confusion, I have not changed the numbers in this volume.

50 Humm, "Multidisciplinary".

extraordinary" Leonard noted in his autobiography.[51] Not surprisingly, both Woolfs might wish to willingly mistake a Greek building or two.[52]

I take the first paragraph first.

The "earlier photograph, taken in 1932" is rather strangely introduced. Instead of telling the reader that it was taken in Athens, Humm quotes a remark of Virginia in "a letter to Ottoline Morrell". That "letter" is actually a brief (twenty-word) message, written in Athens on 7 May 1932 on a picture-postcard that shows the Propylaea (entrance gate) of the Acropolis. Omission of this information makes Virginia's "this is where we are, not much like Gower Street" unintelligible to the reader unfamiliar with the postcard.[53]

Immediately after this puzzling mention of Virginia's communication to Lady Ottoline, Humm claims that I "corrected Virginia's misattribution of the Acropolis in the image (and following Woolf, misattributions by critics …)". She is referring not to the postcard sent to Lady Ottoline, but to the photograph showing Leonard and Virginia and the Frys at the Olympieion (temple of Olympian Zeus) in Athens.[54] However, I did not correct Virginia's misidentification of the scene, and there is a very good reason for that, which is that neither she nor Leonard ever did misidentify it! Under the photograph in the Album, Virginia has simply written "Athens. May 1932" and then identified the four persons in the picture; and on the back Leonard has identified the persons, but not the place.[55] A duplicate of the photograph, found loose in the Album, is included in the Houghton Library's online catalogue,[56] and in this case only the four persons are identified. The misidentification of the building is entirely the doing of later writers, so what Humm considers "the most important question" ("why the misattribution by Woolf?") does not arise at all.

Humm's statement that "the building in the photograph is the temple of Olympian Zeus not the Acropolis" confirms the suspicion, already generated by her descriptions of temple locations in Humm, *Snapshots*, that she is under the misapprehension that the Acropolis is a temple rather than the

51 In view of Leonard's "of this man", Humm's "whose" is inappropriate, and her sentence requires rewording.

52 Humm, "Multidisciplinary", 6–7.

53 The photograph of the Propylaea was not taken by the Woolfs and is not in Monk's House Album 3. The description of the scene, very faintly printed in Greek beneath the image, shows that the postcard was commercially produced in Greece. It is in the Harry Ransom Humanities Research Center, University of Texas at Austin, Ottoline Morrell Collection, Box 34, Folder 6.

54 Plate 28.

55 Smith, 72 = Essay 4, 111.

56 See n. 49 above. In the catalogue the duplicate is no. 54a.

site of temples, most notably the Parthenon, and other ancient buildings. Given that these buildings are among the greatest and best-known architectural treasures in Europe and indeed in the world, the confusion of the Olympieion with them by Humm, Hermione Lee, and others was extraordinary, and it is not in any way excused, as Humm seems to imply, by the proximity of the Olympieion to the Parthenon, any more than a confusion of (say) St Bride's Church in Fleet Street, London, with St Paul's Cathedral could be excused on that ground.

The questions of who took the photograph, and why it is a postcard, are reasonable ones, although to my mind less important than Humm thinks. She considers but rejects the possibility that the photograph was taken with a Kodak self-timer. That leaves two possibilities. One (not explicitly considered by Humm) is that another visitor to the Olympieion took the photograph with the Woolfs' camera. The other is that the photographer was a local professional. The second alternative seems the more probable one. If correct, it would explain why the image is unique in the "Greek" collection both in being on a postcard and in having been duplicated. Whether the prints were made in Athens or after the Woolfs returned home, one may guess that there were at least four copies – at least two for the Woolfs and at least one each for Margery and Roger. The postcard format has obvious convenience if one wants to mail a photograph, and one probably does not need to look for a more profound reason for its use by the Woolfs for their own photographs from time to time.

In the second paragraph quoted from Humm's paper the fiction that Virginia misidentified the scene of the Olympieion photograph as the Acropolis is repeated and elaborated. The suggestion that the memory of her 1906 visit to Athens meant that "the photographic representation had to be the Acropolis" is, with respect, sheer nonsense, as is the extension of the same suggestion to Leonard. The claim that "Leonard also associated the Acropolis with photography," even if true, would not justify the assertion that "not surprisingly, both Woolfs might wish to willingly mistake a building or two", but there is no evidence that he, any more than Virginia, connected the Acropolis with photography. The Greek with whom Leonard had a long conversation on the Acropolis was not, as Humm informs us, "a photographer", but a "tout of postcards" or "tout selling photographs" or "seller of postcards", and the conversation was about Leonard's walking stick, "Greece and England", "Greece and the economic conditions and Greek politics", and "life, his life and mine". Leonard makes no mention of any discussion of photography.[57]

---

57 Leonard Woolf's account of the encounter is to be found, chronologically out of place, in Leonard Woolf, *The Journey*, 184–185, 189. Humm ("Multidisciplinary", 11, n. 13) cites only the abbreviated account given by Victoria Glendinning (300).

If, as Humm contends, photography was so important to the Woolfs in connection with the Acropolis, one has to ask why it is that neither of them seems to have taken a single photograph of it or of any of its monuments during their 1932 holiday, despite having visited it at least three times. It is a question I asked in my earlier essay (4). The only explanation I was able to think of then, and can think of now, is that perhaps they did not trouble to photograph places of which picture postcards could be bought.[58] Whether this explanation is correct or not, one cannot escape the conclusion that, although the Acropolis and its buildings were important to the Woolfs, taking photographs of them was not.[59]

Acknowledgements

I warmly thank the following: Annabel Cole for permission to quote unpublished letters of Roger Fry; Jenny McAleese, Chief Executive of The Retreat, York, for permission to quote unpublished letters written by past members of its staff; Henrietta Garnett, the copyright holder, for permission to quote from letters of Vanessa Bell; Random House for permission to quote the edition of Virginia Woolf's letters published by The Hogarth Press; The Borthwick Institute for Archives, University of York, for permitting me to work on archive material relating to Helen Fry and supplying copies of correspondence between Roger Fry and staff of The Retreat, York, with special thanks to Katherine Webb, Archivist; Tate Gallery Archive for supplying

58 Smith, 72 = Essay 4, 111. As I point out there, Mycenae and Delphi are other notable places not represented in the Monk's House collection.
59 Maggie Humm, "Psychobiography and Virginia Woolf", takes issue with some of my criticisms, but her arguments are negated by further mistakes. For example, she claims (599) that I have maintained that psychobiography as a method is flawed, when I have only drawn attention to the serious errors of fact in her attempt to apply that method to one particular case. She is at pains to emphasise the importance of the Acropolis to the Woolfs, but that is not in dispute. What I dispute is whether photography of the Acropolis was, as she had tried to show, important to the Woolfs. She has no answer to my question of why, if she is right, neither of them seems to have taken a single photograph of it during their 1932 holiday. Her suggestion (597) that the photograph of the Woolfs and Frys at the temple of Olympian Zeus may have been taken on the same day that Virginia wrote a letter (to Ethel Smyth) mentioning "changing into thin clothes and going up to the Acropolis" is plain wrong: the letter is dated 20 April [1932], the party's first full day in Athens, whereas the visit to the Temple of Olympian Zeus was on 8 May 1932, the Woolfs' last full day in the city. Here, as elsewhere in her discussions of the Woolfs' visit to Greece in 1932, it would be preferable if Humm would pay more attention to the facts and indulge less in speculation.

copies of letters from Vanessa Bell to Roger Fry; King's College Cambridge Archive Centre for supplying a copy of a letter from Roger Fry to Cecilia Widdrington; Special Collections, University of Sussex, for supplying copies of the following items in the Monks House Papers (Virginia Woolf) collection dating from the eight-month period 1 July 1913–28 February 1914: the relevant pages of Leonard Woolf's diaries for 1913–1914, correspondence between him and Virginia Woolf, and letters written to him by Vanessa Bell, Janet Case, Ka Cox, Jean Thomas, and Virginia's doctors; Surrey History Centre, for providing copies of the records of Laura Makepeace Stephen's stay at Earlswood Asylum in 1893–1897; Micah Jared Hoggatt, Reference Librarian, Houghton Library, Harvard University, for information and advice about Virginia Woolf Monk's[60] House Photograph Album no. 3 (MS Thr 560) in the Library's Harvard Theatre Collection; Rick Watson, Head of Reference Services, Harry Ransom Humanities Research Centre, University of Texas at Austin, for supplying a high-resolution scan of the Greek caption printed on Virginia Woolf's postcard to Ottoline Morrell; and Stuart N. Clarke, Secretary of the Virginia Woolf Society of Great Britain.

References

Bell, Quentin. *Virginia Woolf: A Biography.* 2 vols. London: The Hogarth Press, 1972.

Bell, Vanessa. *Selected Letters of Vanessa Bell.* Edited by Regina Marler. London: Bloomsbury, 1993.

Borthwick Institute for Archives, University of York. Records of The Retreat, York.

Caramagno, Thomas C. *The Flight of the Mind: Virginia Woolf's Art and Manic-Depressive Illness.* Berkeley: University of California Press, 1992.

Digby, Anne. *Madness, Morality and Medicine: A Study of the York Retreat, 1796–1914.* Cambridge: Cambridge University Press, 1985.

Garnett, Henrietta. *Anny: A Life of Anne Isabella Thackeray Ritchie.* London: Chatto and Windus, 2004.

Glendinning, Victoria. *Leonard Woolf.* London: Simon and Schuster, 2006.

Holland, Sydney. [Letter concerning remuneration of nurses]. *The Spectator,* 14 June 1913, 16.

Humm, Maggie. "Multidisciplinary Woolf / Multiple Woolfs." In *Interdisciplinary / Multidisciplinary Woolf: Selected Papers from the Twenty-Second Annual International Conference on Virginia Woolf, University of Saskatchewan, Canada, 7–10 June, 2012,* edited by Ann Martin and Kathryn Holland. Clemson, SC: Clemson University Digital Press, 2013.

---

60 The Houghton Library spells Monk's with an apostrophe, University of Sussex Special Collections without one. This variation is preserved in the citations all through this essay.

————. "Psychobiography and Virginia Woolf." *English Studies* 96 (2015), 596–600.

————. *Snapshots of Bloomsbury: The Private Lives of Virginia Woolf and Vanessa Bell*. London: Tate Publishing, 2006.

Hunt, Harold Capper. *A Retired Habitation: A History of The Retreat, York (Mental Hospital)*. London: H. K. Lewis, 1932.

King's College Cambridge Archive Centre, Cambridge. Correspondence of Roger Fry.

Lee, Hermione. *Virginia Woolf*. London: Chatto and Windus, 1996.

Monks House Papers (Virginia Woolf). Special Collections, University of Sussex, Brighton. Material dating from 1 July 1913–28 February 1914: Leonard Woolf's diaries for 1913–1914 and selected correspondence.

Newman, Hilary. *James Kenneth Stephen: Virginia Woolf's Tragic Cousin*. Bloomsbury Heritage Series, 47. London: Cecil Woolf Publishers, 2008.

————. *Laura Stephen: A Memoir*. Bloomsbury Heritage Series, 45. London: Cecil Woolf Publishers, 2006.

Ottoline Morrell Collection. Harry Ransom Humanities Research Center, University of Texas, Austin.

Poole, Roger. *The Unknown Virginia Woolf*. Cambridge: Cambridge University Press, 1978.

Smith, Martin Ferguson. "Virginia Woolf's First Visit to Greece." *English Studies* 92 (2011): 55–83.

Spalding, Frances. "New Introduction." In *Roger Fry: A Biography*, by Virginia Woolf, xi–xv. Reprint, London: Hogarth Press, 1991.

Surrey History Centre, Woking. Archives and History. Records of Laura Makepeace Stephen, 1893–1897.

Tate Gallery Archive, London, UK. Correspondence of Vanessa Bell.

Virginia Woolf Monk's House Photograph Album, MH-3, 1863–1938 (MS Thr 560). Harvard Theatre Collection. Houghton Library, Harvard University, Cambridge, MA. Catalogue of Monk's House Album 3. [Cited 21 May 2014]. Available from http://nrs.harvard.edu/urn-3:FHCL.Hough:hou02070.

Woolf, Leonard. *Beginning Again: An Autobiography of the Years 1911 to 1918*. London: Hogarth Press, 1968.

————. *The Journey Not the Arrival Matters: An Autobiography of the Years 1939–1969*. London: Hogarth Press, 1970.

Woolf, Virginia. *The Letters of Virginia Woolf*. Edited by Nigel Nicolson, assisted by Joanne Trautmann. 6 vols. London: Hogarth Press, 1975–1980.

————. *Moments of Being*. Edited with an Introduction and Notes by Jeanne Schulkind. Second ed. London: Hogarth Press, 1985.

————. *Roger Fry: A Biography*. London: Hogarth Press, 1940.

6

Virginia Woolf and "the hermaphrodite": A feminist fan of *Orlando* and critic of *Roger Fry*

1. Introduction

The last book by Virginia Woolf to appear in her lifetime was a biography of the artist and art critic Roger Fry,[1] fellow "Bloomsberry" and close friend from 1911 until his death, which, according to her own account, affected her more deeply than that of any other friend.[2] The work, her only book-length biography, was published on 25 July 1940.[3] The writing of it did not come easily to her, and she was worried about the reception it would receive from reviewers and from those who had known Roger, including members of his family. It was at the request of his sister Margery Fry that she had undertaken the task. In the event, his family did approve – not only Margery and two other sisters, Agnes and Isabel, but also his daughter, Pamela Diamand; and most others who gave their opinions, whether in print or in letters, reacted favourably.

However, there were some exceptions, although the main target of their criticisms was Roger rather than his biographer. One of these exceptions was Herbert Read, who reviewed the book in *The Spectator*.[4] Another was Ben Nicolson, elder son of Vita Sackville-West, in letters he wrote to Virginia on 6 and 19 August 1940.[5] A third was Mary Gordon, who in a letter to Virginia of 4 November 1940 focused on the portrayal of Roger's wife, Helen Fry *née* Coombe, and on the character of Roger.

---

1 Woolf, *Roger Fry*.
2 Woolf, *Letters 5*, 399, [6 June 1935], to Ethel Smyth: "I never minded any death of a friend half as much: its like coming into a room and expecting all the violins and trumpets and hearing a mouse squeak."
3 She completed *Between the Acts* before she took her own life on 28 March 1941, but the book was published posthumously, on 17 July 1941.
4 Read.
5 Monks House Papers, SxMs-18/1/D/103/1. Virginia replied in letters of 13 and 24 August 1940: Monks House Papers, SxMs-18/1/D/103/2 = Woolf, *Letters 6*, 413–415, 421–422.

It is with the letter of Mary Gordon that I am concerned. Beth Rigel Daugherty was the first to publish it, in 2006.[6] She did well to bring it to public attention, but her presentation of it is not entirely satisfactory: her transcript of the letter is not fully accurate; she is not confident of the identity of the writer ("This correspondent may be Mary Louisa Gordon ..."); and her treatment of Helen is limited to a reference to a footnote in which the editors of Virginia's diary comment briefly on the cause of Helen's mental illness.[7] In this essay I discuss Mary Gordon, present a corrected text of her letter based on autopsy of the original,[8] and comment on its content in the context of a discussion of Helen's life and character.

2. Mary Louisa Gordon

The writer of the letter is certainly, not just perhaps or probably, Mary Louisa Gordon. She was known to Virginia, because in May 1936 the Woolfs' Hogarth Press had published her historical novel *Chase*[9] *of the Wild Goose: The Story of Lady Eleanor Butler and Miss Sarah Ponsonby, Known as the Ladies of Llangollen*, which she dedicated to her friend the psychotherapist and writer Emma Jung, wife of the psychiatrist Carl Gustav Jung. She had undergone Jungian analysis in London in 1920. In 1922 she spent nine months with Jung in Switzerland, studying analytical psychology and undergoing analysis herself.[10] She continued to be a disciple and patient of Jung for the rest of her life.[11] Like him, she showed a great interest in spiritualism and mediums.[12]

Mary's book is in three parts. The first, "The Ladies Meet One Another", describes, as well as the two Irishwomen's meeting, their attempts, first unsuccessful, eventually successful, to escape from their families and find a

6 Daugherty, 202–204.

7 Daugherty, 204.

8 Significant misreadings and omissions by Daugherty are mentioned in the footnotes to the text of the letter. Minor errors, mainly of punctuation, are not.

9 Several writers on Mary Gordon mistakenly give the title as "*The Chase* ..." which, as Mary pointed out, "would connote something quite different" from the "symbolic expression" she intended (Hogarth Press Archives, letter to Winifred Perkins of The Hogarth Press, 10 April 1937). Mavor, 205, 206, 232, makes the further mistake of giving the title as "*The Flight of the Wild Goose*".

10 Mary Gordon, letter of 5 December [1922] to Agnes Bennett. Alexander Turnbull Library, National Library of New Zealand MS-Papers-1346–197.

11 Jung, Correspondence with Mary Gordon. No correspondence between Emma Jung and Mary Gordon is known to survive.

12 Jung, Correspondence with Mary Gordon, letters of 10–11 June 1939.

place where they could lead a quiet and cultured life together on the other side of the Irish Sea. The second part, "Meet the Ladies", describes their life at Plas Newydd, the home which they rented, then owned, in Llangollen, North Wales, where, ironically, their life of retirement attracted much local, national, and international attention. Their numerous distinguished visitors included William Wordsworth, who in 1824 composed a sonnet to them in the grounds of Plas Newydd, ending

> … faithful to a low-roofed Cot,
> On Deva's banks, ye have abode so long;
> Sisters in love, a love allowed to climb,
> Even on this earth, above the reach of Time![13]

The most remarkable part of Mary's book is the third, entitled "The Ladies Meet Me", in which she describes how she met and conversed with the two ladies. The reason why this is so remarkable is that Eleanor and Sarah died in 1829 and 1831 respectively, more than a hundred years before Mary's visit to Llangollen in 1934 – a visit she made in response to a dream of Valle Crucis Abbey. She had previously visited Llangollen only once, fifty-six years earlier, when she was seventeen years old.[14] According to Elizabeth Mavor, author of *The Ladies of Llangollen*, Mary had the dream while she was staying in the Jungs' house in Switzerland, and it was Carl Jung who urged her to accept its summons,[15] but she does not give her source for this information. The source is not Mary's book.

Virginia Woolf briefly mentions Mary six times, but never with warmth. The first mention is in her diary for 13 September 1935: "To make matters worse, Dr Mary Gordon rings up to bother us about her life of the Ladies of Llangollen; and it has turned grey and windy."[16] The other mentions of her are in five letters to her friend the composer Ethel Smyth. On 18 [September 1935] she reports that she has just received "a thick dossier from her", but cannot read the manuscript yet,[17] and on [8 October 1935] writes: "I had to send the Ladies of Ll: back to the hermaphrodite. I cant repeat my reasons on this slip; but perhaps, she'll tell you. I thought it quite well done in its way."[18] Although Virginia had speculated that a hermaphroditic or androgynous mind – one that is neither wholly masculine nor wholly feminine – is most balanced and creative,[19] calling Mary "the hermaphrodite" is hardly

---

13 Wordsworth, lines 11–14.
14 Gordon, *Chase*, 240.
15 Mavor, 204.
16 Woolf, *Diary* 4, 341.
17 Woolf, *Letters* 5, 427.
18 Woolf, *Letters* 5, 431.
19 Woolf, *A Room of One's Own*, chapter 6.

intended to be complimentary. The term may refer partly to her rather unfeminine appearance, her interest in the Ladies of Llangollen, who were widely believed to have dressed in a masculine way, and her assumed abstinence from any sexual relationship, but, as we shall see shortly, there is much more to it than that. Writing to Ethel Smyth on [24 October 1935], Virginia repeats the description: "What about the Hermaphrodite? She's writing a sequel to Orlando."[20] One might have expected the editors of Virginia's letters to comment on "a sequel to Orlando", but they are silent. I first supposed that what Mary is said to be writing is not actually a sequel to Virginia's *Orlando*, published in 1928, but the third part of *Chase of the Wild Goose*, in which she brings her allegedly-cross-dressing and long-dead heroines "alive" again and makes them aware of the economic, political, and social changes that have occurred since their lives ended. It seemed plausible that Virginia saw some similarity between Mary's book and her own for two reasons. One was that the eponymous protagonist of *Orlando* undergoes several incarnations and changes of sex in several centuries.[21] The other was the presence of the wild goose both in her novel and in Mary's book, including the title. At the end of *Orlando* a single wild bird springs up over Shelmerdine's head, prompting the protagonist's last words: "'It is the goose!' Orlando cried. 'The wild goose ....'"[22] In Mary's novel, when the young Sarah Ponsonby tries to persuade the older Eleanor Butler to let her come away with her, the latter warns: "We should go on what the world calls a wild-goose chase. Could I take you to such a life?"[23] To which Sarah replies: "I want to hear you say I may chase the wild goose with you. God would help us." Then, at the very end of Part II of the book, after the dying Eleanor has spoken her last words to Sarah, we read: "Now the beat was in the air. And above and before them, in level unerrant flight, the wild goose was leading the way."[24]

These parallelisms between Mary's novel and Virginia's are striking and real, but I was mistaken in thinking that by Mary's "sequel to *Orlando*" Virginia meant Part III of *Chase of the Wild Goose*. I discovered this when I came across a letter in the Hogarth Press Archives. The letter, dated 18 February 1937, is from Mary to Leonard Woolf. The situation is that the first edition of her novel has nearly sold out and the Press does not want to reprint it, which has greatly disappointed her because she is expecting the

20 Woolf, *Letters* 5, 435.
21 On Virginia's interest in the Ladies of Llangollen, and on the influence of their story on *Orlando*, see Jones.
22 Woolf, *Orlando*, 295.
23 Gordon, *Chase*, 53.
24 Gordon, *Chase*, 235.

forthcoming installation of the memorial to the Ladies of Llangollen to generate much further interest in the book. In March the Press was to change its mind and agree to a reprint, but Mary's present assessment is despondent: "It is plain that the wild goose is dead." She goes on to mention that she has two other books under construction. One, to be entitled something like *The Plas Newydd Papers*, would be "an appendix or second volume" to the book already published. The other she describes as "a work that is half finished on a very imaginative theme – the hero being a son of Virginia Woolf's Orlando and a spiritual son of Hermaphrodites". I confess that, when I first read this, I nearly fell off my chair with surprise. But there we have the true explanation of the "sequel to *Orlando*" and probably the main justification for "the Hermaphrodite".[25]

The next appearance of Mary in Virginia's letters to Ethel Smyth is on 16 January [1936]: "We have accepted Dr Gordon's second version of the L. of L: L[eonard] has read it: I've not."[26] The sixth and last mention Virginia makes of her is in a letter of 14 November 1940, written ten days after Mary penned her letter critical of *Roger Fry*:

> Your quondam friend, Dr Gordon, has written me about 10 pages of violent abuse of Roger Fry. Again I ask why. She never met him. She says she hates him; and that he's the spit and image of Russells Viper – a snake whose bite is small but deadly.[27]

Mary's letter, which actually occupies four large pages, is certainly very hostile to Roger, and it is true that she never met him, but she does not say that she hates him, and the comparison of him to a Russell's viper is Virginia's embellishment. It is to be noted that the editors of Virginia's letters misidentify Ethel's "quondam friend" as the harpsichordist (and clavichordist) Violet Gordon-Woodhouse.[28]

It seems that Mary had consulted Ethel about her book, and that Ethel either had suggested The Hogarth Press as a possible home for it or had agreed to have a word with Virginia about it. Even if Virginia had not described Mary as "your *quondam* friend", one would have guessed from her references to her, and not least from her description of her as

---

25 Another letter in the Hogarth Press Archives, dated 25 April 1938, from Mary to Leonard Woolf, probably refers to the same work: "I have decided not to offer my story again yet. I think the whole second half is so much better than the first that I hope to rewrite it."

26 Woolf, *Letters* 6, 6. See also Hogarth Press Archives, letter from Leonard Woolf, 2 January 1936, in which he informs Mary that the Press will publish her book in the spring, provided that she accepts certain suggestions for its improvement.

27 Ibid., 444.

28 Ibid., 444, n. 3.

"the Hermaphrodite", that she and Ethel were not now friends. It is very likely that the two had got to know one another over twenty years earlier. Between 1911 and 1913 Ethel was a very prominent and active campaigner for women's suffrage as a member of the Women's Social and Political Union, and on 9 March 1912 she was sentenced to two months' imprisonment with hard labour for breaking a window of the Berkeley Square residence of Lewis Harcourt, Secretary of State for the Colonies. We shall see that Mary was closely involved with both the suffragist campaign and prisons.

In 1937, the year after *Chase of the Wild Goose* appeared, Mary presented to the Church of St Collen, Llangollen, whose churchyard is the burial-place of the two ladies and their devoted Irish servant, Mary Carryl, and also the location of a memorial to the three, a sculpted marble relief, placed in the south aisle of the church, of Eleanor Butler and Sarah Ponsonby. At a service in the church in the afternoon of Sunday 4 July 1937 the plaque was unveiled by Thomas Evelyn Scott-Ellis, Eighth Baron Howard de Walden, of Chirk Castle, and dedicated by the Venerable James E. Williams, Archdeacon of Wrexham.[29] The sculptor was Violet ("Vi") Labouchere. A niece of the celebrated barrister Sir Edward Marshall Hall, she had recently (early in 1936) been commissioned to sculpt a marble plaque portraying his head in relief.[30] Vi, who lived in affluent circumstances in Kensington, seems to have taken up sculpture in a serious way quite well on in life, after her marriage to William John Richardson ("Jack") Matthews foundered.[31]

---

29 There is a report of the service and of Lord Howard's tribute to the Ladies of Llangollen in *The Llangollen Chronicle*, 9 July 1937, 4–5. See also *Wrexham and North Wales Guardian*, 7 July 1937, 8. In *The Manchester Guardian*, 5 July 1937, 10, there is a photograph of the memorial, reproduced in *Wrexham Leader*, 16 July 1937, 5. The cost was £600, the equivalent of about £42,000 in today's money (Hogarth Press Archives, letter from Mary Gordon to Leonard Woolf, 3 March 1937), which means that Mavor, 206, is mistaken in suggesting that it was paid for with the proceeds of the sale of *Chase of the Wild Goose*.

30 The plaque, which does not carry the sculptor's name, is fixed to a wall in the Inner Temple.

31 Mavor, 206, mistakenly calls Vi, who married Jack Matthews in 1904, "Miss Mathews [*sic*]". Vi, whose only child, Pamela (earlier "Pauline"), died in 1916 aged three, served as a volunteer in the Women's (later "Queen Mary's") Army Auxiliary Corps, in 1918–1919. At some stage she appears to have become a qualified nurse, for on the memorial in Llangollen she has carved "F.B.C.N." after her name – Fellow of the British College of Nurses. The BCN was established by Ethel Gordon Fenwick in 1926 as an alternative to the College of Nursing. It may have been Vi and Mary's shared professional interest in medical matters that brought them together. On 23 October 2010 the Norfolk auctioneers Horners sold a collection of thirteen letters to Vi from James Ramsay Macdonald, Britain's first Labour prime minister (1924,

It is often said that, in portraying the Ladies of Llangollen, she modelled Eleanor Butler on Mary Gordon, Sarah Ponsonby on herself. The tradition is not supported by any firm documentary evidence known to me, and the way Mavor mentions it suggests that her source is not a written one, but an oral one,[32] perhaps one or more of the persons in Llangollen, or elsewhere in Wales, who gave her information when she was doing the research for her book in the 1960s.[33] However, comparison between Vi's portrayals of the Ladies and photographs of her and Mary[34] suggests that the tradition may well be true, although a definite opinion is not possible. If the tradition is true, what does this tell us about Mary's and Vi's attitude to the Ladies and to one another? Mary hugely admired the Ladies and was no doubt happy to be identified with Eleanor Butler. Whether Vi felt the same way about them, we simply do not know. With the Ladies long dead and reliable likenesses of them unavailable, she needed models, and if Mary was willing to be the model for Eleanor, it is not unnatural that she used herself as the model for Sarah. One cannot safely assume that she wanted to identify herself with Sarah, let alone suggest that Mary's and her relationship was in any way like that between the Ladies. As well as being motivated by considerations of convenience, including the fact that the significant age-gap between herself and Mary (nineteen years) was similar to that between Sarah and Eleanor (sixteen years), she may have thought it amusing to model Sarah on herself. Suggestions that she was Mary's lover cannot be disproved, but are unsupported by any evidence.

1929–1931, then 1931–1935 in coalition). The eleven dated ones were written in 1926–1930. It has not been possible to access them, but it seems that the writer found Vi's shoulder a convenient and comforting one to cry on from time to time. Vi petitioned for a divorce from her husband in June 1935, and the decree absolute was granted on 27 January 1936. He planned to remarry, but did not live to do so, dying on 7 April 1936, which was to have been the day of the wedding. Vi, after a brave battle with cancer, ended her life with an overdose of "drugs self-administered while the balance of her mind was disturbed" on 28 October 1940, exactly a week before Mary Gordon wrote to Virginia Woolf.

32 Mavor, 206.

33 Mavor, 14.

34 Thanks to the kindness of Sally Smith QC and John Labouchere, Deborah Cheney and I have been able to examine two photographs of Vi. One shows her as a young woman. The other, in which she poses with one of her sculptures, the head of "a Negro Baby 'Hercules'", as she describes it, was almost certainly taken in the 1930s and therefore is more useful in connection with the memorial in Llangollen. The two photographs we have seen of Mary were taken in 1908 and 1922, and are less helpful, partly because their quality is less good, partly because they are so much earlier than Vi's sculpture of Eleanor Butler and Sarah Ponsonby.

What has been said about Mary so far may have given the impression of an eccentric. Certainly she was a very unusual person, but equally certainly she was no crank.

She came from Lancashire. She was born in Seaforth, Litherland, close to the north entrance to the River Mersey, on 15 August 1861. Her father, James Gordon, was a hide and tallow broker in Liverpool. Her mother, Mary Emily Gordon, was the daughter of John Wilson Carter, an accountant, and Eliza Carter. They married at the Church of St Helen, Sefton, on 29 September 1860. James, a widower, was aged about fifty – more than twenty years older than his new bride. Mary was the eldest of James's and Mary Emily's ten children (seven daughters and three sons), but had an older half-sister (Elizabeth Anne) and half-brother (James Edgar), born in 1852 and 1854 respectively. Elizabeth's and James Edgar's mother, Anne Barnsley Gordon *née* Shaw, had died from consumption when Elizabeth was two and James Edgar not quite nine months old.

Mary's parents must have been comfortably off. At the time of the 1861 census, when they only had James's two children by his first wife and Mary was expected, they were living in Church Road, Seaforth, with three live-in servants. In 1871, when their family was much larger, they were living in Blundell Sands, Great Crosby, with six servants, and in 1881 at Kenmore, Great Crosby, again with six servants.

Nothing seems to be recorded of Mary's early education. A quite thorough investigation of local possibilities, including Liverpool College for Girls and Liverpool Institute High School for Girls (Blackburne House), proved negative. It is possible that she was educated at home by governesses. It is also possible that she attended a school well away from home, but there were not many girls' public schools in the early 1870s, and there is no record of her having attended Cheltenham Ladies' College,[35] to which I addressed an enquiry not only because it was very much in business at that time, but also because it is not far from Colwall, on the Herefordshire side of the Malvern Hills, where her maternal uncle the Rev. Robert Oliver Carter was headmaster of the Grammar School (now The Elms School) from 1863 until his death in 1876. Moreover, Mary's two youngest sisters, Florence Cordelia and (Edith) Jessie, were educated there, entering in 1888 and 1889 respectively.

---

35 There is a gap in the College's admission registers from c. 1874 to 1882. Two girls called "Mary Gordon" are mentioned in the account book for 1878, but their parents and addresses are not given, and their ages (fifteen and fourteen) do not fit Mary Louisa Gordon.

According to her own account, Mary loved books, horses, and dogs,[36] and could have lived a life of leisure, but instead began to study medicine in her early twenties, motivated above all by a desire to learn about people. She mentions six years of study.[37] So it seems that she had already undertaken some medical studies for two years before she entered the London School of Medicine for Women (LSMW) at the beginning of the winter session 1886–1887 with student-number 171. The battle to open the medical profession to women in Britain had only recently been successful, thanks to the determination and pioneering achievements of Elizabeth Garrett (from 1871 Elizabeth Garrett Anderson), Sophia Jex-Blake, and others, and not all obstacles to the training and examination of female medical students had been removed. The LSMW, the first medical school for women in Britain, had opened on 12 October 1874 at 30 Henrietta Street (now Handel Street), Brunswick Square, in Bloomsbury. From 1877 its students were able to obtain clinical practice on the wards of the nearby Royal Free Hospital on Gray's Inn Road. In 1890 Mary Gordon obtained the Scottish triple qualification, becoming a Licentiate of the Royal College of Physicians (LRCP) of Edinburgh, the Royal College of Surgeons (LRCS) of Edinburgh, and the Faculty of Physicians and Surgeons[38] (LFPS) of Glasgow. She also became a Licentiate in Midwifery (LM).

The battle to enable women to enter the medical profession was part of the much wider campaign for women's rights, and Mary Gordon was a thoroughgoing feminist. After qualifying as a physician, surgeon, and general practitioner and being appointed Librarian and Curator of LSMW (a part-time post she held for two or three years), she interested herself especially in social medicine and the problems arising from poverty, prostitution, venereal disease, and alcoholism. By 1892[39] she was working as Clinical Assistant at the East London Hospital for Children and Dispensary for Women in Shadwell, established (on a different site) in 1868 by Nathaniel and Sarah Heckford in an area of dire poverty and deprivation. At some stage, although it is not clear exactly when, she worked also at the

---

36 Her love of animals and wild birds is revealed also in letters of hers in *The Times*, 30 March 1932, 12, and 17 May 1939, 10. In the earlier letter she mentions her tame monkey.

37 *Penal Discipline*, 1–2.

38 Not "Faculty of Physical Surgery", as given by Forsythe in his good article on Mary in *Oxford Dictionary of National Biography*. Surgery is always physical!

39 Cheney, 116 n. 1, gives Mary's tenure of this post as 1893–1895, but she took it up no later than 1892 (see LSMW's Annual Report for 1892 in London Metropolitan Archives, H72/SM/A/02/01) and, after quitting it in or about 1895, she seems to have held it again in 1898 (see *Memorial*, 7) and 1899 (see LSMW's Annual Report for 1899).

Evelina Children's Hospital in Southwark. In her letter to Virginia Woolf she says that she "was often abroad" in the years before Helen Coombe's marriage to Roger Fry, which was in December 1896. It is not clear what her foreign destinations were in the 1890s. It is known that she visited penal establishments in France, Belgium, the Netherlands, and the USA, but her visit to France at any rate took place "a few years before the war",[40] and so presumably later than 1896. Embarkation records reveal that she sailed from Southampton for New York on 3 September 1919, but there is no record of an earlier visit. From February 1891 she was a member of the Association of Registered Medical Women, founded in 1879, and it was she who, on behalf of that body's Acting Committee of five, wrote on 1 February 1898 to the Secretary of State for India, enclosing a memorial, addressed to him and signed by seventy-three Registered Medical Women in the United Kingdom and India, protesting against measures enacted in 1897 to deal with venereal disease in the army in India.[41]

It is an indication of her reputation as an expert on social and socio-medical problems that in March 1908 she was appointed His Majesty's Inspector of Prisons and Assistant Inspector of State and Certified Inebriate Reformatories. She was Britain's first female Inspector of Prisons. She was responsible only for women's prisons, but that responsibility was huge. In 1911 she inspected up to four times a year the Convict Prison at Aylesbury, the Borstal Institution for Girls there, thirty-eight local prisons in England and Wales, and seven Inebriate Reformatories. In those institutions there were about 42,600 female inmates. Also under her inspection regime were over five hundred officers, and she supervised the training of female prison-officers. Her starting salary of £300 a year, rising by annual increments of £10 to £400, was much lower than that of male inspectors of prisons, and in 1920 her salary, still only £400, was just half of the maximum paid to her male counterparts. In 1911–1912 and again in 1919–1920 she attempted to get this inequality rectified, but without success.[42]

Her appointment caused quite a stir in various quarters, both outside and inside the prison service, especially when she made it clear by her words and actions that she meant business and wanted changes. There was still more of a stir in 1914, when during a raid on Lincoln's Inn House, the headquarters of the Women's Social and Political Union (WSPU), on 23 May by Scotland Yard's Special Branch, a file of correspondence between Mary and the leading suffragette Emmeline Pethick-Lawrence was discovered, revealing

40 Gordon, *Penal Discipline*, 209.
41 *Memorial.*
42 National Archives.

that, while in the service of the Crown, Mary had been giving moral, advisory, and financial support to the WSPU between 1908 and 1911. One donation, made in October or November 1909, was earmarked for the Defence Fund of the militant suffragette Mary Leigh, described by Mary as "that Brick of Bricks". Given that Mary Leigh had smashed the windows of 10 Downing Street on 30 June 1908 and thrown roof-slates at the police and Prime Minister Asquith's car in Birmingham on 17 September 1909, Mary's support of her attracted particular attention when the correspondence was passed to the Home Office, but by that time all the letters were at least three years old and Emmeline Pethick-Lawrence had been expelled from the WSPU for opposing a new campaign of militant action. Moreover, the Home Office was still considering what to do about Mary when Britain declared war on Germany (4 August 1914) and suffragette prisoners were released from prison. So she kept her job.

Although she had to be careful about when and how she intervened, she was able to use her position as Inspector to keep an eye on the treatment of suffragette prisoners. One of those prisoners may have been Ethel Smyth.

In July 1916 she applied for paid leave of absence to enable her to join the Scottish Women's Hospitals' Serbian Transport Column in Macedonia. The Home Office was only too pleased to grant permission, commenting: "she will not be missed".[43] It is said that she was one of only two female civil servants released by the Home Office for active service overseas during the First World War, compared with 266 male civil servants.[44] Her secondment lasted five months, until December 1916.

Mary retired in 1921, when she reached the age of sixty. The following year saw the publication of her book *Penal Discipline*. The dedication reads:

> To B.M.
> D.D.
> M.S.
> and all other prisoners and captives –
> this book.

Of her years as an Inspector she writes:

> During my service I found nothing in the prison system to interest me, except as a gigantic irrelevance – a social curiosity. If the system had a good effect on any prisoner, I failed to mark it. I have no shadow of doubt of its power to demoralise, or of its cruelty. It appears to me not to belong to this time or civilisation at all.

43 National Archives.
44 Scottish Women's Hospitals.

My main argument here is that we not only do not deter, but that we do actually make-over our criminal to crime. The fallacy of applying force to a being who is inherently insusceptible of being managed by force, lies in the fact that the proceeding ends, not in the alteration of the prisoner's point of view, but in his spiritually triumphing over us, and bringing the strong arm of the law to naught. We merely ill-treat a man or woman who still ignores and escapes us.

The time is ripe for us to convince ourselves of this. We should turn a fresh leaf in our treatment of the offender, fortified not by precedent, or by age-long prejudice, but by the findings of science which is, at last, in the act of discovering the mechanism of the whole man. ... When we have abandoned penal discipline we must not let ourselves be dismayed by the size of our scrap-heap, or the cost of our new road, but take up the problem anew, and get on with solving it.[45]

The book presents a devastating criticism of the prison system in Mary's time, and indeed in ours. As her anonymous obituarist in *The British Medical Journal* says, "she implied, without explicitly saying so, that she looked upon the criminal as a sick person and not as a wrongdoer".[46] A lucid and interesting account and assessment of her work in prisons and her proposals for reform is provided by Deborah Cheney.[47] Mary's views about prisons and prisoners were so radically different from those of the Establishment that they were never going to be accepted. Nevertheless she managed to bring about significant improvements to the lives of female prisoners.

In March 1907, twelve months before she was appointed Inspector of Prisons, her novel *A Jury of the Virtuous* was published. Written under the pseudonym of Patrick Hood, it tells the story of Richard Ransome, a young man who has served a prison sentence for forgery, and the difficulties he faces in attempting to re-establish himself in respectable society (which constitutes the "jury of the virtuous"), despite the loyal and loving support of Hertha Traquhair, the good woman he marries.[48]

In her retirement Mary moved from London to Crowborough in Sussex, seven miles southwest of Tunbridge Wells. In 1924–1925 her address was

---

45 Gordon, *Penal Discipline*, xi–xii.
46 "Mary Gordon".
47 Cheney. The author, who has been helpful in connection with the present essay, is preparing a biography of Mary.
48 The novel, 368 pages and twenty-seven chapters long, was considered "much too long" and "wearisome" by the young Orlando ("Orlo") Cyprian Williams, who reviewed it, anonymously at the time. He was unaware of the real identity of the author. See [Williams].

Crest Hotel, but soon after that her home became Hawk Wood, Old Lane, St John's, a house that has been demolished to make way for new developments. It was from there that she wrote to Virginia Woolf, and it was there that she died on 5 May 1941, thirty-eight days after Virginia, no more than twenty miles away, committed suicide by drowning, and seventeen days after her body was recovered from the River Ouse. Mary was three months short of her eightieth birthday. The causes of her death are given as "a. Coronary Atheroma (Cardiac Asthma) b. Senile c. arteriosclerosis". The informant of the death, Winifred M. Preece, also of Hawk Wood and described as "Inmate", was very likely her housekeeper.[49]

3. Mary Gordon's letter to Virginia Woolf[50]

HAWK WOOD,
CROWBOROUGH,
SUSSEX.

Nov 4, 1940

Dear Mrs Woolf

I have just been reading your biography of Roger Fry – (the "Apostle[51] of Modern Ugliness" –) His life aim[52] and work make no appeal to me – a man so little aware of himself could not be aware of a great deal else. Your book brings back to me the most painful memories – for from[53] my early twenties I was a very great friend of Helen Coombe.

In your book she is only the pitiful nebulous ghost she had to be, but there was another Helen who does not appear at all – it is as though all trace of her had been lost. I have to remind myself that

---

49 From 1929 on, Mary placed several advertisements in *The Times* for domestic staff, including a "working housekeeper".
50 Monks House Papers, SxMs – 18/1/E.
51 Daugherty, 202, has "Assault" for "Apostle" – a strange misreading. Other artists who were called "the Apostle of Ugliness" include Delacroix, Courbet, Manet, Liebermann, Matisse, and Picasso. Mary gives Roger this title because he introduced the British public to modern artists, including Cézanne, Gauguin, Van Gogh, Matisse, and Picasso, in his Post-Impressionist Exhibitions in 1910 and 1912 and was influenced by them in his own work.
52 Daugherty, 202, has "aims".
53 Daugherty, 202, has "in".

that may have been the fact, for as I am in my 80th year perhaps there is no older friend of hers[54] now living. I think I was very little older than she was – An aunt of mine discovered her, and her son, my cousin, brought us together. She had just done excellently at the Academy schools, I was a young medical student, my cousin a brilliant "double first" Oxford man of the same age. For some years we met frequently and were a most harmonious trio, all developing the same ideas and ideals. We had of course to separate to go to our respective[55] work – Two of us never married, but to the end we were all friends. My home was not in London but I was invited to Helen's home. They were a large family without a father and all had to work. I remember Mrs Coombe as a lady and a very good mother. I also saw Helen a good deal at the house of her friend and mine Mrs Henry Crompton. Mrs Crompton was always good to her, as long as was possible and I know paid the expenses of the birth of Helen's son, and other expenses. For the years before her marriage I was often abroad and did not see much of her. She had a very hard life and after a starvation year in Paris came home looking very ill and could not have been well when she married. I wished your book could have said something about the courageous charming young Helen of those days, so eager to live and learn, so full of ideas, the most promising open minded of women. I dont use the silly word "unconventional" – for she was much more than that – She opened windows – and round her was always clean air.

The last time I saw her she had been in her home for about a year, she wrote and asked me to come to dinner with her at Willow Walk[56] and she had her little son[57] there. Her husband (whom I had never seen) must I think have been in America –.[58] My visit horrified me for although she was supposed to be quite well, I considered she was far from it – she was entirely changed, looked battered and dissipated, and was bitter and cynical and unhappy – That she had made the right marriage I shall never believe.

54 Daugherty, 202, has "her".
55 Daugherty, 202, has "separate".
56 22 Willow *Road*, Hampstead, was Helen's and Roger's home for five years from 27 February 1903. Daugherty, 202, has "Willows".
57 Julian Edward Fry, born 2 March 1901. Helen and Roger also had a daughter, (Agnes) Pamela Fry, born 29 May 1902. In July 1904 Helen lost a third child, who was unplanned, through miscarriage.
58 Roger left England for his first visit to America on 28 December 1904. He returned in February 1905.

I never saw her again.

I should like to tell you of an occurrence in our younger days.

In London I used to play about with[59] various men and women, and one of the men thought he was in love with me. He told me all about his life which had included experiences with chorus girls and bought women. The Trio had always believed that quite another personal standard than that was a sine qua non for a happy marriage. I told him I did not share his ideas, and turned him down – I was not in any case attracted to him.

Later he was seeing a good deal of Helen, and one day she came to see me and asked me if I cared about him, she had an idea that we had been friends. He had asked her to marry him but she had given him no reply, and of course if I, in any sense, came first, she would not consider it. Of course the young women of today dont do that. I replied that I was not in love with him, and she could do as she wished with a free conscience. She seemed very doubtful about marrying him[60] – but I said no more. When she had gone, I sent for him and asked him if he intended to marry Helen. He said he did. I said "Helen is my friend, I know what she feels and thinks about the necessary conditions for marriage. You would not suit her. She is free to marry you if she wishes, but you must first tell her what you told me." "She would refuse me." "All the more reason why she should know where she stands. I will not interfere in any way – if you will tell her yourself."

I imagine that Helen herself asked the questions, and got some very mitigated replies – but he came back to me and said "She has refused me. How am I ever to marry at this rate"?

"That is no business of mine. You understand perfectly well why you cannot have me, and cannot have Helen."

Helen said when next she saw me – "Mary I have to thank you I believe." We neither of us saw him any more.

We had no conventional outlook, but these things are a question of feeling,[61] insight, attitude, weltanschauung,[62] all good psychological values. This is why I have always thought that Helen

---

59 Daugherty, 203, omits "with".

60 Daugherty, 203, omits "about marrying him".

61 Daugherty, 203, has "feelings".

62 "World-outlook", "philosophy of life". Daugherty has "weltauschauung". "Analytical Psychology and Weltanschauung" is the title of an influential lecture first given by Jung in 1927. "Attitude", "introvert", and "extravert" are psychological terms in his thought, so this paragraph of Mary's letter is much coloured by her study of and with him.

would not be, and was not made happy by marriage. Of course her mental condition had introverted her, and in later years, had she recovered, I do not see how a feeling introvert could have lived with the explosive scattered sensational extravert that Roger Fry became with his advancing years.

You tell the story of a man without relationships – without women, without even the one woman – she is obliterated by his shock, and nothing is left in the foreground or the background of his soul. All that is left is a not too sane chase after his own ideas. His other "affairs" and anaemic traces of women are mere mouldy spots on the landscape of his restless unbalanced being. It is even hard on Helen that you claim so little for them. I who had talked with her so often upon the problem of human relationship,[63] cannot help the[64] phantasy of how things may still strike her in the "house not made with hands."

Your book is a story seen through the eyes of the most able of crystal gazers[65] – written with a matchless pen – but it is quite inhuman. The truth probably is that it beats you to tell it as it was.

You must forgive me, who even at my age have the vivid contrasting images before me of the young sane Helen I knew – and then of the heavy inert wreck alone in her dull poor home and about to be drawn again into the abyss of the unconscious – as I saw her last.

I need not ask you to keep this letter to yourself. And will you excuse the writing, which I am having to do lying down.

With my best regards

Yours sincerely
Mary Gordon.

Given Virginia's close friendship with and great admiration for Roger, one would expect her to have made a robust reply in his defence. But we shall probably never know whether she answered Mary's letter.

4. Helen Coombe, later Fry

Helen Coombe was born in Lee, Kent, on 23 March 1864, the eighth child of Joseph Coombe and his wife Laura Beaumont Coombe *née* Russell. The

---

63 Daugherty, 204, has "relationships".
64 Daugherty, 204, has "this".
65 Daugherty, 204, has "gazes".

couple were to have twelve children – six sons and six daughters – but the eldest daughter died, aged four, four years before Helen was born. Joseph and Laura were English, but Joseph was brought up in Waterford, Ireland, where his father, John Coombe, had established a successful business as a corn and flour merchant. Joseph joined the business and, after marrying Laura, the daughter of a doctor in Gravesend, Kent, in 1853, remained in it until 1863, when the whole family moved to England. Helen was the couple's first child not to have been born in Waterford.

From Lee the family soon moved to Hampstead, London. Joseph, now in partnership with William Raymond, continued to be involved with the buying, storing, and selling of corn, operating from wharfs and warehouses on the south side of the Thames. For ten years or so, until the mid-1870s, Raymond & Coombe flourished and the Coombe family lived in comfortable circumstances. But for a combination of reasons the business then underwent a sharp decline. The Coombes had to move from their fine house in Hampstead to a much more modest one in Hammersmith, and, when Joseph died in March 1883, the family's financial position was weak and would have been weaker still but for the generosity of Laura's parents.

Sometime in 1881, when she was seventeen, Helen entered the St John's Wood Art Schools ("The Wood"), established by the Peruvian artist Abelardo Álvarez-Calderón and opened probably in 1879. The teaching at The Wood had the main aim of preparing its pupils for entry to the Royal Academy Schools (RAS), and it fulfilled this aim with far greater success than any other school of art. Competition to enter the RAS, where tuition was (and still is) provided free of charge, was fierce, and the required standard of achievement was very high. Helen was admitted as a probationer on 30 December 1882, to study painting, and qualified as a full student on 13 March 1883, ten days before her nineteenth birthday and just three days before the death of her father.

In Helen's time the maximum period of a studentship in the RAS was six years. This period was divided into two three-year terms, and a stiff examination had to be passed before a student could proceed from the lower school to the upper school. Many students failed to make the grade – more than half of them in the years 1883–1890. Helen most certainly did make the grade, and moreover in December 1885 received from Sir Frederic Leighton, President of the Royal Academy, the prize of £10 (about £1,200 in today's money) awarded for the best drawing of a statue or a group. In the upper painting school there were separate classes for male and female students, and in December 1883 Helen had been one of sixty-four female students who signed a petition to the President and Council of the RAS that a life-class for the study of the partially-draped figure be established for female students.[66] The petition, supported by twenty-six women from outside the RAS, was successful.[67]

There is no record of when Helen left the RAS. She would have been entitled to stay until the end of 1888, but may have departed earlier than that. The courses in the RAS were traditional, and by the autumn of 1889 she was working and learning in a very different artistic environment, having joined the circle of decorative artists, designers, and writers, in which Arthur Heygate Mackmurdo, Herbert Horne, and Selwyn Image were the most prominent artists. The Century Guild, established by Mackmurdo and Horne in 1883, was formally dissolved after about five years, but the circle, which constituted an important branch of the Arts and Crafts Movement in the late nineteenth century, continued to flourish, based from October 1889 at 20 Fitzroy Street. Another manifestation of the broadening of Helen's artistic experience and development is that she studied at the National Art Training School in South Kensington.[68] It is not known exactly when she did this, or for how long, but it was probably in or about 1889.

It was not later than 1889 that she became closely acquainted with Lucy Henrietta Crompton, wife of the barrister Henry Crompton, and their sons, Paul and David. Her friendship with the Crompton family, who lived in Bloomsbury at 42 Mecklenburgh Square, is mentioned by Mary Gordon in her letter to Virginia Woolf. She says that she too was a friend of Lucy Crompton. Henry Crompton had a long record as an advocate of trade unions and workers' rights, as a supporter of women's education, and as a vigorous opponent of colonial oppression and injustice in all its forms. Mary is likely to have had much sympathy with a man who was so sociopolitically "progressive". Henry was also a leading Positivist, that is to say a follower of the Religion of Humanity founded by Auguste Comte. Arthur Mackmurdo too was for a time a Positivist, and what may well be the earliest of Helen's surviving paintings, a copy of *The Virgin and Child with St John and an Angel* assigned to the workshop of Botticelli,[69] belonged to James and Emily Geddes, who married one another in a Positivist ceremony in 1871. Representations of the Madonna and child played a significant part in Positivist worship, and it is likely that Helen was commissioned to make the copy, which, soon after Emily Geddes's death in 1929, her daughter, also named Emily Geddes, gave to the Corporation of Coventry.[70]

---

66 Royal Academy, RAA/SEC/8/15.
67 Royal Academy, RAA/PC/1/XVIII, p. 92.
68 Peacock, 87–88
69 National Gallery, London (NG275).
70 Helen's painting, in oils, is in the Herbert Art Gallery and Museum, Coventry.

Later, Helen was to paint the portrait of Lucy Crompton,[71] and it is not unlikely that she received other commissions from the family, perhaps including contributions to the adornment of the Positivist church in Chapel Street, when extensive alterations were made to it, under the direction of Henry Crompton and with the assistance of Paul Crompton, in 1893. Lucy and Paul were to be two of the witnesses at Helen's marriage to Roger Fry on 3 December 1896.

Apart from the painting owned by the Geddes family, the first artistic production of Helen known to survive and be on public display is a fine stained-glass window, installed in March 1896, in the Church of St John the Evangelist at High Cross, Hertfordshire. It was not her only stained-glass work to be much admired. It was followed by her beautiful decoration of the so-called "Green Harpsichord" made by Arnold Dolmetsch and exhibited at the Fifth Exhibition of the Arts and Crafts Exhibition Society in October–December 1896. Three years later she exquisitely decorated another instrument for Dolmetsch – a clavichord exhibited at the Sixth Exhibition of the Arts and Crafts Exhibition Society in October–December 1899 and at the First International Exhibition of Modern Decorative Arts in Turin in May–November 1902. At the same time she continued to paint pictures and earned high praise for them too.

Mary Gordon does not say exactly when she first met Helen, but she can hardly be right in telling Virginia Woolf that it was when she was in her *early* twenties. She was already twenty-five when she began her studies at the London School of Medicine for Women in 1886. That year may be considered the *terminus post quem* for her first meeting with Helen for another reason too. This is that the cousin who brought them together was not working in London before that. Although Mary does not name him, he can be identified with certainty as Frank Carter, eldest son of the Rev. Robert Oliver Carter and Elizabeth Fortune Carter *née* Peyton. He was educated at Uppingham School and Balliol College, Oxford, where he did indeed achieve a double first, as Mary says, in Classics (1881, 1883). He then taught Classics at King's School, Ely, for a year before doing the same at St Paul's School, London, from 1886 to 1896. Later he taught at McGill University in Canada before serving Winchester College as Sixth Form Classics master from 1903 to 1922. He was a first cousin of Mary, her mother and his father being sister and brother. The information that Helen spent "a starvation year in Paris" is "new". Again, no date is given. Mary makes it sound as though it was not very long before Helen's marriage in December 1896, but it was not in 1895–1896, when she was in London, and it was most likely sometime between spring 1891 and late 1894. Her

---

71 Sir William Rothenstein Correspondence.

studies there may have been at the Académie Julian or at the cheaper Académie Colarossi. It is also possible that she studied in more than one establishment. Both Académie Julian and Académie Colarossi attracted foreigners and accepted female students. Women were usually catered for in separate studios. At this time Académie Julian had several studios for them.[72] Roger Fry spent the first two months of 1892 studying in that institution, but, even if his time in Paris coincided with Helen's, they would not have been taught in the same studio.

Mary wishes Virginia "could have said something about the courageous charming young Helen of those days, so eager to live and learn, so full of ideas, the most promising open minded of women". In suggesting that Virginia is silent about Helen's charm and qualities of mind, she is being rather unfair. Unlike her sister, Vanessa Bell, Virginia never met Helen, but in 1938, when she had begun writing *Roger Fry*, she asked Robert ("Bob") Calverley Trevelyan, who knew both Helen and Roger very well, for his opinion of her, and she quotes this at some length.[73] Here are extracts from it:

> She was certainly one of the most charming and intelligent women I have ever known – I will not say intellectual, because she was a little impatient of purely intellectual discussions and ways of thinking – even in Roger. ...
>
> [She] may not have been really very beautiful; but she gave me the impression of being so. It is often so hard to distinguish charm and intelligence from beauty. Her movements were always graceful and unhurried and her way of talking too. She had a beautiful and expressive voice, and a quiet, humorous, often rather satirical smile.

In a letter to his Dutch fiancée, Elizabeth des Amorie van der Hoeven, written nearly forty years earlier, Bob Trevelyan went even further. Helen was quite a heavy smoker, who at least before her marriage smoked a pipe as well as cigarettes, prompting Roger to address her in jest as "mia madonna della pipa".[74] Elizabeth had expressed disapproval of her smoking, on the ground that it was detrimental to her health. In response, Bob allowed that smoking may have been somewhat harmful to her lungs, but maintained that it helped her art and her conversation, adding (somewhat tactlessly, one might think, given that he is writing to his future wife!):

> I always found her more interesting and amusing than any woman I have ever met, more original intellectually and aesthetically, with what I call genius, that is with a completely original personality.[75]

72 See Fehrer.
73 Woolf, *Roger Fry*, 102–103.
74 Letter of Saturday [31 October 1896], King's College Cambridge Archive Centre, REF/3/58/1.
75 Letter of 12 April 1900, Trinity College Cambridge Library, RCT 9.124.

Bob was far from alone in expressing high admiration for Helen. Goldsworthy Lowes Dickinson called her "that brilliant beautiful woman".[76] Richard Williams Reynolds, the subject of Essay 10, recalled her thus:

> One of the most interesting and attractive women I knew in London was Helen Coombe. Who introduced me to her, I do not remember. Perhaps it was George Street, who, I know, admired her, but it may equally well have been one of my socialist or artist friends. She was an artist herself of real talent. … Tall and graceful with pale wavy hair and light blue eyes, she suggested a Norse goddess, but she was clever and witty, and excellent company.[77]

Helen's striking appearance, strong personality, and independence of mind are also indicated in the comparison of her, made by a group of friends with whom she was staying in France, to the writer Ménie Muriel Norman *née* Dowie, famous in the 1890s for her adventurous travels, her "progressive" views on social and sexual issues, and her flamboyant dress.[78] The opinions of Helen selected so far all relate to the period when she was still single. But she continued to arouse admiration in the early period of her marriage. When Bernard Berenson, the authority on Italian art in the Renaissance, first met Helen and her husband in Florence in April 1898, he gave his sister Senda his impressions of them:

> Mrs. Costelloe has staying with her now a charming couple, Mr. and Mrs. Fry. They have not been married long, and they are both painters, but he is a university man and scholar to boot. She is the superior person, exquisitely humorous, and altho' relatively silent, is eloquent in her quiet looks. They are delightful to converse with, and she is very beautiful.[79]

Another eminent art historian, Tancred Borenius, friend of Roger Fry, wrote about Helen in his generally favourable but not uncritical review of Virginia's biography:

> as one who had the privilege of knowing Roger Fry's wife, I am specially appreciative of the graceful silhouette which Mrs. Woolf, from, I gather, no such first-hand contact, has drawn of her. Helen Coombe's was indeed a mind of singular distinction, fortunate also – the fact is worth recording – in having been nurtured on an early friendship with Oscar Wilde. And as to her gifts as an artist, I find it difficult to speak of them with moderation – I remember in particular an impression by her of some chalk pits in brilliant sunlight, fixed

---

76 Dickinson, *The Autobiography*, 116.

77 Typescript memoir, King's College Cambridge Archive Centre, REF/13/27, quoted by kind permission of the executor of the estate of Hermione Jolles.

78 Letter, written in late March 1896, perhaps from Barbizon, from Helen Coombe to Roger Fry, King's College Cambridge Archive Centre, REF/3/58/17.

79 Berenson Papers, letter of Easter Day, 10 April 1898.

on the canvas with a justness and certainty akin to Manet in his last phase. ...
It is, indeed, my full conviction, that in Helen Coombe there was lost one of
the truly great "might-have-beens" of English art.[80]

These and other comments fully confirm Mary Gordon's picture of "the
young sane Helen" as an exceptionally talented and attractive woman.

It was only about seven weeks after the meeting with Bernard Berenson
that Helen suffered her first major mental breakdown. It came suddenly and
explosively in late May 1898, but the first signs of problems had appeared
many months earlier. The illness, now recognised to have been chronic
paranoid schizophrenia, almost certainly had a genetic origin,[81] but there
is no evidence that Helen had any significant mental-health issues prior to
her marriage, and, although these would probably have developed in any
case, Mary's belief that her marriage to Roger Fry was not helpful to her
may well be correct.

It is not that he was unloving or uncaring towards her. On the contrary,
the indications are that he fully reciprocated her love for him and, when
she was unwell, spared no trouble and expense to assist her recovery. But
his exceptional energy and stamina, and his determination to make full
use of every moment of the day, could have been very tiring and trying for
someone whose inclinations, energy, and body-clock were more normal,
and especially for one whose physical health was not robust, as was the
case with Helen. No longer could she proceed at her own pace, no longer
was she independent. The loss of her independence was clearly something
she thought long and hard about before agreeing to marry Roger, and it is
significant that, when she had her first major breakdown, she turned against
him so emphatically that he was unable to visit her for three months.
Another problem for her was that, as well as having lost her independence,
she had married a man who was frequently away from home, lecturing,
rushing around the Continent in pursuit of pictures, and making extended
visits to America.

Virginia represents the Frys' honeymoon as "a time for both of them
of 'perfect happiness'".[82] But it was not exactly free from stress. After a
night in Rouen (4 December 1896), the couple spent several days in Paris

---

80 Borenius, 101.
81 See Essay 5, 128.
82 Woolf, *Roger Fry*, 96. She says that the Frys returned from their honeymoon in the
    autumn of 1897 (*Roger Fry*, 100). According to Spalding, 61, they returned in the
    spring of 1897 before leaving London in April 1897 "for an extended honeymoon in
    Italy" after Helen fell ill with pleurisy. Both of them are mistaken. The Frys returned
    to London about 10 August 1897, and Helen's attack of pleurisy occurred on or
    about 5 September 1897.

before continuing south. It was in Paris that their friend the writer Hubert ("Bertie") Crackanthorpe had disappeared a month earlier, and they spent much time assisting a solicitor who was there to make private enquiries on behalf of Bertie's wife. Bertie's body was recovered from the Seine on 23 December 1896, and a few days later the Frys learned the grim news from a French newspaper in Algeria. More bad news awaited them in Palermo: on 12 February 1897 Roger found a letter from Bertie's mother complaining that she had not heard from him and sending copies of his last letters, and Helen received news of the unexpected death of a very dear friend. Between Algeria and Sicily the Frys were in Tunisia. They spent the whole of January there. One evening they were taken by the British vice-consul in Bizerte, with whom they were staying, to witness a service of the Aissaoua, a Muslim sect whose devotees performed frenzied dances and ecstatic rituals. The party watched the worshippers abusing their bodies in various ways, which included the swallowing of nails and the munching of glass. Roger was fascinated. Helen's reaction is not recorded, but it is hard to believe that the event had no impact on a woman of her sensitivity and intelligence, and it is possible that it helped to trigger the mental disturbances that were to afflict her later in 1897 and, more dramatically, in 1898. It may well be significant that the reports of her behaviour in mental institutions mention violence involving glass. In one episode she broke through a plate-glass window before being held on a parapet by a nurse. In another she bit glass out of a tumbler and had to be stopped from jumping on broken glass.

If Mary Gordon is right in thinking that Roger was in America when she last saw Helen, the visit was probably in January–February 1905. In 1904 Helen's mental health had improved after a second spell in an asylum late in 1903, during which her mother died, but in the second half of the year her physical health had been poor: in July she suffered a miscarriage; in August she had a minor gynaecological operation; for most of September and October she was confined in an isolation hospital with a severe attack of scarlet fever; and in the same period she also had an attack of rheumatic fever.

Early in 1907 her mental health deteriorated again, and in July she was received and detained in a mental asylum under the 1890 Lunacy Act. She was there for eight months, until March 1908. After this third spell in an asylum she never properly recovered, and on 7 November 1910 she was admitted to The Retreat, the Quaker mental institution in York. She was never released and never saw her children again before her death from a cerebral haemorrhage on 30 April 1937, aged seventy-three. Roger, who, despite his affairs with Vanessa Bell and other women, remained married to her, had died on 9 September 1934, and his sister Agnes commented on

Helen's death: "it matters to v. few".[83] It is touching that three years later Mary Gordon vividly remembered the times when Helen was young, sane, and successful, when her life mattered to many.

Acknowledgements

I warmly thank the following: Alexander Turnbull Library, National Library of New Zealand; Deborah Cheney; Suzanne Foster, Archivist, Winchester College; Foundation of the Works of C. G. Jung for permission to receive copies of correspondence between Jung and Mary Gordon; Hochschularchiv der ETH Zürich, especially Yvonne Voegeli; Jill Irving, Herbert Art Gallery and Museum, Coventry; Hugh James Solicitors, acting for National Westminster Bank plc (NatWest), for advising that Mary Gordon's letter of 4 November 1940 to Virginia Woolf is out of copyright;[84] Danell Jones; Peter Jones, Llangollen Museum; King's College Cambridge Archive Centre; King's College London Archives; Guyon Labouchere; Joan Labouchere; John Peter Labouchere; Liverpool Record Office; London Metropolitan Archives; National Archives, Kew; Celia Pilkington, Archivist, Inner Temple; Rachel Roberts, Archivist, Cheltenham Ladies' College; Random House for permission to obtain copies of documents in the Hogarth Press Archives on deposit in University of Reading Special Collections; Royal Academy of Arts Library and Archive; Lucinda Ferguson Smith; Sally Smith, QC; Somerville College Oxford Library; Anne Thomson, Archivist, Newnham College Cambridge; Trinity College Cambridge Library; University of Reading Special Collections, especially Alexandra Fisher; University of Sussex Special Collections for permission to publish in full Mary Gordon's letter of 4 November 1940 to Virginia Woolf; Villa I Tatti, Fiesole, and its Archivist, Ilaria Della Monica; Judith Walton, Durham University Library; Wellcome Library, Special Collections, especially Lesley A. Hall, former Senior Archivist, and Amanda Engineer.

---

83 Margery Fry Collection, Box 19.6, letter from Agnes Fry to Margery Fry, 6 May [19]37.

84 Mary Gordon was unmarried and childless and did not appoint a literary executor. In her Will dated 15 August 1939 she appointed as her executor and trustee the National Provincial Bank Ltd, which was absorbed into NatWest in 1970. I therefore asked Hugh James, who act for NatWest in matters of probate, for permission to publish the letter if it were judged still to be protected by copyright.

References

Berenson Papers. Bernard and Mary Berenson Papers (1880–2002). Biblioteca Berenson, Villa I Tatti – The Harvard University Center for Italian Renaissance Studies, Fiesole, Italy. Letter from Bernard Berenson to Senda Berenson, 10 April 1898.

Borenius, Tancred. Review of *Roger Fry: A Biography*, by Virginia Woolf. *The Burlington Magazine* 77, no. 450 (September 1940), 100–102.

Cheney, Deborah. "Dr Mary Louisa Gordon (1861–1941): A Feminist Approach in Prison." *Feminist Legal Studies* 18 (2010), 115–136.

Daugherty, Beth Rigel. "'You see you kind of belong to us, and what you do matters enormously': Letters from Readers to Virginia Woolf." *Woolf Studies Annual* 11 (2006), 1–212.

Dickinson, G. Lowes. *The Autobiography of G. Lowes Dickinson and Other Unpublished Writings*. Edited by Dennis Proctor, with a Foreword by Noel Annan. London: Duckworth, 1973.

Fehrer, Catherine. "Women at the Académie Julian in Paris." *The Burlington Magazine* 136, 1100 (November 1994), 752–757.

Forsythe, Bill. "Mary Louisa Gordon (1861–1941)." *Oxford Dictionary of National Biography*. Oxford: Oxford University Press, 2004; online edition, January 2008, accessed 8 February 2015.

Gordon, Mary. *Chase of the Wild Goose: The Story of Lady Eleanor Butler and Miss Sarah Ponsonby, Known as the Ladies of Llangollen*. London: The Hogarth Press, 1936.

———. *Penal Discipline*. London: George Routledge & Sons, Ltd.; New York: E. P. Dutton & Co., 1922.

Hogarth Press Archives MS 2750/129. File on Mary Gordon, *Chase of the Wild Goose*. Deposited by Random House in University of Reading Special Collections.

Hood, Patrick (pseudonym of Mary Gordon). *A Jury of the Virtuous*. London: Hurst & Blackett, Limited, 1907.

Jones, Danell. "The Chase of the Wild Goose: The Ladies of Llangollen and *Orlando*." In *Virginia Woolf: Themes and Variations: Selected Papers from the Second Annual Conference on Virginia Woolf*, edited by Vara Neverow-Turk and Mark Hussey. New York: Pace University Press, 1993, 181–189.

Jung, Carl Gustav. Correspondence with Mary Gordon. Her letters of 31 July 1928 (Hs. 1056.236) and 10 June 1939 (Hs. 1056.7953), his of 28 June 1930 (Hs. 1056.737) and 11 June 1939 (Hs. 156.8482). Among the C. G. Jung Papers deposited in the Hochschularchiv der ETH Zürich.

———. *Introduction to Jungian Psychology: Notes of the Seminar on Analytical Psychology Given in 1925*. Edited by William McGuire, introduced by Sonu Shamdasani. Princeton: Princeton University Press, 2011.

Margery Fry Collection. Somerville College Oxford Library.

"Mary Gordon, L.R.C.P.&S." *The British Medical Journal*, 24 May 1941, 800. Anonymous.

Mavor, Elizabeth. *The Ladies of Llangollen*. London: Michael Joseph, 1971.

Memorial Addressed to the Secretary of State for India on the Subject of the Measures Recently Adopted for Dealing with Contagious Disease in the Indian Army. London: Her Majesty's Stationery Office, 1898.

Monks House Papers (Virginia Woolf). Special Collections, University of Sussex, Brighton. Correspondence between Ben Nicolson and Virginia Woolf, August 1940; letter from Mary Gordon to Virginia Woolf, 4 November 1940.

National Archives, Kew. Home Office File on Mary Gordon's Service as HM Inspector of Prisons. Reference HO 45/10552/163497.

Peacock, Sandra J. *Jane Ellen Harrison: The Mask and the Self*. New Haven: Yale University Press, 1988.

Read, Herbert. "Roger Fry". Review of *Roger Fry: A Biography*, by Virginia Woolf. *The Spectator*, 2 August 1940, 124.

Royal Academy of Arts Library and Archive, London. Records of the Royal Academy of Arts Schools.

Scottish Women's Hospitals. "Home Office Civil Servants in the SWH". http://scottishwomenshospitals.co.uk/home-office-civil-servants-in-the-swh/, posted 27 April 2014, accessed 8 February 2015.

Sir William Rothenstein Correspondence and Other Papers (MS Eng 1148/1727). Houghton Library, Harvard University. Letter from Helen Coombe to Alice Knewstub, dated Sunday.

Spalding, Frances. *Roger Fry: Art and Life*. London: Paul Elek / Granada Publishing, 1980.

[Williams, Orlando Cyprian]. Unattributed review of *A Jury of the Virtuous*, by Patrick Hood [= Mary Gordon], *The Times Literary Supplement* 271 (22 March 1907), 94.

Woolf, Virginia. *The Diary of Virginia Woolf*. Edited by Anne Olivier Bell, assisted in vols 2–5 by Andrew McNeillie. 5 vols. London: The Hogarth Press, 1977–1984.

———. *The Letters of Virginia Woolf*. Edited by Nigel Nicolson, assisted by Joanne Trautmann. 6 vols. London: The Hogarth Press, 1975–1980.

———. *Orlando: A Biography*. London: The Hogarth Press, 1928.

———. *Roger Fry: A Biography*. London: The Hogarth Press, 1940.

———. *A Room of One's Own*. London: The Hogarth Press, 1929.

Wordsworth, William. "To the Lady E.B. and the Hon. Miss P." In *The Poetical Works of William Wordsworth*, edited by Thomas Hutchinson. London: Humphrey Milford, Oxford University Press, 1920, 272.

7

"I am afraid I am not Irish": Letters from Rose Macaulay to Katharine Tynan

1. Introduction

Among the Papers of Katharine Tynan and Pamela Hinkson (KTH) in the University of Manchester Library are thirteen letters, previously unpublished,[1] from Rose Macaulay to Katharine Tynan (Hinkson). The letters, written between 1913 and 1930 and not a complete collection of those Rose wrote to Katharine,[2] discuss the work of writer and addressee and comment on family matters and literary friends. No letters from Katharine to Rose survive: any that were saved would have perished when Rose's flat in London was destroyed by a German bomb during the night of 10–11 May 1941,[3] but Katharine writes about Rose and her contacts with her in her memoirs and elsewhere.

Born in Dublin on 23 January 1859, Katharine was Rose's senior by twenty-two years and by 1913 was well established as a novelist and poet. Her output was, and continued to be, prodigious, despite her very poor eyesight. Rose, born in Rugby on 1 August 1881, had published six novels between 1906 and 1912. Although she had written some poetry and was to publish collections of it in 1914 and 1919, she was at this stage known as a promising young novelist. Her output was to continue to be steady – good by normal standards, but less prolific than Katharine's. Katharine was Irish and Roman Catholic, Rose British and Anglican; Katharine was a

---

1 LeFanu, the only one of Rose's biographers who was able to consult the archive, which was donated in 1986, makes a brief quotation from Letter 1 (LeFanu, 98) and two longer quotations from Letter 2 (112).

2 A transcript of a list of correspondence, compiled by Pamela Hinkson, mentions "22 letters and cards" from Rose Macaulay to Katharine, without giving any dates or other details, and it is not known if the nine missing items survive. The transcript is in a private collection.

3 In the last paragraph of Letter 1 Rose states her intention to keep Katharine's first letter to her "always".

married woman until the death of her husband, Henry Albert Hinkson, in 1919, with three children living,[4] Rose unmarried and childless, but from 1918, unknown to Katharine and almost everyone else in the world, in a relationship with a married Irishman, Gerald O'Donovan, a former Roman Catholic priest.

The correspondence and friendship between the two writers was initiated by Katharine. In 1911 both had entered the publisher Hodder & Stoughton's £1,000 Prize Novel Competition[5] – Katharine with *Molly, My Heart's Delight*, described by her as "a somewhat painstaking study of Mrs. Delany and her times",[6] Rose with *The Lee Shore*. On 30 July 1912 it was announced that Rose had won the first prize of £600. Katharine's entry, in her own words, "had not passed the weeder-out".[7] In April 1912 Rose and her father, George Campbell Macaulay, had met the judge Sir John Ross and his son Ronald on a Hellenic cruise, and she accepted an invitation to stay with the Rosses at their home in Co. Tyrone, Ireland, in August of that year, just after she was awarded the prize, but before *The Lee Shore* was published. After the book appeared on 18 October 1912 she sent her hosts a copy, which the Rosses lent Katharine when she was staying with them. In *The Years of the Shadow* Katharine recalls:

> I must confess that I took the book with no great anticipations. I had an unfounded suspicion that a Prize Novel could not be a good novel from a literary point of view. … Ever since *The Lee Shore* I have been making my apologies to the distinguished literary men who sat in judgment.[8] … This delicate, humorous, gently satiric, tender book, like the others of Miss Macaulay's making, stands out as something most satisfying to the literary sense … I wrote to Miss Macaulay to tell her how I loved *The Lee Shore*, and established a friendship with her which is added to by my friendship with her creatures. The Crevequers – those fascinating vagabonds who crop up again and again in Miss Macaulay's books – Peter of *The Lee Shore*, Benjy[9] of *Views and*

---

4 Katharine and Henry, who was a Protestant, married in London on 4 May 1893. Her first baby was stillborn in May 1894; her second, Godfrey Assumption Francis Hinkson, died on 30 September 1895, when only six weeks old.

5 The deadline for submissions, originally 31 August 1911, was extended to 1 January 1912. See *The Bookman* 40, no. 238 (July 1911), 151.

6 Tynan, *The Years of the Shadow*, 97.

7 Tynan, *The Years of the Shadow*, 97.

8 The three adjudicators were not all men. One was Beatrice Harraden. The others were William Robertson Nicoll and Clement King Shorter. In dealing with "the hundreds of manuscripts submitted", they were assisted by a team of readers. See *The Bookman* 42, no. 251 (August 1912), 190–191.

9 The correct spelling is "Benjie".

Vagabonds, all the other sweet, impracticable, humorous, delightful creatures walk the world with me since I have met them.[10]

Evidently the comments Katharine made in her first letter to Rose were equally warm, and it is no wonder that they were so well received, coming from a well-regarded senior writer. One cannot help but notice the similarity of some of Katharine's comments here and in her later article on Rose in *The Bookman*[11] to some of those of an anonymous reviewer of *The Lee Shore* in *The Spectator* in October 1912,[12] who starts by expressing doubt about the value of prize competitions, whether in art, music, or literature, but continues:

> Let us hasten, then, to admit that these generalizations do not in the least apply to the success of Miss Rose Macaulay. ... To begin with, ... she has already made her mark by at least three novels of quite uncommon merit. ... But this is not all. *The Lee Shore* is emphatically not the sort of book that any well-conducted competitor would write who wanted to win the prize.
>
> ... [I]n an age when the worship of success is perhaps more pronounced than it has ever been before, it is unusual to find a book succeeding by its exceptionally sympathetic treatment of unsuccess, by its tender handling of ineffectual lives. ... We congratulate the judges on their discernment and Miss Macaulay on her triumph.

Although it is possible that the similarities either are coincidental or result partly from Katharine having read the review in *The Spectator*, it is tempting to identify her as the reviewer. Whatever the case may be, there is a chronological problem with Katharine's account in *The Years of the Shadow*. This is that, whereas her letter to Rose about *The Lee Shore* was written not later than early May 1913, in her memoir she places her visit to the Rosses and her first acquaintance with the novel in the autumn of 1913.[13] She did indeed stay with the Rosses in October 1913,[14] but she must have read *The Lee Shore* not later than the spring of that year. I can find no record of her having made a visit to the Rosses between October 1912 and May 1913, but it seems that such a visit did take place.

10 Tynan, *The Years of the Shadow*, 97.
11 See n. 59 below.
12 "Fiction: The Lee Shore", *The Spectator*, 26 October 1912, 652–653.
13 Tynan, *The Years of the Shadow*, 90, 96.
14 See Atkinson, 358.

2. The Letters

Editorial note

In general, the way in which the letters were written has been faithfully preserved, but, for the sake of clarity, some minor alterations have been made. Dates of letters are presented in a full and standardised form, e.g., "7 January 1926" for "7.1.1926" in Letter 11. Titles of books, periodicals, and newspapers are italicised, while those of articles and individual poems are placed in quotation marks. Also italicised are words that were underlined for emphasis. Ampersands have been converted to "and". Square brackets indicate an editorial supplement, e.g., "2 October [1925]" in Letter 10. Angled brackets indicate a correction, e.g., "16 January 191<6>" in Letter 3, where Rose mistakenly gave the year as "1915".

Letter 1 (KTH 6/23/2)

Southernwood,
Great Shelford,
Cambridge.
6 May 1913

Dear Madam

I feel very proud and honoured by your letter. I have for so long got pleasure from your writings – may I say more especially from your poetry? Perhaps that is chiefly because I know it better than the novels, perhaps because poetry one cares for is more unusually met with. I remember when I was a child coming across your verses about an orchard, and being haunted for many days in a hot summer by "Good is an orchard, the saint saith, to meditate on life and death, with a cool well, a hive of bees ..."[15] It seemed to me, and still seems, to convey the cool peace and loveliness of an orchard on a hot day so extraordinarily vividly. So, you see, that alone would be a reason for feeling proud of your letter. But I think I love all your poetry. I am ashamed not to know the novels better – those I do know I like so much, but I must read some more. I don't know why the office boy should have turned yours back and let mine through – these things are mysteriously arranged, and

---

15　"Of an Orchard", lines 1–3 (Tynan, *Collected Poems*, 316). In June 1916 Katharine's daughter, Pamela, aged fifteen at the time, composed a poem entitled "In the Orchard" (KTH 14/3/5). Unlike her mother's poem, it is melancholic.

I should very much like to know just how. I was extremely startled when I heard I had got the prize – it was the last thing I had ever expected – and not all the jeers of my friends at my having won a Novel Competition could damp my joy in my £600, which is being enormously useful and profitable. Money *is* nice to have.[16]

Really, I am so very glad that you liked my book, and my Peter.[17] I wish I knew your little Peter.[18] I hope he will have better luck in his life than mine, and end with something more than a donkey cart. I am glad you liked the Italian parts of the book – I was brought up in Italy as a child, and feel it is more home than anywhere else.[19] It is certainly the best country in the world.

I am afraid I am not Irish: I wish I was. I was staying there last summer, with the Rosses in Tyrone, and loved it very much. It always seems to me to have more sheer charm, that is quite unexplainable, than any other country.

I hope you won't read *Abbots Verney*, or *The Valley Captives*, they are rather dull. I like *The Furnace* better, and *Views and Vagabonds* – this sounds gross conceit, but I don't mean they are particularly good, only I expect you would like them better than the others. *Abbots Verney* is an extremely early effort, written when I was barely grown up,[20] and I fear it is stodgy and badly lacks form, and would bore you. *The Furnace* I can't help being most attached to, not because it has merits, but because it is about my home in Italy partly. I expect you too know that one cannot help having favourites in one's own books, quite regardless of their worth.

I am writing one now, but I don't know when it will come out.[21]

---

16 £600 in 1912 is equivalent to about £70,000 today. The money was particularly welcome to Rose because it consolidated her position as a professional writer and made it easier her for to spend time in London even before late 1913, when, with help from her wealthy uncle Regi Macaulay, she acquired a small flat there.

17 Peter Margerison ("Margery"), the androgynous anti-hero of *The Lee Shore*. On the way many of Rose's characters do not conform to conventional types of masculinity and femininity, see Smith, vii–viii, and for detailed discussion, Passty.

18 For Katharine's "little Peter", see Letter 2 and n. 25.

19 Rose's family moved from Rugby to Varazze, near Genoa, in 1887, when she was six, and remained there until 1894. The last chapter of *The Lee Shore*, entitled "On the Shore", has "a young man, with a small donkey-cart and a small child and a disreputable yellow dog" (Macaulay, *The Lee Shore*, 299), selling embroidery, made by himself, in and near Varazze. The young man is Peter, and for him, as for Rose when she was a child, the place is an Eden.

20 Rose's first novel, published on 7 December 1906, when she was twenty-five.

21 *The Making of a Bigot*, published on 2 March 1914.

I should be most honoured and interested if you reviewed it – I hope you will, but perhaps you won't like it. I don't know its name even yet.

  Thank you extremely for your gracious and delightful words about my book – I shall always keep your letter as a great treasure. Appreciation from those whose work one has so long admired is a great joy and honour.

Yours with gratitude
Rose Macaulay

Letter 2 (KTH 6/19/2)

More than thirty months separate Letters 1 and 2. It is not certain, but seems likely, that there was no communication between the two writers in the interval. What is certain is that Rose has not written since the death of her father on 6 July 1915, and if there had been an exchange since the publication of *The Two Blind Countries*,[22] her first collection of poems, on 1 April 1914, one might expect her to have sent Katharine a copy of it then rather than now. Her father's death explains why the first side of the paper on which Letter 2 is written has a mourning border.

Southernwood,
Great Shelford,
Cambridge.
Xmas Day 1915

My dear Mrs Tynan Hinkson

It was very nice to get your letter this morning, and very nice of you to write to me again. I nearly wrote to you some months ago, when I got your book *Flower of Youth*, because I wanted to tell you how very much I liked it. Best of all, perhaps, that poem itself (which thank you much for sending me – also the charming Xmas one)[23] but so many of the others too – "All Souls," and the lovely "Song for the New Year," the "Prayer for those that return" (perhaps

22 Macaulay, *The Two Blind Countries*.

23 "Flower of Youth", in Tynan, *Flower of Youth*, 54–55, and Tynan, *Collected Poems*, 195–196, is a five-stanza poem of consolation for parents who have lost their sons and for wives who have lost their husbands, picturing the young men in Heaven as happy, safe, and retaining their youth. Such was its popularity that the publishers sold copies of it separately at twopence each, with the profits going to Dublin Castle Red Cross Hospital. Evidently Katharine sent Rose one of these and also a copy of another poem in the collection, "Christmas in the Year of the War", printed in Tynan, *Flower of Youth*, 68.

nursing wounded soldiers in a Red + hospital brings that one especially home to me)[24] and "To Two Bereaved" – I can't name them all, but they are very beautiful. "Flower of Youth" itself, of course, I simply love. I first came across it when I was feeling rather unhappy about the death at the war of several intimate friends of mine – Rupert Brooke was one – the sort of people who just can't be spared – and it gave me a feeling of comfort that nothing had before. So thank you very much. It is a book you must be tremendously glad to have written, because it must have comforted so many people this last horrible year, when everyone needs all the comfort they can get. You must be thankful that your "Peter" (I like to think of him as that) isn't old enough yet to fight; and I hope the other one won't have gone *very* far from home before it's all over.[25] My own brother[26] is in Serbia – a horrid place to be, because one doesn't hear much. We've not had a word from him since that week of fighting that began about Dec 6th, and it makes one anxious, though of course we know the Serbian posts are very bad and comfort ourselves with that. Xmas, of course, is a [*sic*] especially sad time for everyone this year. We've not only a brother in Serbia, as well, of course, as all the friends and relations killed that everyone must love, but my father has also died in the last few months; and I think there are times when one's father seems a greater loss than any other could be.

I am not writing much just now, I think my brain is gone, with all this nightmare horror; also I am very busy working in a V.A.D.[27] hospital here. It is rather absorbing work. The soldiers are dears; I love them.

24 From the summer of 1915 Rose had been working in the Red Cross auxiliary hospital near her home. Later in this letter she calls the work "rather absorbing", but her service there was not a success, and early in 1916 she became a land girl, although she continued to do part-time work at the hospital for a while longer.

25 "Peter" in this context is the younger of Katharine's surviving sons, Giles Aylmer Hinkson, known to family and friends as Pat or Bunny. Born on 7 February 1899, he was soon to be seventeen. He had attended Shrewsbury School in 1914–1915 and was now at Sandhurst Royal Military College. He joined the Royal Dublin Fusiliers and served in France and Belgium until the Armistice. His brother, Theobald ("Toby") Henry Hinkson, born 12 August 1897, had joined the Royal Irish Regiment and was to serve in Macedonia and Palestine. Both survived the war.

26 William ("Will") John Conybeare Macaulay, who had taken up farming in Canada in 1906, served in the King's Royal Rifle Corps. He was to be wounded in France on 3 October 1918. He lost his left lung and the use of his left arm, but returned to his farm in Alberta.

27 Voluntary Aid Detachment.

I have a copy doing nothing of my poems,[28] so I am sending it in case you care to see it (at least I must wait till the Post Office opens again) – but to me they seem very remote and anti-war, and I can't feel like that now – the other worlds seem to be a long way away behind very thick veils while this one is so insistent and so horrible.

I think it is wonderful you were able to induce "Peter" to write letters with his pencils! My brothers never would have![29]

It has just occurred to me (since you kindly asked if I'd like the book) that though I have got it for myself, I would so love to have a copy of your poems from you, with your name in it, and if I had I would send my own to my sister who is nursing in France,[30] who would love it! Is i<t>[31] a very bold and grasping thing to ask? Don't hurry, anyhow – only it would add so much value to the book.

With very many thanks

Yours very sincerely
Rose Macaulay
P.S. I'm sorry my ink is so smudgy

Letter 3 (KTH 6/19/1)

Rose's dating of this letter, 16 January 1915, is incorrect. Rupert Brooke is dead, and he died on 23 April 1915. Moreover, reference is made to the withdrawal from Gallipoli, which took place on 8–9 January 1916.

Southernwood
Great Shelford
Cambridge
16 January 191<6>

My dear Mrs Tynan Hinkson

Thank you so much for your letter, and for saying you will send me your poems,[32] and thank you too for liking mine, which pleases me much and makes me proud. Tell Pamela I am glad she likes

---

28 *The Two Blind Countries.*

29 Will was Rose's only brother alive. Her other brother, Aulay Ferguson Macaulay, was murdered on 11 February 1909 while serving with the Royal Engineers in the North-West Frontier Province of India.

30 Jean ("Jeanie") Babington Macaulay was with the French Red Cross.

31 Rose has written "is".

32 Probably the signed copy of *The Flower of Youth*, requested in Letter 2, but perhaps *The Flower of Peace*, mentioned later in this letter.

them too. And I like hers – please thank her. I love the last 3 lines especially – the golden street.[33] I shall keep it.

I am glad she likes Rupert Brooke. I love "When Beauty and beauty meet",[34] too; – one of the best, I think. I think those early things of his are very uneven – some beautiful extremely, others jarring in parts, many both. Don't you love – and doesn't Pamela love – "Grantchester"?[35] He lived there for some time, you know, in an old house among deep meadows, by the river. I've paddled about there with him so often. He was one of the most loveable people I have ever known – such a refreshing sense of humour and comedy, with all the other things he had. I've known him always – we played cricket together when we were children.[36] There never was a poet more alive or more unselfconscious or more

---

33 Pamela Mary Hinkson, born on 19 November 1900, was now fifteen. From an early age she showed herself to be a chip off the old block in respect of literature. She was only just fourteen when she had five reviews of books for girls printed in *The Bookman* (Hinkson, "Post Scriptum"), and still fourteen when her poem "A Song of Autumn" was published. Her first novel, *The End of All Dreams*, and a story for girls, *The Girls of Redlands*, appeared in 1923. As well as being successful herself, she was of great assistance to her mother, when the latter's eyesight went from bad to worse. The poem on which Rose comments here is unidentified.

34 Brooke, 101. The poem was composed in 1912.

35 "The Old Vicarage, Grantchester" (Brooke, 93–97).

36 The Macaulays moved to Great Shelford, about three miles from Grantchester, in early October 1906, which happened to coincide with Rupert's entry into King's College, Cambridge. But the Brookes and Macaulays already knew one another well. Rupert's father, William Brooke, and Rose's father, George Macaulay, were both masters at Rugby School, and the two families lived in the same road. When the Macaulays left Rugby for Italy on 15 September 1887, Rupert was only a few weeks old, but the families kept in touch and saw one another when the Macaulays came to England from Varazze for holidays and after they returned to live in Oxford in 1894. Rose and Rupert's friendship became close, but never more than platonic, from 1906 on. They enjoyed boating and swimming, as well as talking, together, and the young poet Michael Travis, the hero of Rose's third novel, *The Secret River*, published on 5 March 1909, is partly modelled on Rupert, as are two characters in *Views and Vagabonds* – Benjie Bunter, the protagonist, and his younger brother, Jerry, a minor figure. The latter novel, Rose's fifth, was published on 8 February 1912, and in it she pokes gentle fun at Rupert's Fabian ideas. Quite often she had his company in London. Late in her life she recalled that he "walked about the streets without a map, often with a plaid rug over his shoulders, as if he was Tennyson, which seemed to me a very good idea and gave him prestige, and people turned to look at him as he strolled through Soho with his golden hair and his rug, and I was proud to be with him" (Macaulay, "Coming to London – XIII", 32).

sweet-tempered and sane. His poetry was getting more and more, I think, and would have.[37]

Tho' one is glad to have left Gallipoli, it brings home to one the awful *waste* of lives like his – given for nothing. Three of my friends have died there – and so many thousands of other people's. But when it seems all waste, then is the time to read your poetry, I think! I would love to read *Flowers of Peace*.[38] I haven't ever, yet. I suppose, as you say, it came out at a bad time. But I know I should like it. And I *am* glad there is going to be another one soon.[39] They are very comforting, you know, as well as lovely. I am going to read *Twenty-five Years* too.[40]

I suppose my poems perhaps *are* sad. Perplexed, perhaps, more. And because the world – or worlds – are so very perplexing! Were, even then;[41] and now, much more. It is difficult to see clearly what anything leads to or means. But anyhow there is beauty every-where, which perhaps should be enough.

I *hope* your boy won't to [*sic*] have to go out too soon. Ours is in Salonika now,[42] or just outside it – and I hope they won't attack him yet awhile. I must stop – it's got later than I thought. Thank you again very very much, and thank Pamela.

Rose Macaulay

Letter 4 (KTH 6/20/1)

> Southernwood
> Great Shelford
> Cambridge
> 4 March 1916

My dear Mrs Tynan Hinkson

I came home from London last night and found the book[43] waiting for me. I do love to have it – and the inscription, which makes me proud and pleased beyond measure.

---

37 Meaning "would have continued to develop".
38 An error for *The Flower of Peace*.
39 *The Holy War*.
40 The book ends with the death of Charles Stewart Parnell in October 1891.
41 *The Two Blind Countries* was published four months before the start of the war.
42 Allied forces had landed at Salonika in neutral Greece on 5 October 1915 in order to help Serbia. Troops from Will Macaulay's regiment had reached Salonika from Marseilles in November and early December 1915.
43 Tynan, *The Web of Fräulein*. It was first advertised in *The Times*, 8 February 1916, 6. The novel describes how a German governess employed by a British family takes

I do love your poetry so much! I happened on "The Wall Between" in *The Westminster* [*Gazette*], – or rather my mother[44] happened on it, and told me what a nice thing she'd found. Please write lots more like that: I shall love to have *Flowers of Peace* and *The Holy War*. Thank you so much for the novel in proof; I only had time to begin it last night, but liked the opening. My aforesaid mother has got further, and I am to tell you from her how much she likes it. She loves *Flower of Youth* too, you know. She is one of the people who live a lot, because they have to, on thoughts of "t'other side o' the wall."[45] Please forgive me for sending this very scrubby copy of *The Lee Shore*! The fact is, it's the only one I can lay hands on in the house that hasn't someone's name on it. I don't know how I came by it, but it looks suspiciously as if one of the family had bought it from a library at some time – cheap. I'm sorry! But it brings none the less gratitude and admiration.

I expect you are in Dublin now.[46] I hope you are able to see your soldier boy. It must have been horribly disappointing missing him. We don't see ours, ever – Greece is so far, the war so long. He is busy in the hills and coast, catching Greeks in wire[47] and digging trenches. It is better than if he was in France, in spite of his not getting home ever. But I don't know how long this Salonika business is going on – no-one seems to. I wonder what regiment the Brigade Major is in, and where he is. I do think your Pamela sounds a joy. It would be fun to meet you and her if ever you were in London.

control of the household and exerts a malign influence on its members. One reviewer described her "as a subtle personation of all that is most aggressive, ruthless, over-mastering in the German psychology" (*The Bookman* 50, no. 300 [September 1916], 174).

44 Grace Mary Macaulay *née* Conybeare.

45 Rose quotes Katharine's poem "The Wall Between". The third stanza (lines 9–12) goes: "The people go, the people flow / T'other side o' the wall / With silken rustle and laughter low / As to a festival." For the whole poem, see Tynan, *The Holy War*, 13–14.

46 Katharine was up in Dublin from her home in Claremorris, Co. Mayo, from 25 February to 13 March 1916. See Atkinson, 417–420. Katharine describes the atmosphere in Dublin at that time, a few weeks ahead of the Easter Rising, in Tynan, *The Years of the Shadow*, 188–190. The following chapter, "A Priest's Story", describes the dramatic events witnessed by two priests who arrived in Dublin on Easter Monday to visit a sick friend, also a priest, in hospital.

47 So much wire was used in the defence of Salonika that part of its territory was called the Birdcage.

If you meet the Rosses ever in Dublin, will you remember me very kindly to them. I think they are there all the winter, aren't they.

I am honoured by the thought of having a share in the paper on "Some Poets."[48]

I wish I could write poetry in these days: I somehow can't. The war seems to have killed all that; I can only just struggle with prose. I am trying to get through with a novel, in moments snatched from nursing in a V.A.D. hospital and working on the land for 3d an hour. I'm rather glad yours is written from the Catholic point of view: that is interesting, and must help to get life and people and things in the right perspective – open doors and thin the wall, which seems rather the only thing worth doing in these horrible days. Do you, by the way, know and like Mr de la Mare's poetry? "Thinning Walls" reminds me. He is a dear.[49]

With my love and thanks

Rose Macaulay

Letter 5 (KTH 6/20/2)

Southernwood
Great Shelford
Cambridge
23 July [19]16

My dear Mrs Tynan Hinkson

The poems[50] came the other day, and I have had no time to write till to-day, though I had time to read them, and have done so several

---

48 This paper has not been traced.
49 Rose was introduced to Walter John ("Jack") de la Mare by her friend Naomi Royde-Smith, who worked for *Saturday Westminster Gazette* – from 1912 as its literary editor. For several years, from 1911, he was infatuated with Naomi. Rose recalls that, like Naomi, he "had more charm than anyone else" and continues: "He was very beautiful, and had a fantastic wit and funniness, and his poetry was exquisite and full of ghosts and shadows and dreams. ... In his serious as well as in his nonsense poetry he wholly blurred the frontiers of reality and dream, which is what poetry ought to do, for we do not want to know which is which, but to travel about freely in both countries, not conditioned either by facts or dreams" (Macaulay, "Coming to London – XIII", 32). Katharine did indeed know and like de la Mare's poetry, even at the early stage of his poetic career, when he was writing under the pseudonym of Walter Ramal (letter from him to Katharine, 19 December 1928, transcript in KTH 2/40).
50 Tynan, *The Holy War*.

times. I can't tell you how much I love them. There's "The Wall Between," that I liked so much when it came out that I stuck it into *Flower of Youth*. I'm not sure I don't still like it best of all, but it is hard to choose. I love "Speeding," and "The Long Vacation," and "The Bulbs,"[51] and "The Mother of Three" and "Riding Home" and "New Heaven" – and also lots of others. They made me cry, they are so sad – but comforting too. Thank you very much indeed for sending them.

I shall send my novel *Non-Combatants* [*and Others*] when it appears, which I think will be any day now.[52] I think very likely you won't like it much.

We were wondering is Mrs Weigall, to whom "They who return"[53] is dedicated (by the way I think I like that almost the best of all) someone we know very slightly, who writes novels under the name of Kate Horn? Very likely not – only I know she had a soldier son.[54] We hear rumours about the rebels being up again in Dublin, but I daresay it's not true.[55] I *love* your rhythms and words – the sound of them; they have a magic. My sister says I am to tell you she likes the poems better than any she has read for many years.[56]

Yours with much gratitude
R. M.

51 "The Bulbs" is not correct as a title. Rose means the poem "What She Said" (Tynan, *The Holy War*, 63–64). Its first stanza reads: "She said: Would I might sleep / With the bulbs I plant so deep, / Forgetting all the long Winter / That I must awake and weep." The bulbs appear again in the last line of the sixth and last stanza.

52 Dedicated "To my brother and other combatants", the novel was published on 30 August 1916. "It is the only book of Rose's to have been published during the Great War. Among novels written about the war and during it, it is unusual for its focus on those at home, including those who have returned from the Front, for its recognition of the psychological damage caused by war, and for its whole anti-war message" (Smith, 11).

53 Tynan, *The Holy War*, 17–18.

54 The tentative identification mentioned by Rose was quite correct. The dedicatee of Katharine's poem was Constance Emma Cromwell Weigall *née* Warner, the daughter of a Lincolnshire clergyman. Her elder son, Lieutenant Richard Edward Cromwell Weigall, was killed in action at Neuve Chapelle on 11 March 1915. For a letter of condolence Katharine wrote her on 3 August 1915, see Atkinson, 411–412. Constance Weigall did indeed write novels under the pseudonym of Kate Horn.

55 Just three months had passed since the Easter Rising in Dublin (24–29 April 1916).

56 Rose had three sisters living – Margaret, Jeanie, and Eleanor Macaulay, the last of whom, a teacher and missionary in India, can be excluded. She might mean Margaret, who was a deaconess in East London, but Jeanie is more likely, given that near the end of Letter 2 Rose mentioned her intention to send her *Flower of Youth*.

I think you have so wonderfully caught the feeling of the closeness and interpenetration of the 2 worlds. That matters so much
just now.

Letter 6 (KTH 6/20/3)

Southernwood,
Great Shelford,
Cambridge.
11 November [1916]

My dear Mrs Tynan Hinkson

I have been trying for some days to get a moment to write and thank
you for what you wrote about me in *The Bookman*[57] – moments
are hard to come by in these days, I'm so busy preparing for our
house-move.[58] There is only my mother and myself, and she is an
invalid, so I have to see to things – the sorting of things to throw
away etc. is an endless and tiresome job. I did like your article –
only it was much too nice and more than I deserved, in what you
said of me. What you say of my people I value enormously – I don't
think anyone else ever understood so well what I meant them to
be.[59] May I some day send you *The Furnace*, since you like the
Crevequers, because that is the book about them, in which they
first come in. I wrote it when I was very young and crude, but I
loved writing it, because it is partly about my own old home in
Italy, and partly about Naples, which I love. The Crevequers are
very disreputable vagabonds[60] – but I think you won't mind that?

What is your boy in Greece doing, I wonder? Is he up at the
front?[61] Ours tells us very little news – he says the air of Macedonia
is bad for letter-writing.

57 Tynan, "Rose Macaulay".
58 In early December 1916 Rose and Grace moved from Great Shelford to Beaconsfield,
Buckinghamshire.
59 Katharine's two-page article in the November 1916 issue of *The Bookman* is full of
praise for Rose. It begins: "Rose Macaulay is of the very small band of writers in our
day whose work counts. She is not for the great multitude who follow the kingdom
of this world and worship success. She lavishes all her art on the failure, the beloved
vagabond who loses the world and saves his own soul." Although she mentions *The
Lee Shore*, *The Making of a Bigot*, and *Non-Combatants*, she focuses most attention
on *Views and Vagabonds*, whose author reintroduces Betty and Tommy Crevequer
(sister and brother), who first appear in her second novel, *The Furnace*.
60 A reviewer of *The Furnace* described Betty and Tommy Crevequer as "this feckless,
guileless pair" (*The Spectator*, 30 November 1907, 872).
61 Toby was posted, and seeing action, on the Struma Front (Atkinson, 429).

I'm reading, with enormous interest, James Stephens' book on the Rising[62] – when I have time to read anything, which is seldom – oh dear, moving is fearful! Don't you rather like the little Anthology-Catalogue? I'm glad they've got that of yours in it.[63] I *do* write badly, I'm afraid – I believe short-hand is spoiling my long-hand!

Yours with much gratitude
Rose Macaulay

Letter 7 (KTH 6/21/1)

Hedgerley End
Beaconsfield
22 March [19]18

My dear Mrs Tynan Hinkson

I love the poems[64] – thank you so much for them. They came this morning, just as I was starting off to my day's work in town[65] – so I unselfishly handed them over to my mother, who loves *all* your poems, you know, and she has had a happy day with them. And this evening I've been reading them. So many of them are lovely that I don't know which I like best. We have a special feeling for the Salonika one,[66] because of Will! And I like "After Jutland", only I wish you'd let them have some ships in heaven and go sailing, not only look out for ships from land. And "All Souls", and "The Welcome", and "The Message", and "The Airman"[67] – but at this

---

62 *The Insurrection in Dublin.* The author, a poet, novelist, and Irish nationalist, was a friend of Katharine and her husband (Atkinson, 365; Tynan, *The Years of the Shadow*, 24–29). Henry Hinkson reviewed the book in *The Bookman* 51, no. 304 (January 1917), 128–129. In 1925 Stephens moved to England and, early in the Second World War, declared himself "an Englishman for the duration" (*The Times*, 19 June 1940, 7).

63 Rose refers to *A Selection of Poems from Recent Volumes Published by Sidgwick and Jackson Ltd*, a booklet issued at sixpence and described by the publisher as "this little Anthology-Catalogue" (20). Among the poems chosen were Katharine's "Flower of Youth" (24–25) and Rose's "The Thief" (16–17), taken from *The Two Blind Countries*.

64 Tynan, *Late Songs.*

65 At the time of writing Rose was working either in the War Office, as in 1917, or in the Foreign Department of the Ministry of Information. For detailed discussion, see Smith, 12.

66 "At Parting".

67 "For an Airman".

rate I shall go through them all. "The House of Life" fascinates me – it is rather eerie, and frightfully true. But thro' all of them there is that lovely "thin-wall" feeling which makes your poetry so different from other people's, and so suggestive, and at the same time *resting*. I do like it.

I was going to write and thank you for your nice article about me in *The Queen*,[68] which I hadn't seen till a cousin sent it me two days ago.[69] I think *The Queen* ought to have sent me a copy. My cousin enquired, very naturally, why I hadn't shot the photographer – it is an awful thing, and one I told Hodder and Stoughton before (at my mother's special desire) must not be used! But he will do it. I don't usually photograph well, but they aren't all quite as bad as that![70] Your mention of Rupert Brooke reminded me of how my father found him chuckling before a bookshop in Cambridge one day, having seen that photograph in the window, enormously delighted with it. But I don't suppose it's worse than either of the other 2 on the same page of *The Queen*. It was dear of you to write of me like that.

I wonder if you will like, or not, my next novel.[71] I don't much think you will, it deals less with people than with departmental politics, and is really meant more for a joke than earnest. I hope you'll like the poems better.[72] But neither are coming out for a long

68 Tynan, "Women Novelists. – XX: Miss Rose Macaulay", *The Queen, The Lady's Newspaper & Court Chronicle*, 2 March 1918, 249. The piece on Rose (there are also pieces on three other writers) is highly laudatory: "Miss Macaulay is the poet and the novelist of the happy vagabond. ... [She] seems to me in the very front of women novelists of to-day. She stands alone in her odd, delightful unworldliness. ... [Her poems] have the unique distinction of her prose. She was a friend of Rupert Brooke – by divine right. She is full of poetry to the lips, and while her poetry in metre is beautiful and strange and sometimes a trifle crabbed – not every man's meat – her prose poetry is limpid and lovely and has all the colours and fragrance of the earth and sky. She is a true earth-lover. She scents it, she burrows in it, like the master, Thomas Hardy."

69 Probably Dorothea Conybeare, younger daughter of Rose's uncle Edward Conybeare and his wife, Frances.

70 The photograph, showing an unsmiling Rose in a broad-brimmed hat, was taken by the renowned photographer Emil Otto Hoppé. Other writers who had their portraits taken by him include Aldous Huxley, Rudyard Kipling, George Bernard Shaw, and H. G. Wells.

71 *What Not: A Prophetic Comedy.* Rose's ninth novel is a satire on bureaucracy inspired by her experience of government offices. It includes a love story that undoubtedly owes much to her affair with Gerald O'Donovan.

72 *Three Days.*

time, probably, because of the difficulties these days of printing and binding and getting paper.[73]

Wasn't it in the Jan: *Bookman* that you said portraits of 2 of your children were to be?[74] I've ordered it and ordered it, in vain; the newsagent hasn't yet given up hope, he says, but I almost have. It is tiresome, just this one number; I must get hold of it somehow. I shall write to Hodder and Stoughton about it myself, I think.

I do hope you haven't got a boy in France, have you, now? We have been so thankful we haven't, these last 2 days. This seems the worst battle we've had yet. I do hope it won't be protracted for weeks and weeks; it is awful. And so little ever comes of these attacks and counterattacks – they can't be worth while.[75] It'll only be worth while, at least, if it shows the Germans they can't get a military victory and dispose<s> them for peace on our terms, or something near enough to our terms for us to accept. But the Russian events make that so much more remote.[76]

It must have been a wonderful experience for your boy in the Palestine campaign. Where is your Patrick now? I do hope he didn't go to France.[77] One is thinking all the time of those boys in France just now, and their people. If prayers could help, they would come through all right – only, alas, prayers don't always save lives. Oh but I do believe they sometimes do – they must wrap them round in a sort of garment of love, anyhow, that must give them confidence – like Julian Grenfell – "knowing, nor caring much to know ..."[78]

---

73 *Three Days* was published in October 1919. *What Not* was scheduled for publication in November 1918, but did not appear until March 1919, because, after it had been printed and bound, a libel was detected, necessitating the rewriting and substitution of two pages. See Smith, 37.

74 The photograph of "Pamela Hinkson and Giles Aylmer Patrick Hinkson, Lieut., Royal Dublin Fusiliers" is in *The Bookman* 53, no. 316 (January 1918), 129. It is reproduced by Atkinson, 447. Katharine sent a copy of it to her friend Alice Meynell, commenting: "The preternatural seriousness is holding giggles in check" (Atkinson, 445).

75 The Germans launched an offensive on the Western Front on 21 March 1918. The Allied counter-offensive began on 18 July.

76 Under the treaty of Brest-Litovsk (3 March 1918), between Russia on the one hand and Germany and Austria–Hungary on the other, Russia ceded Russian Poland and the Baltic provinces to Germany and Austria–Hungary and recognised the independence of the Ukraine and Finland.

77 He was serving, or about to serve, in France (Atkinson, 453).

78 Captain Julian Grenfell died on 26 May 1915 from head wounds sustained at Ypres. Rose quotes, not entirely accurately, part of lines 39–40 of his poem "Into Battle",

With my love and *many* thanks, both for the book and for your article.

Rose Macaulay

On 11 January 1919 Katharine's husband, Henry, died, after a short illness, at their home in Claremorris, Co. Mayo, aged fifty-two. From mid-February until late May and again from early October Katharine and Pamela occupied a furnished house in Killiney on the coast of Co. Dublin. In the interval they were in England, based in rented accommodation in Ealing, west London. A few days before heading back to Ireland and having a long and eventful journey on account of a national rail strike,[79] they and Pat, on weekend leave from army barracks at Aldershot, visited Rose and her mother in Beaconsfield. That was on Saturday and Sunday, 20 and 21 September. The coming visit is mentioned by Rose in a letter of 15 September to her cousin Jean Smith:

> Well, it will be nice to see you this week-end. I hope you won't mind being mixed up with Tynan Hinksons, who will be staying at the Inn and coming in on Saturday afternoon and Sunday lunch. Mrs T. H. will amuse you; she is very ruddy and jolly, with a very fat Dublin brogue. She is bringing Pam and Pat, aged 19 and 20 or thereabouts.[80]

The likelihood is that Jean, who was a budding poet, so far from minding being "mixed up" with Katharine and her family, warmly welcomed the opportunity to meet them.

We do not hear from Rose how things went, but we do have Katharine's account of the weekend in Beaconsfield,[81] during which she and her children visited G. K. Chesterton and his wife as well as the Macaulays. She reports that the inn, probably the Royal White Hart, was unsatisfactory, because, when they arrived, their rooms were full of the luggage of a party of cinema actresses. It was well on in the evening when they at last got access to their

---

composed in Flanders in April 1915 and first published in *The Times*, 28 May 1915, 9. The stanza containing the quotation is the penultimate one of the poem: "Through joy and blindness he shall know, / not caring much to know, that still / Nor lead nor steel shall reach him, so / That it be not the Destined Will." "He" is "the fighting man" (line 9). In a letter of 8 March 1916 to Grenfell's mother, Lady Desborough, Katharine expresses her and Pamela's unbounded admiration for him (Atkinson, 419–420).

79 Atkinson, 465.
80 Smith, 47–48.
81 Tynan, *The Wandering Years*, 147–149.

accommodation, and they slept badly because of the overpowering smell of the cheap powder used by the women.

Katharine was charmed by Grace Macaulay:

> We spent most of the Sunday with Rose Macaulay, and her dear little mother, who drove about the Beaconsfield lanes in the most delicious little donkey shay, that might have belonged to the days of *Cranford*,[82] she herself in her proper setting, for nothing could be prettier and more Quakerish. I am sure the little mother had a Quaker soul, and that she had come back somehow to the place her own people had inhabited, for that is the Quaker corner of England. How she came to mother anything so brave and adventurous as Rose Macaulay I cannot well imagine. The little mother was a primrose, the daughter, a sturdy and honest Rose, with the sweetness of briar-rose.[83]

Grace (who was an Anglican, not a Quaker) certainly could be charming, but it is unlikely that any of her close family ever thought of her as "a primrose". As a mother, she wanted sons, not daughters, which was unfortunate since she started by having three girls and, after having two boys, finished with two more girls. The youngest daughter, Gertrude, died as a young child. The next youngest, Eleanor, was never loved by her mother and was cruelly excluded from family activities and holidays. It speaks volumes for Grace's behaviour as a mother that none of her children married, and that all wanted to get away from home as soon as possible. Aulay, the elder son, went to India with the Royal Engineers; Will, the younger son, went to farm in Canada; the third daughter, Jeanie, left to take up nursing; the eldest daughter, Margaret, to become a deaconess in London; and Eleanor to be a teacher and missionary in India. Rose too craved independence, but, after the escape of her sisters and then the death of her father, felt obliged to live with her mother for most of the time. Their relationship was far from harmonious, and in her novel *Dangerous Ages*, published in 1921, Rose upset her mother by using her as the model for the character of Mrs Hilary, whom her children "knew … to be a muddled bigot, whose mind was stuffed with concrete instances and insusceptible of abstract reason".[84] Grace was not much mollified by Rose's dedication of the book:

TO MY MOTHER
DRIVING GAILY THROUGH THE
ADVENTUROUS MIDDLE YEARS[85]

---

82 Novel by Mrs Gaskell (1853).
83 Tynan, *The Wandering Years*, 148.
84 Macaulay, *Dangerous Ages*, 29.
85 Macaulay, *Dangerous Ages*, [v].

"Driving" is intended to be understood literally as well as metaphorically, referring to Grace's use, thought so delightful by Katharine, of the donkey-chaise.[86]

After giving her impressions of the mother, Katharine assesses the talents of the daughter:

> I am very glad Rose Macaulay has come to her own. Only yesterday I heard *Dangerous Ages* quoted in a speech by the Head of a Woman's College, who perhaps would have been unaware of *The Furnace*, *The Lee Shore*, *Views and Vagabonds*, all the lovely, early books of the time when Rose Macaulay was a romantic writer and not a brilliant satirist. I keep Peter and the Crevequers and Benjy of *Views and Vagabonds* in my heart. The brilliant Rose is the world's Rose. The Rose of the early books and the poetry – her poetry has not yet received anything like its due – is my own and I keep her also in my heart.[87]

Letter 8 (KTH 6/21/2)

University Club for Ladies,[88]
4, George Street,
Hanover Square,
W.1.
as from Hedgerley End
Beaconsfield.
17 October 1920

My dear Mrs Tynan Hinkson

It was delightful to get your letter, and to have all your news. We were so much interested to hear both of your boy's East African appointment and of his engagement.[89] I hope we shall see him sometime before he goes out. I wonder if you will be in town at all. What about your Cambridge plans? Did they fall through? Did you manage to hear of a house? And have you been there yet

---

86 See Smith, 33 and fig. 4.

87 Tynan, *The Wandering Years*, 149.

88 In 1921 the Club changed its name to the University Women's Club and moved to 2 Audley Square, where it remains.

89 Toby had joined the Colonial Office. From 20 January 1921 he was to be a Cadet in the Administration Service in Kenya, and from 15 March 1921 Assistant District Commissioner at Embu in Kenya Province. His fiancée was (Ellice) Moira Charity Gertrude Pilkington, and they were to marry at University Church, St Stephen's Green, Dublin, on 8 January 1921. They had a son, Alexander ("Alec"). In 1929 Katharine reported that the marriage "went on the rocks" (Atkinson, 562). Toby remarried twice, in 1938 and 1956, and died in 1966.

to see your boy?[90] You must let us know when you are in these parts.

Will is in Canada now, on his ranch. His arm is much the same; he can't use it yet, and won't for at least a year; but he manages to do a lot of work with the other, and he can even swim in the river!

I see your new book is out – or is it only just going to come out?[91] I've not seen it yet. Mine will, I hope, come in the spring sometime.[92] Thank you very much for your kind words about *Potterism* – it seems to have been more popular than any of my others, for some reason – the idea caught on, somehow.[93] I don't know a bit if people will like the next.

Have you seen *The Romantic*, May Sinclair's new one?[94] I've just been reviewing it. It is very clever – and rather horrid, I think.

90 Pat had just entered Magdalene College, Cambridge. He was to join the Anglo-South American Bank (later Bank of London and South America), working first in Chile, then in Argentina. From 1935 until his death on 23 September 1957 he combined banking with journalism, serving as the Buenos Aires correspondent of *The Times*, for which he was a fearless reporter throughout the Perón dictatorship. He did not marry.

91 Tynan, *Denys the Dreamer*. According to *The Spectator*, 17 July 1920, 86: "A charming Irish story in which the world is viewed through rose-coloured spectacles. The reader tired of post-war conditions will find it very restful and refreshing."

92 Macaulay, *Dangerous Ages*, published on 20 May 1921. Its publication was delayed for a few weeks by a coalminers' strike, which adversely affected other areas of the economy (Smith, 88, 89 n. 5).

93 *Potterism* was published in late May 1920. Writing to Jean Smith on 15 December [1919], when the book was nearly finished, Rose described it as "an unholy jumble of irrelevant and incoherent odds and ends, I'm afraid – murders, manners and morals. I'm nearly sure it's bad" (Smith, 60). But it was a critical and financial success on both sides of the Atlantic. The novel, which holds up a mirror to a section of con- temporary society, takes its name from the Potter Press, owned by Percy Potter, and from the outlook of him, his popular-novelist wife, and other members of his family. In the words of one of the narrators, Arthur Gideon, "the very essence of Potterism is going for things for what they'll bring you, what they lead to, instead of for the thing-in-itself. Artists care for the thing-in-itself; Potterites regard things as railway trains, always going somewhere, getting somewhere" (Macaulay, *Potterism*, 82). The book's popularity can be attributed not only to the way in which it knocks so many social nails on the head, but also to its being a detective story.

94 Katharine had known May Sinclair (pseudonym of Mary Amelia St Clair Sinclair) for twenty years, and the two were close friends. At the end of June 1920 May had supported Katharine's successful application for a grant from the Royal Literary Fund (Atkinson, 473). *The Romantic* was inspired by the writer's brief and con- spicuously unsuccessful spell as a member of a volunteer ambulance unit in Belgium in 1914.

You should read *Conquest*, Gerald O'Donovan's new book, which is coming out at the end of this month, and is about the Irish question. (Nothing about the Church this time!)[95]

My love please to Pamela. Mother would send hers to you, but I am not with her at the moment. She is very well just now. I hope you too? Mind you let me know when you come to London.[96] With much love – you are always so kind to me!

Yours always
Rose Macaulay

Letter 9 (KTH 6/21/3)

2, St. Andrews Mansions,
Dorset Street, W.1.
14 September 1925

Dear Mrs Tynan Hinkson

It was delightful to hear from you again. The only thing I am sorry for is that you should have ever have felt a wall between us![97] I never have – except that of distance and absence. I am always hoping you will let me know when you are in London. I hope we may meet this autumn. I am per<m>anently here now, since my

---

95 Gerald O'Donovan's first two novels, *Father Ralph* and *Waiting*, were based on his unhappy experience of the Roman Catholic Church in Ireland. *Conquest* was criticised by some for being too sympathetic to Sinn Féin, and by the reviewer in the *The Times Literary Supplement*, 25 November 1920, 777, for its dullness, being "a succession of dinner parties" with "interminable conversations on the Irish question".

96 Until late October 1920 Katharine and Pamela were in Shankill, Co. Dublin. They then spent four months in London before visiting Italy and returning to Shankill in late April 1921.

97 There is no way of knowing why Katharine felt this, but the surviving correspondence strongly suggests that she was the one who usually, if not always, initiated the contacts between her and Rose. Given the praise that she heaped on Rose in her articles and reviews, perhaps she regretted that Rose was content to let her make most of the running. In fairness to Rose, after the death of Henry Hinkson, Katharine was without a permanent home and often on the move, now in Ireland, now in London or elsewhere. In 1922–1923 she and Pamela spent much time in Germany. Katharine recorded their experiences in her book *Life in the Occupied Area*. From October 1924 to the end of November 1925 Katharine and Pamela, with Toby's young son and his nurse, were living in France.

dear mother's death deprived me of our home at Beaconsfield and her companionship.[98]

I hope you have been faring well – I am sorry you cannot read much, though: that must be a *very* depressing trial.

Thank you for telling me about *The Victors*.[99] I don't review now – I found it took too much time – but I shall certainly read it. I will get it from the Times Library[100] from whence I get my novels now that I don't review. And if I ever get a chance to mention it anywhere, I will – I am writing a kind of review of the year's literature, for some paper, and will mention it there when I've read it.

I wish I had some new poetry of yours to read! And what is Pamela writing?

Forgive this bad handwriting – I would type it, but am in a train returning from a week-end at Deal.[101]

With love
Yours ever
Rose Macaulay

Letter 10 (KTH 6/23/1)

2, St. Andrews Mansions,
Dorset Street, W.1.
2 October [1925]

My dear Mrs Hinkson

Thank you so much for sending me *The Victors*, which I would have acknowledged before, only I failed to read your address with certainty![102] Now I think I can decipher it. I am bad at these things – with no excuse, for I am illegible myself.

I went to 29 Dorset Square to-day (it is close to Marylebone station – a nice quiet square, about 10 minutes walk from this street). I saw the Commander, and the house, but not the rooms,

---

98 Grace Macaulay died on 5 May 1925, aged sixty-nine, after suffering a heart attack. Although Rose was often with her mother in Beaconsfield, she had obtained the tenancy of her London flat (2 St Andrews Mansions) in January 1925.

99 See Letter 10.

100 The Times Book Club, 42 Wigmore Street, close to Rose's flat.

101 Rose had been staying with her sister Jeanie, a district nurse in Deal, Kent.

102 Katharine and Pamela were still in France (see n. 97). When they arrived in London at the end of November, they took accommodation not at 29 Dorset Square, which Rose visited at Katharine's request, but at 44 Pembroke Road, Kensington. Katharine was, as often, short of money and needed to be as economical as possible.

as they were occupied, and he didn't like to disturb the people. Two flats (besides the one advertised) may be vacant by the end of October, one for certain. The certain one is on the 1st floor (I think) and would be £70 for 6 months – (he doesn't let for less time), or £130 a year. It has one large double bedroom, a sittingroom, and usual offices. The other is on the ground floor (I think I am right about this, unless it is the other way round!) and has 2 bedrooms and sittingroom etc. Kitchen in basement. For this he asks £100 for 6 months. As I didn't see the rooms, I can't say much about them. The Commander struck me as quite a nice one. He seems to let his whole house in flats. If you think one of these might suit you, would you write to him about it. I am sorry I couldn't see the rooms. Do you want rooms for so long as 6 months, or just for the winter? He never lets for less than six. Everyone seems to be letting their flats just now.

I was interested in *The Victors* – a sad tale indeed. But I'm not sure that Michael *would* have turned the gas on. After all, he could have gone to Canada as a government emigrant, or lived on the dole till things were better, or something. I don't believe I should ever turn the gas on because I couldn't get a job – I'm sure that, as so many people have to do, one would hang on somehow till the demand and supply of labour righted itself. I've known so many people, of all classes and both sexes, who couldn't get work and had no money – and they are very miserable, poor dears, but they somehow scrape along, with odd-jobs and court-relief,[103] and private charity, until they get something regular. However, of course Michael *might* have got so depressed that he ended it. I dare say the war had been bad for his nerves. Well, it is a badly organised world in which we are dependent for our livelihood on somehow providing someone with something they will pay us for doing. I always wonder so many of us do succeed in getting paid for anything! Poor Michael ought to have drawn the dole, at least. I never heard of Peter Deane before. Do you know him? Has he – (or she?) written anything else? It sounds rather like a pseudonym. But he doesn't know about gas – those thus slain are found black and distorted in the face, I believe. (It suddenly occurs to me, from your

---

103 A process, also known as "judicial relief", "judicial remedy", or "legal remedy", whereby a court of law gives redress to an individual who has been wrongfully treated in some way and (for example) seeks the return of property or compensation for an injury.

inscription in the book – it's not by your son, is it, by any chance?) Anyhow, I thought it very well done.[104]

Do let me know when you come to London – I shall *so* much like to see you both. Do write to Commander Gleig and ask about his rooms. Only you can't, of course, take them without seeing them.

With love and thanks

Yours aff[e]ct[ionately]
R. M.

104 Peter Deane was the pseudonym of Katharine's daughter, Pamela Hinkson. Dedicated "To Michael's Comrades in Victory", the novel, in the words of the blurb, "tells of a young officer [Michael Foster] who, emerging from the horrors of war, finds that there is no place for him in the 'peace economy' of his country, and that where once was adulation and willing service is now a cold indifference and neglect". In despair, he used a gas stove to poison and kill himself (Deane, *The Victors*, 114). In death, "he didn't look as if he had suffered at all, and his face seemed younger and rounder than ever. He looked quite smiling and happy, and the lines seemed to have gone from his face, leaving it as young as when I knew him first at Stowick" (Deane, *The Victors*, 115). The day after Michael gassed himself, a letter arrived from the Colonial Office, accepting his application for an administrative appointment in New Caledonia.

Around the time Katharine sent a copy of *The Victors* to Rose, she sent one also to Desmond MacCarthy, literary editor of *The New Statesman*, with a plea to publicise it. She adds: "*The Victors*, I will tell you in confidence is the story of my Pat and Michael Foster is a very living portrait of him. He was just saved from turning on the gas and he is now in a South American bank where he will make good if they don't kill him with hard work. ... The book is written by a friend who knew and loved him nearly as well as I do. The writer was 23 when the book was done" (Letter of [October 1925] in Atkinson, 540). In the Katharine Tynan and Pamela Hinkson archive in the University of Manchester Library is a copy of the novel signed by Pamela. Inside it is an undated newspaper cutting headlined "OFFICER'S ATTEMPTED SUICIDE. UNSUCCESSFUL ATTEMPTS TO GET WORK". The article concerns the case of Captain Cyril George Royston, a former Indian Army officer with a fine war record, charged with "attempting to commit suicide in circumstances reported in *The Times* of September 24". (Until the enactment of the Suicide Act 1961 attempting suicide was a crime in England and Wales.) The cutting is from *The Times*, 1 October 1925, 11. The article in *The Times*, 24 September 1925, 9, entitled "ATTEMPTED SUICIDE CHARGE. SCENE IN HOSPITAL CASUALTY WARD", describes how the accused was found lying on his kitchen floor with his head immediately in front of the gas oven. The gas was switched off, but the room reeked of gas. Royston was taken to hospital and, while being treated there, stabbed himself in the chest with an Indian dagger which he had concealed in his trousers. He missed his heart and survived.

Letter 11 (KTH 6/22/1)

Hedgerley End
Beaconsfield.
7 January 1926

My dear Mrs Hinkson

Thank you so much for your kind note. It is good hearing that you are in London, and I shall call, if I may, some Sunday soon after I get back there. All this month I am down here, with my brother and sisters, very busy sorting, dividing and disposing of our household goods, as we have sold the house from the end of January.[105] It is a melancholy job, and I shall be glad when it is finished with. I hope to see you in February.

I hope you are both well. May I send remembrances to Pamela too.

Yours affectionately
Rose Macaulay

Letter 12 (KTH 6/22/2)

10, St. Andrews Mansions,[106]
Dorset Street,
W.1.
22 October 1927

I was so glad to have your letter, and I will certainly send a book for the sale. Yes, I like animals – at least a great many animals. Not all. In fact, I feel I might almost as well say "I like people" – animals are even more different from one another. But they certainly ought all to be looked after when ill, poor things, and I hope the sale will make a lot for the dispensers.[107]

---

105 Rose describes the clearing and sorting operation, undertaken by Will, Margaret, Jeanie, and Eleanor Macaulay and herself, in a letter of 30 January 1926 to Jean Smith (Smith, 140–141).

106 Rose moved from no. 2 to no. 10 St Andrews Mansions some time in the second half of 1926.

107 The sale was in aid of the St Francis Dispensary, Dublin, for sick animals, founded in 1926, after Katharine had had a letter published in *The Irish Times* in support of the Irish Animals' Protection League (Atkinson, 546). Rose had owned, and been devoted to, a notoriously aggressive dog called Thomas (Smith, 88, 89, n. 4). She did not like cats (Smith, 213, n. 6). Pamela followed her mother in being a vigorous campaigner against cruelty to animals.

I hope you are well, and all of you. I am much too busy, writing against time to finish a book.[108] Forgive a typed letter, I type all my letters now, out of mercy to my friends, as my hand grows worse and worse.

Are you ever in London now?

Yours affectionat<e>ly,
Rose Macaulay

Have you read Elizabeth Bowen's *The Hotel*? It is clever.[109]

Letter 13 (KTH 6/22/3)

10, St. Andrews Mansions,
Dorset Street, W.1.
7 July 1930

My dear Mrs Hinkson

It was delightful to get your letter. Indeed I should love to come and see you,[110] if I may – I was to have come up to the Lynds one evening when you were there,[111] but I was still not recovered from concussion, after a fall I had on my head in the spring, and could not go. I am still a little giddy at times, but am staying in London till I have finished a novel[112] I am struggling with, when I may go to my sister's in the country.[113] May I come and see you sometime during the last week of July, when I hope to have done the book? I should love to do that.

---

108 *Keeping Up Appearances*.

109 On the friendship between Elizabeth Bowen and Rose, and on the former's debt to the latter, see Smith, 166, n. 2.

110 Katharine and Pamela had come to London from Blackrock, Co. Dublin, in May 1930. At the time Rose wrote this letter they were staying at 18 Bedford Gardens, Campden Hill, W8. By October 1930 they had moved to a flat at 3 St John's Road, Wimbledon, and it was there that Katharine died, of cerebral thrombosis and congestion of the lungs, on 2 April 1931, aged seventy-two. After a requiem Mass at the Church of the Sacred Heart, Edge Hill, Wimbledon, on 8 April, she was buried in St Mary's Roman Catholic Cemetery, Kensal Green, near her close friend Alice Meynell.

111 Robert and Sylvia Lynd were good friends of Rose as well as of Katharine. Robert, born and educated in Belfast, was a prolific writer of essays and reviews. For many years, from 1912, he was literary editor of *The Daily News*, then the *News Chronicle*. Sylvia Lynd was a novelist and poet. The couple frequently hosted literary gatherings at their home, 5 Keats Grove, Hampstead.

112 *Staying With Relations*, published on 22 September 1930.

113 Margaret Macaulay's house in Liss, near Petersfield, Hampshire.

I read Pamela's book with great pleasure: the publishers kindly sent it me.[114] Please tell her I liked it.

I hope you are well. It is a long time since I last saw you – far too long.

With love and remembrances,

Y[ou]rs,
Rose Macaulay

Acknowledgements

I warmly thank the University of Manchester Library for allowing me access to Rose Macaulay's letters to Katharine Tynan and for giving me every assistance and encouragement, with special thanks to Fran Baker, Archivist, and Thomas Gordon, Special Collections Assistant; the Society of Authors, the copyright holder, for permission to publish the letters; the Rev. Philip Hanson, copyright holder, for permission to quote writings of Katharine Tynan and Pamela Hinkson; Peter van de Kamp, for much information and advice about Katharine Tynan and for commenting on this essay; Damian Atkinson for reading the essay and undertaking a search in the Bodleian Library, Oxford, on my behalf; Durham University Library, especially Judith Walton and Gail Pitty; and Lucinda Ferguson Smith.

References

Atkinson, Damian. *The Selected Letters of Katharine Tynan: Poet and Novelist.* Newcastle upon Tyne: Cambridge Scholars, 2016.

Bowen, Elizabeth. *The Hotel.* London: Constable, 1927.

Brooke, Rupert. *The Collected Poems of Rupert Brooke: With a Memoir* [by Edward Marsh]. London: Sidgwick & Jackson, 1928.

Deane, Peter (pseudonym of Pamela Hinkson). *The Victors.* London: Constable, 1925.

Hinkson, Pamela (*see also* Deane, Peter). *The End of All Dreams.* London: Fisher Unwin, [1923].

———. *The Girls of Redlands.* London: Partridge, 1923.

———. *The Ladies' Road.* London: Gollancz, 1932.

114 *Wind From the West.* Katharine did not live to see the publication of Pamela's most successful novel, *The Ladies' Road*, in 1932. Pamela continued to be a successful writer of novels, travel books, and short stories. In July 1934 she became engaged to Eric (later Sir Eric) Hallinan of the Colonial Office, but in May 1935 the engagement was called off, and she never married. She died in Dublin on 26 May 1982.

———. "Post Scriptum." *The Bookman* 47, no. 279 (December 1914), 83–84.

———. "A Song of Autumn." *The Windsor Magazine* 42, no. 250 (October 1915), 532.

———. *Wind from the West.* London: Macmillan, 1930.

KTH. Papers of Katharine Tynan and Pamela Hinkson. The University of Manchester Library.

LeFanu, Sarah. *Rose Macaulay.* London: Virago, 2003.

Macaulay, Rose. *Abbots Verney: A Novel.* London: John Murray, 1906.

———. "Coming to London – XIII." *The London Magazine* 4, no. 3 (March 1957), 30–36.

———. *Dangerous Ages.* London: Collins, 1921.

———. *The Furnace.* London: John Murray, 1907.

———. *Keeping up Appearances.* London: Collins, 1928.

———. *The Lee Shore.* London: Hodder & Stoughton, 1912.

———. *The Making of a Bigot.* London: Hodder & Stoughton, 1914.

———. *Non-Combatants and Others.* London: Hodder & Stoughton, 1916.

———. *Potterism: A Tragi-farcical Tract.* London: Collins, 1920.

———. *The Secret River.* London: John Murray, 1909.

———. *Staying with Relations.* London: Collins, 1930.

———. *Three Days.* London: Constable, 1919.

———. *The Two Blind Countries.* London: Sidgwick & Jackson, 1914.

———. *The Valley Captives.* London: John Murray, 1911.

———. *Views and Vagabonds.* London: John Murray, 1912.

———. *What Not: A Prophetic Comedy.* London: Constable, 1918.

O'Donovan, Gerald. *Conquest.* London: Constable, 1920.

———. *Father Ralph.* London: Macmillan, 1913.

———. *Waiting.* London: Macmillan, 1914.

Passty, Jeanette N. *Eros and Androgyny: The Legacy of Rose Macaulay.* Rutherford [NJ] / London: Fairleigh Dickinson University Press / Associated University Presses, 1988.

Sinclair, May. *The Romantic.* London: Collins, 1920.

Smith, Martin Ferguson. *Dearest Jean: Rose Macaulay's Letters to a Cousin.* Manchester: Manchester University Press, 2011; 2017 (paperback).

Stephens, James. *The Insurrection in Dublin.* Dublin / London: Maunsell, 1916.

Tynan, Katharine. *Collected Poems.* Macmillan, 1930.

———. *Denys the Dreamer.* London: Collins, 1920.

———. *The Flower of Peace: A Collection of the Devotional Poetry of Katharine Tynan.* London: Burns & Oates, 1914.

———. *Flower of Youth: Poems in War Time.* London: Sidgwick & Jackson, 1915.

———. *The Holy War.* London: Sidgwick & Jackson, 1916.

———. *Late Songs.* London: Sidgwick & Jackson, 1917.

———. *Life in the Occupied Area.* London: Hutchinson, [1925].

———. *Molly, My Heart's Delight.* London: Smith, Elder, 1914.

———. "Rose Macaulay." *The Bookman* 51, no. 302 (November 1916), 37–38.

———. *Twenty-five Years: Reminiscences.* London: Smith, Elder, 1913.

———. *The Wandering Years.* London: Constable, 1922.

———. *The Web of Fräulein.* London: Hodder & Stoughton, [1916].

———. *The Years of the Shadow.* London: Constable, 1919.

8

A teenage star:
The forgotten contribution of
Dorothy L. Sayers to a pageant

Dorothy Leigh Sayers, the only child of the Rev. Henry Sayers and his wife, Helen Mary Sayers, *née* Leigh, was born in Oxford on 13 June 1893. Her father was headmaster of Christ Church Cathedral School. Dorothy was educated at home until January 1909, when she entered the Godolphin School, Salisbury, as a boarder.

Her time at the Godolphin, the subject of the next essay, was important for her development as a writer, thinker, and person. But, even before she went there, she had displayed unusual talents both as a modern linguist and as a writer, a passion for poetry and drama, and a love of music. The way in which she flourished in the cultured and enlightened atmosphere of her parents' home under the tuition of governesses and her father is well known, but what seems not to be known is the way in which her talents were exploited and appreciated in a major local event that took place several months before she went to school. That event is the subject of this essay.

I chanced upon Dorothy's involvement in this event when I was researching her time at the Godolphin. I was curious to discover if any photograph of her, taken in her schooldays, exists. Careful searches of the numerous Godolphin photographs held by the School and by Wiltshire and Swindon County Archives in Chippenham proved fruitless. But the Marion E. Wade Center, Wheaton College, Illinois, has two photographs showing Dorothy as a teenager in costume for some sort of performance, and Barbara Reynolds, who published both of them, one in *The Letters* (opposite 108), the other in *Dorothy L. Sayers* (112), tentatively or definitely identifies them as having been taken at school. In the former and earlier publication her caption is: "Dorothy, possibly acting in *Coriolanus* at the Godolphin"; in the latter and later one it is: "Dorothy in costume for *Coriolanus*".

The photograph reproduced by Reynolds in *Dorothy L. Sayers* is a full-length portrait (Plate 30). Dorothy stands, right hand on hip, facing half-left. She is wearing a white sleeveless batwing-style bodice with dark ribbon-edging, and a floor-length non-white dirndl skirt with dark ribbon-edging at the hem, double ribbon-edging at the side seam, and a dark-coloured sash hanging down the front. Behind her is the decorated frame of part of a large picture or panel. The photograph chosen by Reynolds for inclusion in the earlier *Letters* is a three-quarter-length portrait (Plate 31). Wearing the same costume as in the other portrait and looking almost at the camera and with her head tilted slightly to the right, Dorothy stands with her hands behind her head. She has a solid bracelet on her left wrist and a three-band bracelet on her right wrist. Like the other photograph, this one was probably taken indoors, but in this case the background is plain.

Although Dorothy did take minor parts in scenes from *Coriolanus* performed by the Upper Fifth form at the Godolphin School on 20 March 1909,[1] towards the end of her first term, Reynolds's identification is mistaken. The Wade Center's photographs are copies of originals that are thought to be still in the possession of Dorothy's descendants, but the Center has a record that the back of one of the original photographs, the three-quarter-length portrait, is inscribed "Somersham Pageant, 1908" at the top, and "your very loving cousin / *Dorothy Leigh Sayers*" at the bottom. A dark and poor photocopy, made many years ago at the time when the Wade Center was lent the two original photographs, indicates that the original of the three-quarter-length portrait is set in a photographer's matt that carries in the lower left corner the name of the photographer: "Maddison & Hinde, St. Ives".[2]

The Huntingdonshire village of Somersham is about five miles from St Ives and only about two miles from Bluntisham, where Dorothy's father was rector from late December 1897[3] to 1917. So the pageant was very near to home, and it took place before Dorothy entered the Godolphin in far-off Salisbury. Although the correct identification of the occasion means that we still have no image of Dorothy during her schooldays, the photographs are the key to something much more interesting, for they direct us to the important contribution she made to a public event that occurred just two months after her fifteenth birthday. The pageant, considered significant enough to

1 The class was studying the play for Higher Certificate. The Godolphin School *Diary* (a manuscript compilation, with many items pasted in), in the School's archives, reveals that Dorothy was one of the five citizens of Rome, one of the three servants to Aufidius, and one of the six Roman and Volscian patricians.

2 Maddison & Hinde's premises were in Sheep Market. They also operated from 120 High Street, Huntingdon.

3 The Sayers family moved from Oxford to Bluntisham in January 1898, but the mandate for Henry's induction is dated 20 December 1897, and 1897 is the starting date of his rectorship given in *Crockford's Clerical Directory*.

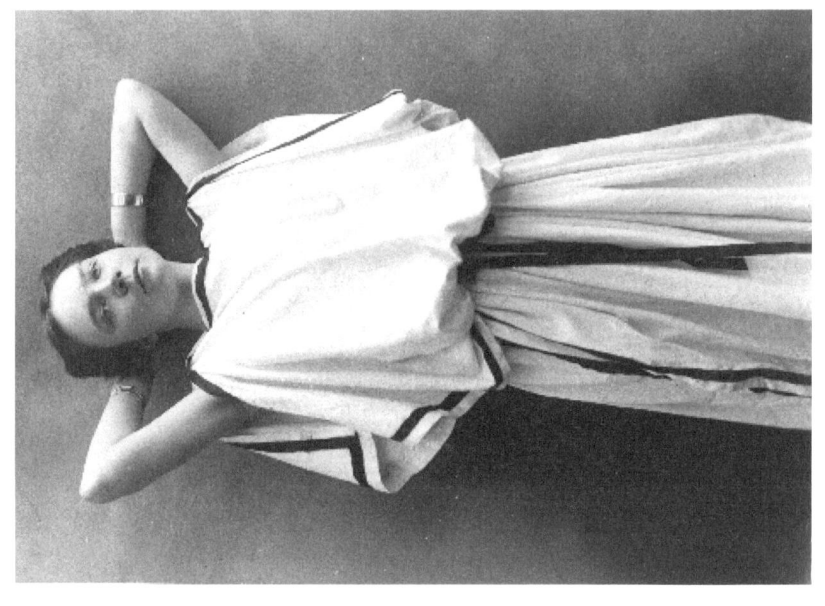

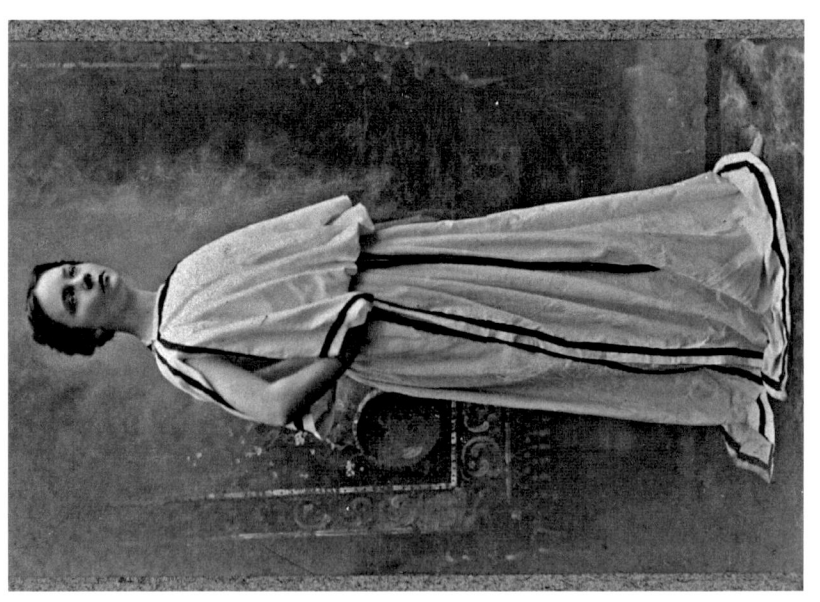

30–31 Dorothy L. Sayers in costume for the Somersham Pageant, August 1908.

receive extensive coverage not only in local Huntingdonshire newspapers, but also in a national one,[4] is not mentioned by any of her biographers.

In the late nineteenth and early twentieth centuries historical pageants were in great vogue in England, so much so that the term "pageantitis" was coined to describe the widespread enthusiasm for them. A pageant was a colourful outdoor spectacle depicting and dramatising, in a series of episodes or tableaux, the history of a locality. The great majority of participants were amateurs, even if the event was professionally organised and directed. The spread of pageantitis in the ten years before the First World War was in no small measure due to Louis Napoleon Parker, who, after organising a brilliant large-scale pageant at Sherborne Castle in 1905, put on spectacular shows in other historic places, including Colchester, Dover, Warwick, and York.[5] But Parker was not the only important and influential pageant-master, nor was he the earliest.

Another significant figure, and one who started his pageant-making career twenty years earlier, was D'Arcy de Ferrars[6] (Plate 32). Born Ernest Richard D'Arcy Ferris, he changed his surname to de Ferrars by deed poll in 1889. He was a talented composer, conductor, and teacher of music, and a singer with a good tenor voice. He was much concerned with recreating Merrie England, and he is an important figure in the revival of morris dancing. He also had artistic ability, historical interests, and a passionate belief in the aesthetic, educational, social, and moral benefit that pageants, festivals, and other wholesome traditional (or supposedly traditional) entertainments brought to performers and spectators alike. He was a frequent lecturer. A member of the Catholic Apostolic Church, he had a firm Christian faith, but, as well as being a man with a mission and a thoroughgoing romantic, he possessed remarkable organisational abilities and advertised himself as a professional designer and master of pageants and other functions.

---

4 *The Morning Leader* (see below). The pageant is briefly mentioned as a forthcoming event in *The Times*, 7 August 1908, 9.

5 One who caught the "bug" from Parker was Frank Lascelles, who was master of a grand pageant in Oxford in 1907 (27 June to 3 July). Writing to her cousin Ivy Shrimpton on 27 January 1907, Dorothy says that she and her mother have been invited by Aunt Maud (Maud Leigh) to stay with her in Oxford at the time of the pageant. She refers to the visit again in a letter to Ivy of 7 March 1907: "You will be pleased to hear that we are going to stay some little time in Oxford when we go – about a fortnight, I believe. Won't it be jolly?" So there is a strong probability that Dorothy saw the Oxford pageant, although there does not seem to be an account of it in her surviving letters: her next letter to Ivy is dated 3 September 1907, when Ivy had just spent four weeks (30 July to 27 August) at Bluntisham (*Visitors' Book*).

6 For helpful information, see Judge, "D'Arcy Ferris" and "Ferrars". But a full account of de Ferrars's varied life and career has yet to be written.

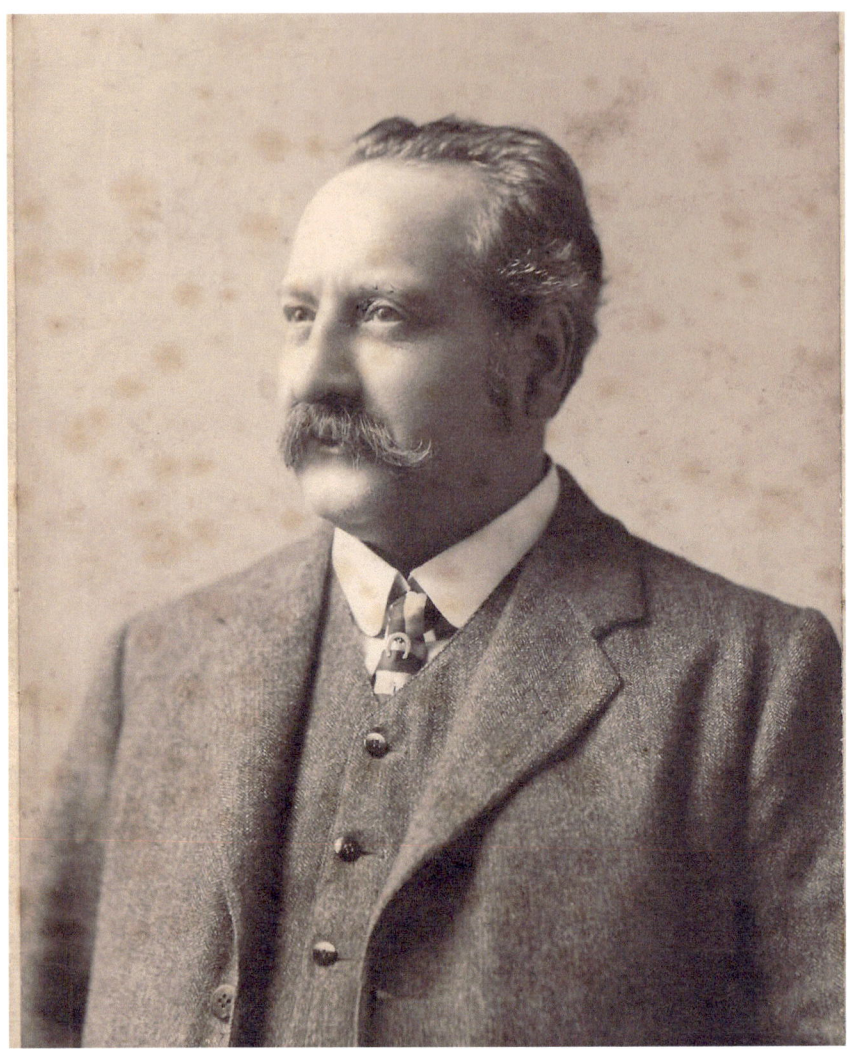

32 D'Arcy de Ferrars in 1907.

The first major event he was commissioned to organise was the Ripon Millenary in August 1886.[7] Many other commissions were to follow, the most prestigious of which was the pageant staged in Liverpool on 3 and 5–6 August 1907 to celebrate the city's seven-hundredth birthday. The Somersham pageant, of which he was master, was of course in no way

---

7　The millenary festival was held on 27–28 August 1886. For a full account, see *Ripon Millenary*.

comparable with the Liverpool one in terms of scale, cost, sophistication, and prestige. The population of Liverpool was then about seven hundred thousand, that of Somersham and its immediate area under two thousand. Why was it chosen as a venue at all? The answer lies in the friendship and family ties between D'Arcy de Ferrars and the vicar of Somersham with Pidley, Fenton, and Colne, the Rev. Magens de Courcy-Ireland (Plate 33). Unusual names were not the only thing they had in common:[8] the two men were related by marriage,[9] Magens being a first cousin of D'Arcy's wife, Isabel Mary Caulfeild Browne. Evidently he shared D'Arcy's enthusiasm for pageants. According to Bell, he is said to have taken part in the Ripon Millenary and to have "got the bug" then (*History*, 6). However, Bell's unnamed source is almost certainly mistaken: Magens, who was only nineteen in 1886, is not mentioned as having been a participant, and it is doubtful if at that time he had even met D'Arcy, who did not marry his first cousin until 1889. But when D'Arcy was invited back to Ripon to be master of revels at the city's Historic Festival in August 1896,[10] Magens, who was curate of Holy Trinity Church, Ripon, from 1890 to 1896, contributed three guineas to the festival's Guarantee Fund and may well have given other assistance, although this is not mentioned in the detailed record of the event, *Boadicea to Victoria*. It is possible that he gave some help when D'Arcy was master of revels at a Ripon festival for the third time in July 1906, but again there is no mention of him in reports of the event,[11] and at that time he was vicar of Somersham.

The Somersham pageant began on Monday, 10 August 1908 and continued on Tuesday and Wednesday, 11 and 12 August. The Tuesday programme was a repetition of the Monday one. On the Wednesday a

---

8 Magens derived his first name from his maternal uncle Captain Magens James Caulfeild Browne, who had died at the age of twenty-nine a few months before "our" Magens was born. According to his death-notice in *The Times* (12 March 1955, 1), the younger Magens preferred to be known as Tom!

9 Bell (*History*, 6) curiously refers to Magens (whom he calls "Magems") and D'Arcy as brothers.

10 The 1896 festival was held on 18–19 and 22 August, to commemorate both the city's one thousand and tenth birthday and "the entry of our Sovereign Lady Queen Victoria on the sixtieth year of her glorious Reign".

11 The 1906 festival was held on 19–21 July. Unlike the festivals of 1886 and 1896, it was not followed by the publication of a book describing and illustrating the events, but there is a detailed account, with the names of the participants, in *The Ripon Gazette* (see "Ripon Historic"). As at Somersham, there was a *Masque of the Flower Queen*, for which D'Arcy wrote the libretto and composed or chose the music. No doubt the same libretto was used at Somersham, and probably much of the same music as well.

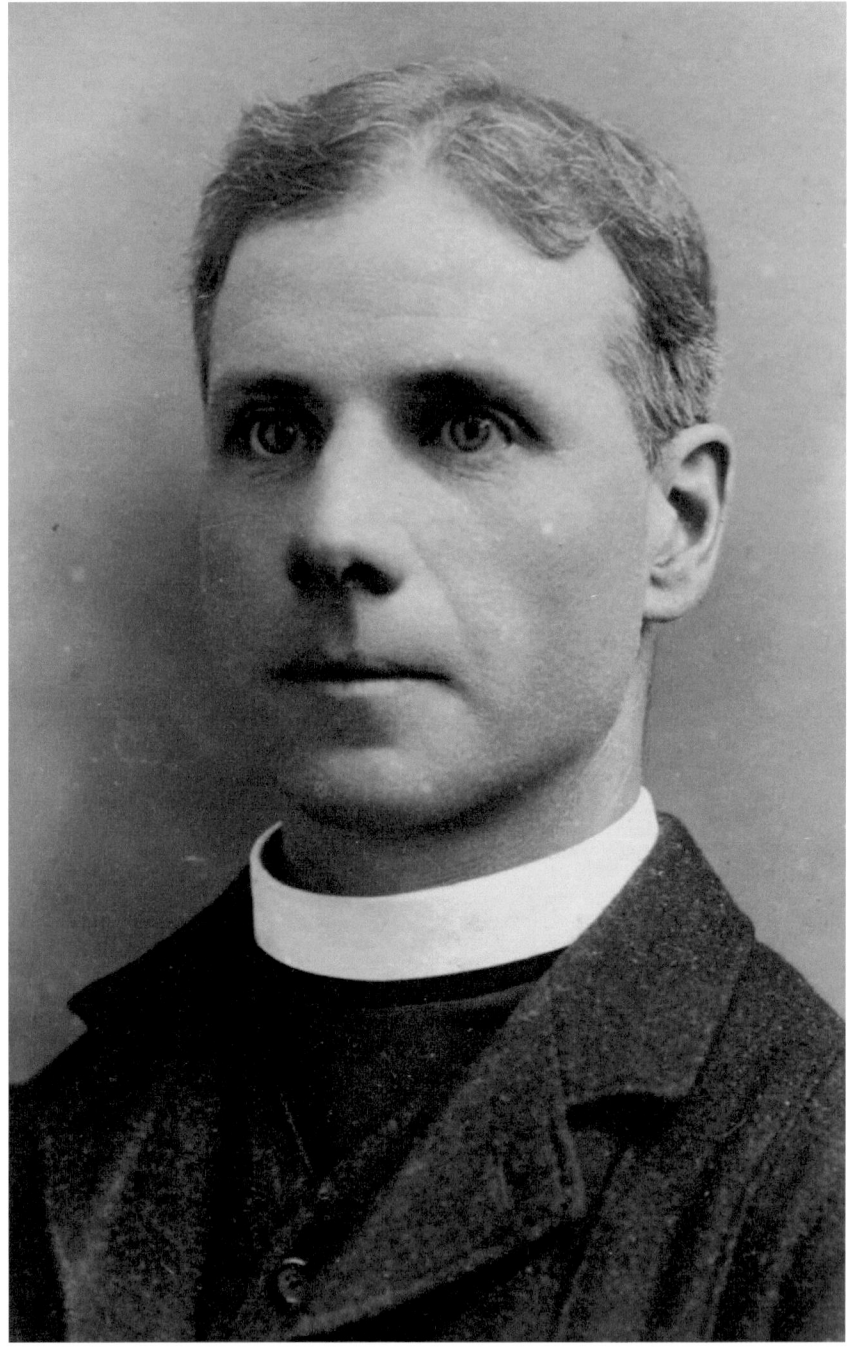

33 The Rev. Magens de Courcy-Ireland, vicar of Somersham, 1904–1911.

shortened version was put on for those parishioners who could not afford the admission fee charged on the first two days (one shilling and sixpence). The event was held at short notice and organised with great speed. The first mention of preparations for it seems to be in *Somersham Parish Magazine* (*SPM*), July 1908, probably printed in late June 1908: "The various Committees are hard at work and sparing no pains to make the production as artistic and accurate as possible, the Choruses are learning their parts and the Costume Making will soon be in full swing." At that stage the intention was to hold the pageant in the autumn. But around 20 July the decision was taken to bring it forward to 10–12 August, allowing only three more weeks for preparation and rehearsal. The decision is likely to have been influenced by at least three considerations. The first was the desirability of holding the event before harvesting began. The second was probably the hope of having better weather in August than later, although this hope was to be somewhat disappointed: in the afternoon of the first day conditions turned wet and windy, and the programme had to be curtailed. The third consideration was the availability of costumes: the making of them could have been a difficult, time-consuming, and costly business, but D'Arcy and Magens managed to borrow about seventy that had been used in the festivals D'Arcy had directed in Ripon in 1886, 1896, and 1906, and also some that had been worn by performers in the Thirsk Historical Play, of which D'Arcy had been joint master on 25–26 June 1907.[12]

Magens's seven years as vicar of Somersham (1904–1911) were marked and marred by a series of serious disputes with some of his parishioners. The disputes, which involved a variety of issues, are described by Bell (*Somersham*, 14–23) and Williams. The details are interesting but do not concern us here. The organisation and execution of the pageant were, it seems, completely harmonious: certainly the reports of it give no hint of any problems between Magens and his parishioners. The profit made was amicably shared in the village, 60 per cent of it going towards the re-roofing of the Parish Church and 40 per cent to the nonconformists (Baptists and Wesleyans) "for Philanthropic Objects" (*SPM*, October 1908).

It was Magens who, in the afternoon of Monday, 10 August 1908, began the proceedings in the grounds of the Vicarage. In a speech calling upon the Earl of Sandwich to declare the pageant formally open, he praised and thanked all who had worked so hard to make the event possible. According to the report in the *Huntingdonshire Post* ("Somersham Pageant"), reproduced in *SPM*, September 1908, he named just two individual contributors.

---

12 "Somersham Pageant." The Thirsk event was held on 25–26 June 1907. For the text of the play and the names of the officials, patrons, and performers, see *Thirsk Historical*.

One of course was the pageant-master, D'Arcy. The other was a girl from a neighbouring parish:

> Their [i.e. everyone's] thanks were also due to the persons who had written the words for the narrative chorus, amongst whom he especially mentioned Miss Dorothy Sayers, of Bluntisham Rectory.

Dorothy was one of six contributors of original words for the pageant. All six are listed in *SPM*, September 1908, and *Hunts County News* ("Pretty Pageant"), but Dorothy was singled out for special mention not only by Magens, but also by the writer of the report ("Rural Pageantry") in *The Morning Leader*:

> All the local poets had contributed right nobly. One or two halted occasionally in their muse, but Mr. D'Arcy de Ferrers [*sic*] coupled poetry with pageant-mastership most cunningly, and did much towards the success of the show. He also wrote the music. Miss Dorothy Sayers, of Bluntisham Rectory, was another most successful poetess – quite young, but amazingly fervid, and with just the right sort of fire in her.

This is likely to be the earliest mention of Dorothy in a national newspaper.

The pageant began with the *Masque of the Flower Queen* performed by children. Rather mirroring the way the weather behaved during the pageant, the performance told the story of how the Summer Queen is attacked by the grim Tempest Queen, but eventually overcomes her. Then there were displays of morris dancing by boys and maypole dancing by girls (Plate 34), and the masque ended with a battle of flowers. One element of this opening event has yet to be mentioned: between the morris dancing and the maypole dancing Madame Klauwell[13] sang "Somersham Triumph Song", the words of which were composed by Dorothy:

> Bring the harp and merry lute,
>   With a thankful heart and voice

13 Marie Klauwell (or Lang-Klauwell) came from a talented musical family. She was the daughter of Adolf Klauwell, a well-known teacher of the piano in Leipzig, and she was a first cousin of Otto Adolf Klauwell, composer and music-teacher and -writer. Born in Leipzig on 27 January 1853, she was aged fifty-five at the time of the pageant. A soprano, she was with the Vienna Court Opera (Wiener Hofoper) in 1872–1873 and in those years also sang at concerts in Leipzig and Dordrecht (Netherlands). Internet sources do not record any more appearances for nineteen years, and it is probable that marriage interrupted her professional career. I have not discovered when she moved to Britain, or why. It is likely that her husband, who seems to have been dead by 1891, was British. In any event, she became a British subject, and by 1891 was living in Brighton and teaching singing. When "God Save the Queen" was sung at the unveiling of the town's Preston Clock Tower on 17 June 1892, she gave a solo rendering of one of the verses. She died in Brighton in 1911, aged 58.

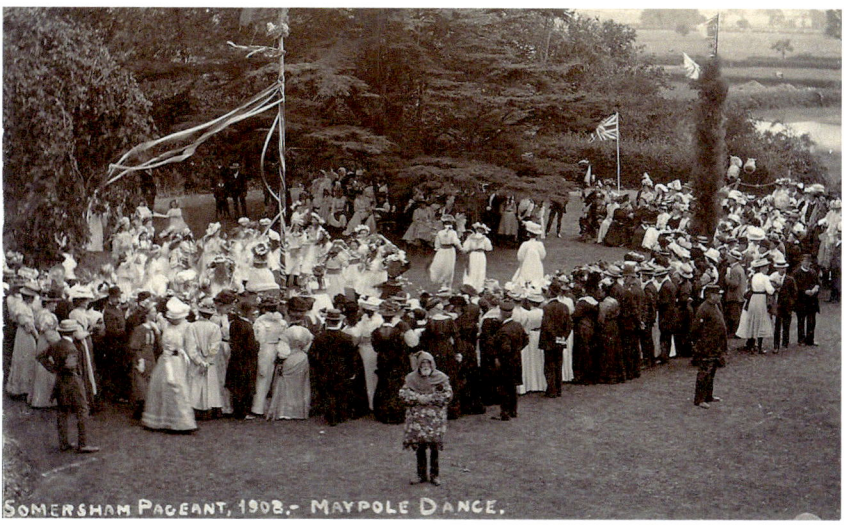

34 The Somersham Pageant, August 1908: maypole dancing.

Come young, come old,
  Be glad and rejoice,
For heaven hath blessed our store
  Throughout the ages long –
Bring the harp and the lute
  With a glad and joyful song.
Come and sing with a merry noise,
  With shouts of joy and mirth,
For the fruit and the corn
  And the fair bright flowers of earth.
With cymbal[14] and with dance
  Let songs of joy abound,
Come, sing with merry noise,
  With a glad and joyful sound.

These preliminaries were followed by twelve tableaux, all concerned with local historical events, ranging in time from Boadicea and the Romans to 1882, when King James the First's grant of the rectory of Somersham to the Regius Professor of Divinity at Cambridge was terminated by an Act of Parliament. Devised by D'Arcy, they were performed on a low stage

14 *SPM*, September 1908, the only source for the words, has "symbol", a homophonous error. In the absence of Dorothy's manuscript, one cannot prove that the error is not hers, but it is perhaps most likely to have been perpetrated by whoever copied the poem for *SPM*.

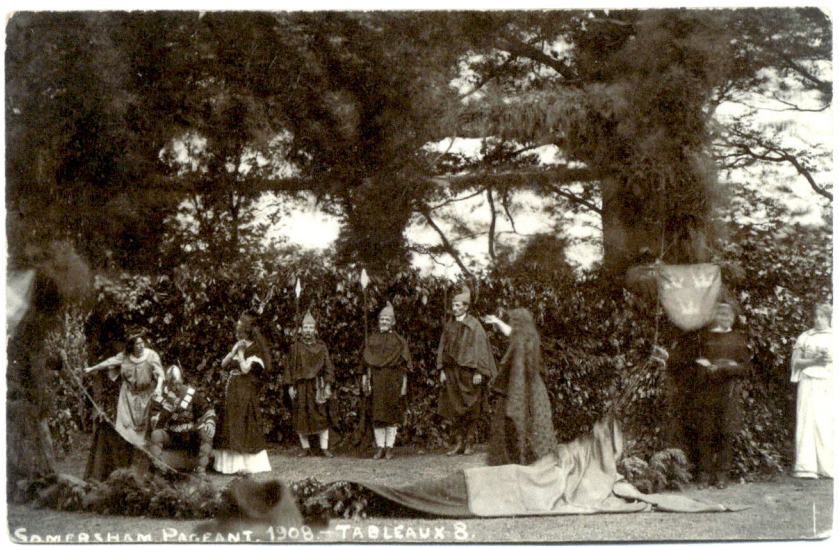

35 The Somersham Pageant, August 1908: Hereward the Wake tableau.

(Plate 35). Magens contributed explanatory remarks, and a musical narrative was provided by a choir or a solo singer.

The real names of some of those who took parts in the tableaux sound marvellously fictional, notably Goodenough and Gotobed. The Miss Goodenough who "made an excellent Boadicea" was clearly more than good enough. Dorothy did not have any role as an actor, the reason being that she was one of three musical accompanists. She played the violin, the others the piano and organ. Since she was passionate about drama and loved acting, she may have been a little disappointed not to have an acting part. One who did have such a part was her father, the Rev. Henry Sayers, who in the fifth tableau, about the dispute between Bishop de L'Isle of Ely and Lady Wake (Blanche Plantagenet), "was particularly good as the bishop" ("Pretty Pageant"). The costume Dorothy wore, the one she is wearing in Plates 30 and 31, is meant to be ancient Greek, like the costumes of the pageant chorus (*SPM*, August 1908).[15] The costumes are misinterpreted as "kind of Druidical" in "Somersham Pageant".

15 The question of exactly where the photographs of Dorothy were taken cannot be answered with certainty: one possibility is that Maddison & Hinde set up a temporary studio in or near the grounds of Somersham Vicarage or even in the Vicarage itself; another is that the photographs were taken at their premises in St Ives; yet another possible location is Bluntisham Rectory. If Maddison & Hinde were permitted to enter the Vicarage grounds to conduct their business, one would expect them to have paid a fee. There is no mention of a payment in the "Epitome of Pageant

Only in the case of five tableaux is the author of the verses sung by the choir or by a soloist named. Dorothy is named as the author in the case of the eighth and tenth tableaux. The omission of the authors' names in seven cases leaves open the possibility that she composed the verses for one or more of them. If one had to conjecture which, if any, of the seven she is most likely to have composed, one might be tempted to choose the second tableau, depicting Hereward the Wake (Plate 35), for, as we shall see, she was to be asked to write about Hereward for a proposed event in 1909. The tableau told the story of how Hereward hid in the forest from the soldiers of William the Conqueror and managed to evade them until he was betrayed by an informer. The story is summarised in the choral narrative:

> Bend your boughs, ye forest trees,
>> Shelter noble Hereward,
>> The foe is on the rearward,
> The dauntless warrior flies apace,
>> From Norman William's tyrant sword;
> Alack! the hope of Saxon rule
>> Hopeless treads our woodland sward.
> Brave, his stand against the foe,
>> Fierce the curse the witch did hurl[16]
> Against the invader – all in vain,
>> Betrayed was he by Norman girl.

On Dorothy's possible authorship of these lines one has to keep an open mind, but my instinct is that the rather painful "Hereward … rearward … sword … sward" would not have been penned by her even at the age of fifteen.

The eighth tableau depicted a visit of King Charles I and his queen consort, Henrietta Maria, to Somersham. It was celebrated in the following verses composed by Dorothy:

> From the pomps of proud St. James',
>> From the splendour of Whitehall,
> From the pageant and the revel,
>> From the purple and the pall,
> The majesty of England hath turned his steps away;
> Ho! gallants, raise a lusty cheer to welcome him to-day.
> To the stalwart sons of labour,
>> To the yeomen of the fen,

Balance Sheet" printed in *SPM*, October 1908, but it might have been included under "Donations and Sundry Receipts".

16 I have deleted a comma printed in *SPM* and "Rural Pageantry" after "hurl".

To the steadfast deep devotion,
  Of true-hearted Englishmen,
Comes the King of royal England,
  With his fair and gentle Queen;
Ho! maidens! Strew their joyous path,
  With flowers across the green.
From the sword of rebel foemen,
  From the hand of traitor earles;
In war and storm and tumult,
  In dangers and in parles,
May England's loyal gentlemen,
  Defend their gallant King;
Pray God protect the Sacred throne,
  Beneath His mighty wing.

The tenth tableau could hardly be described as a tableau. It presented a facsimile of an inscription in the Parish Church chancel in memory of Sir Charles Howard's son, William, who died aged two in 1646. The words, sung mainly solo by Mrs Menagh, partly by the chorus, were written by Dorothy:

Oh! Somersham's leas[17] are[18] green and fair,
And the woodlands sing and the flowers blow there,
  To welcome thee, sweet child.
The winds of the fen ride forth to meet thee,
Hark! How their song doth greet thee.
  Son of Suffolk's lordly line,
  Love and hope and joy be thine,
  See the crimson roses twine;
  Oh! but the wind blows wild!
There is a bed, so dark and deep –
A bed that is made for lasting sleep,
A cradle that's hewn for thee,
Where a wreath of white lilies they shall weave thee,
And the chanting priests receive thee.
In the chancel the tomb is made,
And a grey stone is over thee laid,
And the cypress weeps in the churchyard shade,
And the willow sighs "Woe is me."

Although Dorothy nowhere seems to mention, let alone describe, the pageant, there are several letters in which she mentions the two men who

---

17 *SPM* has "Leas", but there is no reason for a capital letter.
18 *SPM* gives "a green and fair", where "a" would be equivalent to "all", but the next two lines strongly suggest that "are" is intended.

were chiefly responsible for it. Magens first appears in a letter of 24 January 1909, the first letter she wrote to her parents from the Godolphin School. Dorothy reports that her head of house "is a fat girl in spectacles, called – what do you think? – Marjorie Wolley-Dod – isn't that an awful surname? Worse than de Courcy-Ireland."

Her first mention of D'Arcy is in a letter dated 23 February 1908 and written from Bluntisham to her beloved cousin Ivy Shrimpton, who was eight years her senior. Ivy, who lived in London, usually stayed at Bluntisham Rectory once or twice a year. One of her visits was from 4 to 29 August 1908 (*Visitors' Book*), which means that she was with the Sayers family at the time of the pageant, and she is the cousin to whom Dorothy inscribed one of the photographs of herself in costume for it. The letter includes a description of a concert in Somersham on 17 February:[19]

> It was a lovely concert. They had got a splendid tenor rejoicing in the name of d'Arcy de Ferrars – down from London – he sang most beautifully. He was a stout, grey-haired, middle-aged person, with a seal-ring and a seraphic smile. (Reynolds, *The Letters*, 9)

As well as her seeing and hearing D'Arcy in performance, probably for the first time, he saw and heard her, for she played three violin solos – "Shepherds' Dance", "Moto Perpetuo" (Paganini), and the final movement of "Seventh Concerto" ("Somersham: Enjoyable Concert"). Her playing was well received by the audience, for she tells Ivy that it demanded an encore. No doubt D'Arcy was impressed, and it is not surprising that he wanted her to play again at the pageant.

Her second mention of D'Arcy is in the letter in which she comments adversely on Magens's surname:

> I had a letter from dear D'Arcy de Ferrars this morning; it appears he wants *me* to write the whole Hereward play. Rather cool, isn't it? I shall tell him I have very little time. However, I dare say it won't come off this year. (Letter to parents, 24 January 1909)

The proposed play is mentioned in the two spring 1909 issues of *SPM*. The April issue contains the following announcement:

> AN OPEN-AIR PASTORAL PLAY. – We are suggesting to have a Summer Garden Fête, Pastoral Play and dance, etc., perhaps early in August, or about the same time as the Pageant which is being discussed to be held at Ramsey. Mr. De Ferrars has kindly offered to act as the Director of both events, and is preparing an outline of a Musical Play from scenes in "Hereward the Wake,"

---

19 The concert, organised by Magens, was held in the Somersham schoolroom in aid of the fund for the new church organ.

the words of which Miss Sayers is composing so as to fit in with most of the "Pageant" music of last summer.

Dorothy's scepticism about whether the play would "come off this year" turned out to be fully justified. *SPM*, May 1909, carries the following report:

> THE PASTORAL PLAY which was suggested to be given of "Hereward the Wake" during the summer months has been discussed at two public meetings, and Mr. De Ferrars very kindly gave a most interesting descriptive account of the proposed subjects, or events in Hereward's life, to be incorporated in the play, and read some of the verses composed by Miss Sayers, for the illustrative choruses; but there seemed very little desire or interest shewn in the meetings for an open-air play – taking the Parish as a whole – or if it were intended to include all the people. It remains to be seen whether we shall be able to take advantage of Mr. De Ferrar's [*sic*] kind offer and of his able services, of which we may not have the chance again, later on in the summer and find the actors to impersonate the characters and members of a chorus, &c., who are willing to get up the play, for though it is not possible to do so by the Fair-time,[20] it might be about the second week in August.

This describes the situation as it was in (late?) April. A few days later the idea of staging the play at any time in 1909 had been abandoned, for, in a letter of [9 May 1909] to her mother from the Godolphin School, Dorothy writes: "I had a note from little Ireland[21] this morning. He hopes to bring 'Hereward' off next year in June – if he does, I'll eat my armour." It is certain that she did not have to eat her armour. There is no further mention of the Hereward play in her letters or in *SPM*. Although an outdoor event was held in Somersham in June 1910 (see below), the Hereward play was not part of it. It is not clear whether Dorothy completed her writing of it. What she did write is not known to have survived, but it is possible that it is among papers retained by her descendants. The same may be true of other juvenilia from 1909–1911, including issues of *The Belfry*, the magazine, edited and produced by herself, to which she and other members of her Owl Society contributed while she was a pupil at the Godolphin School.[22]

---

20 Somersham's three-day fair was in late June, marking the birthday of St John the Baptist (24 June).

21 It seems that Magens was of small stature. Since the only clear photographs I have seen of his whole figure show him seated, it is difficult to judge his height. It is possible that Dorothy thought it amusing to call him "little" because "Magens" has the ring of "big" – not that the name is actually connected with the Latin *magnus*.

22 The name Owl Society arose out of Dorothy's and some of her schoolfriends' admiration for Florence Mildred White, her French and (sometimes) German teacher at the Godolphin School, the owl being the bird of the goddess Athene whose part Miss

Dorothy mentions D'Arcy again in a letter of 21 March 1909 written to her mother from school:

> About Mr. de Ferrars' concert, or Dr. Barlow's, or whoever it is. I have got from Miss Harding a charming little "Harlequinade" by Squire, which I intended for Warren's entertainment. It would be rather too short, I think, for Somersham. Do you think they would like some of the Bohm [*sic*] suite – say the "March" and the "Intermezzo"? Or of course there's the last de Bériot – the one I played at Cambridge.[23] That's all I can think of at present – have you any ideas on the subject.

Dorothy, who has been invited to play the violin (Miss N. Harding was the Godolphin School's violin teacher), goes on to discuss who might accompany her on the piano. We learn from *SPM*, April 1909, that the concert and the following performance of a farce were to take place in the school in Somersham in aid of the local cricket club on Wednesday, 14 April 1909. We are also told: "The Committee have secured the services of Mr. and Miss de Ferrars, Mrs. Malcolm King, Miss D. Sayers, and Mr. Turner (St. Ives)". However, the quite detailed account of the concert in *SPM*, May 1909, does not mention Dorothy at all, although it does mention the four other artistes, all of whom were singers, and names the pieces they sang. The question arises whether the writer's omission of Dorothy, the only instrumentalist, was an oversight, or whether she did not after all perform. Unfortunately the local newspapers seem not to have reported the concert, so the question cannot be answered.

In 1910 and 1911 D'Arcy was involved in two more events in Somersham. One was a "pageantetta" held as part of a garden fête at the vicarage on 23 June 1910. The other was a mystery play, illustrative of the life of St John the Baptist, performed on the lawn of the vicarage on 28 and

---

White took in a mistresses' play (Sayers, Letter to parents, [12 December 1909]). Known "Owls" and/or contributors to *The Belfry* are Dorothy and her schoolfriends (all to be met in Essay 9) Constance Wollaston, Violet Christy, Anna Hoffmann, Marjorie Gabain, Mollie/Molly Edmondson, and Eleanor Chase. On one occasion Dorothy's father joined the "Owls" in submitting to *The Belfry* an English translation of a sonnet by Sully Prudhomme in a competition that was judged by Miss White. It was arranged that Dorothy would write out all the entries in her own hand, so that they would be anonymous. A recently unearthed letter, written to Dorothy by a schoolfriend who is certainly identifiable as Eleanor Chase, reveals their Owl Society names: Dorothy was "Scops", Eleanor "Strix" (Strix, 31 August 1911). It is likely that the other members too had owl names.

23 The Cambridge concert, organised by a Miss Beale, who sometimes accompanied Dorothy's violin playing on the piano, was on 14 November 1908 (Sayers, Letter to Ivy Shrimpton, 7 November 1908).

29 June 1911. Dorothy did not participate in either event. She was away at school in Salisbury in June 1910. In June 1911 she was at home, despite it being term-time, because she missed the whole of the summer term after falling seriously ill in February, but arrangements for the play, interspersed with vocal solos and choruses, were made very early in the year, before her illness. She may well have seen the play, the libretto of which, taken largely from Scripture, was devised by D'Arcy, with some assistance from local clergy, including her father (*SPM*, February 1911). In 1911 Magens moved from Somersham to Melbourn in Cambridgeshire, and D'Arcy's association with Somersham seems to have come to an end.

Although the pageant of 1908 and the other Somersham events of which mention has been made were local affairs and involved performers who were almost all amateurs, the professional direction and participation of D'Arcy ensured that the enthusiasm and talent of local performers were exploited to the full. The pageant, the first to be held in Huntingdonshire, was an important and memorable event in the locality. It is remarkable that one who had only recently had her fifteenth birthday should have made such a notable contribution to it, gaining for herself special mention in the opening address, in the local press, and even in a national newspaper. The verses she composed may not have been the very best that she penned in her mid-teens, but one must remember that she was writing to order for a musical and to a very tight timetable, and they are very good indeed for one so young. She was probably as modest about her success (one is tempted to say "triumph") as she was to be when she went on to achieve great things at school, but her highly praised part in the pageant must have given her pleasure and increased her confidence in her ability as a writer.

Acknowledgements

I gratefully acknowledge the valuable assistance of the following: David Higham Associates for giving me permission, on behalf of the Trustees of the late Anthony Fleming, to receive photocopies of Dorothy L. Sayers's letters to her parents and Ivy Shrimpton and to make quotations from them as well as to publish the three (perhaps four) "new" poems of hers presented in the essay; the Marion E. Wade Center, Wheaton College, Illinois, for permission to publish the photographs reproduced as Plates 30–31, and for giving me every possible help and encouragement in con-nection with my research on Dorothy, with special thanks to its former Head of Public Services and Archivist, Heidi Truty; The Godolphin School, Salisbury, for allowing me to study and use its archival records; Alan

Draper of Somersham for his extraordinary industry, thoroughness, and kindness in retrieving century-old issues of *Somersham Parish Magazine* from Somersham Church and finding and copying for me accounts of the Somersham Pageant and other local events, in giving me a guided tour of Somersham, and in providing the photographs reproduced as Plates 33–35; Jean Draper; Cedric Williams of The Old Rectory, Somersham, for allowing me to see his scholarly notes on the Rev. Magens de Courcy-Ireland's time as vicar, and for permitting me to visit the Vicarage garden, in which the 1908 pageant was held; John Bell, formerly of Somersham, author of a booklet on the pageant, for much useful information; three officers of Somersham History Society – (Mrs) Julyan Hunter, Helen Cole, and Brian West; Kilmaine de Ferrars and James de Ferrars, grandson and great-grandson respectively of D'Arcy de Ferrars, for information about their ancestor and for kindly supplying the photograph reproduced as Plate 32; Malcolm Taylor, Library Director, English Folk Dance and Song Society at Cecil Sharp House, London; Huntingdon Library and Archives; Christopher Dean, Chairman of The Dorothy L. Sayers Society; the Rev. Sheila Anthony, Rector of Bluntisham; Mike Bateman (churchwarden, Bluntisham); Christine Holgate of Ripon Library; Leofranc Holford-Strevens; the editorial staff of *SEVEN*, especially Assistant Editor Rachel Mink, and the anonymous readers of this essay; and Sally Dowding for being my research assistant, companion, and chauffeuse during visits to Somersham and Huntingdon in January 2011.

References

Bell, John. *The History of Somersham as Dramatised for the Pageant of 1908, Including the Stories of Queen Boadicea and Hereward the Wake*. St Ives, Cambridgeshire: Popular Publications, 1998.

———. *Somersham Parish: 2000 Years in and around the Churches of Somersham, Pidley and Colne*. In six parts. Somersham: Parochial Church Council, 2001. Part 4.

Boadicea to Victoria: A Souvenir of the Ripon Historic Festival, 1896. Ripon: William Harrison, 1897.

Judge, Roy. "D'Arcy Ferris and the Bidford Morris," *Folk Music Journal* 4 (1984), 443–480.

———. "Ferrars, Ernest Richard D'Arcy de (1855–1929)." *Oxford Dictionary of National Biography*. Oxford: Oxford University Press, 2004. www.oxforddnb.com/ view/article/57233. Accessed 2 January 2011.

"Pretty Pageant at Somersham." *The Hunts County News*, 15 August 1908, 8.

Reynolds, Barbara (ed.), *Dorothy L. Sayers: Child and Woman of Her Time: A Supplement to* The Letters of Dorothy L. Sayers. Vol. 5. Swavesey, Cambridge: The Dorothy L. Sayers Society, 2002.

———. *The Letters of Dorothy L. Sayers: 1899–1936: The Making of a Detective Novelist*. London: Hodder & Stoughton, 1995.

"Ripon Historic Festival, 1906." *The Ripon Gazette*, 26 July 1906, [4–5].

Ripon Millenary: A Record of the Festival, also a History of the City, Arranged Under Its Wakemen and Mayors from the Year 1400. Ripon: William Harrison, 1892.

"Rural Pageantry: Historical Display in Huntingdonshire." *The Morning Leader*, 11 August 1908, 1.

Sayers, Dorothy L. *Cat O'Mary. Dorothy L. Sayers: Child and Woman of Her Time*. Ed. Barbara Reynolds. Swavesey, Cambridge: The Dorothy L. Sayers Society, 2002, 23–165.

———. Letter to Ivy Shrimpton. 27 January 1907. Folder 53, p. 81. The Dorothy L. Sayers Papers. The Marion E. Wade Center, Wheaton College, Wheaton, IL.

———. Letter to Ivy Shrimpton. 7 March 1907. Folder 52, p. 10. The Dorothy L. Sayers Papers. The Marion E. Wade Center, Wheaton College, Wheaton, IL.

———. Letter to Ivy Shrimpton. 23 Feb. 1908. Folder 54, pp. 47–48. The Dorothy L. Sayers Papers. The Marion E. Wade Center, Wheaton College, Wheaton, IL.

———. Letter to Ivy Shrimpton. 7 November 1908. Folder 53, p. 55. The Dorothy L. Sayers Papers. The Marion E. Wade Center, Wheaton College, Wheaton, IL.

———. Letter to mother. 21 March 1909. Folder 70, pp. 54, 53. The Dorothy L. Sayers Papers. The Marion E. Wade Center, Wheaton College, Wheaton, IL.

———. Letter to mother. [9 May 1909]. Folder 71, pp. 5–6. The Dorothy L. Sayers Papers. The Marion E. Wade Center, Wheaton College, Wheaton, IL.

———. Letter to parents. 24 January 1909. Folder 70, pp. 2, 3. The Dorothy L. Sayers Papers. The Marion E. Wade Center, Wheaton College, Wheaton, IL.

———. Letter to parents. [12 December 1909]. Folder 72, p. 63. The Dorothy L. Sayers Papers. The Marion E. Wade Center, Wheaton College, Wheaton, IL.

Smith, Martin Ferguson. "'Golliwog', Wolley-Dods, Wollaston, and Others: Some Contemporaries of Dorothy L. Sayers at The Godolphin School, Salisbury." *Proceedings of the Dorothy L. Sayers Society 34th Annual Convention, 14th–17th August, 2009*. Hurstpierpoint, West Sussex: The Dorothy L. Sayers Society, 2010, 85–106.

———. "The Godolphin Schooldays of Dorothy L. Sayers (1909–1911)." Text of the Godolphin Lecture given at the Godolphin School, Salisbury, 19 January 2011. Unpublished typescript.

"Somersham: Enjoyable Concert". *The Hunts County News*, 22 February 1908, 8.

"Somersham Pageant: Historic Day in Huntingdonshire." *The Huntingdonshire Post*, 15 August 1908, 8.

Somersham Parish Magazine. July 1908.

Somersham Parish Magazine. August 1908.

Somersham Parish Magazine. September 1908.

Somersham Parish Magazine. October 1908.

Somersham Parish Magazine. April 1909.

Somersham Parish Magazine. May 1909.

Somersham Parish Magazine. February 1911.

Strix [Eleanor Chase]. Letter to Dorothy L. Sayers. 31 August 1911. Folder 614, pp. 42–65. The Dorothy L. Sayers Papers. The Marion E. Wade Center, Wheaton College, Wheaton, IL.

The Thirsk Historical Play. Thirsk: Z. Wright, 1907.

Visitors' Book of the Sayers family at Bluntisham, 1899–1923. "Sayers Family Papers, 1879–1941", Box 1, Series 2.12. The Marion E. Wade Center, Wheaton College, IL.

Williams, Cedric. Notes on the Vicarship of the Rev. Magens de Courcy-Ireland at Somersham, 1904–1911. Unpublished typescript.

9

"She had quite unusual gifts": Dorothy L. Sayers at school

At the time the original version of this essay was written,[1] the Godolphin School's website listed eighteen "notable alumnae". Rather remarkably, no fewer than four of them were writers of detective novels, which makes one wonder if there is not something in the atmosphere of Salisbury that inspires writing in this genre. Of the four none is more notable than Dorothy Leigh Sayers.[2] Local historian the late Richard Durman calls her "perhaps the most distinguished Old Godolphin"[3] — a judgement that is subjective, but not absurd.

Although known to many only as the writer of the Lord Peter Wimsey novels, which have achieved a wide readership and were successfully adapted for television, with first Ian Carmichael, then Edward Petheridge, playing Wimsey, Dorothy was a versatile author, who also wrote poetry and plays, and who in the last twenty or so years of her life[4] gave the bulk of her time and attention to religion and theology and to the translation of Dante's *Divine Comedy*. It is probably not widely known that words of hers used to be read by many millions across the land: in the 1920s she worked for an advertising agency and, in collaboration with the artist John Gilroy, devised the famous Guinness advertisements, one of which featured a toucan with its large beak arched over two pints of Guinness and Dorothy's punning jingle below:

If he can say as you can
Guinness is good for you
How grand to be a Toucan
Just think what Toucan do.

---

1 That version was "The Godolphin Lecture", given in the Blackledge Theatre at the Godolphin School, Salisbury, on Wednesday, 19 January 2011. The lecture, marking the centenary of the beginning of Dorothy's last year at school, was illustrated.

2 The other three writers are Josephine Bell, Elizabeth Lemarchand, and Minette Walters.

3 Durman, 49–50.

4 She died on 17 December 1957.

Dorothy entered the Godolphin in January 1909 and left in December 1911. She was aged fifteen and a half on entry. Until then, she had been educated by her father, the Rev. Henry Sayers, in the rectory at Bluntisham in what was then Huntingdonshire, and by various governesses. So going to boarding school a long way from home was an awfully big adventure, and she was understandably apprehensive as well as pleasurably excited about it. The momentous decision had been made not later than June 1908, and the choice of the Godolphin in July 1908.[5] It is not clear why she did not start there in September of that year.[6]

Why did her parents decide to send her to school? And why did they choose the Godolphin? The answer to the first question is that they wanted her to go to university, preferably Oxford, and realised that she needed more comprehensive and intensive teaching than she could receive at home. No doubt they also thought that more interaction with other girls would be beneficial to her. The answers to the second question are not all known, but, where not known, can be plausibly guessed. Her parents wanted a school that was not in a big city and had pleasant surroundings with plenty of fresh air, and the Godolphin fulfilled this requirement. No doubt it was a bonus that Salisbury is a cathedral city. Henry Sayers had been headmaster of Christ Church Cathedral School, Oxford, and it amused Dorothy to boast that she had been baptised in one cathedral (Christ Church) and confirmed in another (Salisbury). Obviously her parents were looking for a school that combined high academic standards with a caring and stimulating atmosphere, and the Godolphin admirably met that requirement too.

A major attraction of the Godolphin was its headmistress, Mary Alice Douglas. Although the school had been founded in 1726, it had been very small until it was taken over and virtually refounded by her in 1890.[7] Starting what was to be a thirty-year "reign" with just twenty-two pupils, of whom only seven were boarders, she built it up rapidly, expanding its numbers,[8] adding to its buildings and other amenities, and gaining for it a deserved reputation for academic achievement and a wholesome atmosphere with just the right balance of competition and co-operation. To the

---

5 Sayers, Letter to Ivy Shrimpton, 28 June [1908]; postcard to Ivy Shrimpton postmarked 20 July 1908.
6 According to Brabazon, 31, she missed the whole Autumn Term because of a bout of chickenpox. It seems that he is assuming that Dorothy suffered the same illness as Katherine Lammas in Sayers, *Cat O'Mary*, 79. Perhaps she did, but the assumption is unsafe, and it is to be noted that Katherine did not miss the whole term, only the first three days of it.
7 On the history of the School down to its bicentenary, see Douglas and Ash.
8 In 1908, according to the School Diary, there were over two hundred girls in the School.

amusement of the girls (and she could find it amusing too), her initials spelled out "MAD", but that is the last thing she was. Although she insisted on punctuality and tidiness, her regime was free of petty rules: believing in self-discipline, she gave the girls space to be themselves and to develop their own interests and talents. A clergyman's daughter (and one of his and his wife's sixteen children), she was committed to Christian values and expected high moral standards, but she was far from being concerned only to prepare girls to become good wives and mothers. She appointed teachers who really knew their subjects and were good at communicating that knowledge. That applied not least to modern languages, which were Dorothy's main interest. The school was also strong in drama and music, about both of which, especially drama, Dorothy was passionate. Like all her fellow pupils, she regarded Miss Douglas with considerable awe, but also with respect. It is worth noting that, while some of the girls' nicknames for staff-members were unflattering, the headmistress was neutrally or even affectionately called "The Doug".

To illustrate Miss Douglas's enlightened treatment of Dorothy, one may mention two incidents. One was when Dorothy revealed that she would like to become a professional actor. The Doug's response was not to pooh-pooh the schoolgirl's theatrical ambition, but to comment, wisely, that she would probably have more success as a dramatist.[9] The other incident occurred in Dorothy's last term. On 28 October 1911 a troupe of French actors came to Salisbury to perform in the Picturedrome plays by Labiche and Molière. They were directed by a Monsieur A. Roubaud. They had been to Salisbury before in 1909 and 1910, and Dorothy had impressed and charmed Roubaud with her fluent French and had written a favourable review of the 1909 performance (in French of course) for the *Godolphin School Magazine* (henceforth *GSM*).[10] During the October 1911 performance Roubaud spotted her, and they exchanged a bow and a smile. When the performance was over and the audience was making its way out, Roubaud stood by the door and spoke to her. She tried to reply, but almost before she could say "*Bonsoir, Monsieur*", she was dragged off by the School Matron and School Secretary, who were determined to prevent any conversation and contact. When she protested that she only spoke when Roubaud spoke to her, she was told that she should have ignored him. The Secretary's name was Violet Parson, and V or Vi followed by a P, combined with her perceived poisonous character, easily suggested the nickname "The Viper". Dorothy did not take what had happened lying down, as

---

9 Sayers, Letter to parents, 9 October 1910 = Reynolds, *The Letters*, 49 (misdated by her 8 October 1910).

10 *GSM* 50 [Autumn] (mistakenly shown as "Summer") Term 1911, 28.

she explains in a triumphant letter she wrote to her parents the following day:

> I came up from the town in a fury. Arrived at School, I went straight to Miss Douglas and told her all about it – she was *perfectly ripping* [a favourite word among Godolphins a hundred years ago, but one discouraged by their teachers] and said I had done perfectly right, and Matron and Miss Parson hadn't quite understood, and it was quite right of me to come to her about it. I was awfully glad I had, for that confounded Viper had been before me – Miss D. said: "Miss Parson said something to me about it, but I explained to her, and I think she understands now." I hope to Heaven she gave that woman a good dressing down. Pompous, interfering, conceited ass!!!![11]

Although Dorothy's biographers have described and discussed her time at the Godolphin, rightly recognising its importance in her development as a writer, thinker, and person, they have not always made the best use of the available sources of information. Moreover, they have had little or nothing to say about the fellow-pupils with whom she formed friendships and/or was in close contact. Elsewhere I have written about sixteen of them,[12] and I will briefly mention some of them in the present essay. Although few of them remained in touch with her for long after they left, her interaction with them, whether she got on well with them or not, must have had a significant influence on her; and it is of interest to see what kinds of girls she liked and disliked, for this illuminates her own character.

The main sources on which I rely are: the letters, many of them unpublished, which Dorothy wrote while at the Godolphin; *GSM*, sets of which are to be found in the School Library and in the Wiltshire & Swindon County Archives, Chippenham; and a variety of other material both in Chippenham and at the school. Particularly important among the material at the school is the School Diary, handwritten, but with many items pasted in. I am very grateful to the school for permitting me to study and use its unpublished records.

Dorothy's biographers have not consulted the School Diary, and most have made little or no use of the unpublished letters. At the same time some of them have placed too much trust in Dorothy's unfinished novel *Cat O'Mary*.[13] It is true that the experiences of Katherine Warwick Lammas at the Beaufort School, Carisbury, have much in common with those of Dorothy Leigh Sayers at the Godolphin School, Salisbury. Many of the names in the novel are adapted from the names of Dorothy's Godolphin days. This applies to places: Salisbury becoming Carisbury is one example;

11 Letter to parents, 29 October 1911.
12 Smith, "Golliwog".
13 Sayers, *Cat O'Mary*.

others include the conversion of Cathedral Hotel into Minster Hotel and Nelson House into Wellington House. It applies also to people, both staff and girls. To take some staff names – real name first, fictional name second:

Douglas, Dando
Bagnall, Bellows
Brett, Pratt
Gillman, Goodman
Hancock, Peacock
Jeffreys, Jenkins
Jones, James
Taylor, Naylor
Westlake, Waterhouse
White, Greene[14]

But the correspondences between the names do not mean that the characters and situations in the novel are identical to those encountered by Dorothy in real life. *Cat O'Mary* is a novel with autobiographical elements, not an autobiography. The differences between fiction and fact can be seen at once with reference to Katherine's and Dorothy's arrival at school: Katherine arrives three days after the start of the Autumn Term, Dorothy at the beginning of the Spring Term – not, as has been speculated, an almost solitary arrival, but, as the School Register shows, one of fifteen new girls. Katherine starts in School House, Dorothy started in another house, from which she was transferred to School House after four terms. Katherine's Head of House has red hair and is "an apt classical scholar", Dorothy's, although given the same Christian name, was neither red-headed nor a classicist. When Katherine is about to go to school, Miss Dando is "getting on for seventy"; when Dorothy entered, Miss Douglas was forty-nine. One could mention scores of other differences. And yet several of Dorothy's biographers treat her account in *Cat O'Mary* as essentially factual. It is bad enough to accept details as factual, when they are certainly or possibly fictional; it is worse to identify Dorothy's whole outlook with Katherine's. Take the matter of religion, for example, and specifically that of Dorothy's confirmation on 23 March 1910. In *Cat O'Mary*, which she began writing in 1934, she represents Katherine as hostile to the religious instruction she received at school and as reluctant to be confirmed, but there is no hint of such hostility or reluctance in her letters from school; on the contrary, she seems very happy with what the school offered, and, as for the big day, the day of the confirmation service, the unfavourable description in *Cat*

---

14 For detailed lists of correspondences between the names of staff and pupils in the schools attended by Dorothy in real life and by Katherine Lammas in *Cat O'Mary*, see Smith, "Golliwog", 99–100.

O'Mary is in sharp conflict with the account in letters Dorothy wrote at the time. Contrast these extracts. First, *Cat O'Mary*:

> The veils provided for the candidates were of an excessive ugliness. ... The dead white made Katherine's plain eyes and high forehead look plainer than even she could have believed possible. ... The day was wet, and the candidates went down to the Cathedral in three moth-eaten fourwheelers, smelling like damp and ill-ventilated loose-boxes.

As for the service: "Katherine fixed her eyes on the hymn-sheet and thought how awful it was and what a hypocrite she was."[15] And now the letter she wrote to her parents on the day, immediately after returning to the school from the service:

> It was an awfully nice service. ...We drove down to the Cath[edral] – it was a glorious day – I was quite hot in my muslin frock. ... Our veils were most awfully nice – chiffon – very simple, with just a little ruche at the top. I thought they looked nicer than any others, and people who could see better than I could say the same.[16]

It cannot be the case that Dorothy is giving a favourable report just to please her clergyman father and her mother, for what she tells her cousin Ivy Shrimpton is equally positive. After telling her that "the Lent term ... was awfully nice this year", she writes of the confirmation: "It was a lovely day, and it all went off beautifully."[17] The only plausible explanation for the divergent accounts is that the experiences and views attributed to Katherine on the day of her confirmation in *Cat O'Mary* are as fictional as the conversion of a gloriously fine day, which in fact it was,[18] into a dismally wet one and attractive veils into ugly ones. One might add that, as photographs of the young Dorothy show, she was not the plain-looking girl described in her novel.

Among the biographers who believe that the novel's portrayal of Katherine as unhappy at school more accurately represents Dorothy's feelings at the Godolphin than the letters she wrote at the time is James Brabazon, who in his chapter on her schooldays cites *Cat O'Mary* thirteen times, but her letters from the Godolphin only five times.[19] Although he

---

15 Sayers, *Cat O'Mary*, 114–115.
16 Letter to parents, 23 March 1910.
17 Letter to Ivy Shrimpton, 9 April [1910].
18 Meteorological forecasts and reports in *The Times* on 23 March 1910, 10, and 24 March 1910, 19, show that the weather throughout England, under the influence of an anticyclone, was dry and settled. No rain fell anywhere on 23 March, the day of the Confirmation, and many places in the south enjoyed prolonged sunshine.
19 Brabazon, 31–41.

allows that Dorothy "did not feel homesick" and "was interested" and, while interested, "could never be totally miserable", he calls her "unhappy" and claims that "in her letters home she found it quite impossible to speak of her mental and physical distress". The same line is taken by David Coomes, who in his Godolphin pages cites *Cat O'Mary* nine times, but the letters only once. He calls Dorothy's years at the Godolphin "mostly miserable".[20] According to Janet Hitchman, Dorothy "soon began to loathe the place".[21] Catherine Kenney describes her schooldays as "an unhappy experience which [she] later recalled in *Cat O'Mary*".[22] A notable absentee from this list of writers who take a dismal view of Dorothy's Godolphin days is her goddaughter Barbara Reynolds.[23]

Of course her letters describe reverses as well as triumphs, disagreeable events and people as well as agreeable ones, and she often says how much she is looking forward to the holidays, but the overall impression she gives is of interest, enthusiasm, enjoyment, and merriment. Adjectives like "ripping" and "killing" abound. It is impossible to believe that she is putting all this on for the sake of her parents. What is certainly true is that 1911 was a less happy year for her than 1909 and 1910 had been, but that is hardly surprising because, as we shall see, she very nearly died during the Spring Term and missed the whole of the Summer Term; it is also true that her time at the Godolphin came to an abrupt end, in mysterious circumstances, before the end of the Autumn Term 1911.

In *Cat O'Mary* Katherine is represented as a fish out of water when she arrives at school. She cannot find her way about the place, keeps doing the wrong things, and makes a poor impression on most of the other girls. She dreads the idea of playing games. Nothing much goes right until she has her first French lesson in the Lower Fifth. On entering the classroom, the mistress asks in French if anyone can tell her who Molière was. She is met with blank looks and silence. She asks again with a similar response until a shy hand goes up in the back row. In perfect French Katherine tells the class exactly who Molière was, mentioning not only his best-known plays, but also an obscure one. Her star performance brings every head round to gape at this prodigy, hitherto regarded with contempt. Nobody is more stunned than the mistress, "who had never before in her life heard the subjunctive accurately and readily placed within the walls of the Lower Fifth".[24] How closely does this account describe Dorothy's own experiences

---

20 Coomes, 40.
21 Hitchman, 13.
22 Kenney.
23 Reynolds, *Dorothy L.* Sayers, 27–43.
24 Sayers, *Cat O'Mary*, 87.

in her first days at the Godolphin? Well, it is perfectly normal to encounter initial problems with the topography, regulations, and routine of a new boarding school, but Dorothy's early letters do not mention anything really worrisome. As for games, it is certainly true that she did not care for them, especially team games. What of her performance in the French lesson? One would love to believe that the incident actually occurred as described, as several of her biographers assume. But Dorothy does not make any mention of it in a letter home, which one might expect her to have done. So some scepticism is in order. What is not in doubt is that she had an outstandingly good knowledge of French language and literature, and very early in her first term she was promoted from the Lower Fifth to the Upper Fifth.

The house in which she was placed on arrival was very small, accommodating nine girls. It was called Oakhurst. For games and all school competitions it was combined with a house called Glenside with just four residents, the combination being known as Glenhurst. From Dorothy's first letters home we learn what sort of girls she likes and dislikes.

The house prefect was definitely not to her taste. "The head of Oakhurst is a fat girl in spectacles, called — what do you think? — Marjorie Wolley-Dod — isn't that an awful surname?" So she wrote in a letter home.[25] In a letter of the same date to her cousin Ivy Shrimpton, she offers an alternative version of the name – Woolly Dog.[26] She found Marjorie too full of her own importance, too loud, and too bossy. Marjorie, the daughter of a pioneer rancher in Canada, was not at all academic, and she and Dorothy had no common interests. Dorothy's relief when Marjorie left in December 1909 was short-lived, for January 1910 saw the arrival of the latter's two younger sisters, Rosamond and Nancy. Dorothy, who shared a bedroom with them, describes their jarring accents and calls them "rude and tiresome — they are an awful nuisance, those children — quite untamed, and one in particular most objectionable".[27] Being spared further close contact with them must have been one of the reasons why she was pleased to be transferred to School House at the beginning of Summer Term 1910. (Another, incidentally, was that School House had electric light.) But, as we shall see, she was not going to be able to forget the Wolley-Dods.

Much more to Dorothy's taste was a girl in her bedroom in Oakhurst, Violet Christy. Writing to her mother, she describes Violet as "a nice quiet girl, not one of your 'loud, robustious women', and she's fond of reading and writing and acting and things like that, and she bicycles …".[28] Her

25 Letter to parents, 24 January 1909.
26 Letter to Ivy Shrimpton, 24 January 1909.
27 Letter to parents, [23 January 1910].
28 Letter to mother, 7 February 1909.

friendship with Violet was close and important to her during her first term as she settled into the Godolphin, and Rose Mason, who is kind and helpful to the newly arrived Katherine in *Cat O'Mary*, owes something, but by no means everything, to Violet. But during her second term Dorothy became very friendly also with a School House girl called Constance Wollaston, nicknamed "Coney", and by the time Violet left the Godolphin at the end of Spring Term 1910, her friendship was much less congenial to Dorothy than Coney's. Why? Well, for one thing Violet had resented Dorothy having another close friend. Also, as Dorothy got to know her better, she increasingly perceived her as self-satisfied and boring. The girls she liked most were those who genuinely shared her passions for languages, literature, and drama, and who were somewhat unconventional in their tastes.

Coney was just such a person, as Dorothy explains in letters to her mother: she likes her "because she's rather less conventional than the rest of the school, and she's got very much my tastes. … I am rather sorry for her; she isn't awfully popular at school and I don't think she has a frightfully good time of it at home."[29] There is the bonus that "she is a very quiet sort of person", although Dorothy warns her mother that "she is not awfully prepossessing at first sight. She is one of those unfortunate people who never look well put together."[30] The context of this assessment is that Dorothy wants Coney to come to stay. Coney was three years older than Dorothy, but evidently the age-difference was as unimportant to Dorothy as Coney's unprepossessing looks. What mattered was that Coney had good French and German, loved drama, and was generally on her wavelength.

Unconventional at school, Coney took an unconventional step in the First World War, when she became a policewoman. She was promoted Sergeant in June 1917. In joining the police, something that was impossible for a woman before the First World War, she anticipated the unexpected career-change made in her mid-forties by Dorothy's and her beloved Modern Languages teacher Florence Mildred White (known among the girls as Fanny Maud), who left the Godolphin in 1917 and the following year became the first female police officer in Wiltshire.

Another older girl with whom Dorothy formed a friendship during her second term was Marjorie Gabain. Marjorie was two years senior to Dorothy and, like Coney, in the Sixth Form. Dorothy describes her as an "awfully nice girl",[31] "a ripping sort and so frightfully clever".[32] Like

---

29 Letter to mother, [13 June 1909].
30 Letter to mother, 12 December 1909.
31 Letter to mother, [13 June 1909]. Marjorie Gabain is not named, but there is little doubt that she is meant.
32 Letter to parents, 1 October 1911.

Dorothy, Marjorie was a fluent French speaker, in fact a native French speaker, for her father was French and she had been born and brought up in Le Havre. Like Dorothy and Coney, she also spoke good German. What made her especially attractive to Dorothy was that she was passionate about drama, including French drama, and acting. She showed her talent for acting, as well as for music and dancing, at the Godolphin, and, after reading Moral Sciences at Newnham College, Cambridge, became a professional actress, whose stage career, spanning the years 1915 to 1939, was pursued in Paris, with la Comédie Française, as well as in London and Bristol.

Marjorie Rawlings in *Cat O'Mary*, a girl "who was potty about the theatre",[33] suits Marjorie Gabain, but also Mollie Edmondson, who entered the Godolphin in April 1910 and soon became a close friend of Dorothy, who liked her because "she, like myself, is considered a 'weird freak' by the conventional part of this establishment".[34] Mollie, like Dorothy, a clergyman's daughter, loved drama and acting, and the two stayed in one another's homes in the holidays.

Coney, Marjorie, and Mollie were among those who contributed to Dorothy's home-produced magazine, *The Belfry*.[35] Another was a German girl, Anna Hoffmann, who came to Oakhurst at the beginning of Dorothy's second term and was put in her bedroom, probably because her English was imperfect and Dorothy's German was good. Anna stayed for only a year, but her friendship with Dorothy survived the two World Wars.[36] Yet another contributor was Eleanor Chase, represented in *Cat O'Mary* by Elizabeth Cornish. Eleanor too was at the Godolphin for only a year (1910–1911) before going on to Girton College, Cambridge, and Dorothy was absent for half of that time, but the two got on well and were in contact from time to time until at least 1951. Dorothy calls her "a very nice girl and very clever".[37] In 1913, when Eleanor was in her second year at Cambridge and Dorothy in her first at Oxford, Eleanor caused irritation when she stayed with the Sayers family. It was her fifth stay with them and, significantly, her last! Writing to a Somerville friend, Dorothy complains that Eleanor

has adopted the dreadful "pose of being natural" which is the posiest pose I know. You know what I mean. She dresses all anyhow and does her hair hideously, and sprawls about all loose at the joints in ugly attitudes and wears

---

33 Sayers, *Cat O'Mary*, 129.
34 Letter to mother, 19 June 1910.
35 See Essay 8, 214 and n. 22.
36 Reynolds, *The Letters*, 24 n. 4.
37 Letter to mother, 20 November 1910.

no stays. ... She is also very keen on Socialism and suffrage and eugenics and God knows what.[38]

As we have seen, Dorothy liked people to be "unconventional", but the unconventionality had to be sincere. Anyhow, the First World War soon put an end to all that "posy" nonsense described by Dorothy! Eleanor worked for the War Office and the Russian Commission of the Board of Trade before in 1917 joining the Air Ministry, where she was the officer in charge of the Translation Section of the Air Intelligence Department. Dorothy and her contemporaries had their schooling in a period of calm before storm, and the War was to alter the lives of many of them, sometimes painfully, but often taking them into areas of employment and responsibility that had not been open to women before.

After Dorothy's death in December 1957, *Godolphin Gazette* printed an obituary of her.[39] The contributor is not named, but is known to be one of her contemporaries in School House, Ivy Phillips. While acknowledging Dorothy's "extraordinary ability and great talent for Modern Languages and everything dramatic", she regrets that she "came to a public school too late" and so "found it hard to play a full part in the school community", and she stresses her loneliness. As we have seen, Dorothy was not keen on games, but to suggest that she was lonely and did not participate fully in the life of the school is nonsense. Her letters make clear that she enjoyed the company of selected friends, enjoyed school outings, and enjoyed school dances, concerts, and plays, whether as a spectator or as a participant.

During her first term she had parts in two plays, first an unusual adaptation of *Red Riding Hood*, in which, according to *GSM*, she was "excellent" as the Wolf,[40] then *Coriolanus*. She was to continue to be an enthusiastic participant in and organiser of dramatic activities throughout her time at the Godolphin. She was also a member of the School Orchestra, in which she played the violin. From Autumn 1909, when she had moved into the Sixth Form, she was a regular contributor to *GSM*, writing reviews in French, original poems, and poetic translations. One of her poems was addressed "To Sir Ernest Shackleton and his Brave Companions".[41] Shackleton, who had nearly reached the South Pole, had given a lecture on his expedition in the County Hall, Salisbury, on 11 October 1910 and the school had heard it. Dorothy sent her poem to Shackleton, and was thrilled to receive

---

38 Letter to Catherine Godfrey, 28 March 1913, in Reynolds, *The Letters*, 72–73, where the letter is misdated April 1913.

39 *Godolphin Gazette* 160 (September 1958), 46–47.

40 Dorothy describes the production in a letter to Ivy Shrimpton, 28 February 1909.

41 *GSM* 48 (Spring Term 1911), 21.

a reply. As one would expect of one destined to become a famous author, the quality of her writing is extraordinarily good. This is well illustrated by her translation of the sonnet "La mort du soleil" ("The Death of the Sun") by the French poet Leconte de Lisle. The poem was given to the Sixth Form by Miss White as a translation exercise, in the expectation that her pupils would translate it into English prose. Dorothy was not content to do that, and produced a sonnet so brilliant that Miss White went into raptures and insisted that it be published in *GSM*:

> As break the sounding billows far away,
>   With murmur of regret and nameless woe,
>   Down the long glades the autumn wind sighs low,
> O Sun! and all the dusky copses sway,
> Red with thy blood. In wild, fantastic play
>   Whirls the sere leaf, and in the crimson glow
>   Great nests on the bare boughs swing to and fro,
> Rocked into slumber at the close of day.
>
>   Sink, radiant star! Thy glory floods the west
> In streams of splendour from thy wounded breast,
> So falls from great soul a love sublime –
>   Sink! For we know that thou shalt rise ere long;
> But when the sad heart breaks for the last time,
>   Who shall give back its light and life and song?[42]

In Autumn 1910 Dorothy became editor of *GSM*, succeeding my aunt Jean Smith. At the same time she also succeeded Jean as Secretary of the Debating Society. The Debating Society, open to staff and girls from the Sixth and Fifth Forms, met twice a term. Dorothy took an interest in it from the beginning, and in October 1909, when Jean, a classicist, proposed the motion "That the study of the Classics is more beneficial than that of modern languages", Dorothy led the opposition, which easily won. Jean was Head of School House, to which Dorothy was transferred in Summer Term 1910, and Head of School in 1909–1910; the two were in the Sixth Form together; and they acted together in a play, Dorothy's preparation for which included sending an urgent request to her parents: "Could you please send me my dagger paper-knife … I *must* have it, please, … because I have to offer to stab Jean in my scene."[43] Despite their sharing of activities, and despite their having some significant common interests, including poetry (Jean was to have a slim volume of hers published by Oxford University Press), no close friendship developed. One suspects that Dorothy regarded

---

42 *GSM* 45 (Spring Term 1910), 11.
43 Letter to parents, 17 July 1910.

Jean as too conventional, and that Jean thought Dorothy not conventional enough. The same sort of relationship, cordial and co-operative but not involving close friendship, existed between Dorothy and Natasha Harris, future cipher specialist at Bletchley Park, who succeeded Jean as Head of School House and Head of School. Natasha too had things in common with Dorothy: she was a good musician, actor, and linguist, with fluent Russian as well as French, but again probably too conventional for Dorothy.

Academically, Dorothy was not the School's best all-rounder. That was Barbara Tracey, yet another clergyman's daughter, represented in *Cat O'Mary* by Barbara Haines, "who, of all Katherine's contemporaries, was the best able to hold her own with her intellectually".[44] Dorothy was unimpressive in some subjects, including mathematics, despite the best efforts of her teacher Miss Hancock, whose birdlike appearance and unusual opinions (she considered drama immoral) are vividly described by Dorothy in a letter home.[45] But in Modern Languages she was unsurpassed. In the Higher Certificate Examination in summer 1909, when there were six distinctions in papers sat by Godolphin candidates, no fewer than three were obtained by Dorothy – in French, German, and English. The following summer she took French and German again, and again obtained distinctions, although probably the greater triumph for her was that she passed Arithmetic and Algebra.

On 18 January 1911, when the school re-opened for the Spring Term, Miss Douglas proudly announced that Dorothy had passed Group B in the Cambridge Higher Local Examination, obtaining distinctions in spoken and written French and spoken German and coming top of all the candidates in England in these languages. Although Dorothy claims to be sickened with all the fuss, she must have felt pleased with herself, and she had plans. She was preparing to sit for a scholarship in French at Oxford, probably at Lady Margaret Hall. And she was excited about stage-managing an act of *Les Femmes Savantes* to celebrate the 238th anniversary of her beloved Molière's death on 17 February. The performance was her idea, warmly approved by Miss Douglas. But these plans were to be thwarted. In the days before there were effective inoculation programmes, outbreaks of infectious diseases were frequent in boarding schools. In November and early December 1908 an outbreak of diphtheria at the Godolphin caused all the girls to be sent home for Christmas two weeks early. In Spring Term 1911 the problems were measles and mumps. The measles epidemic started on the second day of term. Dorothy reports the case thus:

44 Sayers, *Cat O'Mary*, 129.
45 Letter to mother, 7 February 1909.

I ought to inform you that there is a case of measles at Nelson House – a Wolley Dod of course – but it has gone to the San[atorium] and the whole house is in quarantine so it probably won't spread. Wolley Dods were made to plague their neighbours.[46]

So Dorothy is quite relaxed and jokey about the situation. But she was wrong in thinking that the infection would not spread, and what was to happen to her was no joking matter.

In the absence of the headmistress, the school doctor isolated Nelson House from the rest of the school, but, when Miss Douglas returned three days later, she stopped this prudent arrangement, whereupon the infection spread rapidly. Out of about two hundred girls, ninety succumbed – almost all of those who were not already immune. Dorothy went to the Sanatorium in the week beginning 5 February and developed the complication of pneumonia in her left lung. On the night of 23 February her condition suddenly deteriorated, and her life was in the balance. According to *Cat O'Mary*, where Katherine is given the same experience, the specialist who had been summoned in this crisis did not arrive, and it was the school doctor who saved the patient's life by giving her a saline injection. Perhaps he did, but I hesitate to follow Dorothy's biographers in accepting this particular as factual, for it is not contained in the detailed account Miss Douglas gave governors and parents in a circular dated 24 February;[47] in fact, she says that Dorothy was seen by a London specialist on the 24th. One possibility is that the school doctor gave the injection on the recommendation of the specialist in advance of the latter's arrival.

Dorothy did not return to school that term, and she was absent for the whole of the Summer Term 1911. Her Molière production, to which she had been looking forward so much, did not take place, and she did not sit her Oxford scholarship papers. Given the seriousness of her illness, it was completely understandable that she missed what remained of the Spring Term. But why did she not return at the beginning of the Summer Term, when her convalescence was over? Presumably she did not want to do so, and her parents thought a longer break would be beneficial. One must not underestimate the traumatic effect of her near-dying experience, and there was the further point that, as a result of her illness, she lost all her hair and for a while had to wear a wig.

She returned to the Godolphin in September 1911, to prepare for the scholarship examination in 1912. This time she was aiming for Somerville. She was now eighteen. She had been appointed a form prefect a year before.

46 Letter to parents, 22 January 1911.
47 The letter is in the School Diary.

Now she was a house prefect as well. In her second letter of the term she is amused to report: "the night before last I had to give the whole House a fearful blowing up on the subject of – what do you think? – untidiness!!! I did feel such a hypocrite!"[48] If she was unhappy about returning to the Godolphin after an interval of six months, her letters give no hint of that. She is thrilled that School House is going to stage *The Merchant of Venice*, and that she is to play Shylock. Although Ivy Phillips claimed that Dorothy "was obliged to wear a wig for the rest of her schooldays", she is refuted by Dorothy herself. Writing home about her costume for the play, she says: "I don't think I shall need a wig, unless I had a nice grey half-bald one; my own hair is rather thick on top for Shylock."[49] One must not forget the outrage in the Picturedrome, when the Viper and Matron tried to prevent her from speaking to Monsieur Roubeau, but the Doug had sided with her over that, so that she emerged in triumph. She finished the editing of the Autumn Term issue of *GSM*. She was very chuffed that in mid-December she would be playing the violin at a concert in the Albert Hall, the School Orchestra having been invited to join other schools in a huge orchestra. She was going to sing a solo in the end of term concert. So the picture looked very positive.

But she was not to make it to the end of term. She did not act in the house play; she did not sing at the school concert; she did not play in the Albert Hall. Why not? Her biographers quote *GSM*'s version of what Miss Douglas said to the school on 19 December 1911: "It was a great disappointment that Dorothy Sayers had to leave on account of illness. She is going to try at home to win her scholarship."[50] But the School Diary gives the full – or a much fuller – version of the Headmistress's words, and it increases rather than lessens the mystery:

> Dorothy Sayers – It is a great disappointment – a double one – it is strange. We thought last spring that she was going to bring honour to her school and win a scholarship at Oxford. She had great gifts, quite unusual gifts, and she had made good use of them. She came back again to have another try, but it was not to be – she has had another illness, though she is well again, it is a great disappointment that she has to leave. She is going to try at home to win her scholarship. None of her work is lost, or of Miss White's or Frl Seipp's, it will be all right.

The nature of the illness is nowhere specified. In her last letter from school to her parents, written on Sunday, 26 November, Dorothy says that she is

48 Letter to parents, 8 October 1911.
49 Letter to parents, 29 October 1911.
50 *GSM* 51 (Spring Term 1912), 7.

longing to come home and counting the days to the holidays. She also says: "I say, I hope you're not being alarmed by this scarlet-fever scare. I don't think there's much danger – I wish I did – I'd give my ears to come home – but really I don't see how I could catch it." When her parents read this, they probably did not take seriously her wish to fall ill, and it is doubtful if Dorothy meant it seriously. But, given that she quickly recovered from whatever illness she had, but still withdrew from school, one must accept that she could not face staying on for the Spring Term 1912. But what exactly occurred is a mystery. Was the illness physical, psychosomatic, or even partly feigned? We do not know. All we can say is that, whatever happened, happened between 26 November and 3 December, when she was due to write her next letter home.

Miss Douglas was as shrewd a judge of ability as she was of character, and she was quite right in predicting that, with the help of the school's French and German teachers, there would be a happy outcome to Dorothy's preparation for the Oxford scholarship. The School Diary records that on 28 March 1912: "Miss Douglas … announced that in spite of all the drawbacks through illness *Dorothy Sayers had won the Gilchrist Scholarship for Somerville College, Oxford*. There was great clapping."[51] Dorothy was not present to hear the announcement. It seems that she returned to the school only on one occasion. That was for Commemoration in September 1912, at which she exhibited some of her photographic work and won a prize for it. The last occasion on which she took the initiative in contacting the Godolphin may have been in 1920, when she communicated some news of herself. She did not become a member of the Old Godolphin Association.

That her memories of her time at school were mixed is very understandable in view of what happened to her in 1911, and one suspects that things would have been rather different if she had not been taken seriously ill, had won a scholarship in 1911, and left the Godolphin in April or July of that year. That unfortunate third year, during which she was in school and well for no more than twelve or thirteen weeks, seems to have coloured her perception of her whole time in Salisbury, and this jaundiced perception is reflected in *Cat O'Mary*, whose picture is, as we have seen, often in conflict with the picture presented by her letters.

Whatever the exact truth may be about the degree of happiness or unhappiness she experienced at school, and about the reason for her abrupt departure before the end of Autumn Term 1911, her time at the Godolphin had a significant impact on her educational and personal development. She found certain aspects of school life irksome from time to time, but undoubtedly

---

51 The Gilchrist Scholarship, awarded triennially and tenable for three years, was worth £50 p.a., the equivalent of about £5,600 p.a. in 2018.

she benefited a great deal, and much more than she was prepared to admit, from the high standard of education it gave her, from the civilised and stimulating atmosphere fostered by its exceptional headmistress, and from the varied contacts she had with her fellow-pupils as well as with her teachers.

Acknowledgements

I repeat the grateful acknowledgements recorded at the end of Essay 8 to the Godolphin School, Salisbury, David Highman Associates, and the Marion E. Wade Center at Wheaton College, Illinois, adding my warm thanks to the Godolphin School for inviting me to be the Godolphin Lecturer, 2011, and to the present archivist of the Marion E. Wade Center, Laura Schmidt.

References

Brabazon, James. *Dorothy L. Sayers: A Biography*. London: Victor Gollancz, 1981.

Coomes, David. *Dorothy L. Sayers: A Careless Rage for Life*. Batavia, IL: Lion Publishing, 1992.

Douglas, M. A. and C. R. Ash (eds). *The Godolphin School 1726–1926*. London: Longmans, Green, 1928.

Durman, Richard. *Milford: Sarum Studies 1*. Salisbury: Hobnob Press, 2007.

Godolphin School Magazine (GSM).

Hitchman, Janet. *Such a Strange Lady: A Biography of Dorothy L. Sayers*. New York: Harper & Row, 1975.

Kenney, Catherine. "Sayers, Dorothy Leigh." *Oxford Dictionary of National Biography*. Oxford: Oxford University Press, 2004, www.oxforddnb.com/view/article/35966, accessed 1 May 2006.

[Phillips, Ivy]. Obituary of Dorothy Sayers, *Godolphin Gazette* 60, September 1958, 46–47.

Reynolds, Barbara. *Dorothy L. Sayers: Her Life and Soul*. London: Hodder & Stoughton, 1993.

———. (ed.) *The Letters of Dorothy L. Sayers: 1899–1936: The Making of a Detective Novelist*. London: Hodder & Stoughton, 1995.

Sayers, Dorothy L. *Cat O'Mary*, in *Child and Woman of Her Time: A Supplement to The Letters of Dorothy L. Sayers*. Vol. 5. Edited by Barbara Reynolds, vol. 5. Swavesey, Cambridge: The Dorothy L. Sayers Society, 2002.

———. Letter to Ivy Shrimpton, 28 June [1908]. Folder 54, pp. 86–87. The Dorothy L. Sayers Papers. The Marion E. Wade Center, Wheaton College, Wheaton, IL.

———. Postcard to Ivy Shrimpton, postmark 20 July 1908. Folder 54, p. 78. The Dorothy L. Sayers Papers. The Marion E. Wade Center, Wheaton College, Wheaton, IL.

———. Letter to Ivy Shrimpton, 24 January 1909, Folder 53, p. 6. The Dorothy L. Sayers Papers. The Marion E. Wade Center, Wheaton College, Wheaton, IL.

———. Letter to parents, 24 January 1909, Folder 70, p. 3. The Dorothy L. Sayers Papers. The Marion E. Wade Center, Wheaton College, Wheaton, IL.

———. Letter to mother, 7 February 1909, Folder 70, p. 15. The Dorothy L. Sayers Papers. The Marion E. Wade Center, Wheaton College, Wheaton, IL.

———. Letter to Ivy Shrimpton, 28 February 1909, Folder 53, p. 11. The Dorothy L. Sayers Papers. The Marion E. Wade Center, Wheaton College, Wheaton, IL.

———. Letter to mother, [13 June 1909], Folder 71, pp. 28–30. The Dorothy L. Sayers Papers. The Marion E. Wade Center, Wheaton College, Wheaton, IL.

———. Letter to parents, 23 January 1910, Folder 73, p. 4. The Dorothy L. Sayers Papers. The Marion E. Wade Center, Wheaton College, Wheaton, IL.

———. Letter to mother, 12 December 1909, Folder 72, p. 61. The Dorothy L. Sayers Papers. The Marion E. Wade Center, Wheaton College, Wheaton, IL.

———. Letter to parents, 23 March 1910, Folder 73, pp. 48–49. The Dorothy L. Sayers Papers. The Marion E. Wade Center, Wheaton College, Wheaton, IL.

———. Letter to Ivy Shrimpton, 9 April [1910], Folder 47, p. 19. The Dorothy L. Sayers Papers. The Marion E. Wade Center, Wheaton College, Wheaton, IL.

———. Letter to mother, 19 June 1910, Folder 75, p. 41. The Dorothy L. Sayers Papers. The Marion E. Wade Center, Wheaton College, Wheaton, IL.

———. Letter to parents, 17 July 1910, Folder 75, pp. 55–56. The Dorothy L. Sayers Papers. The Marion E. Wade Center, Wheaton College, Wheaton, IL.

———. Letter to parents, 9 October 1910, Folder 74, p. 13. The Dorothy L. Sayers Papers. The Marion E. Wade Center, Wheaton College, Wheaton, IL.

———. Letter to mother, 20 November 1910, Folder 74, p. 45. The Dorothy L. Sayers Papers. The Marion E. Wade Center, Wheaton College, Wheaton, IL.

———. Letter to parents, 22 January 1911, Folder 76, p. 4. The Dorothy L. Sayers Papers. The Marion E. Wade Center, Wheaton College, Wheaton, IL.

———. Letter to parents, 1 October 1911, Folder 77, p. 3. The Dorothy L. Sayers Papers. The Marion E. Wade Center, Wheaton College, Wheaton, IL.

———. Letter to parents, 8 October 1911, Folder 76, p. 4. The Dorothy L. Sayers Papers. The Marion E. Wade Center, Wheaton College, Wheaton, IL.

———. Letter to parents, 29 October 1911, Folder 77, pp. 22–23, 26–27. The Dorothy L. Sayers Papers. The Marion E. Wade Center, Wheaton College, IL.

Smith, Martin Ferguson. "'Golliwog', Wolley-Dods, Wollaston, and Others: Some Contemporaries of Dorothy L. Sayers at The Godolphin School, Salisbury". *Proceedings of the Dorothy L. Sayers Society 34th Annual Convention, 14th–17th August, 2009*. Hurstpierpoint, Sussex: The Dorothy L. Sayers Society, 2010, 85–106.

10

The secret love-child of an American Civil War commander: The strange story of Tolkien's schoolteacher

Daniel Harris Reynolds (Plate 36) is well known to historians of Arkansas for his distinguished service in the Confederate Army and for the lively and illuminating diary that he kept throughout the Civil War.[1] Born near Centerburg in Hilliar Township, Knox County, Ohio, on 14 December 1832, he was the fourth of the ten children of Amos Reynolds and Sophia Houck, farmers.[2] After the deaths of his parents, he studied at the recently founded Ohio Wesleyan University from 1850 to 1854 and became a freemason in 1853. From Delaware, Ohio, he moved to Iowa in 1854, then to Somerville, Tennessee, three years later to study law.

After qualifying as an attorney at law, he established his own practice in Lake Village, Chicot County, Arkansas, taking up residence there on 15 June 1858.[3] The settlement, which was to be his home for the rest of his life, was small but had gained significance in 1857, when it became

---

1 A typescript transcription of the diary is item no. 131 in the Daniel Harris Reynolds Papers [hereinafter DHR Papers], MS R32, Special Collections, University of Arkansas Libraries, Fayetteville. It has been published, edited by Robert Patrick Bender, as *Worthy of the Cause for Which They Fight: The Civil War Diary of Brigadier General Daniel Harris Reynolds, 1861–1865* (Fayetteville: University of Arkansas Press, 2011). The DHR Papers were given to the University of Arkansas by Martha Hill Williams, the elder daughter of Reynolds's eldest acknowledged child, Kate Reynolds Hill. It is a reasonable assumption that Kate inherited the original of the diary after her mother's death in 1924, that Martha inherited it when Kate died in 1943, and that the transcript, described in the catalogue of the papers as a "carbon copy of a typewritten copy", was made or commissioned by a member of that branch of the family, very likely by Martha herself. In the absence of the original manuscript, one cannot be sure that the typescript version is complete and wholly accurate.

2 On Reynolds's parents, ancestors, and siblings, see his manuscript notes, written on 1 September 1867, from memoranda made in 1856–1858: "The genealogy of myself as taken from records and obtained from old relatives". DHR Papers, item no. 116.

3 The exact date is given in his diary under 15 June 1865, the date of his return to Lake Village after the war, which was seven years to the day after he arrived as a settler; Bender, *Worthy of the Cause*, 186.

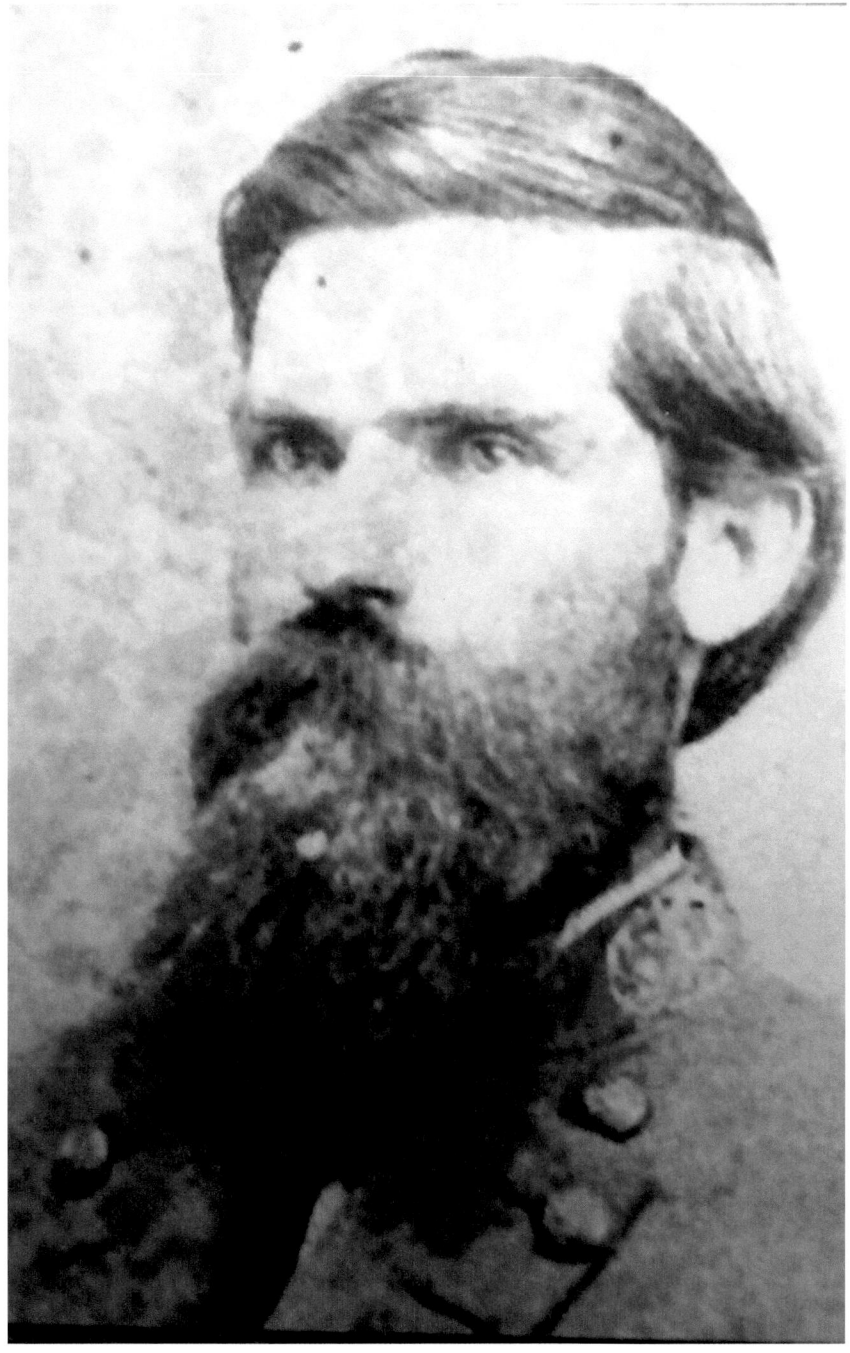

36 Daniel Harris Reynolds, c. 1864, aged about thirty-two.

the county seat. The main attraction of the area for new settlers was the prosperity created by its cotton plantations. The population increased from 5,115 in 1850 to 9,234 in 1860, when the county produced more cotton than any other in Arkansas. Of the 1860 population, 7,512 were slaves.[4]

Reynolds prospered professionally and began to invest in property – but he did not buy slaves. The 1860 census shows him resident on 1 June in Parker House (Hotel) in Old River Township, along with four other lawyers and a dozen or so others of various trades and professions. His real estate was valued at $8,500, his personal estate at $500.[5]

At the same time, he was becoming prominent on the local political front as a vigorous proponent of the secession of the southern states. The only surviving antebellum issue of the *Chicot Press*, dated 17 January 1861, includes his announcement of his candidacy for election as delegate to the proposed secession convention in Little Rock and of arrangements for him to address meetings at nine locations in Chicot County before the balloting on 28 January. The same issue contains appeals for support of the Chicot Rangers, a body of cavalry that he recruited, which was to become Company A of the First Arkansas Mounted Rifles in the Confederate Army.[6]

Reynolds was not elected delegate to the secession convention, but during the war he gained great prestige, showing much political astuteness as well as fine military judgement and leadership. After the battle of Pea Ridge in March 1862, his unit fought in the Western Theatre as part of the Army of Tennessee. Starting as a captain, he achieved the rank of colonel in November 1863 and brigadier general in March 1864. His active service ceased on 19 March 1865, shortly before the end of the war, when, during the battle of Bentonville, North Carolina, a cannonball killed the horse on which he was mounted and destroyed his left leg, which had to be amputated above the knee. He endured the whole ordeal with great stoicism. On 2 June he ordered a wooden leg from a doctor in Baltimore. On 15 June he was back home and wrote the final words in his diary:

> The war is over and we failed. I have many things to regret and many things to be proud of, but of none am I prouder than that of having commanded "Reynolds's Arkansas Brigade" and nothing do I regret so much as the loss of our cause. We lost many noble men, but those who did their duty like men will

---

4 Scott Cashion, "Chicot County", *Encyclopedia of Arkansas History and Culture*, www.encyclopediaofarkansas.net (accessed 12 July 2016).

5 Manuscript census returns, Eighth Census of the United States, 1860, population schedules, Chicot County, AR. Two years later, his property was valued at $7,650 by Judge Henry Hayes in a letter to Reynolds of 8 February 1862; DHR Papers, item no. 7.

6 *Chicot Press* (Lake Village), 17 January 1861.

ever be held in grateful remembrance by their relatives and friends, and by the friends of constitutional liberty everywhere. Peace to their ashes.[7]

On 21 August 1865, Reynolds wrote to President Andrew Johnson, making a special application for the benefits of the amnesty proclamation of 28 May 1865 – an amnesty from which he, as a senior Confederate officer, was excluded. Having received no reply, he wrote again on 15 January 1866.[8] Again, no reply was received, and it was not until 13 November 1866 that he was granted a full presidential pardon.[9] In August 1866, the citizens of Chicot, Ashley, and Drew Counties elected him to the Arkansas state senate, but he served only for a matter of months before the legislature was disbanded by Reconstruction authorities. After that, he concentrated on his work as a lawyer, his political prospects dimmed by the enfranchisement of Chicot County's black majority. Reynolds did run for a seat in the state's constitutional convention in 1874, but lost. He continued to invest in land, and, at one stage, owned about 60,000 acres in Chicot County.[10]

A bachelor until after the Civil War, Reynolds married a woman whom he is said to have met and courted "shortly after his return to Lake Village".[11] Martha ("Mattie") Jane Wallace was born in Holmes County, Mississippi, on 23 May 1845, the only child of Jeremiah Wallace, a Scottish immigrant, and Eleanor Wallace *née* Waddell. She was only three years old when her father died. She and her mother, surnamed Avent by 1868, are said to have moved to Lake Village in 1859.[12] They remained there throughout the war. Reynolds and Mattie were married in a Presbyterian ceremony in Lake Village on 24 November 1868.[13] He was thirty-five, she twenty-three. The couple were to have five children – three daughters and two sons, born between 1869 and 1883. He died in Lake Village on 14 March 1902, aged sixty-nine, and is buried in Lake Village Cemetery. She survived him by twenty-two years, dying on 23 March 1924. Her grave, too, is in Lake Village Cemetery.

7 Bender, *Worthy of the Cause*, 186–187.
8 DHR Papers, item nos 108–109.
9 Bender, *Worthy of the Cause*, 6.
10 Mrs J. W. McMurray, "Sketch of Mrs. D. H. Reynolds, of Lake Village", in *Confederate Women of Arkansas in the Civil War: Memorial Reminiscences, Originally Published in 1907 by the United Confederate Veterans of Arkansas, Revised, and New Material Added with an Introduction by Michael B. Dougan* (Fayetteville: M & M Press, 1993), 133; *Arkansas Gazette* (Little Rock), 30 June 1874, 4.
11 Bender, *Worthy of the Cause*, 6. See, also, McMurray, "Sketch", 132.
12 However, they are not shown as being there in the census of July 1860.
13 The marriage license is recorded in Chicot County Minister's Credentials and Marriage License Book C, 46, Chicot County Courthouse, Lake Village.

The marriage has been called "a lovely uniting of two fine characters".[14] No doubt it was, but Reynolds's private life after he returned from the war was less regular than has been hitherto represented. Apparently unknown to all those who have written about him, he had an affair with a widowed British woman prior to his marriage and fathered an illegitimate son by her.

The British woman was Anne ("Annie") Franklin. The daughter of John Williams, a millwright (a highly skilled profession, like that of a mechanical engineer), and Winifred Williams *née* Wynne, she was born in Liverpool on 11 April 1829. She had at least three brothers and two sisters. On 28 July 1853, when residing in Dexter Street, Toxteth Park, Liverpool, she married William Inch Franklin. She was twenty-four, four years younger than William, who is described on the marriage certificate as a "merchant".[15]

Soon after their marriage the couple went to Chicot County, where William had already been living. The census of 1850 shows that on 27 September he was a resident of Oden Township.[16] His profession is not given, so one cannot tell if he was already a merchant. After he returned to Chicot County with Annie, they had two daughters – (Mary) Elizabeth ("Bessie") Franklin, born on 14 May 1854, and Ruth Franklin, born on 3 April 1856.[17] In his will, dated 11 August 1858, William declared that he was "of the town of Columbia, in the County of Chicot".[18] At that time, when there was no railway into southern Arkansas, Columbia, on the west bank of the Mississippi River, was a prosperous settlement, especially important for the shipping of cotton grown on local plantations. In the years before the Civil War, the export of cotton, picked by slaves, from the southern states to England was at its peak, and most of it was landed in Liverpool. William's will does not specify the nature of the business he carried on in Columbia, but his mention of "goods [and] fixtures" suggests that he was still a merchant, and this is amply confirmed by entries in Deed Books H and J in the archives of the Chicot County Courthouse.

---

14 McMurray, "Sketch", 132.

15 In this essay, certificates of births, deaths, and marriages in England and Wales are often used as sources of information, as are wills and probate records and census returns. Copies of certificates for events since 1837 can be ordered online from the General Register Office, www.gro.gov.uk. Probate documents and wills for those who died in or after 1858 can be found and ordered online from the website GOV. UK. Census returns from 1841 to 1911 are available online from ancestry.co.uk (1841–1891) and findmypast.co.uk (1901, 1911).

16 Manuscript census returns, Seventh Census of the United States, 1850, population schedules, Chicot County, AR.

17 No Chicot County birth or death records from this time survive. The birth dates come from a descendant of Annie.

18 Chicot County Will Record Book C, 153–154, Chicot County Courthouse.

They reveal that, from 1855 on, William, sometimes jointly with Annie, was involved in several real estate transactions. He acquired town lots and owned stores in both Columbia and Lake Village. The most noteworthy document is a debenture, dated 14 April 1859, between him and Reynolds. It reveals that he was in debt to the tune of over $18,700, owed to a string of businesses and individuals. In several cases, court action to recover the money had already been taken. William wished to pay off all his debts as soon as possible and, in return for a nominal payment of one dollar, he assigned specified lots of land and his two stocks of goods to Reynolds in trust to sell on the most advantageous terms and to use the proceeds to pay off his creditors in a designated order of preference. Reynolds was "to receive as compensation for his services a reasonable percent on the amount of assets by him collected and paid to the beneficiaries".[19]

As well as being a businessman, William was a public servant. Despite his unsuccessful management of his own finances, he held the post of Chicot County treasurer from 1858 to 1860.[20]

In the 1860 census, taken on 18 July, William's occupation is not stated, perhaps because he was no longer working. His business had collapsed, and it may be indicative of a serious illness that a physician, William H. Makie from Kentucky, is shown as residing in the same house as the Franklins. In view of William's recent financial problems, one need not be surprised that the value of his real estate is estimated at only $200, his personal estate at $500.[21]

William died on 22 November 1860. In his will, he had expressed full confidence in his "beloved wife Annie" to do what was best for the disposal of his estate so far as their children were concerned and stated that he did not wish "to embarrass her in any manner in case she may wish to remove from Arkansas". By 1864 Annie was living in Lake Village, and she may well have moved there early in the war, if not before it, for the sake of security. There is no way of knowing whether she considered going back to England after William died, and, if so, why she decided not to,

---

19 Chicot County Deed Book J, 48–51, Chicot County Courthouse, Lake Village.
20 His name appears in published lists of county officers as W. F. Franklin, but he is the only male Franklin over the age of five in the Chicot County census lists for 1850 and 1860, and the treasurer's correct initials, W. I., are given several times in Chicot County Record Book E, 250, Chicot County Courthouse. I warmly thank local history expert Blake Wintory for searching the Chicot County Courthouse archives on my behalf and for locating and copying not only the mentions of W. I. Franklin as treasurer but also the pages of the deed books that record William Franklin's property agreements, including his agreement with Reynolds.
21 Manuscript census returns, Eighth Census of the United States, 1860, population schedules, Chicot County, AR.

but her decision very likely implies that she liked the life in Chicot County and already had a feeling of belonging there. Her daughters had known no other home, and the family would have made friends, some of whom could have been expected to be supportive of them. Moreover, although in hindsight a move away from Arkansas might seem to have been wise, she could not have predicted the course, duration, and outcome of the war. It is possible that she discussed her options with William's executors, Johnson Chapman and Anthony Harpin Davies. Both were wealthy men of long experience and great influence in Chicot County. Chapman was a plantation owner and also a lawyer. Davies owned the Lake Hall plantation on Lake Chicot and had served two terms as county judge.[22] In view of the professional assistance that Reynolds gave when William was in financial difficulty, he is another person whom Annie may have consulted.

The witnesses of William's will, Daniel H. Sessions and John MacLean, were also prominent figures in Chicot County. MacLean, born in Scotland, lived at Bayou Macon, to the west of Lake Village, and served in the Chicot Rangers until 1 May 1862, first as a private, then, from 24 September 1861, as a second lieutenant. Three letters from him to Reynolds survive, reporting on the situation in Chicot County during the war and indicating a firm friendship between the two.[23]

Another prominent Chicot man who corresponded with Reynolds during the war mentioned Annie three times in two letters and gives us some picture of how difficult life was for her. He also provides the valuable information that Annie and Reynolds wrote to one another, at least in 1864. The writer signed himself "H. H." or "H." Both from the content of the letters and from the handwriting, he can be identified with certainty as Henry Hayes (born c. 1830), Chicot County judge from 1860 to 1866.[24]

22 Manuscript census returns, Eighth Census of the United States, 1860, population schedules, slave schedules; Blake Wintory, *Chicot County (Images of America)* (Charleston, SC: Arcadia, 2015), 14.

23 Bender, *Worthy of the Cause*, 29, 212–213; John MacLean to Reynolds, 10 March 1864, 16 October 1864, 24 February 1865, DHR Papers, item nos 39, 93, 101.

24 The handwriting is identical to that in Hayes to Reynolds, 8 February 1862. That letter is concerned mainly with taxation matters but also announces a forthcoming "grand exhibition and entertainment given by the Ladies of Chicot at the Court House for the benefit of sick soldiers at the Nashville Hospital". The programme was to include: "Tableaux/Music, By Worthingtons Band / Ditto a number of times – / Supper – Embracing all the delicacies of the season including oysters etc. / Music – / *Field cleared – Guns unlimbered* / Drinks / Dancing, all night till broad day light etc." Chicot County had not yet suffered the full effects of the war. For Hayes's dates as judge (given incorrectly in some lists), see Chicot County Record Books E and F, Chicot County Courthouse.

The letters, both sent from Lake Village, are dated 24 July and 9 October 1864. In the earlier letter, Hayes wrote:

> I have partially recovered my equanimity after the severe trials, afflictions and losses inflicted by the d—d thieving, lousy, cowardly, servile yankees. They find they can't conquer our soldiers, so they vent their spleen and indulge their avarice in pillaging and robbing unarmed citizens, women and children, whenever they get the opportunity.[25]

These actions followed the battle at Ditch Bayou on 6 June 1864. A Confederate force of cavalry and artillery under the command of Brig. Gen. John Sappington Marmaduke had arrived in Chicot County around mid-May and effectively blockaded the Mississippi River by bombarding passing gunboats and transports. A Union force of six thousand men aboard twenty-eight steam vessels was sent to deal with the situation. Half the force landed on 5 June, and the following day attacked six hundred Confederate troops, who, although outnumbered five-to-one, inflicted much higher casualties on the enemy than they suffered themselves.[26] The Federal troops moved on to Lake Village and gave its inhabitants a rough time, as Hayes described:

> The yankees camped here over night robbing all hen roosts, kitchens, pantries, meat houses, and in some instances every thing else, womens and childrens clothing etc, and tearing down much of the fencing, destroying gardens etc. Mrs Franklin fortunately escaped with the loss of her provisions, kitchen wares and a few small articles.

Annie may have come off lightly compared with some other residents, but the experience must have been a terrifying one, and, indeed, there would have been many scary times during the war as the opposing sides fought and skirmished in the locality. Obviously, it was worse when Federal soldiers or lawless bandits were on the scene, but the presence of Confederate forces could also be a cause of concern, partly because they needed to live off the land, partly because their presence was all too likely to provoke enemy attention and retaliation, as happened in summer 1864.[27] Hayes complained to Reynolds that Marmaduke "did much more harm than good". "[H]e has some of the qualities of a good general", Hayes conceded, but he criticised Marmaduke's planning and alleged that he squandered "one of the finest opportunities here, of gaining a most brilliant victory". Hayes

---

25 H. H. to Reynolds, 24 July 1864, DHR Papers, item no. 65.

26 For a detailed account of the battle, see William L. Shea, "Battle at Ditch Bayou", *Arkansas Historical Quarterly* 39 (Autumn 1980), 195–207.

27 On the war in Chicot County, see Daniel Doyle, "The Civil War in the Greenville Bends", *Arkansas Historical Quarterly* 70 (Summer 2011), 131–161.

gave a lively and entertaining account of Marmaduke's conduct and reception after his arrival in Lake Village in May 1864:

> He made his Head Quarters in the woods back of the jail. He spent most of his time at Mrs Franklins – he complaining of being indisposed – where he was beset and placed *hors de combat* by the adulations and caresses of a number of old and young female parasites. It was amusing and disgusting to witness the two widow Rs from over the Lake, one holding to each of his coat tails (figuratively) in the most beloving manner, seemingly first experiencing the maidenly sensations of the thrilling passion, while the younger dames were exhibiting not the spread-eagle, but spread skirts in front, apparently vieing [*sic*] with each other as to who should be the fortunate one to get on his *staff*.[28]
>
> What c[ou]ld have produced amongst the fair se[x s]uch a sensation in favor of Marmaduke I cannot divine, unless it is that he was the first *line*-general that they have had amongst them, and had that *nonchalant* air, and a good deal of small talk which they seem to relish.[29]

There is no suggestion that Annie was star-struck or man-hungry in the way the other women were, but it is interesting that she is the one who acted as Marmaduke's hostess.

In the second letter, written eleven weeks later (9 October), Hayes replied to a letter of 6 September from Reynolds and updated him on the situation at home. He himself had been without light or fuel since Union soldiers stole or destroyed everything except his books. But he seemed less sorry for himself than for another resident:

> Mrs Franklin is well, but at times quite low spirited. I sympathize with her deeply, she is so far from her relations, and it is difficult for any one here who has no family connexions to produce the means of subsistence. The planters here have forgotten the many favors and kindnesses they received from her and her husband in his lifetime. I hope they and she will yet receive their reward. She recd your last letter, and wrote you a long letter in July which I suppose you had not recd. Bessie is well and growing like a weed. She will soon be a young lady.[30]

The information that Reynolds and Annie were corresponding with each other at this stage is telling.[31] He had not been home since January 1863, so one can reasonably assume that friendly contacts between the two went

---

28 An obvious *double entendre*, emphasised by Hayes's underlining of the word.
29 The square-bracketed letters in this sentence are missing from the manuscript.
30 H. H. to Reynolds, 9 October 1864, DHR Papers, item no. 92.
31 Unsurprisingly, there are no letters from Annie among the DHR Papers. He is likely to have destroyed them. The possibility that letters he wrote to her survive is mentioned below.

back at least as far as that and very likely began when her husband was still alive, in view of the help that Reynolds gave him in April 1859. In any case, the affair Annie and Reynolds had in 1866 did not come from nowhere but arose out of several years of friendly acquaintance and communication.

At what stage the relationship between Annie and Reynolds became sexual one cannot know. But it is certain that the two had sexual inter-course in spring 1866, probably in late April or early May. One can imagine that Annie, who had been widowed for several years and was likely to have desired a man for her and her family's security as well as to satisfy her physical and emotional needs, would have considered Reynolds a prize catch, despite the loss of his left leg. He was handsome, courageous, clever, influential, and comfortably off. Photographs of Annie as a young woman (Plate 37), and indeed one of her when she was probably in her mid-sixties (Plate 38), show that she was good-looking, and the indications are that she was not only kind and friendly but also determined and brave. Clearly, Reynolds found her attractive, but in 1866 she was thirty-seven to his thirty-four, and perhaps her age may have seemed a disadvantage to him. Certainly the woman he chose to marry was much younger and without children. She is also more likely than Annie to have had some money. There survives a receipt, dated 30 June 1864, issued to Martha J. Wallace for the purchase of $500 of Confederate registered bonds.[32]

Annie probably knew or suspected that she was pregnant by the end of June 1866. After presumably discussing with Reynolds what to do, she arranged to leave Chicot County and go back to England, from which she had been absent for thirteen years, and have the baby there. Family tradi-tion, as reported by one of her descendants, is that there was an agreement that he would join her in England. According to the same descendant, there may be letters in the family from Reynolds to Annie, but this informant has not read them and does not at present have access to them. Given the huge commitment Reynolds had shown to Arkansas and Chicot County during the Civil War, it might seem surprising if he was prepared to follow Annie to England and start a new life there. It is true that he had been on the losing side, but he had land in Chicot County and in August 1866 would be elected to the state senate. At the time Annie became pregnant, he was still awaiting a presidential pardon, but, after he obtained that in mid-November 1866, he would have been free to do what he wanted. Anyhow, for whatever reasons, he did not follow her to England.

Whether Annie realised the affair with Reynolds was over before she left Arkansas or only after she arrived in England, her unhappiness about

32 DHR Papers, item no. 113.

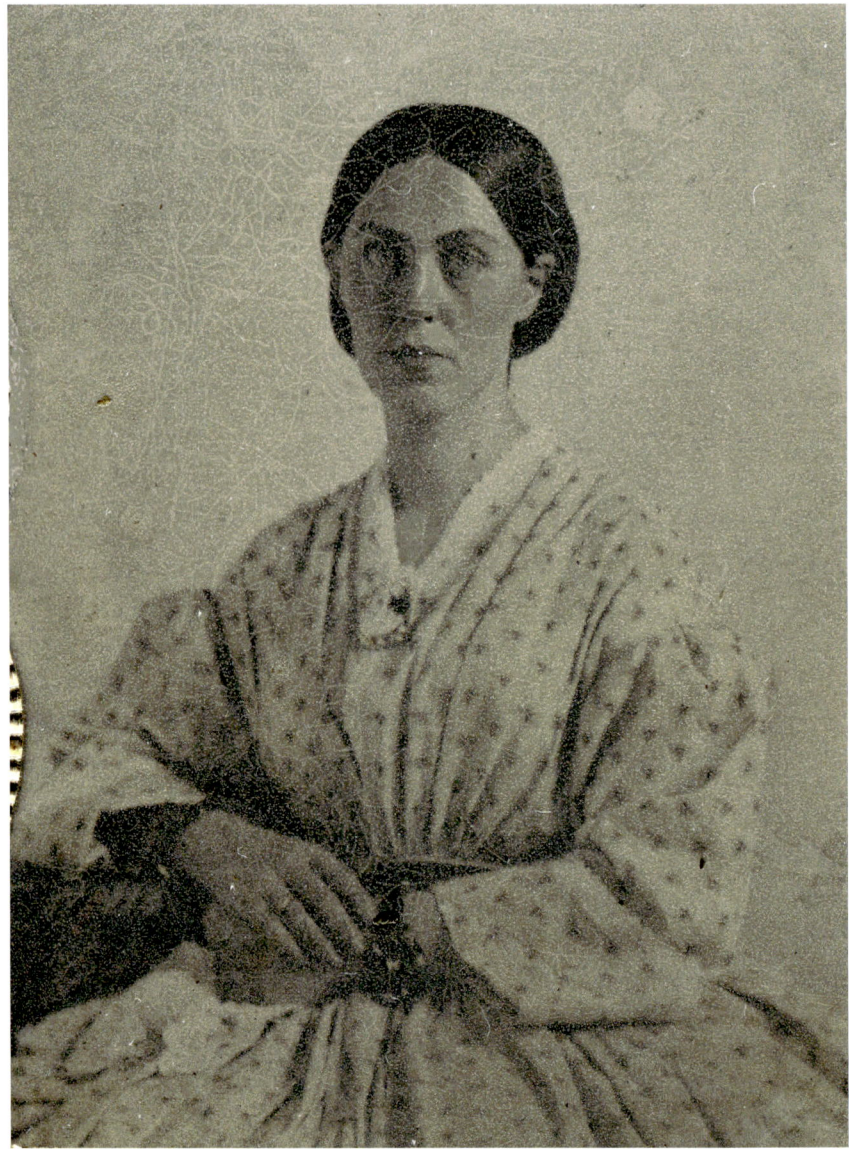

37 Annie Reynolds, *née* Williams, probably soon after her marriage
to William Franklin in 1853.

the situation can be imagined. She probably left Chicot County in July or
August 1866, before it became obvious that she was expecting a baby.
Bessie would have gone with her. She is shown as living with her mother,
unmarried and without occupation, in the English census records of 1881,

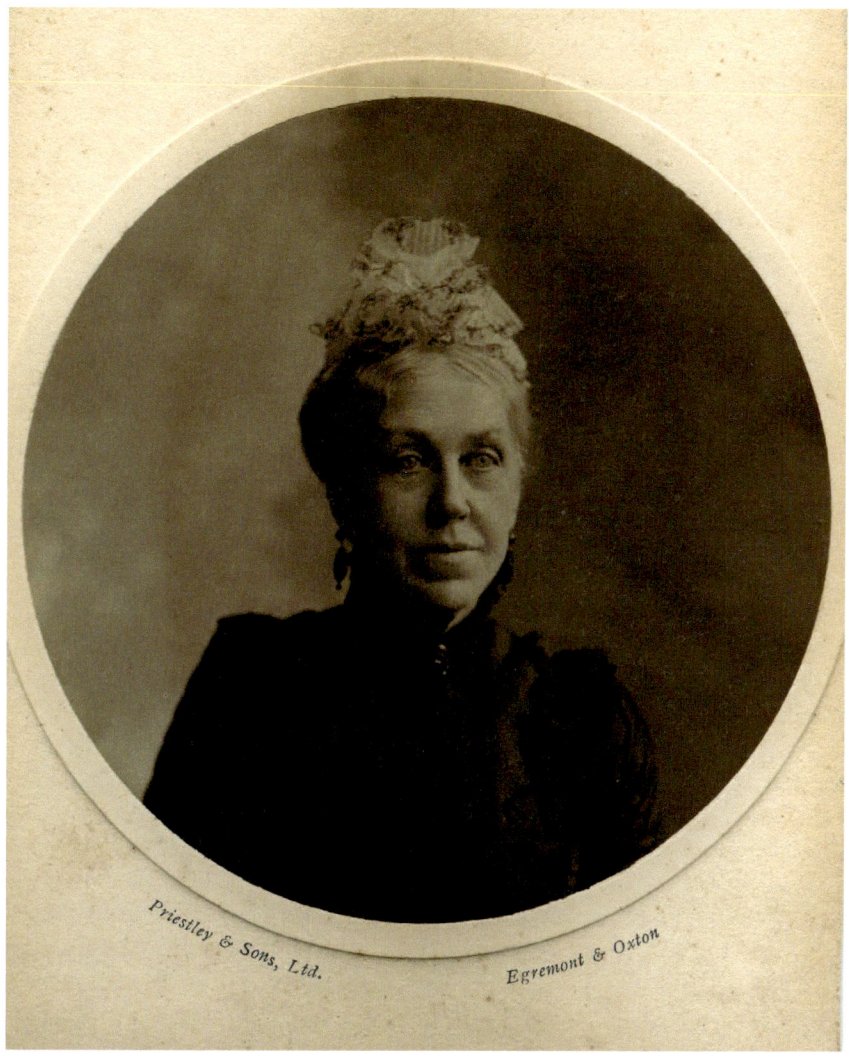

Priestley & Sons, Ltd.

Egremont & Oxton

38 Annie Reynolds, probably c. 1895, in her mid-sixties.

1891, and 1901.[33] There is no mention of Ruth in the English census records and no mention of her in Henry Hayes's letter of 9 October 1864. It seems certain that she died in childhood in Arkansas between 1860 and 1864.

Annie and Reynolds's son was born in Liverpool on 4 February 1867, and named Richard ("Dickie") Williams Reynolds. Williams was Annie's

33 Bessie was not at her mother's address on the day of the 1871 census. She may have been staying with relatives or friends or at a boarding school.

maiden name, and she almost certainly called her son Richard after one of her elder brothers, Richard Williams, who, when she got married, had given her away, their father being deceased. The baby's birth certificate gives the place of birth as 161 Admiral Street in the sub-district of Toxteth Park. It names his mother as "Anne Reynolds formerly Williams", his father as "Daniel Reynolds", and his father's occupation as "Attorney at Law". The informant is "Anne Reynolds Mother Lake Village Chicot County Arkansas America". The birth was registered on 12 March 1867, thirty-six days after the event, which makes one wonder if Annie delayed to allow time for an exchange of letters with the child's father.[34]

The mother was to call herself Annie or Anne Reynolds for the rest of her life and from 1871 presented herself as a widow.[35] Although it is true that she was a widow, she was not the widow of Daniel Reynolds, not only because she was never married to him but also because until 1902 he was still alive. On her death certificate, she is explicitly described as "Widow of Daniel Reynolds Barrister Attorney at Law". Admittedly, that was after Reynolds's death, but the information, supplied by her son, is false. The younger Reynolds knew who his father was and, according to a descendant, knew that he had married Mattie Wallace in 1868, but it seems that he never revealed that his parents were not married to one another. This is not surprising for that day and age, but the question arises whether Annie ever told him before she died. Perhaps she did not.

It is noteworthy that Annie gave her residence on Richard's birth certificate as Lake Village rather than Liverpool. Likewise, when he was baptised into the Church of England at St Paul's Church, Prince's Park, Toxteth, on 17 April 1867, the abode of his parents, "Daniel & Annie", was recorded in the baptismal register as "Arkansas U.S.".[36] One wonders whether Annie was just intending to prevent awkward questions about the whereabouts of Richard's father or still hoped for a future with him.

Annie did not remain in Liverpool for long. By 1868 she had moved to Birmingham, England.[37] Again, a wish to avoid possible questions about her marital status and her son's paternity may have been one reason for

---

34 Not all of the information on the certificate is accurate. The birth could not have taken place at 161 Admiral Street, for, according to the Liverpool Record Office, no such number existed at that time. So, unless the registrar made a mistake, Annie seems to have supplied incorrect, and possibly deliberately misleading, information

35 1871 census.

36 Reynolds's profession is given in the register as "Solicitor". The register is held by the Liverpool Record Office.

37 Her name appears in Birmingham directories (Kelly's, Hulley's, and White's) from 1869, and an 1869 directory will have been compiled in 1868. She is always shown as "Mrs".

the move away from her home area. But a powerful positive reason for choosing Birmingham was that her brother Richard and his wife, Margaret ("Peggy"), lived in Wednesbury, a few miles northwest of the city. They had been in the town since 1844, when Richard Williams began a fifty-year career with the Patent Shaft and Axletree Company there. He became a prominent member of the local community, serving as a justice of the peace and as Wednesbury's first mayor (1886–1888).[38] Annie found accommodation in Handsworth, on the same side of Birmingham as Wednesbury, but just two or three miles from the city centre. She was to spend the rest of her life there, although not always at the same address.

Her occupation is shown in the 1871 census as "Rents from houses", as is that of her sister-in-law Peggy, who was staying with her. In the censuses of 1881, 1891, and 1901, she is shown as having no occupation but as having a resident female servant, so, although she was not very wealthy, she was not poor either. After she died in 1907, the gross value of her estate was £3,674, the equivalent of about £438,000 in 2019. One would hope that Reynolds gave her financial assistance when and after she left Arkansas. Richard and Peggy may have helped too, and they would have been a valued source of support in other ways. For young Richard, without a father on the scene, his uncle is likely to have been a significant presence in childhood, and, given that his aunt and uncle were childless, he is likely to have been a welcome arrival in their lives.

The Williams family was educated, practical, industrious, and ambitious, with a strong sense of social responsibility, and Annie ensured that her son received the best local education available. Whatever school he first attended, probably in Handsworth, its teaching must have been good, for, on 20 January 1879, about a fortnight before his twelfth birthday, he was admitted, with a Foundation Scholarship, to King Edward's School (KES), Birmingham. Established by King Edward VI in 1552, this boys' school had high academic standards.

The younger Reynolds was at KES until July 1886. His record, chronicled in the school's class lists, was impressive.[39] Starting in the Ninth Class in January 1879, he was elevated to the Fifth Class in 1879–1880, the Third Class in 1880–1881, and the Second Class in 1881–1882. During these years, he won many prizes. In July 1881, he was awarded a Junior Scholarship and, in July 1883, a Senior Scholarship. The senior award was made at the end of his first year in the First Class (1882–1883), which he had entered at age fifteen, and in which he remained for four years.

38 "Richard Williams (1817–1909)", *Grace's Guide to British Industrial History*, www.graces-guide.co.uk/Main_Page (accessed 11 June 2017).
39 The class lists are in KES's archives.

Membership of the First Class was restricted to just twelve pupils, and it was very unusual to join it at such a young age.[40] He continued to win prizes in a wide range of subjects. In his final year, he was School Captain (head boy). Throughout his time at KES, he excelled outside the classroom as well as in it, making notable contributions to the Debating Society, drama, and care of the library.

In 1885, during his last year at KES, he was awarded an Open Classical Exhibition, worth £70 a year, at Balliol College, Oxford. He entered in October 1886, when he was nineteen. In the matriculation register of the University of Oxford, he is shown as the first son of "Daniel [Reynolds], of Liverpool, gent.".[41] In 1888, he was placed in the second class of Classical Moderations ("Mods"), in 1890, in the first class of Literae Humaniores ("Greats"). The Master of Balliol throughout his time there was Benjamin Jowett, a notable educational reformer whose liberal influence transformed the college. In recruiting students, he was much more interested in their ability than in the names of the schools they had attended. It would be surprising if Jowett did not leave his mark on Reynolds. As at KES, Reynolds was a keen debater, and in his last year he was president of the debating society, the Brackenbury Society. It is also recorded that he rowed in the second Balliol boat for Torpids in Oxford's bumping races.[42]

From Oxford, Reynolds went to London in 1890 to train to become a barrister. His success in the debating societies of KES and Balliol augured well for this career. Whether he was influenced at all by the knowledge that his father was a lawyer, one does not know, but he was certainly aware of his father's profession. He was a member of Inner Temple and successfully took the Pass Examination in December 1892. However, his legal career never took off, perhaps through a combination of bad luck and a distracting interest in other matters, especially politics, journalism, and literature. Despite this, he always took considerable pride in his legal qualification. Although he was a schoolmaster from 1900 to 1922, on his mother's death certificate (1907), his first marriage certificate (1910), the birth certificates of his children (1912, 1913, 1915), his second marriage certificate (1935), and his will he gave his profession as "barrister at law". Only in the 1911 census did he identify himself as "schoolmaster".

As well as studying law, he spent some time translating Greek and Latin texts into English. His versions of Book 22 of Homer's *Iliad*, Euripides'

---

40 Another who achieved the same feat, twenty-five years later, was J. R. R. Tolkien.

41 Joseph Foster, *Alumni Oxonienses: The Members of the University of Oxford, 1715–1886: Their Parentage, Birthplace, and Year of Birth, with a Record of their Degrees*, vol. 3 (Oxford: Parker & Co., 1888), 1188.

42 Information from Balliol College archives.

tragedy *Alcestis*, and Books 1 and 2 of Horace's *Odes* were published by Hodder and Stoughton in its Classical Translation Library series in February 1893. In each case, the translation was presented in parallel with the Greek or Latin original.

From 1893 until 1901, Reynolds had rooms in the Inner Temple. Before that, he often lodged at 88 St James's Street, sometimes, when the tenant was elsewhere, in the apartment of Oscar Browning, former Eton schoolmaster, fellow of King's College, Cambridge, educational reformer, historian, and eccentric. Reynolds may have been introduced to him by George Warrington Steevens, brilliant classicist at Balliol and friend of Browning, or OB, as he was always called. Letters from Reynolds to OB, written between 1892 and 1898, show that the latter took a friendly and helpful interest in the younger man's welfare and career.[43] OB was a homo-sexual and much enjoyed the company of young men, but, although in the summer of 1898 he invited Reynolds to be his travelling companion on a trip abroad, there is nothing to indicate any sort of sexual relationship between them.[44]

Another occupant of no. 88 was the writer George Slythe Street, best known for *The Autobiography of a Boy* (1894), in which he brilliantly satirised the Aesthetic Movement in general and Oscar Wilde in particu-lar. Like Street and Steevens, Reynolds was employed to write for the *National Observer*, a weekly journal edited until 1894 by the poet and critic William Ernest Henley, and the *Pall Mall Gazette*, an evening newspaper, edited from 1892 to 1896 by Henry ("Harry") Cust. It is likely that he, like Steevens, was hired on the recommendation of OB. Both publications attracted writers of real merit. Reynolds was never a signing contributor to either publication, so independent assessment of his journalistic work is not possible. According to his KES obituarist, "he wrote little but fastidiously", and this is true not only of his years in London but of his whole career.[45] For one who had ample leisure for much of his life and also abundant knowl-edge and ability, his literary output was small. Likely restricting factors included modesty, diffidence, a laudable but misguided perfectionism, and the generous assistance he gave to others with their work.

Modesty and diffidence are perhaps discernible in Reynolds's face in a photograph taken in 1906 (Plate 39). His look is markedly different from the confident one of his father. Some physical likenesses between the two can be observed, in the eyes, eyebrows, nose, ears, and hair texture, but the

43 Papers of Oscar Browning, King's College Cambridge Archive Centre, catalogue no. OB/1/1357A.
44 Reynolds to OB, 1 July 1898, OB/1/1357A.
45 *Old Edwardians Gazette*, December 1948, 9–10.

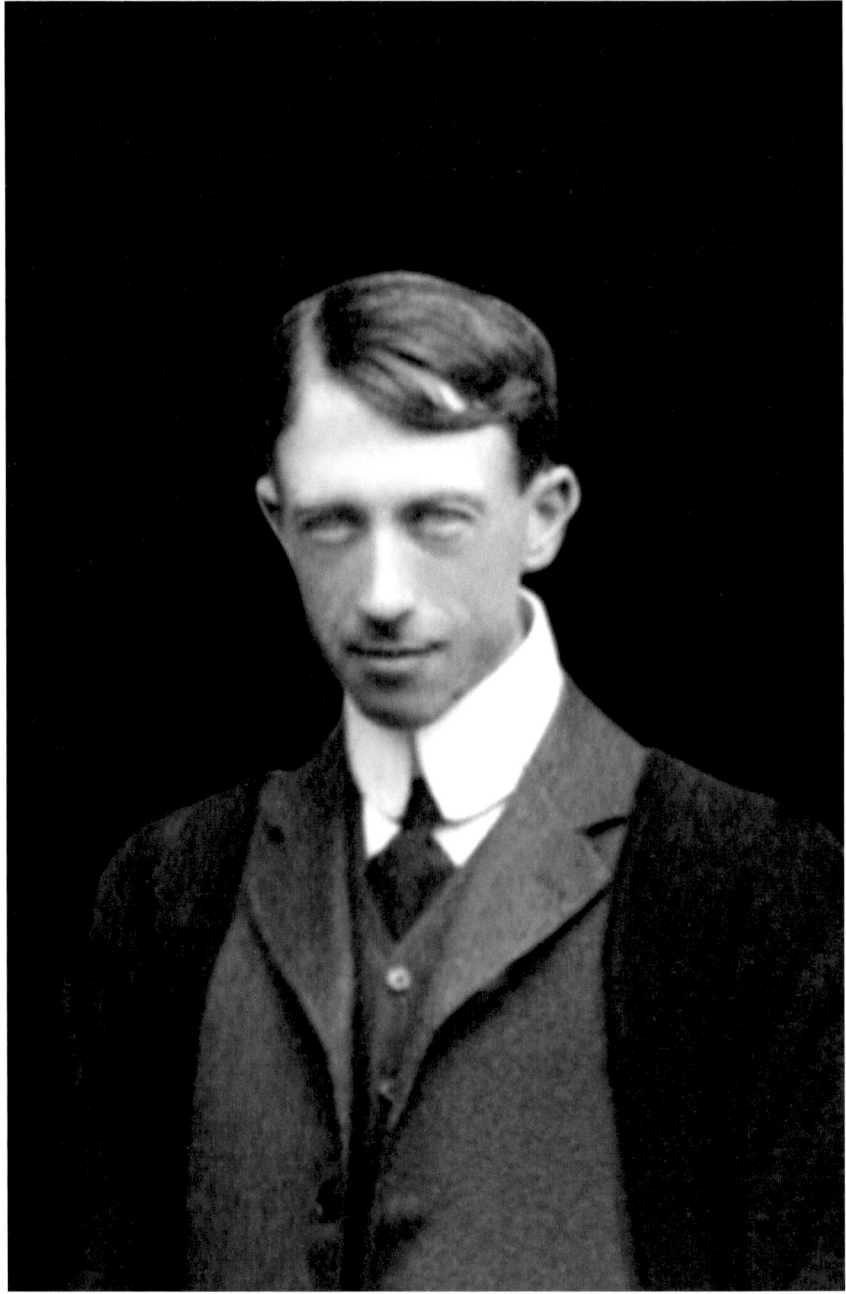

39 Richard Williams Reynolds, 1906, aged thirty-nine.

consensus of opinion is that he looks at least as much like his mother as his father – not that any diffidence is discernible in her face.

While still a pupil at KES, Reynolds had taken a sympathetic interest in socialism. In December 1885, he supported a motion "that private property in land is unjust in principle and injurious to the welfare of the community"; and, in a debate on 19 February 1886, he declared that "he himself went neither with Conservative nor Liberal, but looked down on both parties from a platform of advanced Radicalism".[46] His time in Oxford evidently did nothing to make him change his mind about socialism, for, on 27 May 1890, around the time he graduated, he was elected a member of the Fabian Society, which had been formed in London on 4 January 1884, to promote the peaceful dissemination and adoption of socialist ideas in Britain.[47] It is often stated that he became secretary of the Fabian Society.[48] This is incorrect: he was never even a member of its executive committee, let alone one of its officers. But his membership brought him into contact with, among others, Beatrice and Sidney Webb, Annie Besant, and George Bernard Shaw. Writing to OB on 1 July 1892, he described lunching with OB's Belgian friends, the liberal politician and journalist Auguste Couvreur and his novelist wife, Jessie: "I had Bernard Shaw and one or two other of our Fabian economists in whom M. Couvreur is interested to meet him."[49]

Very importantly for his personal future, the Fabian Society also brought him into close contact with two of its nine founder-members, Hubert Bland and the writer Edith Nesbit. The two had married in 1880. The Blands had three children together. Unknown to Edith at the time of the marriage, Hubert had fathered a son by his mother's paid companion, and, when he had two more illegitimate children with his long-term mistress, Edith accepted them as her own. Given his infidelities, he was in no position to complain when she interested herself in other men, including George Bernard Shaw. After that, she enjoyed the company and attention of a number of young men who loved and admired her, including Reynolds.[50]

---

46 *KES Chronicle*, February 1886, 174; March 1886, 190.
47 Fabian Society Executive Committee Minute Book, 29 April 1890–1 September 1891, p. 20, Fabian Society/C/3, London School of Economics Archives.
48 See, e.g., *Old Edwardians Gazette*, December 1948, 9–10; John Garth, *Tolkien and the Great War: The Threshold of Middle-Earth* (London: HarperCollins, 2003), 93. Edwin Cerio, *L'Ora di Capri*, 2nd ed. (Capri: Edizioni La Conchiglia, 2000), 459, is wide of the mark when he calls Reynolds "one of the founders, with Wells and Shaw, of the Fabian Society". In fact, none of these three was a founder of the Society, and H. G. Wells did not join until February 1903.
49 Reynolds to OB, 1 July [1892], Oscar Browning Papers.
50 See, especially, Julia Briggs, *A Woman of Passion: The Life of E. Nesbit 1858–1924* (London: Hutchinson, 1987).

The loving relationship he had with this attractive, warm, and clever woman was undoubtedly of great importance to him, but to what extent it was given full physical expression is not clear. The relationship was important to her too, although she perhaps never allowed him to monopolise her. When she published her romantic novel *The Incomplete Amorist* in 1906, she dedicated it to him and to Justus Miles Forman, a handsome American novelist. With the dedication is a quotation from Balzac: "*Faire naître un désir, le nourrir, le développer, le grandir, le satisfaire, c'est un poème tout entier.*"[51] Edith established herself as an outstanding writer of books for children, and 1906 saw the publication not only of the novel just mentioned but also of her best known book, *The Railway Children*.

A much fuller picture of Reynolds's time in London during the 1890s, as well as of other stages of his life, would emerge if a typescript memoir he compiled were accessible. Written in Chicago in the early 1940s and said to be about 175 pages long, it is in the possession of his descendants.[52] A tantalising indication of its likely interest and value is given by the only extract from it that seems to be publicly available. This is a delightful and appreciative vignette of the talented artist Helen Coombe, to whom he says he was introduced either by George Street or by "one of my socialist or artist friends".[53]

Reynolds's sources of income during his years in London were limited. It is possible that he supplemented his earnings from journalism with fees from private tuition. In 1900, a teaching opportunity unexpectedly presented itself. He had kept in close touch with KES, Birmingham, ever since he left in 1886. In July 1900, the headmaster, the Rev. Albert Richard Vardy, suffered a stroke and died. In this emergency, Reynolds was recruited as temporary assistant master for the next term.[54] He was able to live with his mother and for the time being retained his rooms in London.

The following summer, the first assistant master at KES, the Rev. John Hunter Smith, retired after many years of service, and on 26 June 1901 Reynolds was appointed to replace him as the form-master of Class Four

51 "To give birth to a desire, to feed it, to develop it, to grow it, to satisfy it, is a whole poem." E. Nesbit, *The Incomplete Amorist* (London: Archibald Constable, 1906).

52 "A letter from Richard R[eynolds] yesterday pleases me. I am interested that he is writing his memoirs for Mynie and Claire"; Achsah Barlow Brewster to Harwood Brewster Picard, 25 May 1941, Willa Cather Collection, Drew University Library Special Collections, Madison, NJ.

53 Papers of Roger Eliot Fry, King's College Cambridge Archive Centre, REF/13/2. The memoir is entitled "Some Notes on Family History", and the page carrying the account of Helen Coombe is numbered 93. Part of it is quoted in Essay 6, 165.

54 *Governors' Order Book*, 31 October 1900, KES Archives.

(Classical) at a starting salary of £200 a year. In his retirement speech, Hunter Smith said: "There is no one in the country whom I should prefer to Mr Reynolds as my successor. He is a favourite old pupil, he has ever been as a son to me, and he brings to the work brilliant scholarship, versatile talents, and a freshness to which I could never, at any time, have laid claim."[55]

As it turned out, Reynolds was not particularly well suited to step into his predecessor's shoes. Most of the boys in Class Four were too young and immature to appreciate his learning and somewhat idiosyncratic teaching methods, and he was a poor disciplinarian. This is made clear in his obituary in the *Old Edwardians Gazette*.[56] In a letter of 9 January 1964, his most famous pupil, J. R. R. Tolkien, told a contemporary at KES, the Rev. Denis Tyndall, that he had found Reynolds's teaching at that stage "boring", although he adds that he was "immensely interesting as a person".[57] As well as being in charge of Class Four, Reynolds contributed to the teaching of classics to Classes Two and Three and taught history to Class One. Also, he took Oxbridge scholarship candidates for "Special History" and "English Essay". It was with these mature, able, and well-motivated pupils that he was most successful. With his excellent knowledge of ancient and modern languages and of classical, English, and continental literature, he was well placed to bring out the best of them, and he took immense trouble with individuals as well as with groups. He also made important contributions to KES outside the classroom, presiding over the Debating and Literary Societies and not infrequently speaking in debates and reading papers. As when he was a pupil, he gave much time to the school library.[58]

Tolkien entered KES in September 1900, aged eight, so that his arrival coincided with that of Reynolds as temporary assistant master. Early in 1902, Tolkien's mother, Mabel, who had converted to Roman Catholicism, transferred him to a Catholic school, but its academic standard was poor, and she soon removed him and taught him herself. Elected a Foundation Scholar at KES, he resumed his studies there in January 1903.[59] He entered Reynolds's Class Four in January 1906, when he was just fourteen, and remained in it until July. Although he found his teacher boring at this

---

55 *KES Chronicle*, October 1901, 186.

56 *Old Edwardians Gazette*, December 1948, 9–10. The writer observes: "it would be foolish to pretend that he wore Hunter Smith's mantle worthily".

57 Humphrey Carpenter, with the assistance of Christopher Tolkien, *Letters of J. R. R. Tolkien* (London: Allen & Unwin, 1981), 342–343.

58 See the assessments not only in his obituary but also his retirement notice in *KES Chronicle*, November–December 1922, 79–80.

59 Not in autumn 1903, as stated by Humphrey Carpenter, *J. R. R. Tolkien: A Biography* (London: Allen & Unwin, 1977), 27.

stage, he undoubtedly learned much from him later, both in and out of class. Reynolds did his best to interest boys in English poets from Milton to Kipling and Walter de la Mare. At a meeting of the Debating Society, he once proposed the daring motion "That Kipling is the greatest English poet since Shakespeare".[60] His interest in early English and Scottish ballads is likely to have appealed to Tolkien; likewise his knowledge of German language and literature as well as of English and classics.[61] That he continued to interest himself in German while on the staff of KES is indicated by his editing, for German students of English, Frances Webster's *The Island Realm, or Günter's Wanderyear, Being Scenes from English Life*.[62]

During Tolkien's last year at school (1910–1911), he and a small number of other senior boys formed an esoteric society for the discussion of literature, mythology, and other cultural topics. It met for tea either in the school library or in the first-floor café of the old-established Barrow's Stores on Birmingham's Corporation Street, very close to KES, which at that time was located in the city centre, in New Street. It came to be known by the acronym TCBS, standing for Tea Club, Barrovian Society. The core members were Tolkien, Christopher Luke Wiseman, Robert Quilter Gilson, and Geoffrey Bache Smith. Gilson's father was the headmaster, Robert Cary Gilson. The four kept in touch with one another until 1916, when Gilson and Smith were killed in action. Reynolds was in no way involved in the TCBS's formation or agenda, but, given that he was closely involved with the school library, the Debating Society, and the Literary Society, he must have been a potent influence. Over fifty years later, Tolkien would recall that when his time at KES had ended, Reynolds gave him a lift to Oxford in his new automobile, which was affectionately known as the "Green Lady".[63] Tolkien kept in touch with Reynolds and sometimes sought his advice on pieces he had written not only soon after he left KES, but at least as late as 1926. Indeed, Tolkien states that he "kept up with him and the Beak until they died".[64] Among the Tolkien family papers deposited in (but not owned by) the Bodleian Library, Oxford, are six uncatalogued letters

---

60 *KES Chronicle*, March 1905, 6.

61 Reynolds read a paper on ballads to the Literary Society on 28 February 1902; *KES Chronicle*, March 1902, 24–25.

62 Frances Webster, *The Island Realm, or Günter's Wanderyear, Being Scenes from English Life* (Bielefeld: Velhagen & Klasing, 1906). The same publisher also issued separately a twenty-six-page appendix containing Reynolds's "Annotations". This probably appeared a year or two later, but no date is given.

63 Carpenter, *Letters of J. R. R. Tolkien*, 343.

64 Carpenter, *Letters of J. R. R. Tolkien*, 343. The "Beak" is headmaster Robert Cary Gilson.

written by Reynolds to Tolkien between 1915 and 1917. In them, he gave his former pupil some advice about the latter's literary compositions.[65]

Reynolds was with his mother when she died, aged seventy-eight, on 18 August 1907, at 4 Holly Road, Handsworth, the home she shared with him and probably also Bessie. Her death certificate lists the causes as "Mammary Carcinoma 2 years" and "Pulmonary Congestion". The only parent he had known, she had brought him up admirably in difficult circumstances.

Three years later, Reynolds married. His long and close friendship with Edith Nesbit had naturally brought him into close contact with her relatives, and for many years he had known and liked her favourite niece, Dorothea Deakin. Born in Manchester on 19 December 1876, she was the daughter of Edith's half-sister, Sarah ("Saretta") Deakin, and her husband, John Deakin, a cashier at the time of Dorothea's birth and later a cotton merchant. Dorothea was a slim, attractive, vivacious, sweet-natured, clever woman, who, with advice and encouragement from Edith, enjoyed some popularity as a writer on both sides of the Atlantic in the first decade of the twentieth century. Between 1903 and 1910, she had seven light and gently humorous romantic novels published, including *Melinda*, *Georgie*, and *The Goddess Girl*. She also wrote short stories for British and American magazines, among them *Strand Magazine*, *Pall Mall Magazine*, *The Queen*, and *The Century Illustrated Monthly Magazine*. Her writing brought her some much-needed income. Her mother had died in 1899, leaving her responsible for her invalid and impecunious father and to some extent her three younger brothers. Reynolds became increasingly interested in her, somewhat to the displeasure of Edith, who did not want to lose his close attention. She did her best to obstruct the love affair.[66] But on 21 December 1910, two days after Dorothea's thirty-fourth birthday, she and Richard, who was nearly ten years older, were married in St Mary's (Anglican) Church, Hendon, in London. His details, entered in the marriage register[67] and reproduced in the marriage certificate, merit some comment. This is the only place where he gave his father a middle name, and he got it wrong – "Daniel Henry Reynolds". He gave his "father's rank or profession" as "Brigadier General" but without indicating that his service was not in the British army.

---

65 Details can be found in Garth, *Tolkien and the Great War*, 76, 93, 279–280. Garth was granted access to the Tolkien papers. Unfortunately, I was refused access to Reynolds's letters and so cannot judge the "chemistry", or lack of it, between the two men.

66 Briggs, *Woman of Passion*, 228–229.

67 Register of St Mary's Church, Hendon, London Metropolitan Archives, on microfilm at X094/184.

After their marriage, Richard and Dorothea lived at 10 Pakenham Road in the affluent Birmingham suburb of Edgbaston. Their detached house was (and is) attractive, with an elegant classical portico in front and a long garden behind. They could well afford to live in comfort because Reynolds, as well as benefiting in a modest way after Annie died intestate, had received a substantial legacy under the will of his uncle Richard Williams, who died on 28 June 1909, aged ninety-two, leaving an estate with a net value of over £30,000, equivalent to about £3,540,000 in 2019.[68] Although Reynolds did not receive all of this, he was the residuary legatee. The census of 2 April 1911 shows four other occupants of the house – Dorothea's bedridden father, a nurse for him, a cook, and a housemaid. His half-sister Bessie was not there. She was to spend her last years in a nursing home near Harlech in Wales. She died there on 1 August 1925, aged seventy-one. Reynolds was the sole beneficiary of her estate, whose net value was just over £3,500.

Dorothea did no writing after her marriage. She no longer needed the money, and at the beginning she would have been much occupied organising the house and giving attention to her father. Also, she soon became pregnant. She was to have three children in quick succession, and she was not only very busy with them, but also, by the time the third child arrived, battling against a serious illness. The first child, Diana, born on 11 February 1912, was followed by Hermione ("Mynie") on 14 November 1913, and Pamela on 24 May 1915. Friends used to say that the third daughter should have been called Victoria, partly because she was born on Queen Victoria's birthday, partly because as a young child she looked remarkably like the monarch.[69] Encouraged by their parents, the girls became voracious readers at an early age. Pamela was especially remarkable for her very early development in speech, thought, reading, and writing. Since the three were close in age, they were good at entertaining one another. Their early childhood was undoubtedly a very happy one, but for Dorothea and Richard life was less idyllic. Dorothea's health was a cause of great anxiety. While expecting Pamela, she was diagnosed with pulmonary tuberculosis, and, a few months after Pamela was born, her condition deteriorated markedly, and she became an invalid. It was mainly for her sake that in 1919 the family left Edgbaston to escape the smoke and smog of a big industrial city.

---

68 If Annie's estate was divided equally between Reynolds and Bessie, he will have received about £1,800.

69 An abundant source of information about Pamela and her sisters in their childhood is Richard Reynolds's memoir "Pamela" (unpublished and undated typescript, private collection). I have made much use of it in my account of the Reynolds family in the years 1915–1929.

Their new home, "Winterholme", sat on four acres in the Worcestershire countryside at Barnt Green, a village about ten miles southwest of Birmingham. Occupying an elevated position on the southern slopes of the Lickey Hills, the spacious redbrick house offered fine views. The children loved it, and the purer air suited Dorothea, whose health significantly improved. The children attended a local school, and Reynolds commuted to Birmingham. But, in autumn 1920, he was struck down by a serious illness, the nature of which he did not divulge. He was off work from October 1920 until September 1921. Although he then resumed teaching, his health continued to be unsatisfactory, and, having been certified as "mentally and physically, wholly and permanently unfit for work", he resigned with effect from September 1922.[70]

For the sake of his and Dorothea's health, the couple took doctors' advice to live abroad. After considering various destinations, they decided upon Capri. Reynolds had visited it thirty years earlier, and it was now the home of his friend the novelist and doctor Francis Brett Young and his wife. Young, too, had health problems and strongly recommended the island. The family arrived in Capri on 30 September 1922, and soon found a house they wanted – a small villa called Casa Monticello, standing by itself outside the village of Anacapri at an altitude of eight hundred feet and looking south across a wooded valley to the sea.[71] For the girls, Capri was a case of love at first sight – an exotic and beautiful playground affording ample opportunities for walking, climbing, swimming, and canoeing. As for education, instead of going to school for long hours, they received tuition from their father each morning from nine until half past twelve. After that, they were free to do what they wanted. Reynolds taught them English, French, Italian, mathematics, and history. He soon arranged for them to receive lessons in music, dancing, and foreign languages. The extra tuition in foreign languages was mainly for Diana, who had an exceptional talent for them as well as for music. Pamela's chief talents lay in poetry, drawing, and philosophy. When she was "at a very tender age", apparently about five, Reynolds tried her with Berkeleian idealism. She understood it at once and quickly put her knowledge to practical use. When her nurse made what she regarded as an unreasonable demand, she gave in under protest, adding, as a Parthian shot, "After all, you're only an idea in my mind." When she had attained the advanced age of thirteen and was visiting Rome, she had a lengthy discussion over lunch with the eminent idealist philosopher Benedetto Croce. She was not in the least overawed, and, when asked on

70 Reynolds, "Pamela", 4.
71 There is a photograph of the house in Riccardo Esposito (ed.), *Versocapri: Antologia poetica del novecento* (Capri: Edizioni La Conchiglia, 2004), 162.

her return to Capri what she thought of him, commented: "His philosophy is sound, but. ..." She had her reservations![72] She remained a committed Berkeleian. "To the end of her life she confessed to being unable to believe in the reality of the external world and protests against such solipsism left her unconvinced."[73]

Among other residents of Anacapri when the Reynoldses arrived were the Swedish doctor Axel Munthe, who had built a villa for himself on the ruins of a palace of Tiberius – the Villa San Michele, celebrated in his most famous book, *The Story of San Michele* (1929). They quickly became friendly with him, and he allowed them to play badminton on his grassy tennis court. His love of animals no doubt endeared him to the Reynolds girls, who kept a variety of pets. But more important than Munthe were the Brewster family. Achsah Leona Barlow Brewster and Earl Henry Brewster were American painters and writers in their mid-forties. They had a daughter, Harwood Barlow Brewster, six months younger than Diana. As soon as Diana, Mynie, and Pamela were introduced to Harwood, they got on like a house on fire, and, whenever all four were on the island, Reynolds included Harwood in his classes.[74] To say that the Brewsters were an unusual couple would be an understatement. Highly spiritual, their union became a celibate one during Achsah's pregnancy and remained so until her death in 1945. She always dressed in white, and he was deeply interested in European philosophy, including Platonism, and especially in Eastern philosophy and religion, becoming a Buddhist, then a Vedanta Hindu. In 1935, the couple left Europe to live in India and never returned.[75] They introduced Reynolds and his daughters to their close friend D. H. Lawrence in 1926.

With the move to Capri, Reynolds's health improved, but Dorothea's declined, and, on 30 November 1923, the family sailed from Naples for Alexandria in the hope that the dry winter climate of Egypt would benefit her. They rented a bungalow in a derelict date plantation on the edge of the desert southwest of Cairo. For the children, it was a great adventure: they rode donkeys to the Pyramids and Sphinx, rode camels as well, saw wolves,

---

72 Cerio, *L'Ora di Capri*, 459–460.

73 Reynolds, "Pamela", 8.

74 Lively and charming descriptions of the numerous activities the four enjoyed together are contained not only in Reynolds, "Pamela", but also in Achsah Barlow Brewster, "The Child: Harwood Barlow Brewster" (unpublished memoir, 1942), 277–310, Willa Cather Collection, Drew University Special Collections. When Harwood was fourteen, she described her contacts with the Reynoldses in "Fourteen Years of My Adventures" (unpublished typescript, 1926), private collection, 4–8, 44–45.

75 On the Brewsters, see especially Lucy Marks and David Porter, *Seeking Life Whole: Willa Cather and the Brewsters* (Madison, NJ: Fairleigh Dickinson University Press, 2009).

heard jackals at night, built towns in the sand, and attended an Arab wedding at which two guests were accidentally shot, one fatally. But the deterioration in Dorothea's health continued, and on 21 March 1924 the Reynoldses sailed from Alexandria heading for Switzerland. They reached Lugano and took rooms in the lakeside Hotel Victoria. At first, Dorothea seemed slightly better, but, on 9 April, she was admitted to the Clinica Luganese with pneumonia. She died there six days later. The girls' ages ranged from nine to twelve. They were old enough to have been indelibly influenced by their mother's fine qualities of mind and character. One of these qualities, cheerfulness and fortitude in the face of adversity and pain, was now to be exhibited in abundance by the whole family as they faced life without her.

Reynolds's first move was to employ a woman to help with the children. Within days of Dorothea's death, he chose a cultivated, polyglot Dane, Eli Laub, who accompanied them back from Lugano to Capri and stayed with them for a year. She proved to be pleasant and stimulating company but was of little practical assistance. She was replaced by a British woman, Hilda Balfour ("Bal"), who was just the opposite – not at all intellectual, but commonsensical, practical, versatile, and energetic. She was also kind and had a keen sense of humour. She was to remain with the Reynoldses for five years, until 1930, by which time the girls were studying away from Capri.

Casa Monticello must have seemed empty when the family returned without Dorothea, but, in addition to the Brewsters, there were other friends to provide company and distraction and new acquaintances, too, including the writer Compton Mackenzie and his wife, Faith, although they were soon to leave Capri.

Soon after the family returned from a visit to England, the first issue of *Genius Burning* appeared, on Monday, 20 October 1924. "[A] domestic magazine written and produced entirely by the girls", its title was inspired by Louisa May Alcott's *Little Women*, in which one of the four March sisters, Jo, accustomed to shutting herself up in her room whenever she wanted to write, was left alone by the rest of the family at such times, except that they occasionally put their heads round the door to ask, "Does genius burn, Jo?"[76] With several breaks, the longest lasting from February 1926 until January 1928, it appeared on Mondays for five years, until 29 June 1929, usually weekly, but fortnightly from October 1928. Each issue, except the last, ran to six pages – five carrying articles, stories, and poems and the sixth an illustration in colour. The main contributors were Diana, the editor, and Pamela, who took over as editor in October 1928

76 Reynolds, "Pamela", 17.

when Diana left home. Harwood was often involved, Mynie less often and then usually as an illustrator. Friends occasionally made guest appearances. The standard of composition was high, and the magazine gives a vivid and charming picture of the girls' interests, thoughts, and activities. Harwood's set of issues, in a blue satin case embroidered by Eli Laub, is in the Centro Caprense Ignazio Cerio, Capri.

Most of the poetry in *Genius Burning* was the work of Pamela, whose talent in this area was outstanding. A year after the foundation of the magazine, four of her poems and one piece of prose were printed in the *New Statesman*, the prestigious and influential weekly review of politics and literature. Pamela was only ten, and four of the pieces had been written when she was younger than that – one when she was seven.[77] Six poems she presented to Edwin Cerio in 1934 were published seventy years later with an Italian translation.[78]

For Reynolds, the education and care of his daughters (Plate 40) were always his chief concern and occupation. This, together with his modesty and diffidence, helps to explain why he did little writing. But his expertise in many areas, including English and European literature, his intellectual abilities, his independence and fairness of mind, and his generosity in sharing his knowledge were soon recognised and exploited by others. Casa Monticello gained a reputation for being a cultural workshop, which some of his friends jokingly called "little Oxford" ("la piccola Oxford").[79] As well as advising authors on books they were writing or had written, he translated one of the chapters of Edwin Cerio's best-selling book *Aria di Capri* for the English edition published in 1929.[80] Later, he produced an English translation of an unusual German work – edited selections from the diary of Cordelia Gundolf, who had accompanied her mother to Italy, and especially to Capri, several times in the 1920s and early 1930s. Essentially, the book contains the sensitive observations and impressions of a young girl.[81]

77 Pamela Reynolds, "Very Early Poems", *New Statesman*, 17 October 1925, 14.

78 Renato Esposito (ed.), "Pamela Reynolds: I sogni e gli incubi di una giovane poetessa," in *Almanaco Caprese*, vol. 12 (Capri: Edizioni La Conchiglia, 2004), 95–106. The typescript originals of the six poems and a letter to Cerio are in the Centro Caprense Ignazio Cerio, Capri.

79 Edwin Cerio, "Parole di saluto a Richard W. Reynolds nel Composanto Acattolico di Capri il 27 Dicembre 1947", unpublished typescript, Centro Caprense Ignazio Cerio, Capri.

80 Edwin Cerio, *That Capri Air*, with a foreword by Francis Brett Young (New York: Harper & Brothers, 1929). The chapter translated by Reynolds is "The Temple of Cybele" (139–154).

81 Cordelia Gundolf, *Myrtles and Mice: Leaves from the Italian Diary of Cordelia Gundolf*, trans. R. W. Reynolds (New York: Dutton, 1935).

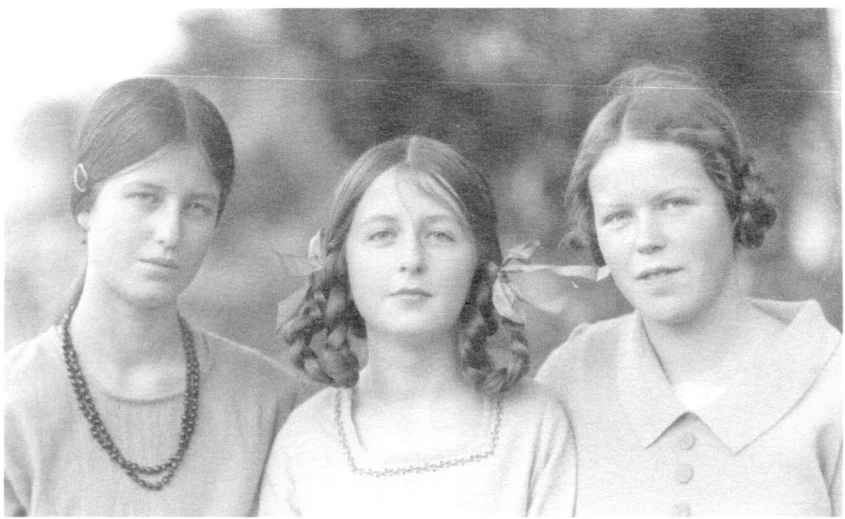

40 L–R: Mynie, Pamela, and Diana Reynolds in 1926.

In October 1928, Diana went to Heidelberg to learn German. In 1929–1930, she passed Oxford University's entrance examinations and, in 1931, entered Lady Margaret Hall to read classics.[82] Mynie and Pamela also went to Heidelberg and England to further their education. After a spell at boarding school, Mynie began but did not complete a nursing course in London. Pamela studied art, first at the Slade School of Fine Art at University College, London, then at l'École des Beaux Arts, Fontainebleau.[83] Diana enjoyed her time in Oxford and made quite an impression.[84] But she left in March 1933 to prepare for marriage to a Frenchman, Georges Levy Picard, an English teacher and former Rhodes Scholar. They married in Paris on 8 February 1934, three days before her twenty-second birthday.[85] A year later, on 5 February 1935, she gave birth to a daughter, Claire Dorothea Picard – "Dorothea" after the baby's maternal grandmother.[86] At first all seemed well, but on 29 March Diana died, apparently from a postpartum infection.

On 1 June 1935, exactly two months after *The Times* printed a notice of Diana's death, its "Deaths" column carried another grim announcement:

82 Information from Lady Margaret Hall (LMH) archives.
83 Information from family source.
84 Obituary, by classics tutor A. M. D[ale], *The Brown Book*, December 1935, p. 35, LMH Archives.
85 *The Times* (London), 12 February 1934, 1.
86 *The Times* (London), 15 February 1935, 1.

"REYNOLDS. – On May 27, 1935, at Anacapri, instantaneously, from an accident, PAMELA, youngest daughter of R. W. REYNOLDS, of Monticello, Anacapri, aged 20." In Italy in recent years, there has been ill-informed, sensationalist speculation that her death was not an accident, but suicide or even murder.[87] But Pamela was not alone when she died.[88] Harwood Brewster recalled: "On May 27, Pam and Mynie were taking a walk near Damicuta [Damecuta], which they had taken countless times. Pam slipped, falling into the sea after hitting her head."[89] Mynie herself wrote on 20 August 1997, to Georges Picard:

> I feel very strange when I think of that year [1935]. It's still very much a series of clear pictures. Diana lying dead as I last saw her, Pam slipping and sliding down the cliff at Orico, and floating on the surface in her bright dress, when I finally got to the water and swam to her, and pulled her out. I've sometimes wondered if I could have saved her by first aid. But the doctor who examined her said she had hit her head on the way down and that had killed her.[90]

If Pamela had wanted to kill herself, she would hardly have made the attempt while out for a walk with her sister, and Capri has many cliffs higher and more precipitous than those of Orrico (as it is now usually spelled) from which she could have made a clean jump. Still, Orrico is a rugged spot, and it is easy to believe that one could have an accident there if one tripped and/or suffered a momentary lapse of concentration. One may add that the idea that Pamela would be so selfish as to inflict a second bereavement on her father and surviving sister contradicts everything that is known about her character.

Pamela, who died just three days after her twentieth birthday, was buried in Capri's historic Non-Catholic Cemetery (Cimitero Acattolico). Twelve years later, her father was buried next to her. According to Dieter Richter in his book on the cemetery, Pamela's gravestone carries the famous Latin dictum "*Quem di diligunt / adulescens moritur, dum valet sentit sapit*", meaning: "Whom the gods love dies young, while the person's physical and mental faculties are intact."[91] But the inscription simply reads:

87 This is the line taken by Rita Monaldi and Francesco Sorti in their "historical" novel *Malaparte: Morte come me* [*Malaparte: Death Like Me*] (Milano: Baldini & Castoldi, 2016).

88 Marks and Porter, *Seeking Life Whole*, 69.

89 Harwood Brewster Picard, "To Frances and Claire: Some Memories of Your Grandparents Earl Henry Brewster and Achsah Barlow Brewster" (unpublished type-script, July 1977), 56–57, Cather Collection, Drew University.

90 Private collection.

91 Dieter Richter, *Il giardino della memoria: Il Cimitero Acattolico di Capri: Storia di un luogo* (Capri: Edizioni La Conchiglia, 2015), 145. The quotation is of Plautus,

"IN / LOVING MEMORY / OF / PAMELA REYNOLDS / BORN MAY 24, 1915 / DIED MAY 27, 1935." At her father's funeral, Edwin Cerio quoted the Latin saying in his remarks about Pamela, and it is highly likely that Reynolds himself thought of it in connection with both Pamela's and Diana's deaths.[92] But he was a man whose behaviour and reactions were understated and undramatic, and the simple inscriptions on both Pamela's and his graves are in character for him.[93]

In summer 1935, Harwood Brewster went to stay at Casa Monticello. When she arrived, Georges was there with baby Claire. Harwood and he fell in love. They married in Paris on 7 May 1936, and the following year moved to the United States. Harwood brought up Claire as her own child. On 1 October 1938, Harwood gave birth to a daughter, named Frances Diana – Diana after Claire's mother.[94] After several years of teaching, Georges served abroad with the US Army. In 1951, he and Harwood divorced. She died in Washington in 1990.[95]

Six months after Pamela's death, Reynolds, after eleven years as a widower, remarried. He was now sixty-eight. His second wife was Edith Harriet Andrews, an attractive sixty-nine-year-old American woman, who had been a resident of Capri for just over forty years. She and her much older husband, William Page Andrews, had moved there from Massachusetts in 1894. He was not exactly enthralling company for anyone not interested in Goethe's *Faust*, which was his main passion and topic of conversation. His only other significant interest was his health. He was a semi-invalid and hypochondriac. Edith was a much more congenial person.[96] Edith and William are represented by Elsie Neave and Joseph Rutger Neave in Compton Mackenzie's novel *Vestal Fire*, set on the island of Sirene with a village called Antisirene. Joseph is always translating Dante and brings Dante into every conversation. Elsie is described as "a little blonde with bright weary eyes who was still pretty enough to make her elderly husband smack his lips at the idea of her being admired by other men", and as having "a genuine simplicity which was rather charming, and completely disarming".[97]

Bacchides, 816–817. The thought is first found in Menander. I have paraphrased the last four words of the Latin.
92 "Parole di saluto."
93 Reynolds's gravestone simply gives his full name and the dates of his birth and death.
94 Frances Diana Picard Holt is much interested not only in the Brewster family but also in the Reynoldses. She is generous with information and encouragement, and the present writer owes her a heavy debt. Claire died on 20 June 2009.
95 Information from Frances Diana Picard Holt.
96 James Money, *Capri: Island of Pleasure* (London: Hamish Hamilton, 1986), 53–54.
97 Compton Mackenzie, *Vestal Fire* (London: Cassell, 1927), 5, 128.

William Page Andrews died in 1916. It was inevitable that Edith would meet the Reynolds family, but it is not clear when she and Richard got to know one another well.[98] They married in London on 27 November 1935.[99] Any hopes that the marriage would bring lasting comfort, companionship, and mutual loving support as the couple moved into and through old age were soon to be shattered. Just ninety-nine days later, on 5 March 1936, Edith died.[100] She is buried in the Non-Catholic Cemetery in a tomb next to that of her first husband.

Reynolds did not marry again. He continued to live at Casa Monticello and in 1938 had the satisfaction of seeing Mynie get married to (Otto Jolle) Matthijs ("Thijs") Jolles, the brother of a Dutch-German friend, in Aberystwyth, Wales, where he was teaching German. She was twenty-four, he twenty-seven. They went to live in Chicago, where he continued to teach German. Reynolds returned to Capri but came to visit them the following spring. It is not known how long he stayed, nor is it clear if he returned to Capri. The next information is that he re-entered the US by road at Detroit from Windsor, Ontario, on 3 May 1940, with permission to be a permanent resident. His immigration card indicates that he had come from England.[101]

It is well that he left Italy before 10 June 1940, when Benito Mussolini declared war on the United Kingdom and France. Otherwise, he would have faced internment. He stayed with Mynie and Thijs until after the end of the war. No doubt he was able to give them financial assistance, and he kept himself busy. He read and played the piano, busied himself with his family memoir, and gave Thijs much help with the latter's translation of Karl von Clausewitz's treatise *On War*.[102] It would be surprising if he did not think often of his father in connection with Clausewitz, not least in reference to a famous passage in the first chapter: "We see, therefore, that war is not merely a political act but a real political instrument, a continuation of political intercourse, a carrying out of the same by other means."[103] As Kim Allen Scott has pointed out, "An interesting example of the Clausewitz maxim can be found in the career of Daniel Harris Reynolds, who fought

98 On 3 November 1931 both were elected members of a new committee appointed to manage the Non-Catholic Cemetery, but they probably met much earlier; Richter, *Il giardino della memoria*, 56.
99 *The Times*, 29 November 1935, 1.
100 *The Times*, 11 March 1936, 1.
101 Card Manifests (Alphabetical) of Individuals Entering through the Port of Detroit, Michigan, 1906–1954, ancestry.com (accessed 29 September 2016).
102 Karl von Clausewitz, *On War* (New York: Modern Library, 1943).
103 Clausewitz, *On War*, 16.

a war that required him to display as much skill in the political arena as in the military".[104]

Arnold Jolles remembers Reynolds, his grandfather, talking about the American Civil War. Although he was careful to explain the importance of Abraham Lincoln, "his sympathies seemed to lie somewhat with the South".[105] Perhaps his viewpoint was influenced by his knowledge of the prominent part his father had played on that side in the conflict and of his mother's years in Arkansas before, during, and after the war.

Reynolds remained in the US until at least August 1945. Harwood's daughter, Frances, who saw him at that time, writes: "My memory is of a very nice old man who was hard of hearing. He had a cumbersome hearing aid, wore a straw hat and maybe a seersucker suit. I think he had trouble with his teeth."[106]

Reynolds returned to Capri and Casa Monticello in 1946 or 1947. The island had suffered occupations and deprivations during the war, and provisions were scarce for some time after it. In the last years of the war, Monticello was occupied by American military personnel, for whom Capri had been designated a rest-camp. Before Reynolds left for the US, his valuables (including a full set of gold teeth!) were packed away in boxes, and these were taken away and stored by Raffaela Celentano, who, since the mid-1920s, had been a faithful employee of the family, cooking, washing, and helping to look after the girls. Such was her devotion to the family that, in memory of Pamela, she gave her own daughter the same name. When Reynolds returned to Capri, she returned all the valuables intact.[107]

In summer 1947, the Jolles family visited Capri. Reynolds had turned eighty in February, and his health was failing. He was composed, quiet, and kind. He managed short walks and wrote letters. Sometimes he fainted at dinner. He died peacefully at home on 22 December. The cause of his death is not certain but was probably heart failure. The funeral took place in the Non-Catholic Cemetery on 27 December. Mynie and Thijs were present with their children to see Reynolds interred next to Pamela and to hear Edwin Cerio deliver in Italian a eulogy that celebrated daughter as well as father.[108] Near the end of his address, Cerio recalled the words of a poem she sent him in 1934, entitled "Shadows":

---

104 Kim Allen Scott, review of *Worthy of the Cause for Which They Fight: The Civil War Diary of Brigadier General Daniel Harris Reynolds, 1861–1865*, edited by Robert Patrick Bender, *Arkansas Historical Quarterly* 71 (Winter 2012), 445.

105 Email to the author, 20 August 2016.

106 Email to the author, 17 September 2016.

107 Information from the Reynolds family and Celentano's daughter, Pamela Viva.

108 "Parole di saluto." The Reynolds graves can be seen in the centre of the colour photograph in Richter, *Il giardino della memoria*, 26, top left.

Do not put out your hand to touch the shadows.
They are so beautiful, the shadows, crimson, vermillion, violet, azure and
  green.
But it is terrible, terrible, to find out that they are intangible and without life.

Cerio continued (I translate the Italian):

Terrible, but not for the shadows – for us, when we want to stretch out our
hands, to stir our bodily senses to touch the shadows, and they escape us.
And that is why we do not want to approach Pamela and recall her father
with bodily senses. We want to come close to them in our thoughts and keep
them together, as together they lie, in our memories. To his surviving daughter, Hermione, and her husband we want to give the assurance that Richard
Reynolds, who became a "fellow countryman"[109] of Capri, blended and
united with our land, will be guarded in our hearts, in the memories of present
and absent friends.

If some satisfaction can be found in Reynolds's peaceful end, one cannot
escape the conclusion that he suffered more than his fair share of disap-
pointments and misfortunes. A lesser man might have been crushed by
them, but he soldiered on. His father had been a man of physical courage,
who had philosophically accepted the loss of a leg in battle. Reynolds's
courage and determination were, perhaps, partly inherited from his father
but at least as much from his mother, who, after suffering the deaths of her
husband and younger daughter in Arkansas and surviving the deprivations
and dangers of the American Civil War, reacted to the disappointment of
losing her lover by making a new life for herself, their son, and her elder
daughter in England.

Acknowledgements

I thank the following for their assistance: two anonymous readers who
reviewed this essay when it was first published in *Arkansas Historical
Quarterly*; Jane Abram; Anna Maria Palombi Cataldi, director, Centro
Caprense Ignazio Cerio, Capri; Victoria Chance; Rita Chiarini; Pam
Donaldson, Chicot County Clerk, Lake Village, AR; Sally Dowding; Drew
University Special Collections, and its catalog(u)er, Cassie Brand; Carmelina
Fiorentino, librarian, Centro Caprense Ignazio Cerio, Capri; Frances Diana
Picard Holt; Arnold Jolles; José Kany-Turpin; Liverpool Record Office;
London Metropolitan Archives; London School of Economics Archives;

---

109 Italian "*paesano*", the opposite of a *forestiero*, "outsider".

Francesca Longo Auricchio; Oliver Mahony, archivist, Lady Margaret Hall, Oxford; Lucy Marks, instructor librarian and Special Collections *cataloger emerita*, Drew University; Katherine O'Donnell, archivist, Somerville College, Oxford; Anna Sander, archivist, Balliol College, Oxford; Lucinda Ferguson Smith; University of Arkansas Libraries, Special Collections, for copies of items in the Daniel Harris Reynolds Papers and for permission to quote passages of Henry Hayes's letters to Reynolds of 24 July and 9 October 1864; Pamela Viva of Capri; Judith Walton, Durham University Library; Kristina West, University of Reading; Alison Wheatley, King Edward's Foundation Archivist, Schools of King Edward VI in Birmingham; Deborah Wilkes; Blake J. Wintory, assistant director, Lakeport Plantation, Lake Village, AR.

11

"A land pre-eminently to inspire a painter": Tristram Hillier's first visit to Portugal

In his autobiography, published in 1954, the artist Tristram Paul Hillier, describing his activities in 1936, writes:

> Most of the year I was to spend in Spain, a country which I came subsequently to love above all countries and where, since the last war, I have worked for several months each year. The translucent light of the south is comparable to that of Greece, which had so deeply fascinated me, with the addition of a dramatic quality, both noble and cruel, with which the landscape as well as the people are invested. The Iberian Peninsula is neither European nor Asiatic in character, a land set apart from all others, but one pre-eminently to inspire a painter.[1]

"The Iberian Peninsula" suggests that Hillier is thinking of Portugal as well as of Spain. The importance of Portugal to him is confirmed by part of the explanation he gives for not wanting to settle in Austria after his marriage to his second wife, Leda Hardcastle, in Vienna in January 1937:

> Austria … is not a painter's country; I imagine that this is due to the quality of its light. There is a lack of subtlety in the landscape, beautiful as it is, and the lovely Baroque architecture, unlike its counterpart under the warm sun of Portugal which was later to provide the theme for so many of my canvases, never excited me in a pictorial sense.[2]

Although Hillier did not set foot in Portugal until after the Second World War, it was to it rather than to Spain that he went to paint as soon as circumstances allowed after the war ended. The visit was an important one for him both for his work as an artist and because it arose out of a crisis in his personal life. The purpose of the present essay is to clarify the context, dating, and itinerary of the visit, and to focus particular attention on the artist's portrayal of scenes in the city of Viseu (Vizeu).

---

1 Tristram Hillier, *Leda and the Goose: An Autobiography* (London, 1954), 39.
2 Hillier, 150. The Hilliers' decision not to stay in Austria was also influenced by the political situation.

After leaving Austria, the Hilliers spent some weeks in Italy and considered settling near Florence, but there, as in Austria, the political climate was uncongenial, and they decided on France. They moved there in the autumn of 1937 and, after a brief stay in Provence, determined to make their home in Normandy. There, in the village of Criquetot-l'Esneval near Étretat, they found a delightful eighteenth-century house called l'Ormerie. Its price was unaffordable for them, but Leda's father generously bought it for her. So attractive were the house and its gardens and trees that Hillier declared: "We had a home in which we felt that we could very happily pass the remainder of our lives".[3] Sadly, however, their idyllic stay there was to be all too brief. Only about twelve days after the birth of their elder daughter, Mary,[4] in Le Havre on 8 May 1940, they were compelled to flee their home, just ahead of the advancing German forces. Their escape was a narrow and dramatic one, and they had to leave behind virtually all their possessions, including Hillier's paintings.[5] After various adventures, the family rested for a few days at Château Mont Gouje, St Maclou, whose owner, Madame Turquet, previously considered a friend, refused them admittance until Hillier demanded sanctuary and, when they departed, charged them for their stay, despite not having had to feed them.[6] They then had an anxious wait of a week in St Malo before they managed to get aboard a ship sailing to Southampton in early June.[7]

Hillier soon volunteered for service in the Royal Naval Volunteer Reserve. He served first ashore, then on local convoy-duty, then aboard a Free French naval vessel heading for Sierra Leone, before being employed ashore in Freetown. He was miserable for most of this time, partly because he missed Leda and Mary, partly because he was unable to paint. Health problems, psychological as well as physical, developed. The ordeal came to an end when he was certified as unfit to serve. On 30 September 1942 he

---

3 Hillier, 158.

4 Hillier, 165.

5 Hillier, 158–173.

6 Hillier, 171, does not name the house or its owner. The information is to be found in the carbon copy of a typescript letter of 30 May 1940 to Hillier from Richard Smart (TGA 20106/1/6/6) – a letter Hillier probably never received.

7 Jenny Pery, *Painter Pilgrim: The Art and Life of Tristram Hillier* (London, 2008), 73, says that they arrived in England in May, but Hillier's artist-friend Edward Wadsworth, writing on 7 June, reports that on 1 June the Hilliers were in St Malo, and that news of their arrival in England was still awaited (letter from Edward Wadsworth to Richard Smart, 7 June 1940, TGA 20106/1/6/70).

sent a telegram from Liverpool to Leda in Somerset, announcing that he would be home the following afternoon.[8]

He was now able to paint again, but did not go abroad until after the war in Europe ended. His first destination, in September 1945, was Normandy. With Leda he shared the painful experience of revisiting l'Ormerie. From their devoted maid, Henriette,[9] they had learned that the house had been trashed by the Germans, apparently when they learned that the owners were English.[10] But, thanks to Henriette, Hillier's paintings had been removed from his studio and hidden in the house of a neighbour, Monsieur Layet. In the spring of 1945, they were passed to Hillier's *notaire*, Maître Maujean.[11] When the Hilliers arrived back in France, they rented a house called Villa la Pivoine in Étretat, l'Ormerie being uninhabitable. The survival of the paintings was extremely welcome from every point of view, including the economic one, for, if they could be got to England, their sale should give a much-needed boost to the family's finances. After a tussle, the Board of Trade gave permission for the pictures painted by Hillier prior to his departure from France in 1940 to be imported, but refused to issue an import licence in respect of any of the work he did after his return to the country in 1945. A condition of the licence was that he agreed to take up permanent residence in the United Kingdom. Life in Normandy at this time was not easy, with shortages of food, fuel, and materials, and it took some time, persistence, and ingenuity to get the pictures packed in readiness for transportation.[12] There were fifty-one of them – thirty-seven paintings and fourteen drawings. They left Le Havre,

---

8 Pery, 78, quotes the telegram, which is in the Hillier Archive. Hillier himself writes: "I was invalided from the service in the autumn of 1944" (Hillier, 174), but he is strangely mistaken about the year.

9 Henriette is portrayed, wearing her maid's uniform and carrying a bottle and glass on a tray, together with the Hilliers and their two dogs, on the lawn of l'Ormerie in a painting by Hillier in a private collection, illustrated in *A Timeless Journey: Tristram Hillier R. A. 1905–1983* (Bradford Art Galleries and Museums, 1983), 25 (fig. 20) and by Pery, 73 (fig. 57).

10 Letter from Hillier to Dudley Tooth and RS, 24 September [1945], TGA 20106/1/6/33.

11 According to Hillier, 174, the pictures "had been hidden throughout the war in my lawyer's cellar", but letters of 21 April 1945 and 18 May 1945 from Hillier to Dudley Tooth make clear that Layet hid the pictures in his house for the duration of the German occupation and then passed them to Maujean, the lawyer – a handover that had to be managed delicately because Layet and Maujean were "sworn enemies" (TGA 20106/1/6/26, 30, 31). Hillier was to meet up with Maujean early in his time in Portugal in 1947 (letter from TH to LH, 28 May 194[7], HA).

12 On the Hilliers' time in Normandy in 1945–1946, see Hillier, 174–177.

along with several packing-cases containing carpets, bedding, clothes, and other items saved from l'Ormerie, aboard a vessel sailing for London on 7 March 1946.[13]

The Hilliers returned to England ten days later,[14] and between 7 May and 1 June Arthur Tooth & Sons Ltd, the London art-dealers through whom Hillier usually sold his pictures, held a successful exhibition and sale of his rescued work in their gallery at 31 Bruton Street.

Hillier's Somerset home was only ten miles, as the crow flies, from Downside Abbey and the school run by its Benedictine monks. On 1 November 1944 Hillier had lunch with Dom Sigebert Trafford, sixth Abbot of Downside, and was asked to paint his portrait.[15] Terms were agreed, and the first of several sittings took place on 15 November.[16] The finished work was delivered to Arthur Tooth in London on 5 March 1945.[17] Hillier had been a boarder at Downside School from 1914 to 1921,[18] and Dom Sigebert had been his headmaster from 1918. In his later years as a pupil and after he had left, Hillier had seriously contemplated becoming a monk, although a Trappist one rather than a Benedictine, but, when he was still a young man, he lost this ambition, and his faith lapsed. It was Trafford who, to his surprise, had encouraged him to train to be an artist, which he did, in the first place, at the Slade School of Fine Art in London under Henry Tonks, enrolling there in February 1926. His renewed contact with the Downside community, in combination with his wartime experiences, brought him back to the Roman Catholic Church. Mervyn Levy says that this happened in 1945,[19] but the year is much more likely to have been 1946, after Leda's and his time in France. The later date is supported by his report of her unexpectedly unfavourable reaction to the news:

> … when I announced my resolve to Leda she flew into a towering rage. I had never spoken to her seriously about my spiritual problems, and although she had known of my discussions with various monks at Downside she had,

13 Letters from TH to RS, 25 February 1946, with enclosed inventory, and 7 [March 1946], TGA 20106/1/7/39.
14 They crossed the Channel from Dieppe on 17 March. Letter from TH to RS, 7 March 1946 (TGA 20106/1/7/39).
15 Letter from TH to Dudley Tooth, 1 November 1944, TGA 20106/1/6/25.
16 Letter from TH to Dudley Tooth, 11 November 1944, TGA 20106/1/6/25.
17 Letter from TH to Dudley Tooth, 18 February 1945, TGA 20106/1/6/28.
18 Hillier's father, Guy Hillier, the manager of the Hongkong and Shanghai Bank in Peking, had converted to Roman Catholicism after going blind. Tristram was born in Peking on 11 April 1905, but brought up mainly in England.
19 Mervyn Levy, "Hillier, Tristram Paul", *Oxford Dictionary of National Biography: 1981–1985* (Oxford, 1990), 194.

I think, regarded them simply as intellectual gymnastics in the company of old friends with whom I had agreed to disagree. My declared intention of resuming allegiance to Rome awoke in her all the bitterness of the Irish Protestantism in which she had been reared.[20] She said that if I persisted in pursuing this superstitious fad she would seek a divorce ... My relationship with Leda at this time became very strained, and since my convictions could permit no compromise I was able to do little in healing the breach between us. Thinking that a temporary separation would restrain her from any impetuous decision and enable her to regard the matter in a more reasonable light I told her that I intended to spend the next five or six months painting in Portugal. She seemed to welcome my decision.[21]

Jenny Pery mistakenly places this first visit to Portugal in 1945,[22] misled by a slip of the pen on Hillier's part when he dated one of the many letters he wrote to Leda from Portugal "28.5.1945" instead of "28.5.1947," the slip very likely having been influenced by the preceding "5" for May. Her mistake is unfortunate, because it involves misdating by two years a visit that was, as I have already indicated, of great consequence for him, both professionally and personally.

Hillier gives a brief account of his time in Portugal on the penultimate page of *Leda and the Goose*.[23] The details of it can be found in the letters he wrote from Portugal to Leda and to Richard Smart of Arthur Tooth. The letters to Leda are in the Hillier Archive. Those to Smart are in the Arthur Tooth & Sons Collection in the Tate Gallery Archive in London and include also letters written before and after the trip.[24]

In a letter to Smart in mid-March 1947, he writes:

20 Leda's father, Engineer-Captain Sydney Undercliffe Hardcastle, RN (retired), was from northeast England (of Yorkshire ancestry, but born and school-educated in County Durham). Her mother, Annie Hardcastle, was the daughter of James Preston, a veterinary doctor of Mallow, County Cork. Sydney and Annie married in Haydon Bridge, Northumberland, on 9 August 1908. Leda Millicent was born in Southsea, Portsmouth, on 28 November 1911. She was only three or four when Annie died, and was then brought up by her mother's family in County Cork.

21 Hillier, 182.

22 Pery, 94, 97.

23 Hillier, 183.

24 Pery's book was published in 2008. The Tate Archive purchased the Arthur Tooth Collection from Simon Matthews, grandson of Dudley Tooth, in April 2010. Although Pery includes Matthews in her list of acknowledgements, she does not appear to have had access to the Hillier correspondence in the collection, which is a rich source of information.

After an uninterrupted winter's work in East Pennard[25] I am feeling very stale and badly need a change of scene if it can be managed, and I am sure that from the point of view of painting Portugal would be the answer.[26]

This statement is the truth, but not the whole truth, Hillier's difficulties with Leda understandably not being mentioned. He had mentioned his intention to Smart earlier, as the preceding lines of the same letter show:

When I saw you last in London you were good enough to say that you would send me Sine Fordham's address if you could find it in order that I could write to her for information about Portugal.
Have you been able to find it or have you forgotten?

Sine Fordham, better known by her maiden name, Sine Mackinnon, was born in Newcastle, County Down, Ulster. Like Hillier, but earlier than he, she had studied drawing at the Slade School of Fine Art, London, under Henry Tonks.[27] She had exhibited several times in London and Paris. She shared Hillier's preference for working abroad and lived mainly in France. In the spring of 1940 Arthur Tooth staged an exhibition of her *Recent Paintings of France, Greece and Portugal*.[28] She had spent the first months of the Second World War in Portugal. An artist who deserves to be much better known than she is,[29] she produced work that has one striking similarity to Hillier's, which is the absence or fewness of human figures in her scenes,[30] but her method of composition was very different from his: unlike him, she always painted *en plein air*, according to her daughter, Jan Fordham.[31] One cannot tell how helpful she was to Hillier about Portugal. Smart immediately sent Hillier her temporary address in Dublin.[32] It is not

---

25 Yew Tree House, East Pennard, Near Shepton Mallet, Somerset, had been the Hilliers' address since 15 July 1946 (letter of 13 July 1946 from TH to RS, TGA 20106/1/7/43), and it was to be his home for the rest of his life.

26 Letter from TH to RS, 17 March 1947, TGA 20106/1/7/50.

27 She entered the Slade in October 1918, when she was seventeen.

28 25 April–18 May 1940. Exhibition catalogue, TGA 20106/6/1/224.

29 A welcome exhibition of thirty-one of her paintings and drawings was presented by Gorry Gallery, Dublin, in 2012 (20 May–2 June). The leading authority on her work is Professor Antoin Murphy of Trinity College, Dublin.

30 Cf. Thomas MacGreevy, "In the World's Art Centres: London: Sine Mackinnon", *Studio* 120, 568 (July 1940), 22: "Human beings seldom appear in the villages of France, Greece and Portugal as seen by Miss Sine Mackinnon".

31 Letter from Jan Fordham to the Tate Gallery, 26 February 1996, cited in the Tate's catalogue entry on Mackinnon's painting *Farm Buildings in Provence 1934*, ref. N05135.

32 Letter from RS to TH, 19 March 1947, TGA 20106/1/7/50.

known whether he received a reply from her before he started his visit, but he did hear from her towards the end of it.[33]

Smart encouraged Hillier to go to Portugal and may even have suggested it as well.[34] As we shall see, he was to join him there for nearly three weeks in August. In a letter to Hillier dated 1 May 1947 he writes, "The Portugese [*sic*] conspiracy goes merrily on", and "I now feel sure that you and Portugal are meant for one another. Could it be otherwise when the way is paved with gold, so to speak? Anyhow I am delighted, not to say envious, that everything has planned out so well."[35] Hillier echoes the term "conspiracy" in a letter, written just over a week later, in which he reports:

> All is now arranged for the Portuguese trip. I recieved [*sic*] this morning the Bank of England's authorisation to transfer £300[36] to Lisbon, and I have just telephoned the American Express and reserved an air passage on saturday the 17th May. It really seems as though the Gods were in on this conspiracy, to send me to Portugal, as I have met both from the B.O.T.[37] and the Treasury with an immediate compliance with my requests, and I am sure that if I had asked for much more than £300 it would have been granted to me.[38]

On the same day that he wrote the above, he wrote again to Smart, requesting his help in contacting another person whose knowledge of Portugal he wanted to tap:

> I cannot remember Sache Sitwell's address and I urgently require some information about Portugal from him before I leave. You probably have it in your lists, but if not could you please find it out for me and forward the enclosed letter.[39]

Sacheverell Sitwell, younger brother of Edith and Osbert Sitwell, was an indefatigable traveller and prolific writer, best known for his books on baroque art and architecture. One of these, *Spanish Baroque Art*, discussed also buildings in Portugal as well as in Mexico, South America, Abyssinia,

---

33 Letter from RS to TH, 8 September 1947, TGA 20106/1/7/53.
34 Postcard from TH to RS, 21 May 1947, TGA 20106/1/7/51; letter from TH to RS, 1 June 1948, TGA 20106/1/7/52.
35 Letter from RS to TH, 1 May 1947, TGA 20106/1/7/51. One would expect "panned out".
36 The equivalent of just under £12,000 in 2018. The normal foreign travel allowance at this time was £75 (just under £3,000) for twelve months, but from 1 October 1947 it was reduced to £35 for fourteen months, and extra allowances for those carrying out business abroad were also more strictly limited (*The Times*, 7 August 1947, 4).
37 Board of Trade.
38 Letter from TH to RS, 9 May 1947, TGA 20106/1/7/51.
39 Letter from TH to RS, 9 [May 1947], TGA 20106/1/7/51.

Goa, and China.[40] That book appeared sixteen years before Hillier's first visit to Portugal. In the preface to *Portugal and Madeira*, published in 1954, Sitwell calls Hillier "my friend",[41] and the frontispiece of the book is a colour photograph of Hillier's painting of the Church of the Misericordia at Viseu. It seems a reasonable conjecture that the information Hillier sought from Sitwell in May 1947 included "the lovely Baroque architecture ... of Portugal" mentioned by Hillier in a passage quoted near the beginning of this essay.

A few months before Hillier decided to visit Portugal, in September 1946, Rose Macaulay's entertaining account of British people who for various reasons visited or settled in Portugal over the centuries appeared under the title *They Went to Portugal* (London, 1946). An important part of the research was done in Portugal in March–May 1943. The book did much to enhance awareness of British links to Portugal and its people. Although there is no evidence that its publication influenced Hillier's decision to go to Portugal, Macaulay, who made an adventurous solo trip to Spain and Portugal by car in the summer of 1947 in preparation for her book *Fabled Shore*,[42] was to have some contact with him. She admired the work he did in Portugal in 1947 and bought one of the drawings he made. When he went to Spain in April 1949, she "strongly recommended" to him Guadix "as a painting terrain".[43] Unfortunately his visit to Guadix that year was not the success she and he had hoped. In a letter to her Portuguese friend Luiz Marques in July 1949, just after Hillier had returned from Spain, she writes:

> Tristram Hillier, the artist, was disgusted because, when he went to the Guadix hill country to paint it (he is very good) the children surrounded him, threw stones and dirt, upset his easel, and made themselves so tiresome that he gave it up and went back to Torremolinos in a temper. He did some beautiful drawings and paintings in Portugal in 1947, of Vizeu and other places. He is among the several people who seem to have gone to the fabled shore after reading my book.[44]

40 Sacheverell Sitwell, *Spanish Baroque Art, With Buildings in Portugal, Mexico, and Other Colonies* (London, 1931).
41 Sacheverell Sitwell, *Portugal and Madeira* (London, 1954), 10. A presentation copy of the book, inscribed "To Birdie Hillier best wishes from Sachie 3 September 1954" remains with the Hillier family. Hillier was always "Birdie" to family and friends.
42 Rose Macaulay, *Fabled Shore: From the Pyrenees to Portugal* (London, 1949).
43 Letter from TH to RS, Thursday [21 or 28 April 1949], TGA 20106/1/7/62.
44 Letter from Rose Macaulay to Luiz Marques, 3 July 1949. Photocopy kindly supplied by Marques' elder daughter, the late Ana Vicente.

Unless Macaulay let Hillier read her book prior to publication, the last statement cannot be correct. Hillier left England for Spain on 9 April,[45] several weeks before *Fabled Shore* appeared.[46] Several years later, he was to return to Guadix to draw and paint it.[47]

On 17 May 1947 Hillier flew with British European Airways from Northolt Airport, London, to Bordeaux and on to Lisbon, where he stayed his first nights in Portugal at the Grand Hotel Borges. In Lisbon he made the acquaintance of Susan and Luiz Marques, who had been very helpful to Macaulay and remained good friends of hers, and were to assist also Sacheverell Sitwell. Susan was a daughter of the author Marie Belloc Lowndes and a niece of Hilaire Belloc. Like them, she was a writer. She was to co-author with Ann Bridge *The Selective Traveller in Portugal* (1949), a book praised by Sitwell.[48] Luiz had been the Lisbon correspondent of *The Daily Telegraph* since 1936 and editor of *Anglo-Portuguese News* since 1937. Hillier met them at the British Institute, where he heard Susan give a lecture on Anglo-Portuguese relations in the arts during the past four hundred years. He took to her and Luiz immediately.[49] They invited him to visit them at their home in Estoril, although he did not manage to do that, but, in deciding where to base himself, he benefited from Luiz's advice. After a brief stay in Nazaré, on the coast north of Lisbon, he went further north to Aveiro, "the Venice of Portugal", but found it "awful", and after what he describes, in a letter to Richard Smart, as "a rather abortive period of travel" and, in a letter to Leda, as "a perfectly ghastly five days", he followed the advice of Luiz Marques to abandon his plan of staying in "those miserable village inns" and go to Foz do Arelho, a little down the coast from Nazaré.[50]

At Foz he found "an extremely comfortable hotel on a long and solitary beach run by a most agreeable Englishman with whom I have become very friendly and have consequently been accorded most reasonable terms".[51] The establishment was Hotel do Facho, and its proprietor was Charles

45 Letter from TH to RS, 28 March 1949, TGA 20106/1/7/61.
46 Letter from RS to TH in Spain, 3 May 1949, TGA 20106/1/7/62: "The Rose Macaulay book is just out but I am afraid there's not much point in offering to send it to you. It would most likely be stolen or even siezed [*sic*] by the Customs as an obscene publication as it happens to be written in English."
47 See Pery, 130–131, 133, figs 109–110.
48 *Portugal and Madeira*, 9.
49 Letter from TH to LH, 21 May 1947, HA.
50 Letters from TH to RS, 1 June 1947, TGA 20106/1/7/52, and to Leda Hillier. 28 May [1947] (misdated by TH "1945"), HA.
51 Letter from TH to RS, 1 June 1947, TGA 20106/1/7/52.

Harbord. Harbord, said to have had links to the British security services,[52] was an elder brother of Felix Harbord, a noted interior designer and theatre designer, with whom Hillier had become friendly years before in London. Another link with Charles Harbord was that "we both at different times enjoyed the favours of the same Lady in Paris – also some years ago – which he seems to consider a bond of real brotherhood".[53]

When still in England, Hillier had heard of Foz from several sources, but had not paid much attention. One of his informants, through Richard Smart (he thought) was the celebrated Australian-born ballet-dancer and actor Robert ("Bobby") Helpmann, who had stayed at Hotel do Facho the previous summer and made a remarkable impression on its manager, a man named Hannibal (probably Anibal).[54] Helpmann was to buy two of the pictures that resulted from Hillier's 1947 visit to Portugal. One of them was *Rocks at Facho*. Early in his stay at Foz, Hillier suggested to Leda that she and Mary fly out to join him in August.[55] This was not to happen, but he was joined by several other visitors from England. One was Richard Smart, who arrived on 5 August and departed on 25 August. Hillier gave him advance warning that he must not expect any lively entertainment, the entertainment being "almost entirely in liquid form (i.e. either the Atlantic or the Bar)".[56] A surprising item he urgently requested him to bring him from London was nothing to do with drawing or painting, but a bottle of Truefitt & Hills' Monte Carlo Special Hair Lotion, because "Portuguese hair lotions are very sticky and smell like a tarts' bedroom".[57]

As well as Foz itself being attractive, "The surroundings", Hillier declared, "are all that I could desire to paint".[58] Nearby places that are scenes of his paintings include Peniche, Obidos, Nadadouro, and Caldas da Reinha. Hotel do Facho remained his base until 11 September,[59] but he was to make several expeditions to other parts of Portugal before he flew back to London on 25 September. In the first week of September, and again later in the month, he stayed at Quinta do Carmo, Estremoz, as a guest of Victor Hunter Reynolds. Estremoz, east of Lisbon, is less than thirty miles from the Spanish border and, during the Second World War, Reynolds, whose mother was Portuguese, played a most valuable role in assisting the escape

---

52 Ana Vicente, *Arcádia: Notícia de uma Família Anglo-Portuguesa* (Lisboa, 2006), 165.
53 Letter from TH to LH, undated but written early in his stay at Foz do Arelho, HA.
54 Letter from TH to RS, 1 June 1947, TGA 20106/1/7/52.
55 Letter from TH to LH, 28 May [1947], HA.
56 Letter from TH to RS, Saturday [12 July 1947], TGA 20106/1/7/53.
57 Letter from TH to RS, 17 July 1947, TGA 20106/1/7/53. Truefitt & Hills, established in 1805, still offers a lotion of this name.
58 Letter from TH to RS, 1 June 1947, TGA 20106/1/7/52.
59 Letter from TH to LH, 11 September 1947, HA.

of Allied servicemen, agents, and refugees from occupied Europe through Spain and Portugal. He suggested to Hillier that he do a small drawing of the nearby house of the Duke of Palmela, the Portuguese Ambassador in London, and give it to him.[60] When the exhibition of Hillier's work in Portugal was held in London the following spring, the Ambassador agreed to be its patron, opened it, and purchased one of the paintings.

Between his two visits to Estremoz, Hillier visited the Douro valley, Oporto, and nearby places in the north in the company of Max Graham and two of Graham's acquaintances. Major Maxwell Graham, who had been resident in Oporto since 1907 or 1908, headed the operations of Grahams Trading Company Limited in Portugal, where it owned textile- and paper-mills and a printing works. His family also owned Graham's Port. It seems that Hillier knew Max Graham before his trip to Portugal, but it is not clear how.

Much the most important destination for Hillier away from Foz and the surrounding area was Viseu, an ancient episcopal city and district capital in northern[61] Portugal, east of Aveiro and southeast of Oporto, situated on a plateau on the left bank of the River Pavia, a tributary of the Mondego. Hillier made two and perhaps three visits. The first was early in his time in Portugal, probably just after his unenjoyable visit to Aveiro. On this first occasion he seems not to have done any drawing.

His second visit, at the end of June and beginning of July, was much more significant. In a letter of 25 June to Leda from Foz, he writes:

> The day after tomorrow I am motoring north with Harbord who goes to his other hotel, in order to spend a few days in a lovely mountain town called VIZEU where I have already made some notes and have several drawings to do.[62]

The second establishment owned by Harbord was the Hotel Urgeiriça in Canas de Senhorim, a little south of Viseu. Hillier briefly described his time in Viseu on a picture postcard from Viseu written to Leda in the morning of Tuesday 1 July:

> Have been staying here last 2 days drawing –. Have completed an ambitious and successful drawing of Cathedral Square – Quite magnificent – for a large picture –. Return this afternoon to URGERIECA [*sic*] Harbord's Northern hotel, which is 30 kilometres away, and back to Foz during the week –.

---

60 Letter from TH to LH, 5 September 1947, HA. The Fifth Duke of Palmela, Domingos de Sousa Holstein-Beck, was ambassador 1943–1949.

61 Although reasonably described as "northern", Viseu is actually in Portugal's Centro region.

62 Letter from TH to LH, 25 June 1947, HA.

V. dirty and cafard[63] accomodation [*sic*] here, but worth putting up with for the drawing … The heat here is really overwhelming, …[64]

The following day he wrote to Leda again from Hotel Urgeiriça:

I arrived here yesterday from Viseu, whence I sent you a card, after an apalling [*sic*] journey which took 5 hours, although the distance is only 25 kilometres … It is wonderful to be in this comfortable hotel of Harbord's again after the very cafard surroundings in which I have been drawing for the past few days. But I did a really fine drawing, which makes any discomfort worth while. The heat up here in the mountains is terrific – enough even for you, I think, – and I manage only to draw outside in the mornings, and work in my room during the afternoons.[65]

In a letter to Leda at the end of August, Hillier announced his intention of making a third visit to Viseu, which Richard Smart had visited without him a few days earlier:

Richard has absolutely insisted that I return to Viseu in the north to make a drawing, and subsequently a large painting of the 'Misericordia' there (which he went to see, and of which I had already made notes) so I am going to spend a week in Charles Harbord's house (which is not far away) from 15th Sept.[66]

In the correspondence I have seen, however, there is no confirmation of a further visit to Viseu, and certainly the plan of spending a week from 15 September in Harbord's Hotel Urgeiriça was not fulfilled. Hillier wrote to Leda from there on 11 and 12 September, when on his way to the Douro with Max Graham and companions, and in the letter of 12 September he reports an accident he had in the swimming pool the previous day, when he dived off the top board into water that was too shallow, hit his head on the bottom of the pool, and "came up with my face streaming with blood and feeling rather gaga"![67]

There is no mention of Viseu. After the Douro and Oporto trip he went to Lisbon and Estremoz and seems not to have travelled north again. If, therefore, a third visit to Viseu was made at all, it seems to have been a very brief one, probably for no more than a few hours in the company of Graham and friends. No drawing he made of the eighteenth-century Church of the Misericordia (Igreja da Misericórdia), directly opposite the Cathedral, survives, and his painting of it is not the large one Richard Smart and he had envisaged, but a small panel (Plate 41). Preserved in the Hillier Archive are

63 "Grotty."
64 Postcard from TH to LH, 1 July 1947, HA.
65 Letter from TH to LH, 2 July 1947, HA.
66 Letter from TH to LH, 31 August 1947, HA.
67 Letter from TH to LH, 12 [September 1947], HA.

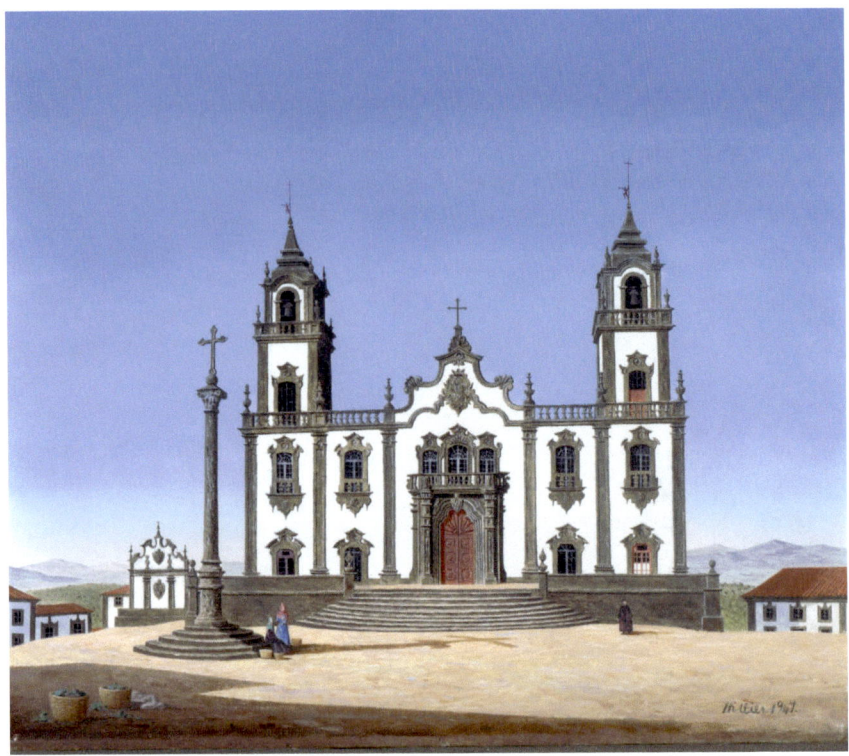

41 *Church of the Misericordia, Viseu*, 1947. Oil on panel, 25.4 × 29.2 cm.

three photographic images of the church. One is a large photograph giving the same view, from the same point, as the painting (Plate 42). Even the shadows are similar. The back of the photograph is stamped "Germano VISEU". Germano was a leading photographic business in Viseu in 1947, and the two cars parked in front of the church suit that sort of date. It is not clear whether the photograph was taken by Germano, or whether it was taken by Hillier and developed and printed by them. The two other images are picture-postcards. One gives a slightly nearer view of the church than the photograph (Plate 43). The other is a more distant view, from just in front of the Cathedral (Plate 44). This second postcard is reproduced, very small, by Pery.[68] In her caption she dates it 1982, which is puzzling: the postcard carries no indication of date, but, like the photograph, it is a production of Germano, and the look of the parked cars points to 1947 rather than 1982, the year before Hillier died.

68 108, fig. 88.

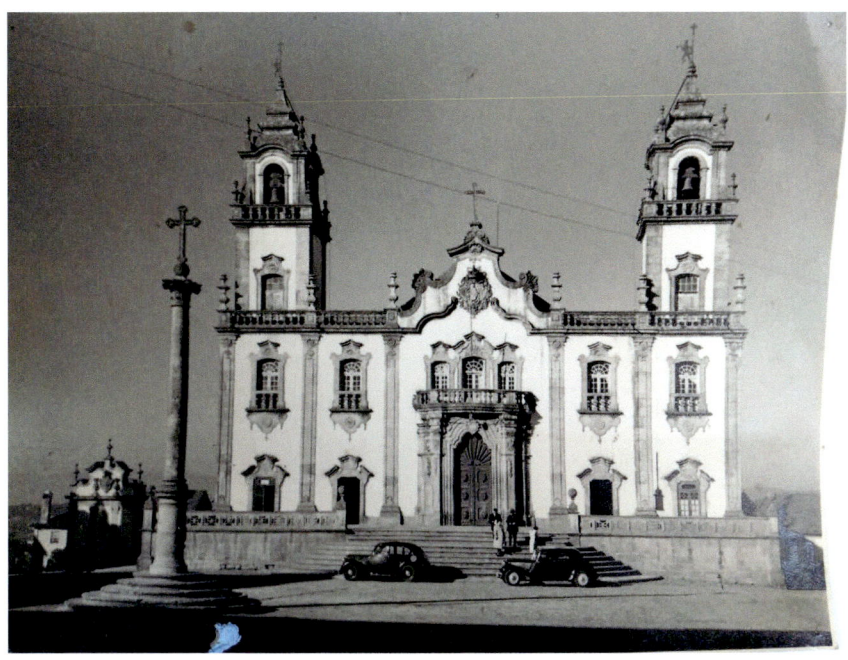

42 *Church of the Misericordia, Viseu*, 1947. Photograph.

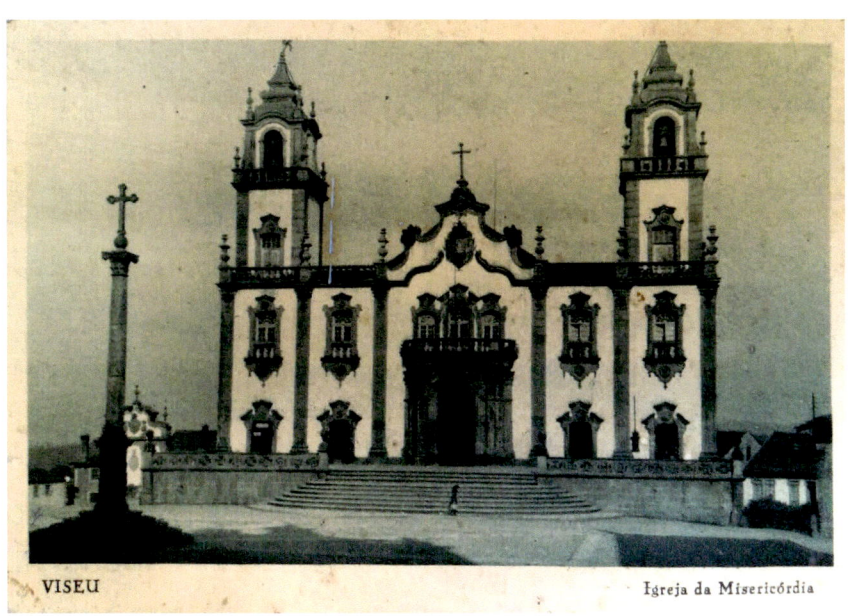

43 *Church of the Misericordia, Viseu*, not later than 1947. Postcard.

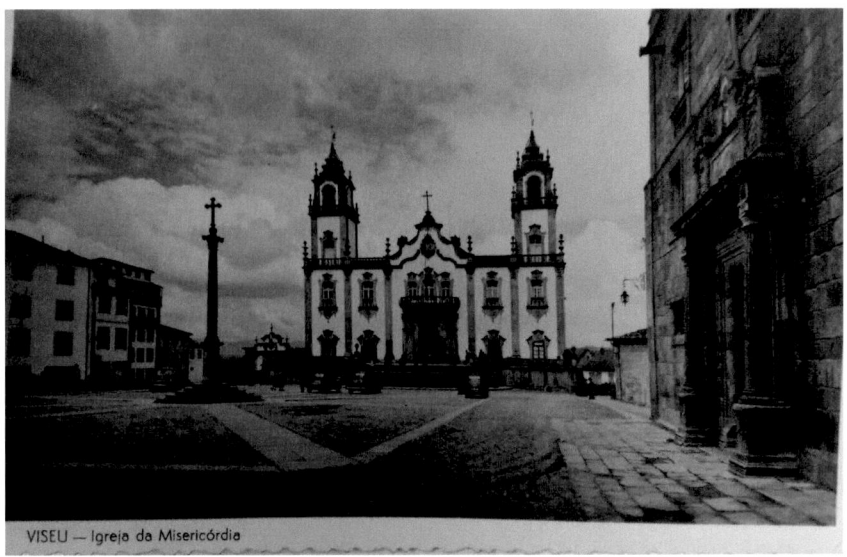

44 *Church of the Misericordia, Viseu*, not later than 1947. Postcard.

Hillier sometimes used photographs as aids when he was painting his pictures,[69] and, although the notes he made on the Church of the Misericordia may well have included some sketches, it seems very likely that he relied on photographs to a greater extent than usual when painting the church. The picture, signed "Hillier 1947" lower right, was painted late in 1947, very soon after he had completed his large Viseu painting – the one for which he made the drawing. He tells Richard Smart that he found the job difficult: "I have done a painting of the Baroque facade of the Misericordia which has nearly sent me blind, but it is rather a 'tour de force' of detail, and now I am on to the large canvas of boats at Peniche, which looks promising."[70] Smart replies: "I feel that the Misericordia facade will be one [large picture] much to my liking. For daring to tackle it you deserve a really high-grade Portugese [*sic*] decoration – if they still hand out such things."[71] It is not known if Smart was disappointed when he discovered that the picture was not the "large" one he had been expecting.

The drawing Hillier made in Viseu on 29–30 June was preparatory to one of his finest and best-known paintings, now in Wolverhampton Art Gallery. The painting (Plate 45), a large canvas signed lower right "Hillier 1947", was

69 Pery, 34, 77–79.
70 TH to RS, 19 January 1948, TGA 20106/1/7/56. In 1975 Hillier developed a severe problem in his left eye – a problem that led to the loss of it.
71 Letter from RS to TH, 28 January 1948, TGA 20106/1/7/56.

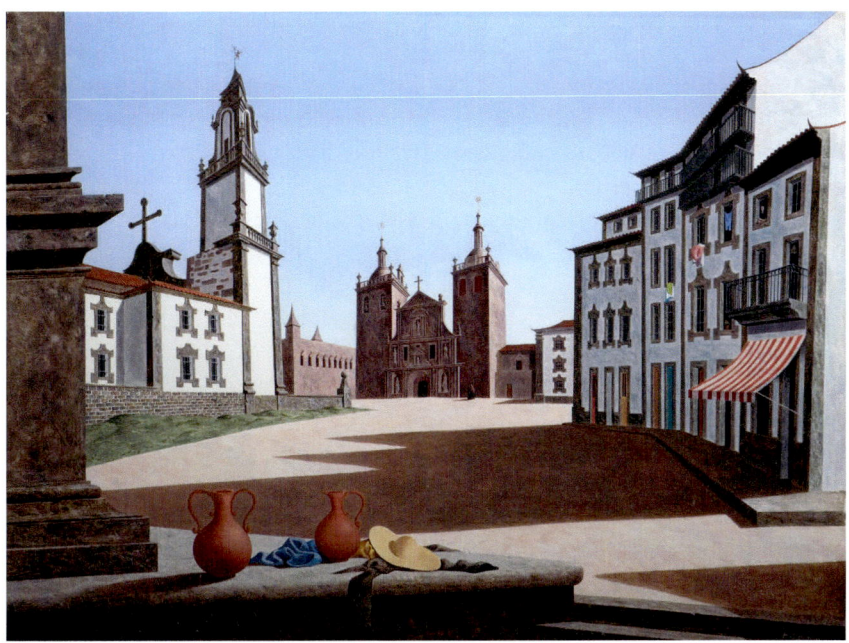

45 *Cathedral Square, Viseu,* 1947. Oil on canvas, 61 × 81 cm.

completed in November of that year.[72] Like the *Church of the Misericordia,* both it and the drawing for it were included in Arthur Tooth's exhibition of Hillier's "Portuguese" work, held at 31 Bruton Street, London W1, from 27 April to 22 May 1948.[73] There are thirty-eight items in the catalogue: twenty-eight paintings and ten drawings. Both the large canvas and the drawing are titled *Viseu, 1947,* but a more helpful title would be the one indicated in Hillier's communication of 1 July 1947 to Leda, *Cathedral Square, Viseu.* It is indicative of the special importance that Tooth and Hillier attached to the painting that it is reproduced on the title-page of the catalogue. Its importance to the artist is confirmed by his choice of it to be one of only six of his paintings reproduced in his autobiography,[74] and by his recommendation of it to be one of three works of his selected to form part of a British Council exhibition "Eleven British Artists" presented at the National Gallery of South Australia, Adelaide, in 1949.[75] His high opinion of

---

72 Letter from TH to RS, 23 November [1947], TGA 20106/1/7/55.

73 *Paintings of Portugal by Tristram Hillier* (London, 1948).

74 Hillier, opposite 109.

75 TGA 9712/2/35. Hillier's recommendation is in a letter to Richard Smart, 30 July 1948, 20106/1/7/59: "I am glad about the British Council and hope they manage

the painting has been implicitly endorsed by others: for example, the Victoria and Albert Museum in London obtained the loan of it from Wolverhampton Art Gallery to make it part of its "Object of the Month" display in August 1985,[76] and Pery has a double-page colour photograph of it immediately before the start of her first chapter as well as a much smaller colour photograph of it as fig. 1 alongside the first paragraph of the same chapter.[77]

The view in the painting is from the northern corner of the public fountain in the Largo da Misericórdia, across the Cathedral Square (Praça da Sé or Adro da Sé), to the west front of the Cathedral, with its two towers. On the right is a row of houses, the nearest of which is, on the ground floor, a shop with a red and white striped awning. On the left, past the corner of the fountain, is part of the Church of the Misericordia. Between the Church and the Cathedral is part of the former Bishop's Palace (Paço dos Bispos de Viseu), home, since 1916, to the Museu Grão Vasco. The only human beings visible are a woman looking out of a second-floor window of the house with the awning and two distant figures in front of the right tower of the Cathedral. Only when one closely views the actual picture can one properly see that the figure on the left is that of a priest holding a furled umbrella, and the figure on the right that of a woman wearing a red shawl.

On the platform in the foreground is a colourful assortment of objects. From left to right they are: a two-handled red jug with a narrow neck; a piece of blue cloth; a one-handled red jug; and a broad-brimmed yellow hat that partly conceals pieces of golden and brown cloth. The inclusion of these "signature" items is an indication of how, despite the transition Hillier describes himself having made in the late 1930s "from abstraction and surrealism to representational painting",[78] he had not shed all his surrealist inclinations. But, although the aforementioned objects are imaginative additions to the scene and have the viewer guessing about their significance and symbolism, they are far removed from the incongruous items "on the pale yellow sands" in Lord Berners' poem "Surrealist Landscape" – items that include.

> A commode
> That has nothing to do with the case.[79]

to borrow 3 pictures which will not dishonour me in tour country. I think Kay [the owner] ought to lend 'Viseu' to make up for all the trouble he has given me!"

76 Information and copies of relevant correspondence kindly supplied by Wolverhampton Art Gallery.

77 Pery, 8–10.

78 Hillier, 151.

79 "Surrealist Landscape", lines 18–19. The poem was first published in *Horizon* 6, no. 31 (July 1942), 5–6.

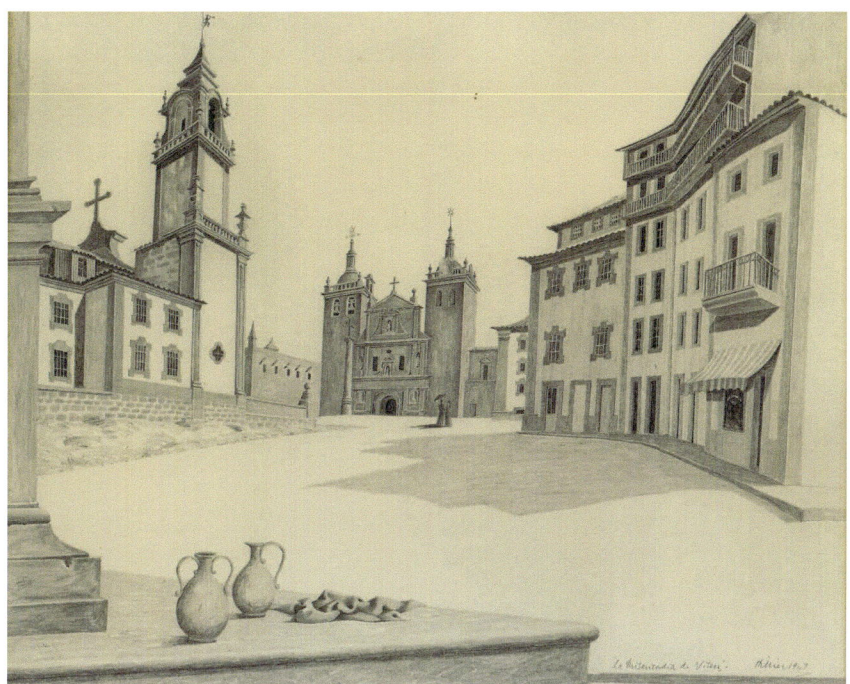

46 *Cathedral Square, Viseu,* 1947. Pencil on paper, 34 × 42 cm.

The hat in Hillier's picture is appropriate to a sunny summer's day, and the jugs are not out of place beside a fountain.

Whereas the painting is well known, the drawing of which the artist was so proud has not been seen in public since it was exhibited over seventy years ago, in the spring of 1948, and has not been published before. It is the work bought by Rose Macaulay and is in my possession. The drawing (Plate 46), in pencil on paper, is a little more than half the size of the painting. Before his signature and the date, "Hillier 1947", lower right, the artist has written the title "*La Misericordia de Viseu*", which is unexpected, given that the church is not the main subject of the drawing. Like the painting, it is best titled *Cathedral Square, Viseu.*

The similarities between the drawing and the painting are obvious, being close and numerous, but there are also differences. Most of the differences are minor, but several are more significant. The most remarkable one is the omission from the painting of the granite column, bearing the episcopal coat of arms and surmounted by a cross, in Cathedral Square, of which it is a prominent feature, as is clear in the Misericordia painting and the photographs. It is to be seen in the drawing in front of the left tower of the Cathedral. Given Hillier's usual attention to detail, it is hard to believe that its omission from the painting is accidental. It is much more likely that he thought that it spoiled the view of the Cathedral and detracted from the symmetry and harmony of the picture. It is probable too that it was aesthetic considerations that prompted him to make several alterations to windows – for example, to give the house at the far end of the row three first-floor windows instead of two, to remove the small diamond-shaped window near the base of the tower of the church, and to tidy up the building's roof by removing not only the second-floor window, but also the second floor itself. In the drawing no face of a woman is to be seen in the window above the shop, no items of drapery are hanging in or out of the windows, and there is no pot of flowers. The two distant figures are easier to make out in the drawing than in the painting, and the priest has his umbrella up, not down. As for the quasi-surrealist assemblage of objects in the foreground, the jugs are in the drawing, but close together. There is just one piece of drapery and no hat.

Another difference between drawing and painting concerns the shadows. They are more extensive in the painting. Some critics detect something unnatural and unsettling about the emptiness of Hillier's scenes and the presence of long shadows.[80] Their judgement is subjective and, with regard to shadows, largely fanciful. There is nothing unnatural about the shadows in either of the Viseu paintings. Pery thinks that the painting of the *Church of the Misericordia*, "with its bare piazza pierced by geometric shadows, has the hushed intensity of a stage before the play has begun". Perhaps, but comparison with the photographic images in Plates 42 and 43 suggests that the shadows in the painting are not exaggerated. It may be added that Plate 43 shows a solitary woman passing the church, whereas the painting shows three figures. It is undeniable that, partly through the influence of the young Giorgio de Chirico, Hillier liked to show squares and other spaces uncluttered with human figures, but it seems that he may have found Viseu's Cathedral Square so quiet in 1947 that he did not need to depopulate it, and this may have been one of its attractions for him.

The drawing of Cathedral Square is of obvious interest and value for being essentially the work Hillier produced *en plein air* in preparation for the painting he executed in his studio, and at least one sensitive viewer has felt that it scores over the painting in respect of immediacy and freshness.

Throughout Hillier's time in Portugal he and Leda exchanged letters. On 17 September, just over a week before he returned home, he received a letter from her containing an astonishing piece of news. His reply began:

---

80 See, e.g., Pery, 109–110.

My darling–,

Your letter of September 9th reached me yesterday in Oporto, and I cannot tell you how happy it has made me. That you should wish to become a Catholic is something I have prayed much for, but others must too have prayed for you, because I cannot imagine that the prayers of such an old sinner as I would be so quickly answered!

Your change of heart is, of course, as you say, miraculous, and I can so well understand the deep happiness it has brought to you and will, I am sure, bring to our life together.[81]

How Leda's conversion had come about is described by Hillier in his auto-biography. Their daughter, Mary, now aged seven, was attending a convent school (in Shepton Mallet) open to all denominations. Leda had become friendly with one of the French nuns, and their conversations and the various books the nun obtained for her had made her want to be instructed in Roman Catholicism and received into the Church.

Leda did indeed become a Roman Catholic, and it would be nice to be able to report that the rift between husband and wife that brought about his first visit to Portugal was as successful for his personal life as it was for his professional career. From the closing paragraph of *Leda and the Goose* one would think that it was:

We have now lived in Somerset for seven years, the longest period I have ever spent in one place. Another daughter has been born to us,[82] and my sons pay me visits from time to time.[83] I spend a few months of each year painting in Spain lest my palette and my mind become as misty as the gentle landscape which surrounds us, but I have found my happiness and my home at last, in Leda and in England.

Sadly, the reality was very different. Despite Leda's conversion and the welcome addition to the family in 1950, the marriage never again became the closely loving one it had been in its earliest years, before Hillier's wartime service and breakdown. The couple had different interests and, although he enjoyed riding horses, he did not fully share her passion for them or her social life. He would have loved them to make their home abroad again. Soon after the war this would not have been possible, because of the undertaking he had given the Board of Trade in 1946 to live in the United Kingdom. Later it would have been possible, but Leda would not

81 Letter from TH to LH, 18 September 1947, continued and completed 19 September 1947, HA.

82 Anna-Clare Hillier, born 8 August 1950.

83 Jonathan Daniel Hillier and Benjamin Paul Hillier, Hillier's twin sons by his first wife, Irene Rose ("Georgiana") Hillier *née* Hodgkins, later Varley.

agree. As early as the summer of 1948, just after the successful exhibition and sale of his "Portuguese" pictures, he was suffering from depression. At the end of July he told Richard Smart: "My long period of gloom and frustration seems to be coming to an end."[84] In earlier letters he had mentioned his depression and inability to paint. Depression was to continue to blight him periodically for much of the rest of his life.

But his memories of Portugal in 1947 will undoubtedly have been happy ones – in complete contrast to those he had of the war years and the months in Normandy in 1945–1946. His concern about the future of his marriage was outweighed by his recently rediscovered faith in Roman Catholicism.[85] Once he had based himself in Foz, he was generally relaxed and happy, and he made friends with several interesting people. The whole visit was artistically congenial, stimulating, and productive and set the pattern for his future way of working – drawing abroad in the summer, painting at home in the winter.

Hillier was to return to Portugal many times, especially from the mid-1960s, when he began a routine of spending the summer months at Quinta da Relva near Portalegre in the east of the country, north of Estremoz and near the Spanish border. His first visit to the estate was in response to an advertisement in *The Times* in 1965, offering accommodation to paying guests. The owner was Letitia Frazer, whose mother was a member of the Robinson family that owned a large cork business. Hillier established a close and enduring friendship with Letitia after her partner, the writer Huldine Violet Beamish, died in October 1965. He loved to be at Relva, drawing, riding, and swimming. Portugal became a second home to him, and it is there that he would gladly have settled.

Provenance of the Viseu paintings and drawing

Church of the Misericordia, Viseu

Arthur Tooth & Sons Ltd to Arthur Tilden Jeffress in 1948 for £65;[86] acquired by Southampton City Art Gallery, along with Hillier's *Portuguese Farmhouse* (1960), as part of the Arthur Jeffress Bequest, in 1963.

---

84 Letter from TH to RS, 30 July 1948, TGA 20106/1/7/59.

85 Hillier, 183.

86 The prices of Hillier's paintings and drawings of Portugal exhibited by Arthur Tooth in April–May 1948 are shown in Richard Smart's copy of the catalogue, TGA 20106/6/1/243. The copy has the initials "RS" on the front cover, lower right.

Cathedral Square, Viseu *(painting)*

Arthur Tooth & Sons Ltd to Major Edwin Ody Kay in 1948 for £200; to Kay's nephews Nicholas and Lt.-Col. Michael Hicks after Kay's death on 7 September 1969; sold for £472.50 by Christie, Manson & Woods, London, on 19 March 1971, lot no. 67, to a London art-dealer whose name Christie's cannot divulge because of a fifty-year client-confidentiality commitment; soon after the sale, Arthur Tooth & Sons, who had left a commission-bid of £400 for the picture, acquired it from the purchaser; bought by Wolverhampton Art Gallery, with assistance from the Victoria & Albert Purchase Grant Fund, at Sotheby's, London, on 23 May 1984, lot no. 206, for £7,600. Sotheby's cannot divulge the name of the consignor.

Cathedral Square, Viseu *(drawing)*

Arthur Tooth & Sons Ltd to Rose Macaulay in 1948 for £21; to Jean Isabel Smith after Macaulay's death on 30 October 1958; to James ("Jim") Stewart Smith, probably c. 1963;[87] to Jim Smith's widow, Rosemary Stella Middlemore Smith *née* Hughes, after his death on 13 February 1987; to Martin Ferguson Smith, November 2001.

Abbreviations

HA: Hillier Archive, private collection, Somerset
LH: Leda Hillier
RS: Richard Smart
TGA: Tate Gallery Archive, London
TH: Tristram Hillier

Acknowledgements

First and foremost, Anna-Clare Hillier for permission to quote her father's writings, published and unpublished, and for much other generous assistance and encouragement; Bridgeman Images, especially Siân Phillips, for copyright permissions; Christie's Archives, London, especially Lynda

---

87 For Jean and Jim Smith, both converts to Roman Catholicism, the drawing had considerable significance, since in March–April 1947, shortly before Hillier's visit to Portugal, they had spent three weeks together in that country.

McLeod, Librarian; Brendan Flynn; John Graham of Churchill's Port and Max Graham, owner of Bar Douro, London, for information about the Max Graham with whom Hillier travelled in Portugal; Jenny Pery; Society of Authors for permission to quote from an unpublished letter of Rose Macaulay; Sotheby's, London, especially Nicholas Hemming-Brown; Southampton City Art Gallery, especially Clare Mitchell, Curator of Art; Lucinda Ferguson Smith for much assistance with research; Tate Gallery Archive, especially Adrian Glew, Archivist; University College London, Special Collections, especially Colin Penman, Head of Records; the late Ana Vicente, for supplying photocopies of letters from Rose Macaulay to her parents, Luiz and Susan Marques; Wolverhampton Arts and Culture, with special thanks to Sophie Heath, Collections Officer, Taz Lovejoy, Freelance Art Technician, and Niki Harratt, Digital Promotions Office. Repeated attempts were made to contact Foto-Germano, Viseu, about the images in Plates 42 and 44, but without success, and it seems that it is no longer in business.

Details of original publications

1. "New" portraits by Roger Fry (1866–1934) of Helen Fry and Vanessa Bell. *The British Art Journal* 17, 3 (Spring 2017), 34–39.
2. A complete strip-off: A Bloomsbury threesome in the nude at Studland. *The British Art Journal* 20, 2 (Autumn 2019), 72–77.
3. Clive Bell's memoir of Annie Raven-Hill. *English Studies* 100 (2019), 824–855. With Helen Walasek.
4. Virginia Woolf's second visit to Greece. *English Studies* 92 (2011), 55–83.
5. "Suicidal mania" and flawed psychobiography: Two discussions of Virginia Woolf. *English Studies* 95 (2014), 538–556.
6. Virginia Woolf and "the hermaphrodite": A feminist fan of *Orlando* and critic of *Roger Fry*. *English Studies* 97 (2016), 277–297.
7. Letters from Rose Macaulay to Katharine Tynan. *English Studies* 99 (2018), 517–537.
8. Dorothy L. Sayers and the Somersham pageant of 1908. *SEVEN: An Anglo-American Literary Review* 28 (2011), 79–96. Reproduced with permission from the Marion E. Wade Center, Wheaton College, Wheaton, IL.
9. The Godolphin schooldays of Dorothy L. Sayers. Not previously published.
10. The British connection: The secret son of Brig. Gen. Daniel Harris Reynolds. *Arkansas Historical Quarterly* 76, 2 (Summer 2017), 144–176.
11. The first visit of Tristram Hillier (1906–1983) to Portugal. *The British Art Journal* 20, 1 (Summer 2019), 90–97.

Index

Note: 'n.' after a page-reference indicates a footnote on that page, 'nn.' more than one footnote. Numbers in **bold** are not of pages, but of illustrations.